I-23-

D0916140

# Women at the Front

KIRTLAND COMMUNITY COLLEGE
LIBRARY
4800 W. FOUR MILE RD.
GRAYLING, MI 49738
989.275.5000 x 246

# Women at the

HOSPITAL WORKERS IN CIVIL WAR AMERICA

CIVIL WAR AMERICA | GARY W. GALLAGHER, EDITOR

# Front

## Jane E. Schultz

The University of North Carolina Press

Chapel Hill and London

© 2004 Jane E. Schultz
All rights reserved
Manufactured in the United States of America

Designed by April Leidig-Higgins
Set in Ehrhardt by Copperline Book Services, Inc.

The paper in this book meets the guidelines for
permanence and durability of the Committee
on Production Guidelines for Book Longevity
of the Council on Library Resources.

This volume was published with the generous assistance
of the Greensboro Women's Fund of the University of
North Carolina Press.

Founding Contributors: Linda Arnold Carlisle,
Sally Schindel Cone, Anne Faircloth, Bonnie
McElveen Hunter, Linda Bullard Jennings, Janice
J. Kerley (in honor of Margaret Supplee Smith),
Nancy Rouzer May, and Betty Hughes Nichols.

Library of Congress Cataloging-in-Publication Data
Schultz, Jane E.
    Women at the front: hospital workers in Civil War
America / Jane E. Schultz.
    p. cm.—(Civil War America)
Includes bibliographical references and index.
ISBN-13: 978-0-8078-2867-0 (cloth: alk. paper)
ISBN-10: 0-8078-2867-X (cloth: alk. paper)
ISBN-13: 978-0-8078-5819-6 (pbk: alk. paper)
ISBN-10: 0-8078-5819-6 (pbk: alk. paper)
    1. United States—History—Civil War, 1861–1865
—Hospitals.   2. United States—History—Civil War,
1861–1865—Women.   3. United States—History—
Civil War, 1861–1865—Medical care.   4. Women—
United States—History—19th century.   5. Women—
Confederate States of America—History.   6. Hospitals
—United States—Staff—History—19th century.
7. Hospitals—Confederate States of America—Staff—
History.   8. Military nursing—United States—History
—19th century.   9. Military nursing—Confederate
States of America—History.   I. Title.   II. Series.
E621.S35   2004
973.7'76'082—dc22                    2003024944

08 07 06 05 04   5 4 3 2 1
10 09 08 07 06   5 4 3 2 1

THIS BOOK WAS DIGITALLY PRINTED.

To my parents
Lloyd Ellman Schultz
Beverly Weenick Schultz

# Contents

# Illustrations and Figures

**FIGURES**

# Acknowledgments

In the decade it has taken me to research and write this book, I have accrued many debts to individuals and institutions. The National Endowment for the Humanities provided me a year-long fellowship to inaugurate the research phase of the project in 1990–91. The School of Liberal Arts at Indiana University–Purdue University–Indianapolis (IUPUI) awarded me several grants-in-aid-of-research to complete the Civil War hospital workers data entry project, which has compiled the most complete statistical survey of paid female relief workers to date. I thank Patricia Hoard of Washington, D.C., for entering data from the thousands of musty nineteenth-century file cards; Bill Stuckey of IUPUI for troubleshooting the computer management of the data; Bill Stuckey and Dana Qualls for producing the quantitative figures summarizing the data; and Joy Kramer for word processing wizardry. My students in Civil War literature at IUPUI, especially Diana Dial Reynolds, helped augment the bibliographic base of this book.

An army of archivists and librarians have aided me in my work. At IUPUI University Library, Marie Wright, Jim Baldwin, and Mary Beth Minick answered detailed reference questions, no matter how obscure the sources, and I received hours of help from Interlibrary Loan. Nancy Eckerman of the Indiana University School of Medicine Library was tireless in tracking down information about nineteenth-century medical history. For the courtesy, patience, and guidance of archivists from Louisiana to Maine, I am also immensely grateful. Cumulatively I logged nearly two years of research at twenty-four sites. Michael Musick and Michael Meyer at the National Archives allowed me to pore over thousands of brittle documents and correspondence from the Union and Confederate Surgeon Generals' Offices and to scurry through the stacks with them in search of registers, letterbooks, and other dusty tomes. Special thanks to Ed Bridges, Rickie Brunner, Norwood Kerr, and Ken Tilley at the Alabama Department of Archives and History in Montgomery; Clark Center of the W. S. Hoole Special Collections at the University of Alabama in Tuscaloosa; Ellen Gartrell in the Perkins Library at Duke University in Durham, North Carolina; Steve Towne of the Indiana State Library Archives in Indianapolis; Susan Sutton of the Indiana Historical Society in Indianapolis; Virginia Lowell Mauch of the Lilly Library at Indiana University, Bloomington; Fred Bauman, Jeff Flannery, Charles J. Kelly, Michael J. Klein, and Mary Wolfskill at the Library of Congress Manuscript Division in Washington, D.C.; Jan Grenci in Prints and Photographs at the Library of Congress; Melissa Delbridge, Anne Edwards, and Faye Phillips of the Louisiana and Lower Mississippi Valley Collections at Louisiana State University in Baton Rouge; Bill Barry, Kate Chapman, and Nick Noyes at the Maine Historical Society in Portland; Haywood Harrell of the Manassas National Battlefield Park; Randy Hackenburg and Jay Graybill of the U.S. Army Military History Institute in Carlisle, Pennsylvania; Fran Blouin of the Michigan Historical Collections, Bentley Historical Library, and Roy Kiplinger, Arlene Shy, and Galen Wilson of the William L. Clements Library, both at the University of Michigan, Ann Arbor; Michael Hennen of the Mississippi Department of Archives and History in Jackson; John White of the Wilson Library's Southern Historical Collection at the University of North Carolina, Chapel Hill; Allen Stokes of the South Caroliniana Library at the University of South Carolina, Columbia; and Ron Chepesiuk of the Winthrop College Archives in Rock Hill, South Carolina. For their help I would also like to thank the staffs of the Special Collections Department at the Robert W. Woodruff Library at Emory University in Atlanta; the Georgia State Archives in Atlanta; the Illinois State Historical Library in Springfield; the Library of Congress Book Division in Washington, D.C.; the North Carolina Department of Archives and History in Raleigh; the University of Iowa Special Collections in Iowa City; and the Virginia State Library Archives and the Museum of the Confederacy in Richmond.

I thank my mentors at the University of Michigan—Cecil Eby, the late John Owen King, and James McIntosh—and at the University of Iowa, Linda Kerber, who urged me to reconceive my dissertation in the form of this book. Colleagues and staff in the Departments of English and History and in the American Studies and Women's Studies programs at IUPUI, especially Chi Sherman, Wanda Colwell, Jon Eller, Barbara Jackson, Jan Shipps, Jack McKivigan, and Bill Schneider, offered support in innumerable ways, as did Bill Chafe, Marilyn Mayer Culpepper, Bob Kieft, Stephen Oates, Mary L. White, Peter Yarrow, and Caroline Zilboorg. The Modern Language Association, the American Studies Association, the Organization of American Historians, the Medical Humanities Seminar at IUPUI, Clare Hall of Cambridge University, and the Society of Civil War Surgeons provided me the forums to present work in progress. Over the years as this project evolved, Jeanie Attie, Bill Blair, Kathleen Diffley, Drew Gilpin Faust, Gaines Foster, Elizabeth Fox-Genovese, Angela Baron McBride, Gina Morantz-Sanchez, Nell Irvin Painter, George Rable, Anne Firor Scott, Karen Manners Smith, Tim Sweet, and Elizabeth Young—all superb scholars—commented on papers and drafts of articles that have worked their way into this book.

Nancy and the late Richard Rocamora, Mary Ann and Aubrey Neely, Carolyn Rast, Miriam Cooke, Lyse Strnad, and Peggy Simpson offered me the hospitality of their homes as I traveled around the country, first with dimes and pencils, later with quarters and a laptop. Not only did my sister-in-law Sue Hoegberg billet me, but she investigated Civil War monuments in Washington, D.C., and did follow-up pension work at the National Archives for me. Kate Douglas Torrey and Paula Wald, director and editor, respectively, at the University of North Carolina (UNC) Press have spent scores of hours with this manuscript without complaint. Kate Torrey's vision for this book was an inspiration to me during the difficult years of its emergence. I am also indebted to Stevie Champion, Kathleen Ketterman, Vicky Wells, and the production staff at UNC Press, whose courtesy and professionalism made me want to cheer.

Thadious Davis, Michael Fellman, Gary Gallagher, Linda Kerber, Elizabeth Leonard, Steven Stowe, and two anonymous readers engaged by the University of North Carolina Press read and meticulously critiqued the manuscript at various stages. I could not have envisioned the final draft of this project without their wit and insight, and I thank them humbly for their time. They and the handful of friends and relatives who kept me at task and rendered service above and beyond the call of duty deserve my greatest thanks. Lady Julia Boyd, Sally Catlin, Elizabeth Heller Cohen, Ruth Hoegberg, Kathleen Junk, Shawn Kimmel, Gina Laite, Therese McCarty, and Susan Shepherd all helped nurse me through a serious illness. Shawn, in particular, provided that rare blend of intellectual and emotional sustenance I needed to keep going. My daughter Miranda was born after I completed the first phase of archival research, and she has come of age as I labored on. It gave me

great pleasure to learn that when her fifth-grade teacher asked the class to impersonate Civil War generals, Miranda asked if she could be Phoebe Yates Pember. My parents, Beverly Weenick Schultz and Lloyd Ellman Schultz, known to all as Bobbye and Bud, have been waiting a long time to hold this book, which I dedicate to them, in their hands.

# Women at the Front

# Introduction

If you turn to page 958 in volume 6 of the behemoth *Medical and Surgical History of the War of the Rebellion* (1875–88), you will see a two hundred–word paragraph on the subject of "female nurses"—the only reference to the topic in the twelve-volume set. As early as 1866, Charles Stillé observed in his *History of the United States Sanitary Commission* that "for some reason, not very apparent, this branch of volunteer relief occupied a very subordinate place in the medical history of the war," despite "extensive arrangements" to supply the Union army with trained nurses.[1] He referred to several weeks of training that physician Elizabeth Blackwell had agreed to give to interested members of New York's Woman's Central Relief Association.[2] As an executive of the Sanitary Commission, Stillé full well believed that plans to initiate war nursing had been extensive, caught up as he was in promoting his organization and anxious to smooth over the fissures that had developed between its largely female force of aid workers and its male governors. Nearly a century and a half later, it is clear that a dearth of trained nurses (*and* doctors) gave rise in the postwar era to substantial changes in the training, regulation, and licensing of medical workers.

More important, Stillé discerned that the story of women engaged in hospital work had escaped the tellers of the medical war. His contemporaries attempted to rectify this oversight with rhetorically expansive but socially exclusive volumes that celebrated women's war work by affirming the models of morality and nurture that constructed their sphere of influence. It is not surprising that, focused on a war story whose central players were men in arms, these early commemorators regarded women as adjuncts to military power brokers. When Elizabeth Cady Stanton, Susan B. Anthony, and Matilda Gage sought the meaning of relief work in the early 1880s, their conclusions reflected their commitment to the legal, political, and economic advancement of women.[3] Putting women at the center of the story—albeit women who were white, well educated, articulate, and elite like themselves—yielded a narrative about progress in which a collective experience of war had prepared women to assume the reins of reform movements that would energize American political life for several decades. In these early assessments of the war's impact on women, feminists saw a group mobilized by remarkable individuals, whereas popular historians saw an indistinct group whose "contributions" were secondary to the narrative of military strife.

More than twenty thousand women in the Union and Confederate states engaged in relief work during the Civil War. Some achieved remarkable results, given the obstacles that work in military hospitals presented. New England educator Amy Morris Bradley proved her mettle early on in Maine infantry regiments and was granted increasing responsibility, first as matron of a brigade hospital, next as superintendent on hospital ships, and later as the prime mover in reforming Alexandria's convalescent camp, where she spoke for five thousand soldiers. The dramatic improvement at the neglected Virginia camp turned official heads and secured for Bradley a place in military memory and a foundation on which to build a postwar career as a public school administrator. Unlike Bradley, the vast majority of relief workers were not positioned to achieve the remarkable. Assigned to domestic drudgery in hospital wards, they built fires to cook soup, washed patients' faces, irrigated noxious wounds, cleaned effluvia from the floors, changed bedding, and scrubbed undergarments. If they were lucky—and literate—they might write letters and communicate soldiers' needs to surgeons and ward staff. Many were like Amanda Jones, who left slavery in Louisiana and worked in Union hospitals for over two years. She did not know her age, did not know her parents, and could not sign her name, though it must be said that her service as a laundress, her subsequent marriage, and her ability to sustain herself were all remarkable achievements. Although well-educated women were poised for success in military hospitals, the story of women's relief work rests as much with those whose social advantages were few.

*Women at the Front* looks broadly at hospital work across regions, races, and classes, insistently foregrounding differences among women and restoring agency to those whose voices did not rise above the pitch of traditional source narratives. Part 1 considers hospital workers during the war: who they were, how they became involved in hospital work, how they adjusted to it, and how they challenged it. Part 2 analyzes the material and psychological conditions of women's war service after the war: how hospital workers fared in postwar life, how and why they pursued military pensions, and how they memorialized the war. I begin with the premise that the most significant wartime labor in which women directly engaged military life was hospital and relief work. Although female intelligence workers and martial cross-dressers have once again captured popular attention, the army of relief workers that labored for millions of hours alongside soldiers instituted greater change in public attitudes about women at work than those who challenged prescriptive notions of femininity.[4] We have too often looked beyond this army of workers perhaps because of the widespread view that the postwar years were a time of social retrenchment when women lost the freedom of movement they had gained during the war. But to see only retrenchment may be to misread their return to private life. The magazines and images that celebrated domestic shelter may have done so as an anxious response to the visible evidence of war workers already moving in more public orbits.[5]

Wherever relief workers served—on the battlefield, in the immediate rear, or at general hospitals far removed from fighting—their presence created a front where gender, class, and racial identities became themselves sites of conflict. As a legitimate channel for patriotic ardor, relief work challenged some prescriptions for masculine and feminine behavior and buttressed others. When sick and wounded men were hospitalized, their weakness and vulnerability were apparent. Though they fought to recover, the martial ideal that led them to the hospital left them. The women who cared for them took on a soldierly aura by going to work against disease, infection, and the medical infrastructure itself. Indeed, the fight women waged to secure a place in military hospitals led to internecine disputes in which class and racial interests trumped job assignments and duties. Thus, in the world of convalescing soldiers, gender roles were often reversed: men were powerless and effeminized, while the women who served them found strength as their advocates, even at the expense of fighting one another. At the same time, relief workers' nursing reinforced nineteenth-century notions that women were born nurturers. Despite the fact that men also served as nurses, the belief that nursing was domestic work performed by women was well established by the 1860s.[6] Although the equation of nursing with domesticity may have eased women's troubled entry into the military medical arena, cultural assumptions about the docility and accommodation of nurturers ultimately undermined their struggle for greater autonomy. If medical officers expected them to be compliant helpers, then it was only with great difficulty that they could claim any share of the authority that governed the care of patients—a preprofessional version of the dilemma that has plagued nursing even to this day.

Although Northern and Southern wartime hospital experience varied widely, women of the two sections confronted similar obstacles to their service. Once they were installed, their encounters with medical superiors reflected ambivalence about the extent of their servitude. So many comparisons can be made, notwithstanding the obvious differences of personal circumstance, that a nursing experience transcending the divisions of region and ethnicity emerges intact. Southern women's hospital work should be seen in the context of their larger social relationships and the more local, provincial, and parochial lives they led, but what their families and medical officials dealt them was not finally so different from Northern women's experience. Greater autonomy, as well as the more cosmopolitan milieu that was Northern urban women's frame of reference, made for more overt conflict in the Union hospital arena.[7] Although Southerners appeared more complacent and resigned to their station in the Confederate hospital service, it would be a mistake to read their milder behavior as constituting assent to higher authority. In their skepticism, they resembled Northern workers.

The network of social relations in Union and Confederate hospitals provides ample material for comparison. The hospital workforce in both sections consisted of a broad spectrum of women; those of higher class and racial standing worked alongside those without privilege, even though the former were usually appointed to jobs of greater status and responsibility. Early historians of women in the Confederacy argued that public prejudice against the use of women in military hospitals, as well as surgeons' opposition to them, "tended to drive the better class of women away from the hospitals and throw the positions open to women of indifferent character and training."[8] This condescension—the writers conflate "better class" with higher class and assume that the working class comprised "women of indifferent character"—reveals a more significant contrast between Southern and Northern hospital work. For black and white Southerners, class was a more essential ingredient in shaping hospital experience than race, perhaps because Southerners were more accustomed to interracial labor. Northerners, on the other hand, experienced race as the more integral and divisive category shaping their hospital work because Northern labor and domesticity were, ironically, more segregated than these areas in Southern society. Thus while Southern women shared a tacit agreement about race relations in military hospitals, their construction of class relations was much less stable. By contrast, Northern workers were more receptive to the intermingling of classes than to the intermingling of races, contrary to the conventional wisdom that the antislavery movement made whites more tolerant of blacks. In sum, Southern women's hospital experience revolved around their perception of class differences, whereas for Northern women, racial division more compellingly structured their work.

By using the work cycle as the locus of analysis—from an individual's decision to perform relief services to the cultural memorialization of that experience—I challenge the notion that the institutionalization of medical work was progressive. In Chapter 1, I debunk the myth that a majority of workers were white and middle class and show that the female workforce was in fact more than twice as large as previously documented. Bearing in mind the differences between Northern and Southern hospitals, *Women at the Front* also explores the links between a worker's social status, her job assignment, and the freedom with which she could accept or decline pay. In a discussion about the propriety of military nursing, I consider women's motivations for seeking service in light of public anxiety over their sexual vulnerability. The household and travel arrangements made by women who left home—and often left their children in the care of others—also illumine motivation. The frequency with which middle-class women traveled without escorts to out-of-town assignments shows how earlier restrictions on their travel relaxed during the war years. Not all of the labor evaluated in this study took place in hospitals, in camps, or on battlefields, however. Some was launched from home when the war spread to villages and farmsteads or when public facilities were unavailable. The circumstances of war required some women—mostly Southerners—to relieve suffering in their own homes. Northerners typically traveled to general hospitals in their own communities or to those a train ride (or two) away.

Once situated, women attempted to domesticate the military hospital. One gauge of their success was the family metaphor that came to characterize the nurse-patient bond, an analogy whereby Mother took care of incapacitated male children who ultimately left the home of the hospital. Her bond with the soldier grew out of the spiritual and religious convictions that defined her work. More important, it forged unexpected cross-class and cross-racial alliances between white middle-class nurses and their black and working-class charges—a connection predicated on the inferior status of both groups within the military-medical complex. Nurses' idealization of the common soldier in contrast to their lack of sympathy for socially inferior coworkers hints at the powerful hold that reverence for manhood exerted over wartime society.

Though recognized by surgeons as superior morale builders, female workers occupied a tenuous place in hospitals. As a matter of workplace survival, veteran nurses learned to meet the needs of their patients without alienating those in charge. But as advocates for patients, they sparred with surgeons over the particulars of diet, medical supply, and procedure. In light of these differences, the patient's body became a symbolic battleground over which nurses fought surgeons to treat patients more humanely. As the growing bureaucracy of military hospitals in both sections frustrated women's attempts to enhance care, they began to question the efficacy of their obedience. Some even risked their positions by exposing corruption, graft, and neglect. Billing themselves as moral watchdogs, hospital workers were shocked to discover that surgeons frequently placed professional allegiance above ethical conduct. Taking the moral high road was consistent with nineteenth-century notions of virtuous womanhood, but in making workplace disputes public, they resisted the model of silent cooperation their society had scripted for them.

Part 2 of this study examines the war's impact on individual workers and the political and cultural legacies of their work. Despite the rhetoric that urged women to return to private life (and women's own collusion in it), relief work gave a number of elite women postwar visibility as agents of change in the public arena. Their postwar work did not, however, threaten the ethos of domesticity: careers in teaching, philanthropy, and health care supported values associated with traditional feminine roles in the antebellum period. Elite women in straitened circumstances found clerical jobs in government offices and wrote their memoirs; few pursued nursing as a profession. The postwar expansion of industrial work appealed to women of more modest means, the war having provided only a temporary "respite" from the tedium of agricultural or paid domestic work. However, the Southern working class — former slaves especially — had fewer industrial opportunities in the war-torn region. The war may not have led directly to more jobs for women in the postwar era, but the much-touted example of their wartime achievement created at least initially an atmosphere of tolerance as they sought work outside the home.

By the 1890s the meaning of women's war work could be measured outside the workplace by veterans' groups lobbying for monthly pensions. Arguing that the nurse's work was comparable to the soldier's, advocates of the Union army Nurses Pension Act of 1892 linked domestic work in hospitals with military defense. Government support through pensioning encouraged a broader definition of what constituted military service and a wider acceptance of women's paid work. The most striking feature of the pension act was that it rewarded the very people who had lobbied for it—Union army nurses. By limiting eligibility to nurses only, the Pension Bureau excluded thousands of other workers from consideration by virtue of their assignment as cooks and laundresses. Hospital administrators who appointed white middle-class women to nursing work and African American and working-class women to custodial work thus set in motion a ranking that excluded poorer women from seeking pensions years later. By 1895 a more liberal provision of the pension law allowed cooks and laundresses to argue that they had done work commensurate with nurses', but the middle-class promoters of the act took no part in pleading their case. Expanding the pool of potential applicants did not ultimately alter the bureau's exclusionary policies or substantially increase the number of former workers granted pensions.

The pensioning of female hospital workers gave public voice to their war work. A more private voice was being constructed up until the second decade of the twentieth century in scores of hospital narratives. Whether given to exaggeration, candor, or faulty memory, former hospital workers used the narrative to illustrate the influence of domestic ideals in the military-medical arena, their developing sense of agency, and their advocacy of the patient. United in the belief that they were putting soldiers' interests before their own, workers represented themselves as triumphing over errant surgeons and a hospital system designed to promote efficiency at the cost of humanity. Increasingly conciliatory in tone as memory of the war receded, narratives after 1880 seldom mentioned sectional enmity and were less critical of the military administration of hospitals. However self-effacing these later representations were, their story remains one of agency and contestation. By the 1880s and 1890s veterans' organizations were supported by middle-class whites who had discovered the expediency of legislative cooperation, but who felt no obligation to former coworkers who did not share their social status. They may have depicted themselves as the soldier's champion but were ambivalent about each other. Ironically but predictably, they used the memory of war and not the war itself to construct a group consciousness.

In a civil war—in this Civil War—domestic space is literally and symbolically a site of conflict. When the front is understood as a place where women are not, we miss the interaction of men and women in the place that fighting occurs. If we define the front solely in terms of its combat function, we may also miss the front that women and men created by virtue of their relief services. If the image of home was never far from the soldier's mind, as one historian has suggested, then the reverse was also true: home took on a war-like aspect.[9] Women with male kin at war fought to maintain a standard of living. Hungry for war news, citizens combed casualty lists after battles. Dismemberment, disease, and death visited so many hearths that the tattered slouch hat, the soldier's letter, and the lock of hair became potent reminders of the war's toll on families. Southern homes materially bore the brunt of war as they accommodated soldiers, were caught in the cross fire of changing lines, or were laid to waste in Sherman's path. Yankee soldiers came to believe that "secesh" women were more virulent in their disunion than soldiers in butternut and gray. If military life invaded the home place, then it is also true, as I show in *Women at the Front*, that the evocativeness of the home place served officially to authorize women's place within military relief work.

As a corrective and an expansion of the two hundred words that the compilers of the *Medical and Surgical History* saw fit to devote to female relief workers, this study offers a portrait of people in difficult places who learned humility at great personal cost. The thousands of pages they wrote and the institutional trail that fans out behind them provide traces of a much larger story whose demographic complexion is not as pure as we once thought. If we are tempted to find a history of Civil War nursing in a photograph of New York sanitary fair workers that graced the society pages in 1864, we must look again, for only one part of the story resides there.

# PART ONE

# On Duty

Who wiped the death sweat from the cold, clammy brow,
And sent home the message:—"'Tis well with him now";
Who watched in the tents whilst the fever fires burned,
and the pain-tossing limbs in agony turned,
And wet the parched tongue, calmed delirium's strife
Till the dying lips murmured, "My mother," "My wife"?
—Clara Barton, "The Women Who Went to the Field," 1892

## CHAPTER ONE

# Women at the Front

Custom inures the most sensitive person to that which is at first
most repellent, and in the late war we saw the most delicate
women, who could not at home endure the sight of blood, become
so used to scenes of carnage, that they walked the hospitals and
the margins of battle-fields, amid the poor remnants of torn humanity, with as perfect self-possession as if they were strolling
in a flower garden.

—Mark Twain and Charles Dudley Warner,
  *The Gilded Age* (1873)

A widely reproduced photograph of three women in dark dresses, white aprons, and beehivelike hats has been used by modern historians as evidence that young, uniformed nurses served in military hospitals during the Civil War.[1] In fact, the women were volunteers in a food concession and were dressed in traditional Norman costumes to sell Normandy cakes at an 1864 Sanitary Commission fair in New York.[2] The twentieth-century historian who first identified the photo expected nurses to wear white hats, even though no female relief worker of the Civil War ever wore professional headgear or a uniform.[3]

Historians' misreading of the photograph exemplifies their misreading of the identity and status of female hospital workers in Civil War America. As early as 1866, assessments of women's wartime contributions read like the lives of saints: the war generation held that the women who nursed soldiers were angelic and motivated by Christian sacrifice. After four years of unstinting labor, the story goes, they returned happily to their homes and domestic routines.[4] What the editors of these early commemorative works did not spell out, however, was that the objects of their praise were exclusively white and middle class. Their depiction of sainted, self-sacrificing, and socially respectable women provided psychological penicillin for an ailing and still sectionalized nation. But it led modern historians away from discovering the demographic truth about more than twenty thousand women who served as domestic workers during the Civil War.

As a point of departure, this study does not restrict itself to a single group of relief workers but instead crosses the boundaries of race, region, and class to re-create the vast complexity of the medical world that women and men inhabited. Female hospital workers were as diverse as the population of the United States in 1860: they were adolescent slaves, Catholic sisters, elite slaveholders, free African Americans, abandoned wives, and farm women. Some were mothers and grandmothers, others childless or unmarried. Most served according to inclination, but a few served under chattel obligation. Northerners had been teachers or reformers before the war; mill operatives, seamstresses, or compositors.[5] Among Southerners, we find plantation mistresses and escaped slaves, genteel widows looking for respectable employment, and yeoman women in need of a living wage.[6] Under the idealized banners of patriotism and religious duty, women from fifteen to sixty-five offered their services. The zeal with which young men enlisted in the first year of the war was matched by women seeking hospital positions. Even though the number pursuing positions tapered off in both sections after 1862, civilian women were writing to the surgeons general as late as 1864 to find them hospital sit-

Three young women (possibly, from left to right, Katharine Prescott Wormeley, Eliza Woolsey, and Georgeanna Woolsey) pose in bakers' outfits and toques advertising a concession at the U.S. Sanitary Commission's metropolitan fundraising fair in New York City in April 1864. Such fairs raised more than $4.4 million for the relief of Union soldiers during the war. (Courtesy of New-York Historical Society)

uations. The evidence of willing Southern hands is particularly remarkable in light of the low morale in the Confederacy by the summer of 1864, when increasing numbers of Confederate women had begun urging their men to return home.[7]

Picnickers who drove eighteen miles to Manassas on a hot July day in 1861 to watch soldiers fight on Virginia soil little anticipated the horrific spectacle that war is. But they began to understand its seriousness when, looking out of their carriages, they saw bloodied, shoeless young men limping along the road to the capital. In lieu of Union or Confederate plans to provide for incapacitated soldiers—few in 1861 imagined how long the war might last—some of those citizens formed local aid societies for soldiers' relief. Historians have estimated that ten thousand groups mobilized in the first year of the war alone.[8] Societies made virtual factories of homes, schools, and churches by sending food, clothing, and medical supplies to the front.[9] As early as April 1861 an alliance of well-to-do New Yorkers envisioned a national organization devoted to soldiers' welfare. By June the U.S. Sanitary Commission (USSC) was trying to bring local aid societies organized by the Woman's Central Relief Association under its wing. Though "manned" by women in the sense that material aid was the result of their labor, the administrators of the Union's Sanitary Commission were primarily men.[10] An early national example of centralized bureaucracy, the commission would distribute over $15 million in supplies, marshal a force of paid relief agents numbering in the hundreds, and work independently of the Union surgeon general's appointment of civilian workers.[11] Not as large but equally ambitious was the U.S. Christian Commission (USCC), established in November 1861 at a meeting of the Young Men's Christian Association, for the purpose of promoting the soldier's "spiritual good" along with his "social and physical comfort."[12] Motivated by an evangelical mission, the USCC distributed hundreds of thousands of Bibles and millions of pages of religious tracts in the hope of returning the errant soldier to the flock. By war's end, it had collected over $3.5 million in aid and organized over 4,800 volunteers.[13]

The Confederate government did not centralize relief efforts until 1862. Where states' rights had constituted an integral part of prewar politics, state relief organizations and individuals took the lead in caring for soldiers. The largesse of prominent Southern citizens, like Alabama's Juliet Opie Hopkins, Arkansas' Ella Newsom, North Carolina's Catherine Gibbon, and Florida's Mary Smith Reid, established state hospitals near the scene of fighting. Governors also relied on ladies' aid societies to manufacture socks, shirts, and "hospital suits" for soldiers from their home states.[14] Newspapers in Charleston and Richmond regularly reported their charitable contributions for hospitalized soldiers and for troops at the front.[15] Judging from the early success of the South Carolina and Alabama hospitals in Charlottesville and Richmond, the state was a productive locus of organization and distribution.[16] After 1862 the Confederate Congress authorized a more centralized relief system, but not on the public-private model of collaboration instituted in the North. The Women's Relief Society of the Confederate States—begun by Nashville's Felicia Grundy Porter in 1864—came closest to a Southern sanitary commission, but it received no aid from the flagging Confederate treasury. Historians have argued that the Confederate government's takeover of citizen-sponsored relief early in the war effectively shut women out of the general hospitals.[17] But by virtue of their proximity to battlefields, Southern women could scarcely avoid providing relief to the sick and wounded.

Women began volunteering for hospital work before the medical departments of either section had adequately assessed the magnitude of their task. Besieged by applicants as soon as Fort Sumter was fired on, the Union's Acting Surgeon General R. C. Wood appointed fifty-nine-year-old Dorothea Dix to supervise the appointment of female nurses in May 1861 soon after Federal troops seized Alexandria and Newport News, and began blockading strategic Southern ports.[18] Nationally recognized for humanitarian work in asylum and prison reform, Dix established the Office of Army Nurses and generated guidelines for the selection of nurses. By October 1863, after the enormous loss of life at Shiloh, Antietam, Fredericksburg, and Gettysburg, Surgeon General William Hammond authorized all U.S. surgeons to appoint female attendants, which circumvented Dix's power. In reality, few surgeons or sanitary commissioners ever acknowledged Dix's authority and her power was ineffectual from the war's first year.[19]

The superintendent ultimately appointed over three thousand nurses. Her selection standards were stringent, and she turned away many able applicants.[20] Dix stipulated that only women between thirty-five and fifty were eligible and that "matronly persons of experience, good conduct, or superior education and serious disposition will have preference." She listed "neatness, order, sobriety, and industry" as prerequisites. Applicants were expected to produce two letters of reference testifying to their "morality, integrity, seriousness, and capacity for the care of the sick" and to "dress plain . . . while connected with the service, without ornaments of any sort."[21] Dix's drab dress code and her preference for middle-aged matrons were meant to discourage thrill seekers from applying. Civilian and military officials feared what might happen to young women in hospitals filled with eager young men; wary of public opinion, Dix did what she could to head off potential romances. In one Washington-area hospital, for example, female workers were not even allowed to stroll the grounds without permission.[22]

Women whose applications had been rejected were persistent in finding ways to serve. New York's Jane Woolsey reported that her sister Georgeanna and a cousin "earnestly wish[ed] to join the Nurse Corps, but [were] under the required age," adding that she knew of women falsifying their ages to gain entry.[23] Though Dix turned them down, the Woolseys' social connections paid off: the Sanitary Commission put Georgeanna, cousin Eliza, and the wife of George Templeton Strong—all elite women—to work on its fleet of hospital ships while Generals George McClellan and Joseph Johnston amassed troops on the Peninsula in 1862.[24] The less well-connected Fanny Titus-Hazen, of Vermont, whose petition was rejected by the Sanitary and Christian Commissions, packed her bags for Washington anyway. Armed with letters of reference, the twenty-three-year-old found leniency because, she reported, Dix "believe[d] [her] heart [was] in the work."[25] New Jersey's Cornelia Hancock, also twenty-three, and twenty-eight-year-old Esther Hill Hawks of New Hampshire thought that Dix had turned them down because of their good looks. Trained at the New England Female Medical College in the 1850s, Hawks spent the summer of 1861 seeking medical employment in Washington. Finding none, she returned to Manchester in December and took over her husband's medical practice. Ten months later she joined him on the Sea Islands, where he was serving the Union army as a plantation superintendent. There Hawks practiced among the predominantly black soldiers and residents of the islands, convinced that military officials, at best uninterested in people of color, looked the other way. Hancock traveled to Gettysburg just two days after the battle under the protection of her surgeon brother-in-law; the need for helping hands was so great in the town of only 2,400 that she was pressed into service with no questions asked.[26]

For African American women who wished to serve, there were other obstacles. No matter what their class or educational attainments, free black women encountered resistance. In August 1862 twenty-five-year-old Charlotte Forten sought a position in the Sea Islands. Daughter of a prominent abolitionist family established in Philadelphia since the eighteenth century, Forten was turned away at the door by the Port Royal Relief Association of Boston. Told that the clerks were "all out of town," Forten determined to press on: she submitted a second application to the Philadelphia Port Royal Relief Association and was accepted.[27] Forten's position as teacher and relief worker privileged her; other blacks were shunted into cleaning and laundering jobs.[28]

Confederate women were as enthusiastic about volunteering for service in 1861 as their Northern counterparts. Although it was not until September 1862 that the Confederate Congress authorized the hiring of female hospital employees in the wake of horrendous losses at Antietam, women answered ads in the *Richmond Dispatch* as early as June 1861 that sought their aid in state-sponsored hospitals. Without a nursing superintendent or formal selection guidelines, Southerners willing to serve met with fewer official roadblocks. Nineteen-year-old Constance Cary of Virginia worked around the clock at Seven Pines in May 1862, learning as Cornelia Hancock would at Gettysburg, that medical emergencies took precedence over youth. Cary remembered that "up to that time the younger girls had been regarded as superfluities in hospital service; but on Monday two of us found a couple of rooms where fifteen wounded men lay upon pallets around the floor, and, on offering our services to the surgeons in charge, were proud to have them accepted."[29] Once the government began to phase out female managers, elite women lost interest in serving. The Confederate Congress ultimately empowered surgeons to appoint two matrons, assistant matrons, and ward matrons to each hospital and as many cooks and laundresses as they saw fit.[30] Although elite volunteers were still reserved for more prized matron jobs, working-class, slave, and immigrant women constituted the majority of Confederate hospital workers.

Much of the hard labor in Confederate hospitals was performed by slaves hired out by their mistresses. Men were detailed to cook, do carpentry work, and lift soldiers. Women also worked as cooks and as laundresses and chambermaids; occasionally they nursed sick white women.[31] When South Carolina's Ada Bacot left her Florence County plantation in 1862 to nurse Palmetto soldiers in Charlottesville, a female slave accompanied her. Ella Newsom, newly widowed like Bacot, left genteel comfort in Arkansas to join the Confederate Army of Tennessee in Kentucky, Tennessee, Mississippi, and Georgia. She took slaves with her and hired dozens of others on location as the army moved its base of operations. Emily Mason depended on her "manservant" Jim for protection as she journeyed away from her Fairfax County, Virginia, home to set up a hospital "in the mountains." Jim slept in a room adjoining his mistress's to protect and "comfort" her at night.[32]

Few Southerners left home to serve, however, because the war usually went to them. As Confederate troops passed through Southern towns, women had the opportunity to work in wayside or field hospitals established in nearby churches, schools, and warehouses.[33] In the absence of adequate public space, they arranged to nurse soldiers in their own homes, like the women of Washington, North Carolina, or those of Abbeville, South Carolina, who met hospital trains with their carriages.[34] In more rural areas, citizens had no choice but to turn their homes into hospitals. Fifty-three-year-old Sarah Hails Bellinger offered her Montgomery plantation in 1861 for a hospital until a larger building could be secured. Another Alabamian, Barbara Moore Simmons, opened her humbler Demopolis home. Elite women in Augusta, Georgia, opened the Millen Wayside Home in the autumn of 1862 and took officers into their own homes until Confederate authorities feared that malingering would result from such comfortable conditions. For Mississippi's Emma Balfour, nursing during the siege of Vicksburg presented unusual challenges: her house was shelled continuously during May and June 1863, causing her to seek refuge in caves while her amputees waited out the bombardments in her home.[35]

Throughout the war, convalescent soldiers were detailed as hospital nurses and orderlies, particularly in the field, where few women were allowed to serve. Surgeons who opposed the use of women in hospitals hired men regardless of their condition.[36] Hospitals ultimately employed more men in spite of a soldierly consensus that women made better nurses.[37] By the war's second summer, Union surgeon general Hammond—who halfheartedly endorsed female workers—allowed that the ratio of female to male nurses could be as high as one to three.[38] Whether women regularly constituted one-third of the Union nursing force is difficult to say when hospital staff fluctuated in response to the supply of sick and wounded. But Hammond's initial acceptance of women in service positions created problems for surgeons later on.

Whether men or women made better workers was subject to debate among surgeons. Using sick men frustrated John Brinton, for one. As brigade surgeon in Mound City, Illinois, Brinton wrote that the medical department would do better to "[secure] permanently the services of men of less rude character, and more suitable to discharge the important duties they are called upon to perform."[39] But as little as he liked using convalescents, he liked using female nurses even less because of the difficulty of accommodating them.[40] Some surgeons came in time to appreciate the services of women, like J. P. De Bruler, who complained in July 1862 that to replace women with convalescents would wreak havoc on his Evansville, Indiana, hospital. "I do not know how it will work," he wrote to Governor Oliver Morton, "but it does seem to me a cruel blow at the efficiency of our Hospitals. How can delicacies suitable for the really sick be prepared by a soldier totally untrained in the culinary art? What kind of sheets and linen will we have?"[41]

Soldiers in both sections preferred female to male caregivers, regularly reporting to kin that a woman's presence did them good.[42] A relative told Confederate nurse Kate Cumming that her ailing brother had been so neglected by soldier-nurses that he had come home "in order to preserve his life[,] the treatment & attendance being so horrible."[43] Women were well aware of the ameliorative influence they had on their patients. Emily Parsons, head of female attendants at Benton Barracks near St. Louis, observed in July 1863 that 416 field-hardened men newly arrived from Vicksburg were docile in her presence: "As I bent over one he said 'It is a long time since a lady had her hand on me.' He seemed so glad to be spoken to, and so were they all. You cannot think how touching it was to see them watch for a greeting and a touch of the hand." Parsons's and other nurses' bonds with the rank and file sprang in part from the scarcity of female relief workers; men were glad to see them.[44]

Estimates of the number of women in hospital work have always been too low. Frank Moore's *Women of the War: Their Heroism and Self-Sacrifice* (1866) and Linus P. Brockett and Mary Vaughan's *Woman's Work in the Civil War* (1867) celebrated the contributions of "the few hundred" white women who shone in Northern hospital work.[45] No volume commemorating Southern women appeared until 1885. Titled *Our Women in the War* and published by the *Charleston News and Courier*, it and John L. Underwood's *Women of the Confederacy* (1906) compiled tracts lauding the spartan mothers of the Confederacy and the paternal benevolence of former slaveholders. Not all contributors supplied their names, and few mentioned unpleasant topics, like caring for the wounded.[46] Later volumes made no mention whatever of black women.[47] Working from the assumptions that elite women were squeamish about publicity and that nonelites were unworthy of historical attention, commemorative editors did as much to censor women's war record as to celebrate it. Northern editors in particular made no attempt to include "disloyal" Southerners in their volumes, which created the erroneous impression that Southerners seldom engaged in hospital work. Not until 1912 did

Mary S. Logan's *The Part Taken by Women in American History* confirm that "brave" Confederate women had "flocked to the hospitals all over the South." In the spirit of restored national unity, Logan insisted that Southerners' sectional proclivities did not dampen their "womanly tenderness" or "righteous impulses."[48]

In the era before its professionalization in the United States and well into the twentieth century, nursing was a manifestation of female identity and a domestic responsibility; every woman was a nurse.[49] Women, by predisposition, were expected to care for others. "The great Father knew whether the male or the female would make the best nurse, when He gave her, instead of him, the care of infants and children," reported one benevolent worker.[50] To nurse also became an extension of Christian duty, the care of the soul integral to that of the physical body. Because nursing was prized above other forms of domestic military work and because nonelites were seldom appointed nurses, the work of cooks and laundresses was scarcely recognized, despite the fact that many of them also performed the work of nurses.[51]

Modern historians have been more generous than their nineteenth-century counterparts, but they have still underestimated the number of women who served.[52] The Carded Service Records of Union hospital attendants, compiled in 1890 by the U.S. Record and Pension Division as Congress debated granting pensions to nurses, list the names of 21,208 women. These records include only Union women who received pay and not the hundreds who donated service gratis. The names of Confederate workers do not appear; nor do the names of women employed in Northern or Southern regiments, in the European tradition, to wash and cook. Harriet Patience Dame, for example, served a New Hampshire regiment for almost five years, but a soldier in her unit noted that "[Dame's] is a name that will not be found on any official roster" though she was "with them" and "of them"—words that implied just how easy it was for women's service to become invisible.[53] That at least 21,000 women served in Union military hospitals alone makes a larger estimate conservative. F. C. Ainsworth, the surgeon responsible for compiling the list, said the figures "do not represent the total number of females employed in the hospital service during the war, but only those whose names have been found of record. Many records are missing and others are so imperfect that the information they contain is of but little value. The total number of female employés of each class *was undoubtedly much larger*."[54]

Estimating the number of women involved in the Confederate hospital service is even more difficult. Many Surgeon General's Office records were lost when Richmond burned in 1865. Also, because so many Southerners nursed soldiers at home or in local churches, their service never became part of official military records.[55] Perhaps most important, Southern hospitals depended on the custodial labor of slaves and white working-class women.[56] Published narratives have led us to conclude, perhaps too hastily, that elite Southerners made up a significant percentage of all Confederate female hospital workers. Bearing in mind that families would have objected to their service, elites probably constituted a smaller percentage of the whole than they did in the North.[57] Given the fragmentary records, the incidence of unofficial service, and the differences in Southern class and racial configurations, we may never know with any certainty how many women served as Confederate relief workers.

By contrast, we know a great deal about the class and racial makeup of women in Union hospitals.[58] Among the 21,208 women named in the Carded Service Records, 6,284 are listed as nurses, 10,870 as matrons, 1,011 as cooks, and 2,189 as laundresses; the remainder are labeled "seamstress," "dining room girl," "chambermaid," or undesignated. (See Figure 1.1.) Five hundred eighty-two of the workers are listed as "Dix" appointees; the nursing superintendent hired women in every category, not just nursing. Dix appointed 371 or 6 percent of the 6,284 nurses, 195 or less than 2 percent of the 10,870 matrons, 4 or less than 1 percent of the 1,011 cooks, and 4 or an even tinier percentage of the 2,189 laundresses. She put only white women to work—amounting to a smaller percentage of nurses and matrons than has commonly been believed.[59] "Contract" nurses, or those who were hired on location and not by the armies or philanthropic organizations, numbered 778. Two hundred eighty-one or 36 percent of the "contract" nurses were black—a statistic that suggests blacks without institutional connections could find on-site hospital work if they happened to be in the right place at the right time.

Two hundred sixty women are listed in the records as "Sisters of Charity," but because many nuns did not accept pay for their services, this number is probably too low. Twelve nuns are listed in work other than nursing. Experts on the sisterhoods, like Frank O'Brien and Mary Denis Maher, have argued that the overall number of Catholic sisters is actually much larger since religious orders were active in both sections.[60]

The breakdown of job classifications by race is illuminating. Black women numbered 2,096 or roughly 10 percent of the total number of workers listed in the records—a percentage consonant with that of African American sol-

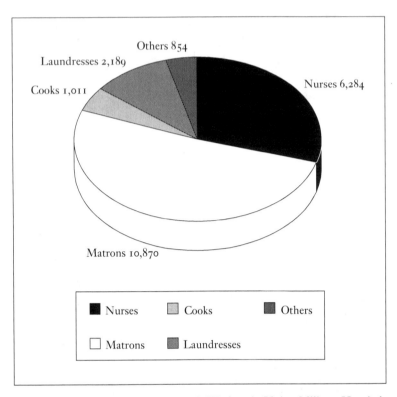

Others 854

Laundresses 2,189

Cooks 1,011

Nurses 6,284

Matrons 10,870

Nurses · Cooks · Others

Matrons · Laundresses

FIGURE 1.1. Job Classification of Female Workers in Union Military Hospitals
*Source:* Carded Service Records of Union Hospital Attendants, Matrons, and
Nurses, 1861–65, RG 94, NARA.

diers in the Union ranks. With breakdowns for job classification and race,
the data list 420 black nurses (6 percent of all nurses), 793 black matrons (7
percent of all matrons), 363 black cooks (36 percent—more than one-third
—of all cooks), and 309 black laundresses (14 percent of all laundresses).
(See Figure 1.2.) Clearly, black women were given the work of cooking and
washing out of proportion to their number in the records, whereas higher-
prestige jobs (nurse, matron) were reserved primarily for whites.

Only 10 percent of all the carded records include information about marital status.[61] Using the 2,335 women for whom we do have marital data, 516
or 22 percent were single. This does not include the 450 who were nuns;
when nuns are included, the percentage of single women rises to 41 percent.
Married or widowed women constitute the remaining three-fifths; we have
no way of knowing what percentage of the married women were also wid-

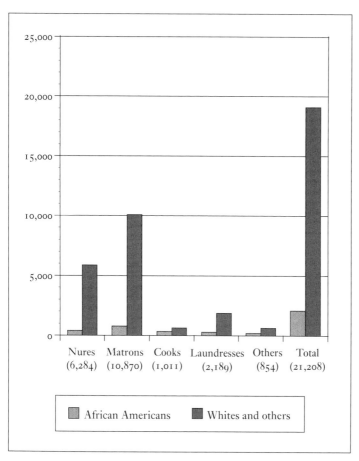

FIGURE 1.2. Racial Breakdown of Union Female Hospital Workers

*Source:* Carded Service Records of Union Hospital Attendants, Matrons, and Nurses, 1861–65, RG 94, NARA.

owed. Although the records make no distinction between women with husbands living or deceased, narrative evidence indicates that a high percentage of widows engaged in the work. (See Figure 1.3.) The records give no age data on single women, making it difficult to know whether specifications that women be above thirty actually kept younger women out of the service, particularly as the war dragged on.

The Carded Service Records report on the female workers of over 500 field, general, and post hospitals, including several in the Far West. Some of these hospitals were temporary; others were closed down when better facil-

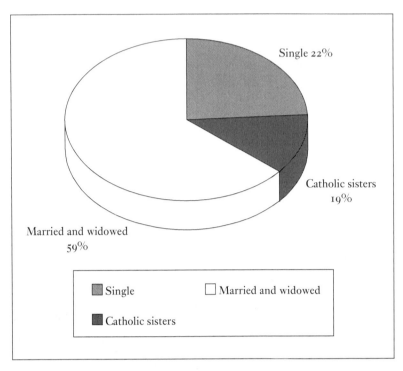

Single 22%

Catholic sisters
19%

Married and widowed
59%

▨ Single        ☐ Married and widowed

▧ Catholic sisters

FIGURE 1.3. Marital Status of Union Female Hospital Workers

*Note:* Based on a sample of 2,335 records.

*Source:* Carded Service Records of Union Hospital Attendants, Matrons, and Nurses, 1861–65, RG 94, NARA.

ities were built; still others were renamed when changes in staff, funding, or physical layout were made.[62] With 25 hospitals, Washington, D.C., and environs had a greater bed capacity than any other city in the Union; Philadelphia, with 27 hospitals, 25,000 beds, and 157,000 admissions throughout the war, was a close second. The Depot Field Hospital at City Point, Virginia, was said to be able to accommodate 10,000 soldiers in its 1,200 tents and 90 log cabins. In the West, St. Louis, Louisville, Memphis, Chattanooga, and Nashville had the greatest hospital presence; by 1864 they could accommodate nearly 30,000 patients.[63] The Union hospitals that employed the greatest number of women were in eastern cities. Whether these hospitals employed larger percentages of female workers relative to all workers or simply had greater turnover is unclear. We do know, for example, that the seven hospitals at City Point, established in June 1864 as a base for the Army of the Potomac besieging Petersburg, employed 46 women.[64] Harewood and Lincoln Hospitals, with the two largest bed capacities in Washington at 2,000 and 2,575, employed 194 and 266 women, respectively, whereas Armory Square, with a bed capacity of just 1,000, employed 297 women—the largest contingent in a Washington-area hospital. There, where Amanda Akin Stearns would observe Walt Whitman haunting the wards at night, 38 or 12 percent of the 297 were black women; at Harewood, on the northwestern outskirts of the city, 21 or 11 percent of the 194 were black—figures consistent with the total percentage of black women hired by the hospital service. However, at Lincoln, a tent hospital established east of the capital on marshy ground, not a single black worker appears in the records. By contrast 161 blacks—exactly one-third of all women—were among the 493 hired at Jarvis General in Baltimore, by far the largest employer of women of both races in either theater during the war. More than 885 women worked in Philadelphia-area hospitals, only 3 of them black. Mower, West, Satterlee, Chester, and Cuyler Hospitals were the largest employers. (See Figure 1.4.)

Hospitals in the western theater, including many below the Mason-Dixon line, also hired hundreds of women throughout the war. Jefferson General at Jeffersonville, Indiana—a pavilion-style hospital built across the Ohio River from Louisville in 1864—had the largest capacity of any institution in the West with 2,400 beds. All 140 female workers listed at Jeffersonville were white. By contrast, more than half the women hired at Asylum General in Knoxville were black—65 of 121. Serving the Mississippi River fleet were large general hospitals at Benton Barracks in St. Louis and at Keokuk, Iowa. Benton Barracks, where Emily Parsons managed the female staff, hired the largest number of women at 209. Thirty-one or 15 percent of these were black; 17 were appointed nurses. Parsons established an unprecedented nurse training program there for blacks in 1863. Upriver in Keokuk, all 87 women hired were white. (See Figure 1.5.)

Hospitals in the West used black workers more readily than many in the East. Mound City General, one of the first established in Illinois, hired 193 workers over the course of the war, 48 or 25 percent of them black. No black worker was hired in 1861, but 8 were on staff by the end of 1862, 10 more by the end of 1863, and 22 more by the end of 1864. Although the gain probably reflected the growing presence of a contraband labor supply in the western theater, it may also have indicated a growing confidence in the use of black workers. Early in the war, Mound City General was under the direction of surgeon John Brinton, whose preference for Catholic sisters re-

Washington's Harewood Hospital, built in 1862 after the summer's fierce fighting, featured fifteen pavilions of rough-hewn boards, about two thousand beds with mosquito netting, and stoves for heating. Located on the outskirts of the Union capital, its grounds were beautifully manicured, and vegetables from its large garden supplemented patients' diets. Pictured here are an army band, civilian staff, and female workers. Harewood employed 194 black and white women during the war. (Courtesy of U.S. Army Military History Institute, Carlisle Barracks, Pa.)

sulted in the hiring of 36, or 19 percent of all workers there. Cumberland General in Nashville hired 24 blacks among its 162 workers (or 15 percent), while Gayoso Hospital in Memphis numbered 14 blacks among its 94 workers (or 15 percent). The general hospital at Little Rock was a racial anomaly: 136 of its 137 workers were black. (See Figure 1.6.)

General Benjamin F. Butler's occupation of New Orleans in 1862 led to a significant Union hospital presence there. Two hundred seven women worked at Corps D'Afrique General Hospital, 5 of whom were black. Virtually all of those employed in New Orleans–area Union hospitals were local women hired on contract—an indication that the promise of a wage was valued above sectional loyalties, especially by 1865, when 153 of the women began their service. General Hospitals No. 2 and No. 3 in Vicksburg employed 40 and 61 women, respectively. Only 2 black women were hired at No. 2, whereas 53 found work at No. 3—a comparison indicating a segregated workforce. (See Figure 1.7.)

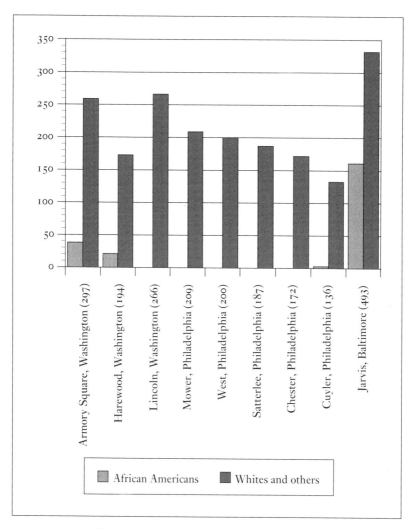

FIGURE 1.4. Racial Breakdown of Female Staff in Sample Hospitals

Source: Carded Service Records of Union Hospital Attendants, Matrons, and Nurses, 1861–65, RG 94, NARA.

Smaller field hospitals often depended on the black labor supply. With over 1,000 contrabands at Fortress Monroe by the summer of 1861 and with 26,000 following Union troops in the Tidewater region of Virginia by 1863, supply was inevitably greater than demand.[65] However, if the labor was difficult or the soldiers being served were black, black women were readily appointed. At Cavalry Corps Hospital—a field installation in the Army of

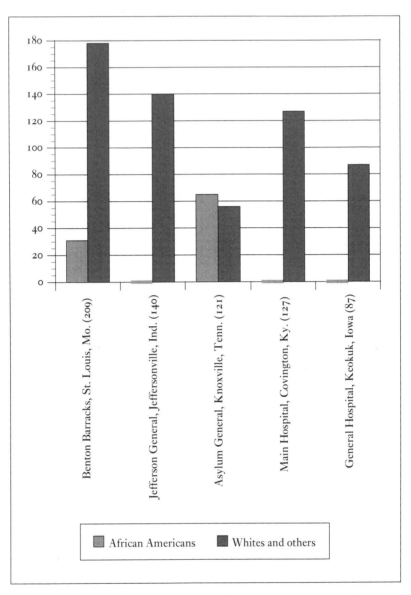

180
160
140
120
100
80
60
40
20
0

Benton Barracks, St. Louis, Mo. (209)

Jefferson General, Jeffersonville, Ind. (140)

Asylum General, Knoxville, Tenn. (121)

Main Hospital, Covington, Ky. (127)

General Hospital, Keokuk, Iowa (87)

■ African Americans    ■ Whites and others

FIGURE 1.5. Female Employment in General Hospitals in the Western Theater
*Source:* Carded Service Records of Union Hospital Attendants, Matrons, and
Nurses, 1861–65, RG 94, NARA.

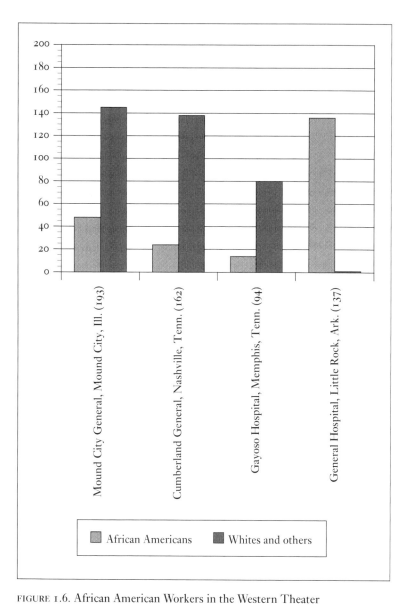

FIGURE 1.6. African American Workers in the Western Theater

*Source:* Carded Service Records of Union Hospital Attendants, Matrons, and Nurses, 1861–65, RG 94, NARA.

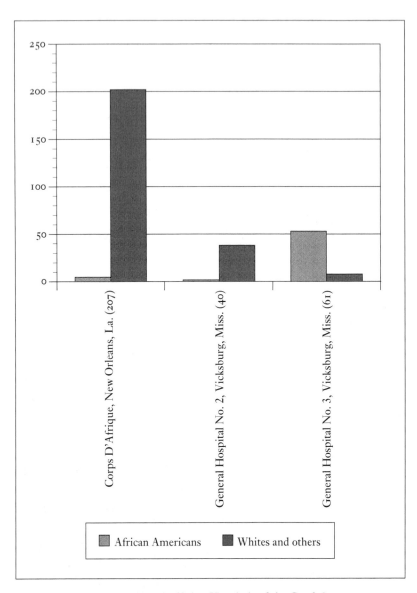

FIGURE 1.7. Racial Breakdown in Union Hospitals of the Confederacy

*Source:* Carded Service Records of Union Hospital Attendants, Matrons, and Nurses, 1861–65, RG 94, NARA.

the Potomac—workers were expected to help with stable work. Surgeons hired only 15 women during its two years of operation; 3 of these, including Charlotte McKay of Massachusetts who later published a narrative of her service, were whites hired as nurses, while the remaining 12 were blacks hired as laundresses.[66] Hospitals for the various companies of the 58th U.S. Colored Troops, also located in the field, hired 38 laundresses, only 4 of whom were white. What is striking is not that black women were hired to nurse black men, but that any white woman was hired to care for black men. (See Figure 1.8.)

Historians have not yet constructed a reliable statistical profile of Confederate relief workers. However, hospital morning reports provide a window into the Confederate system. The Confederacy ultimately sponsored 153 general hospitals, 20 of which were in Richmond. Like the Union capital of Washington, the Confederate capital also had the greatest number of hospital beds. Its medical flagship, Chimborazo, was a pavilion-style hospital of 150 buildings with 8,000 beds. More than 75,000 men were treated during its three years of operation. A city in its own right, Chimborazo employed 50 surgeons, 46 matrons, 30 guards, and 2 druggists. It had icehouses, bathhouses, a bakery that could daily produce 10,000 loaves, a brewery, beef and goat herds, and its own canal trading boat.[67] Richmond also housed its ailing soldiers in private homes and wayside hospitals. The most famous of these was Sally Tompkins's 22-bed Robertson Hospital, where more than 1,300 men were treated over four years with an exceptionally low mortality rate. The Millen Wayside Home in Augusta served 365 men in its first month of operation alone—an indication of how important such establishments were in the treatment of a transient military population.[68]

Women worked in all of Richmond's general hospitals. Morning reports show that on November 15, 1862, 10 of Hospital No. 7's 66 employees and 9 of Hospital No. 11's 45 employees were women. On September 1, 1864, 14 of Hospital No. 4's 77 employees were women (5 laundresses and 9 matrons). Some hospitals experienced little turnover, as with Hospital No. 13, which reported the same women at work on March 31, 1865, as it had on September 1, 1864. As Confederate money lost its value, it is not surprising that people wanted to keep their jobs.[69] Although slaves provided much of the domestic labor in Confederate hospitals, the Confederate surgeon general's records do not generally distinguish between slave and free labor. An exception was Chimborazo Hospital No. 2 (it was divided into five units), which listed 56 black employees in 1864, 3 of whom were women, including

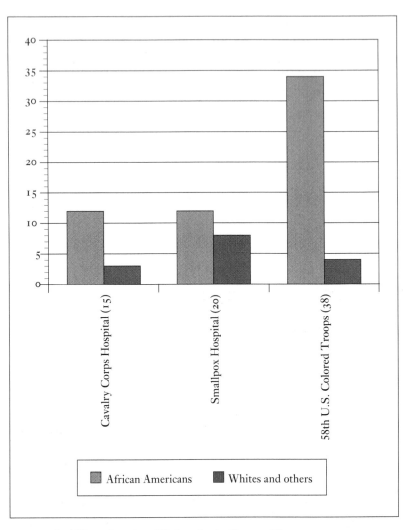

FIGURE 1.8. African American Workers in the Eastern Theater

*Source:* Carded Service Records of Union Hospital Attendants, Matrons, and Nurses, 1861–65, RG 94, NARA.

1 free black. This hospital also listed the names of 3 white matrons—Phoebe Yates Pember, Kate Ball, and "Miss Caffey"—all of whom began service between December 1862 and January 1863 after the battle of Fredericksburg littered Richmond with over five thousand Confederate casualties.[70] There is evidence, admittedly from incomplete records, that black and white women worked alongside one another increasingly after 1862.

Although distinctive labels for nurses, matrons, cooks, and laundresses implied a difference in assignments, workers' duties frequently overlapped. "Nurses" might be called upon to cook or clean hospital wards, "cooks" might also carry food and medicine to patients, regimental "laundresses" might spend weeks at a time nursing ill soldiers, and "matrons" might be called upon to do all of these things. Union administrators used the term "matron" indiscriminately, referring to regimental women hired to nurse, cook, and do laundry in the field; to designate the woman who bore responsibility for ward nurses in general hospitals; and as a label for chambermaids.[71] Confederate administrators used "matron" in lieu of "nurse," the latter term generic and the former, titular. According to Francis Simkins and James Patton, Confederate matrons were "charged with the duties of seeing that the orders of the surgeons were executed, supervising the sanitary and commissary arrangements of the hospital, and satisfying the needs of individual patients."[72]

The great majority of Northern workers served in urban general hospitals; Southern workers' experience was more local because work took place at home or in makeshift hospitals near home. For Confederate and Union workers alike, the kind of hospital and its proximity to military action determined what kind of work was performed. Depending on the hospital's distance from a battle site, workers might encounter freshly wounded men or those already treated in the field. When remote from fighting, general hospitals treated the less critically ill and those who could stand travel; when close to it, ambulances delivered triaged patients to hospitals directly. In Richmond and Washington, D.C., general hospitals regularly received soldiers who had not yet been treated. Confederate women were often closer to battlefield carnage and thus the recipients of more critically ill soldiers than workers in Union hospitals.

A hospital's size, its distance from action, and how recently action took place determined the number of patients that workers cared for. After a battle, nearby workers bewailed the deluge of bodies under their care; when patients died, recovered, or were transferred, workers were left with little to do. The Confederacy's Emily Mason had to prepare 800 beds in a field hospital outside of Fredericksburg to receive incoming wounded during the battles of the Wilderness. Phoebe Yates Pember attended to as many as 600 patients at Chimborazo, while across town at Hospital No. 1 (established in the city almshouse), an order of Catholic nuns cared for 500 at a time.[73] Emily Parson's Benton Barracks could accommodate up to 2,000 patients; by late

1863 her fleet of nurses never handled individually more than 100 at a time.[74] In 1864 Elvira Powers was stationed at a smallpox hospital in Nashville that had only 6 surgeons, 3 of their wives, and 2 female nurses to care for its 800 patients. Scarcely a year later, Powers was transferred to the pavilion hospital in Jeffersonville, Indiana, where she complained that, despite a larger staff, 2,600 patients were accommodated in a space scarcely fit for 2,000.[75]

Although there was variation in hospital size, number of women employed, and number of patients, most hired nurses performed similar activities: they washed, dressed, and fed patients; they wrote letters for, read to, and helped patients endure the tedium of convalescence. Field nurses regularly took on cooking chores. Georgeanna Woolsey reported from Fredericksburg that in one day she had singlehandedly cooked and served 926 rations of soup, farina (a cooked cereal), tea, and coffee.[76] Other nurses were hired to take charge of hospital linen rooms, even to do laundry. When laundresses were unavailable, nurses had to pitch in and do the work themselves or find civilian men who would. Some urban hospitals sent the wash out to private contractors, sparing their own employees this arduous work. At other sites a white middle-class nurse was assigned to manage the black and working-class women hired to do laundry on the premises, although few relished the assignment.[77]

Workers at every level perceived a domestic hierarchy that credited interacting with patients and devalued washing clothes. Rebecca Usher, a middle-class white from Hollis, Maine, wrote home soon after arriving at Chester General near Philadelphia that she was being considered for the dreaded position of laundry manager: "I should not be willing to take it & I could not recommend it to any one. The superintendant [sic] is not expected to wash any of the clothes, but she has about 20 women under her, & is obliged to be there in the steam all the time to arrange the work & see that it goes on well."[78] The questionable value attached to laundry work was apparent as well to ten working-class women at Clay General in Louisville who asked in 1864 for promotion. Sanitary Commissioner James Yeatman denied the request on the grounds that they "were not the kind of women" envisioned by government to perform nursing duties.[79]

Like washing clothes, cooking was not as highly valued among workers as making rounds with surgeons. Though regimental workers were accustomed to cooking and nursing, general hospitals customarily separated these assignments. Convalescent men were assigned to kitchen duty in spite of the presence of more able and knowledgeable female workers. When conva-

Workers in the mess hall at Harewood prepare for the next meal. Only ambulatory soldiers could gather here; black and white relief workers brought meals to the more seriously ill or wounded in bed. Note the woman in a white apron standing second from right. (Courtesy of U.S. Army Military History Institute, Carlisle Barracks, Pa.)

lescent cuisine was unpalatable, women asked for greater control in the kitchen. Kate Cumming observed enormous turnover in kitchen staff with the transient Confederate Army of Tennessee, which sometimes resulted in her having to do the cooking herself—a task that rarely fell to genteel Southerners. To her chagrin Cumming had to fire an intoxicated cook (whom she initially called a "treasure") and replace her with a convalescent soldier.[80] For Fannie Oslin Jackson, another elite Southerner, whose nursing work ended in April 1865, cooking for an officers' mess was the only job she could obtain.[81] When Iowa's Annie Turner Wittenmyer instituted "special diet kitchens" in anticipation of spring and summer campaigns in 1864, cooking gained prestige, largely because the kitchens were staffed by middle-class whites.[82]

Class and racial tensions flared whenever women of privilege were obliged to oversee custodial labor or to perform it themselves. The middle class grudg-

The Army of the Cumberland established Union hospitals in Nashville, where laundresses congregated after hanging up the wash. Urban workers had to make use of limited space to conduct domestic tasks. (Courtesy of Chicago Historical Society)

ingly performed socially stigmatized work, even if it was not custodial. Women hired to nurse took little pleasure in mending soldiers' clothing, which they perceived to be the work of poorer women.[83] Those chosen to staff Union hospital ships by virtue of their connection with elite sanitary commissioners were vexed to find themselves doing heavy chamber work when contraband and immigrant women could not be found to do it. A recent study has suggested that the navy approached contraband women before others to service its fleet because it had little hope that wealthy women would flush the decks of blood, mud, and gore.[84]

To avoid unsavory labor, elite nurses chartered working women's services when they could. During the Peninsula campaign, Maine's Amy Morris Bradley described the "filthy condition" of "several State Rooms filled with soiled clothes" on board the *Knickerbocker*. Quick to take charge, Bradley hired "four girls (colored)" to wash the offending garments and a crew to clean the boat.[85] Emily Parsons, who had to wash floors at Fort Schuyler four months earlier, was not as sanguine about the work ahead of her on the *City of Alton* in March 1863: "Hercules might have cleaned it," she lamented, but "nobody else could; it was awful! We had no regular working-woman on board; only contrabands who had not the slightest idea of neat-

On ships like the *Nashville*, the first vessel the Union Medical Department fitted up in 1862 as a floating hospital, white women on army payrolls routinely ordered black women to do custodial and heavy manual labor on a contractual basis. From its initial docking at Milliken's Bend, Louisiana, the *Nashville* could hold up to one thousand soldiers, who later were transported up the Mississippi and Ohio Rivers to hospitals in the North. (Courtesy of Library of Congress)

ness."[86] Catholic sisters were an exception; they would do chamber work, in addition to doing laundry or chopping wood if need be.[87] Only in settings where the female labor supply was scarce were nurses obliged to carry slop buckets and wash floors. Otherwise these jobs fell to black and working-class women or to convalescent men.[88]

Because work ebbed and flowed with the number of men needing care, the weekly routine varied considerably. Most Northern caregivers spent part of each day writing letters for soldiers and carrying food and supplies to them. Amanda Akin Stearns regularly put in eighteen-hour days at Armory Square: up at six, she dispensed medicines, served breakfast, wrote letters, dispensed medicines, served dinner, wrote letters, dispensed medicines, served supper, wrote letters—the round of chores interrupted only when wounded arrived, as they did from Chancellorsville at three on a May morning in 1863.[89] Elvira Powers described a more varied schedule at Jefferson General: "[Today] I have covered crutches, ripped up arm slings, washed and made them over, gone to commissary with order from doctor for material for pads for wounded or amputated limbs, and manufactured the same." On the same day she helped patients petition for furloughs and back pay, wrote letters, read, sang, and played checkers.[90]

Confederate nurses described similar routines, calling on slaves to perform heavy or onerous labor.[91] Alabama's Kate Cumming, who entered the service after Shiloh, recorded a daily round of carrying food, writing letters, changing wound dressings, keeping track of patients' treatment, and recording their deaths. Martha Milledge Flournoy Carter even helped bury the dead at a Virginia hospital.[92] Phoebe Yates Pember rose to a managerial position as chief matron of Chimborazo Hospital No. 2: she oversaw the work of the other female employees and negotiated with hospital stewards to keep patients supplied with proper food and clothing. Pember also became a one-woman temperance committee, keeping the hospital's medicinal supply of liquor out of the reach of tippling surgeons and ward masters.[93]

In addition to the hospital's size and the patients it served, a worker's seniority affected her workday. Many surgeons required nurses to dress wounds, administer medicines, and communicate dietary requests. Trusted workers accompanied surgeons on their rounds when they became acclimated.[94] Iowa's Amanda Shelton almost vomited from the stench of wounds when she first made rounds at a Louisville hospital in 1864.[95] When a surgeon asked Elvira Powers to help him probe a soldier's gangrenous arm shortly after her arrival in southern Indiana, she nearly fainted: "It will be necessary to imbibe a little more of the heroic before I can be of much help during an operation. . . . All laughed at me, even to the patient; but it isn't expected that a Yankee school-ma'am can be transformed into a dissecting surgeon in a minute, guess it will take about a fortnight."[96] It did not occur to Powers that the medical staff might have been having a joke at her expense in the hope of hastening her departure. Instead, she and others valued the ability to assist surgeons without flinching as a nurse's rite of passage.

Both Union and Confederate women worked in field hospitals, appointed to these more rigorous posts by surgeons who knew their mettle.[97] Virtually all who accompanied regiments became field nurses whose chief duties consisted of providing food and relief for the sick and wounded, and foraging for supplies.[98] At work in the field, nurses encountered skirmishes; some were known to drag men out of the line of fire to attend to their wounds. Even in expected confrontations with the enemy, where they were sent to the rear, field nurses were still likely to be among the first to encounter the wounded. At the battle of Shiloh, Sister Anthony O'Connell of Cincinnati searched the field for wounded, assisted Union surgeon George C. Blackman with amputations and extractions, and accompanied the wounded on transports throughout the Ohio River valley.[99] Elizabeth Hyatt of the 4th Wisconsin Infantry, known for her skill in riding, was deputized to drive an ambulance, as were other nurses in the field.[100]

Massachusetts native Clara Barton was a self-appointed field nurse with the Army of the Potomac. Working beyond the orbit of Dix or the philanthropic commissions, Barton stockpiled supplies in her tiny Washington flat and then drove into the Virginia countryside to disperse them among the wounded. After Second Manassas late in August 1862, Barton lamented that she had only two water buckets, five tin cups, one camp kettle, one stew pan, two lanterns, four bread knives, three plates, and a two-quart tin dish to feed three thousand prostrate men at Fairfax Station. "I assure you," she wrote years later, "that I was never caught so again."[101] At Fredericksburg four months later, Barton's wagons were so laden that she had to get out and walk up every hill. By chance she encountered after the battle a man whose face was so encrusted with blood that his features were undetectable until her scrubbing revealed the face of her church sexton from Worcester.[102] At the request of General Butler, Barton also cared for soldiers in the Army of the James during the fierce summer campaigns of 1864.[103]

Field nurses, who performed more strenuous labor than general hospital workers, were accustomed to tougher assignments. Unhappy about the narrow staircases and poor condition of Mansion House Hospital in Alexandria, Amy Morris Bradley gladly transferred to a tent at Camp Franklin, Virginia, where she thrived on the 5:30 A.M. rising time and the daily fare of coffee, potatoes, fried pork, bread, and molasses.[104] Many enjoyed the exertions of life in the field, preferring to go by horseback instead of ambulance if they had a choice. Energized by regular exercise, they were surprised to discover how much they liked the hard work.

**White Union nurses** who accepted wages were paid forty cents per day and a ration, or approximately $12 per month; black nurses received up to $10.[105] By June 1864 the Surgeon General's Office upped white pay to sixty cents but rescinded the raise just two months later.[106] The Sanitary and Christian Commissions paid workers slightly more.[107] The Christian Commission's

Hannah Cleaver Smith drew an annual salary of $200 for superintending diet kitchens for the Army of the Cumberland and managing the cooking at Nashville's General Hospital No. 14.[108] Cooks and laundresses hired directly by the Union army made less than nurses: between $6 and $10 per month. Regimental laundresses were paid directly by the soldiers for whom they washed, which made regular wages more elusive.

Most women gladly accepted pay, but some let it be known that the amount was inadequate. Six nurses from Knight General Hospital in New Haven resigned in February 1865, "being unwilling to remain under the present compensation."[109] Members of another group at Camp Butler, Illinois, were so irritated when their $18 monthly wage was scaled back to $12 that one of them fired off an angry note to Superintendent Dix: "I can see a shade of rationality in an order dismissing females from this service but I can see none in thus degrading them while in it, and must I think it require a good deal of patriotism to retain an intelligent right minded woman—whether she needs her wages here or not—satisfied to remain in the employ of a Department that issued such an order when greenbacks bear their present value and dry goods their present prices."[110] If the army could not pay women a living wage, argued Emmeline Tenney, then it could not expect to retain competent workers. As a middle-class white, Tenney could not simply say that she needed her wages; like others who shared her class interests, her words betrayed the view that the best workers, indeed the most patriotic ones, were those with more than a common pedigree. Esther Hill Hawks was similarly indignant that the Freedmen's Relief Association of New England had assigned two men at annual salaries of $1,000 to do what she had done the previous year, with more medical experience, for $480.[111]

Southern women said little publicly about their wages. Many were not paid for nursing since they responded to relief emergencies at home without formal contractual arrangements. Some might have declined financial compensation anyway because it signified labor. It was difficult for elite women like Phoebe Yates Pember and Kate Cumming to dodge the ostracism that befell them for working, let alone accepting wages. Confederate nurses' pay was not initially standardized as it had been in the North, but as early as November 1861 Juliet Opie Hopkins paid matrons in her Richmond hospital $20 per month.[112] When the Confederate government formalized the hiring of women in September 1862, it established a pay scale of $40, $35, and $30 per month for chief, assistant, and ward matrons respectively, and $25 for cooks—wages that sound generous until we remember that Confederate inflation limited even wealthy Southerners' purchasing power.[113] An 1864 roster from Chimborazo No. 2 shows that white women were paid the same salaries as free black women. A free black nurse ("Candis") earned $40 per month and was given a clothing allowance, something the Union surgeon general never provided workers—black or white. At the same hospital, "Julia," a cook owned by Mary G. Point, was paid $25 per month but probably surrendered the wages to her owner.[114]

In spite of official efforts to standardize wages in both sections, female workers received pay infrequently. Appointed by Superintendent Dix to nurse at Washington's Union Hotel Hospital in December 1862, Louisa May Alcott made only $10 for six weeks of work instead of the $18 she could have expected as an army nurse.[115] Though Alcott did not attempt to recover her wages, other nurses did. Dix and Surgeon General Hammond had their hands full of petitions from workers in need of back pay. On her way home to Elmira, New Yorker Sarah Palmer, for one, stopped in Washington to see Dix about ten months of wages due her.[116] Surgeons also interceded for female workers when irregular pay brought hardship. One surgeon in Frederick, Maryland, was so distraught that three matrons in his disbanded hospital would not be paid that he told the surgeon general, "Great injustice must be done a class of poor women whom to say the least have well earned their pay."[117] It was difficult for white women at all ranks to draw their pay on a regular basis and even more difficult for black women. A City Point surgeon asked one of the Union's medical directors to see to it that black employees be paid more promptly: "Their services are most valuable," he explained, "and their prompt payment would do away with much suffering and dissatisfaction among them." Another wrote on behalf of Sally Salina, "a worthy colored woman," who had worked for six months in the Convalescent Hospital at St. Augustine, Florida, and whose name had "been omitted from the muster rolls & [was] unable to obtain her hard-earned money."[118]

Too often there was confusion over who was to pay workers, and some got caught in the institutional muddle. Civilians contracted by hospitals were to be paid from hospital funds separate from the government payrolls that took care of military-appointed staff. This meant that while nurses received their pay from the same source as surgeons and soldiers, cooks and laundresses were paid by hospitals or privately by clients. Perplexed surgeons wrote to officials inquiring how to go about paying them. Complained one to the surgeon general in 1863: "I respectfully ask to be informed how Matrons and Laundresses of this Hospital are to be paid. They have re-

African Americans who escaped slavery were able to find work as laundresses in military camps. Though not always paid, they received food in exchange for their labor. (Courtesy of U.S. Army Military History Institute, Carlisle Barracks, Pa.)

ceived no pay in the four months past. The Paymaster refused to pay them as formerly and said they would receive their pay from the Medical Purveyor. There is no Medical Purveyor in this department. There is an acting Medical Purveyor in Cincinnati Ohio from whom we get our supplies of Medicine but he says that he has received no instructions to pay Matrons and Laundresses [and] therefore can not pay any such claims."[119] Workers were at the mercy of an undependable pay system that was also segregated by race. Black women in every job category were usually paid from funds other than those that paid white women—yet another level of red tape that thwarted regular pay for many in need.[120]

Throughout the war, middle-class women who volunteered for service carefully set themselves apart from those who received wages. Although widows and those left indigent by absent male relatives were willing to accept pay as an economic necessity, those not so obliged seized rhetorical advantage over less fortunate earners.[121] They waxed eloquent on their "nobler object" ("I ask nothing for my services, all I do I wish to do out of pure sympathy for the sick and suffering"), assuring hospital administrators that patriotism, not money, motivated them.[122] Surgeons affirmed this patronizing mentality in letters to Dorothea Dix that conveyed a preference for the "purer" motives of those who eschewed wages: women impelled by Christian devotion alone appeared to surgeons to be more compliant and morally better fit to work with all classes of men. Surgeon Willard Bliss at Armory Square went so far as to dismiss paid nurses because he could hire others who would donate their pay to the hospital—the same reasoning that prompted some surgeons to prefer nuns. Religious orders frequently went without pay, such as twenty-three Sisters of Charity who ran a Louisville hospital throughout the war and were compensated only for transportation.[123]

Nurses who took pride in announcing that they were working for free used their unpaid status to apply leverage in negotiations. Chicago's Mary Newcomb believed that because she was not on the payroll, she need not comply with hospital regulations. When a ward master told her that lights must be extinguished at nine o'clock—no matter that she was washing a soldier's wound—she exploded: "You tell that surgeon whoever he is, I will burn just as many lights as I please. I am no hired nurse. I volunteered my services free and there shall be no red tape, but I will break it when humanity demands it." Charlotte McKay believed that she earned a greater measure of respect from soldiers at Fredericksburg when they learned that she "under[went] the hardships and privation of life in a field hospital" for a more exalted purpose than money.[124]

Like Newcomb, middle-class nurses resented the suggestion that their motivation was pecuniary. Amy Morris Bradley bristled when a surgeon asked whether she was a paid nurse: "To think that I, *poor Amy Bradley* would come out here to work for *money* and that, the paltry sum of twelve dollars per month and Rations! . . . Thank God I had a higher motive than a high living & big salary."[125] Clara Barton was not above admitting her financial exigency but became defensive when the Patent Office threatened to remove her from its payroll. "My own living," she shot back in a characteristically imperious tone, "has been such as our Government provides for its troops, hard crackers, often mouldy and wormy salt meat, and water, And from no *person*, or *persons*, or *Society* or *Commission* or *Bureau* or any other conceivable source, have I ever received one dollar of salary or reward, and . . . without doing positive injury to the feelings of a grateful soldier, I have refused all presents, I derived to labor without reward, and I have done it."[126] In a proud display of her martial privations, Barton criticized the institutionalization of hospital work and the monetary recognition of that work. Even if they received wages, some hospital women emphasized their selflessness by distributing them among patients. Annie Johns of Virginia used her first pay to purchase pictures for the wards in Danville. Other Confederate nurses —Virginia's Fannie Beers and Sally Tompkins—and the Union's Mary Newcomb and the Woolsey sisters returned wages to their hospitals. Beers protested that she had no need of money but was later glad to spend it on patients who were suffering for want of comforts.[127]

The nineteenth-century belief that women were natural nurses did not translate into widespread appreciation of their relief services. Opposition to them was apparent early in the war and responsible for discouraging many whose services might have lessened the incalculable suffering that was the fruit of war. Frequent turnover suggests that work was laborious, emotionally draining, and politically inhospitable at times, but some found ways to cooperate with medical staff and grew to care less about accommodations than soldiers' well-being. For others, longevity was simply a function of economic need. All had to negotiate obstacles to their service, which earned them a measure of public approval, but also an unending stream of diseased and battered bodies to care for.

## CHAPTER TWO

# Getting to the Hospital

I have very little experience as nurse, but I hope I could learn, for
my heart is willing—& I think that would influence my hands.
—Lizzie D. Lewis to Juliet Opie Hopkins, June 11, 1861

I would freely give up my time, energies, labours and medical
knowledge for the benefit of the suffering wounded.
—Henrietta Wellington Boate to Dorothea Dix, September 18, 1862

I have felt for sometime that God had called me to lend a helping
hand to those suffering soldiers.... If there is a place for me among
your suffering ones I am willing and should be happy to give you
my servises [sic].
—Mrs. Nathan A. Tinkham to the Secretary of the Christian
Commission, November 28, 1864

**Women of both sections** began to offer themselves for hospital service immediately after the war began. Their ambition grew out of a need to do more than prepare food, clothing, and medical supplies for men at the front. Some felt it a patriotic duty akin to the soldier's; others spoke of religious calling, Christian duty. The death or illness of a loved one might have inspired a woman to do what she could for another woman's son, husband, or brother. For other women, service was not a choice: if a husband's absence led to indigence, hospital work provided sustenance if not steady pay. For still others, the lure of adventure or desire to abandon difficult domestic circumstances may have been a motivator.[1]

Whatever the reasons, getting to the hospital presented material and spiritual impediments. Aspiring workers had to weigh desire against the disapproval of friends, family, and society. Merely securing a position was a difficult task in light of eligibility restrictions. Once appointed, a woman had to make domestic arrangements: Who would care for her children? Where would she live? What must she bring? These matters settled, transportation had to be arranged. For those unaccustomed to solo travel, getting to the hospital meant more obstacles: Would travel be possible under the protection of a male? Would passage be booked by water or rail? Would the distance necessitate several conveyances and overnight stays in unfamiliar cities?

Unlike any other nineteenth-century event concerned with mobilizing people, the Civil War inspired mass production of household goods. Long before government or industry assessed the demand for such goods, American women began producing them. Armies and hospitals benefited from this outpouring throughout the war.[2] After the Union surrender of Fort Sumter, groups of women organized aid societies whose purpose was to manufacture, collect, convey, and distribute food, clothing, and medical supplies. Newspapers North and South, full of the rhetoric of this domestic partnership, called upon women to join sewing circles and donate labor for the soldiers' benefit—"patriotic toil" that Jeanie Attie has recently described as leveraged by philanthropists to consolidate their own class power.[3]

Full of romantic idealism, young women imagined themselves marching off to war to fight disease and privation. Some were satisfied with the prospect of hospital work; others felt slighted that their gender should prevent them from shouldering muskets. In May 1861 Mississippi teenager Cordelia Scales reported to a friend: "I am going in the capacity of Florence Nightingale. Though I would prefer doing a little fighting to dressing wounds."[4] Three months later, when Scales's three brothers enlisted, her sense of injustice was keener: "It seems so hard that we who have the wills of men should be debased from engaging in this great struggle for Liberty just because we are ladies."[5] For Fanny Titus-Hazen, of Vermont, having been born female was no less frustrating: "It seemed the greatest misfortune of my life that I was born a girl. . . . I would have given years of my life could I have taken a place in the ranks with my brother."[6] Elizabeth Wheeler of Massachusetts recalled her jealousy more frankly than Scales or Titus-Hazen: "When the first company enlisted from Worcester, and my brother went with them, my whole soul was aroused, and had I been a man I should have counted one of the number."[7] In Sumter County, young South Carolinian women projected soldierly aspirations by cutting their hair short. One quipped that if they could not go with their brothers, they would "at least look as military as possible."[8]

Youthful fancy and bravado may have fueled women's desire to join men in the fighting, but for many the decision to volunteer for hospital work was like soldiers' enlistment.[9] Women were moved variously by patriotism, self-sacrifice, the prospect of adventure, and, of course, money. Sophronia Bucklin, of Auburn, New York, believed that she felt the same patriotism men did. The labor, she wrote, "was of my own seeking; I had been eager to lend myself to the glorious cause of Freedom."[10] Others coupled patriotism with activism. As agent for a Union ladies' aid society, Anna Morris Holstein spoke of her decision to enlist after Antietam as an "irresistible impulse *to do, to act*." Mildred Duckworth of Selma, Alabama, "felt a strong desire to do something for my country." Louisa May Alcott thought of nursing as a "new way" to "let out my pent-up energy." Massachusetts reformer Hannah Ropes had been moved by Florence Nightingale's *Notes on Nursing* (1860).[11]

Working-class women were not as forthcoming about motivation. Tennessee's Susan "Grandma" Smith spoke of religious visions, but with son and husband absent at the front, she needed to shift for herself. Like Smith, some hid economic motivation behind the more popular rhetoric of Christian duty. Julia Silk's confessed need was highly unusual: she "was willing to lend [her] assistance . . . for whatever remuneration might be judged sufficient."[12] For the thousands who sought hospital work without leaving personal records, the promise of pay was more compelling than they would have admitted.

Drew Faust has argued that elite Confederates devoted themselves to the Cause through self-sacrifice—the rhetorical role planter society assigned them.[13] Equating femininity with self-sacrifice, elite women took pleasure

The wealthy Anna Morris Holstein of Pennsylvania (center, in plaid dress) was impelled to serve after the battle of Antietam, believing that "*we* have no *right* to the comforts of *our* home, while so many of the noblest of our land so willingly renounce theirs." She and her husband William (standing at left) went to work for the U.S. Sanitary Commission. (Courtesy of U.S. Army Military History Institute, Carlisle Barracks, Pa.)

in meeting the crisis through self-denial. As the spirit of self-sacrifice became fashionable, some expressed it by removing themselves from home ties to perform the more sacred work of nursing. Ada Bacot, a young widow from South Carolina, invoked this ideology in her decision to serve: "Now I can give myself up to my state, the very thought elevates me. These long years have I prayed for something to do, perhaps my prayer is now being answered."[14] Arkansas's Ella Newsom, a twenty-four-year-old widow when the war began, wrote in a similar vein: "I had resolved to lay all I possessed of youth, beauty, and wealth on the altar of the Confederacy."[15] If they could not be brides in the usual sense, they could marry themselves sacrificially to the state.

There were also those who confessed to more tangible needs. Juliet Opie Hopkins received a letter on behalf of Mrs. Hunter, of Jackson, Mississippi, "a widow in reduced circumstances desirous of being beneficially employed."[16] Elite Charlestonian Phoebe Yates Pember never characterized herself as a working woman, but as a widow whose family does not appear to have helped her out; she had to support herself. When an acquaintance imputed to her the desire to work, she lost no time setting the record straight—a sure sign of her elite social training: "She had heard from my sister that my work was entirely a matter of choice, but I immediately contradicted this (as the choice of such a life would naturally be considered an absurdity) and said I had no means and it was a necessity. Who would suppose or believe that days passed among fever wards and dying men, in a hospital away from the city, with no comforts and every privation, was voluntary!"[17] Pember enunciated the popular view of work prevalent among women of her class: she worked because need had reduced her to it, not because she wanted to.

Though Pember grew proud of her status as matron in the Confederacy's largest hospital, she found little glamour in hospital work. To some at home, caring for wounded men looked like the stuff of adventure, but few on the other side would have compromised respectability by admitting that thrilling prospects drew them to the work.[18] Such a self-serving motive was indeed at odds with self-sacrifice. Contemporary commentators ensured that women would think twice before embellishing their motives by scorning those who had enlisted "under the pretense of aiding the work in the hospitals, to . . . gratify a taste for romantic adventure."[19] Veterans like "Grandma" Smith, who denigrated thrill seekers, may also have internalized a more powerful social prescription: that hospitals had an aura of sexual impropriety that no respectable young woman would breach.[20]

In the mid-nineteenth century, hospitals were charitable institutions that served the indigent and insolvent. Shunned by the middle class for lack of hygiene and order, hospitals became associated with squalor and moral debility.[21] That genteel women might work in such a slough was appalling to those who aspired to middle-class beliefs. Opponents feared that women would be subject to the whims of sexually aggressive soldiers and that the air of moral laxity in hospitals would encourage romantic attachments and jeopardize reputations. Women who joined the service in 1861 were well aware of the social forces arrayed against them. Some spent time justifying their actions to doubters, insisting that their intent was not to flirt or find husbands. Others sought anonymity for fear that the decision would make them vulnerable to public scrutiny. The power of public disapproval was strong enough to deter some from pursuing positions altogether.

The most vigorous upholder of women's right to nurse was a single, Scottish-born Alabamian—Kate Cumming. Cumming's own family opposed her work despite the fact that two of her sister's female in-laws had nursed with Florence Nightingale in the Crimea. Undaunted, she entered service with the Confederate Army of Tennessee in April 1862, when she traveled to Corinth, Mississippi, after the battle of Shiloh. So pressed by the volume of casualties that she was unable to undress for the first nine days and sought rest on boxes, Cumming was infuriated that more Southern women were not volunteering: "Have we not thousands [of women] who, at this moment do not know what to do to pass the time that is hanging heavily on their hands? I mean the young: the old are not able for the work. If it will hurt a young girl to do what in all ages, has been the special duty of woman—to relieve suffering—it is high time the youth of our land were kept from camp and field."[22] Compared to Northerners, white Southerners typically encountered greater resistance from friends and family; more rigid class and economic systems discouraged them from challenging traditionally received notions of womanhood.[23] If Southerners had been reluctant at the start, Cumming could not comprehend their reticence at midwar. By September 1863 she had lost patience with the view that women damaged their reputations by working in hospitals. "A lady's respectability must be at a low ebb," she protested, "when it can be endangered by going into a hospital."[24] By December, impatience became cynicism: "It seems strange that [Sisters of Charity] can do with honor what is wrong for other Christian women to do."[25] Cumming laid bare the double standard applied to her peers by noting that nuns transcended the laws of virtue to which lay women were vigorously held. If it was all right for some women to nurse, why then not others?

Drew Faust has observed that comparatively few elites served in Southern hospitals; that Kate Cumming and Phoebe Pember were exceptions; and that Mary Greenhow Lee's experience of preparing food but not working beside soldiers was more typical of this group.[26] I do not believe that elite Southerners were more reluctant to serve than their Northern counterparts or that their percentage in the female relief force was appreciably smaller than in the North. The frustrations expressed by Cumming and Pember regarding their peers' poor showing ought to be understood anecdotally and temperamentally. Their consternation can be countered with evidence demonstrating the commitment of others like them to nursing. Emily Mason described the work of Richmond society women in action: "I have seen three or four of these belles drag from an ambulance a wounded man fresh from the lines at Petersburg, washing and dressing him."[27] More important,

Alabama's Kate Cumming and South Carolina's Phoebe Yates Pember insisted that hospital work would not compromise elite Confederate women. One a spinster, the other a widow, both learned how to hold their own with surgeons during the war. (Cumming courtesy of Museum of the Confederacy, Richmond, Virginia; Pember from William C. Davis, ed., *The Embattled Confederacy* [Garden City, N.Y.: Doubleday, 1982], 3:379.)

Confederate hospital records at the National Archives list women in managerial positions, who, as chief or assistant matrons, could claim social superiority over those in their charge. In view of the amount of testimony about such women, the records that confirm their presence, and the fact that Southern women of all ranks were pressed into service when the war invaded their towns, it would seem that elite women were not less likely than others to serve.

Phoebe Yates Pember sought not so much to criticize her peers as to justify her own decision to nurse in light of attacks on her virtue. When a female acquaintance slandered her for working alone, Pember railed in a letter to her sister:

The friend I called on spoke very kindly of the life of exertion and self-sacrifice she fancied I was leading, dilated very strongly upon the sinfulness and scandal making of any woman who would or could say anything reflecting upon me and to make a long story short I found that Mrs. L-y was the mischief maker. She brought no charges it seems against me only that small and mean style of *sur-*

*mising* which is worse than damning with faint praise. *"She* knew what brought
me to Richmond, no one could tell *her* anything about *me*—if I lived alone I
had my reasons"—all this is very bad and very malicious, my life is irreproach-
able now as it morally always has been; there is nothing in the past or the present to touch it—My time is past [*sic*] from morning till night by the bedside
of the sick and dying . . . never considering my personal comfort, being what to
most women would be a life of self-abnegation and sacrifice. . . . Here comes
this woman pretending to know something wrong in my former life and present motives. It is like a small but poisonous sting.[28]

In the private realm of family letters, Pember could afford to be frank about
damaging sexual innuendo. But her public statement on the matter was
more temperate. In *A Southern Woman's Story* (1879), Pember assumed the
safer posture of universalizing women's hospital experience while defending virtue:

> There is one subject connected with hospitals on which a few words should
> be said—the distasteful one that a woman must lose a certain amount of deli-
> cacy and reticence in filling any office in them. How can this be? There is no
> unpleasant exposure under proper arrangements, and even if there be, the cir-
> cumstances which surround a wounded man, far from friends and home, suf-
> fering in a holy cause and dependent upon a woman for help, care and sym-
> pathy, hallow and clear the atmosphere in which she labors. . . . A woman *must*
> soar beyond the conventional modesty considered correct under different
> circumstances.[29]

Pember appealed to a conservative public made uneasy by the social disloca-
tions of war, where contact between men and women that would seem inappropriate during peacetime was necessary. She insisted with words like "holy"
and "hallow" that women's hospital work ought to be regarded as a Christian privilege in which spirits would "soar" rather than sink in tawdriness.
More important, the contrast between Pember's public and private views bids
us to consider how the wish to serve nationalistic interests through a kind of
Confederate performance may have compromised candor.

The Southern debate over nursing strengthened the convictions of some
while it weakened those of others.[30] When Fannie Beers asked Juliet Opie
Hopkins for a job in one of her two Richmond hospitals, Beers's companions made "an earnest protest against my 'quixotic idea' . . . which ended
in a truce of a few days, during which it was hoped I would repent and re-

scind my determination."[31] Unable to gain any ground with Hopkins because of her youth, Beers found a private nursing job in Richmond and spent the next three years working in Mobile and Gainesville, Alabama, Ringgold and Newnan, Georgia, and Omega, Mississippi. Twenty-four-year-old Lizzie D. Lewis of Castalia, Alabama, was not as persistent. After Hopkins had given her the go-ahead, she wrote back in June 1861 to say that "suddenly obstacles were placed in my way by the objections of friends whose opinions I ought to regard."[32] Novelist Augusta Evans Wilson showed similar susceptibility when she wrote to Ella Newsom, then matron at Marietta, that she could not take part: "I feel unwilling to take a step which [my brothers] *disapprove* so vehemently. . . . The boys have heard so much said about ladies being in the hospitals, that they cannot bear for me to go."[33] Gossip and protective male relatives thwarted Southerners who feared disapproval in the face of rigid standards of conduct.

Northern women also confronted opposition to their service but were more willing to brook disapproval. As in the South, assumptions about what constituted appropriate middle-class behavior gave women pause. The extent to which service decisions were influenced by others indicates that it was neither common nor acceptable for middle-class women to act independently. But fewer social restrictions and stronger public support—aided according to one critic by the midwar publication of Louisa May Alcott's *Hospital Sketches* (1863)[34]—allowed more Northerners than Southerners to serve without fear of reprisals. Family and friends, anxious to keep loved ones safe, offered the first line of resistance. In August 1862 John Lynch of Philadelphia begged his fiancée Bessie Mustin not to volunteer for service in local hospitals: "There is a spirit of criticism & I might say sort of *slur* thrown out to those young ladys which attend the Hospitals." Iowa's Mary Shelton was determined to serve despite such pronouncements: "*Will go* though they all object." New Jersey's Elizabeth Tuttle was more secretive, avoiding confrontation by hiding her plans to go to Antietam after it became known that more than eight thousand had been killed or wounded by mid-morning on September 17, 1862.[35] Although Clara Barton had told her father earlier that year that she shrank from service because of the stigma attached to women in military camps, she was soon to change her mind: "My position," she announced, "is one of my own choosing, full of hardship and fraught with danger, one that *I* could not have chosen if I had had a father, a mother, or husband, or child, or even brothers or sisters whose interests centered at all in *me*, in whose home or family circles my absense [*sic*] would leave a vacuum,—at whose fireside my loss would leave a painful void—I am singularly free."[36] Elizabeth Pryor and Stephen Oates have noted that Barton always regretted not becoming involved in war relief sooner; once she had seen the battlefield carnage of 1862, a feeling of urgency supplanted her earlier sense of familial duty.[37] Barton may well have rationalized that she was alone in the world in order to mount the eloquent defense of her actions.

Shelton, Tuttle, and Barton were not daunted by social disapproval, but its insidiousness deterred others. New York socialite Maria Lydig Daly stayed at home, alarmed that friend Harriet Whetten had agreed to serve aboard a hospital transport, "as so much is said about the nurses who have gone. Some of the men say that they are closeted for hours with the surgeons in pantries and all kinds of disorders go on."[38] Others hinted that a good name was not all women would lose; their very femininity was at stake insofar as military life might produce masculine tendencies. Harriet Terry of Connect-icut taunted Harriet Foote Hawley that her service at Port Royal would make her "a perfect amazon, and some day you will reappear in buttons and epau-lettes, singing the Marseillaise in a bass voice." Terry's charge may have di-verted attention from her own patriotic complacency: Hawley's sister re-ported of Terry that "nothing but the strongest advice from her friends prevented her from [joining you.]"[39] Emily Parsons confronted the gossips by clarifying the purity of her motives: "If those who object to women in hospitals could only hear the speeches that are made to us, I think their ob-jections would be answered."[40]

Darts of innuendo were met with expressions of public esteem by 1862. In September *Harper's Weekly* ran a two-page spread on "The Influence of Women" with illustrations of a camp laundress, a nurse composing a letter, and a Sister of Charity standing at a soldier's bedside. "This war of ours," read the caption, "has developed scores of Florence Nightingales, whose names no one knows, but whose reward, in the soldiers' gratitude and Heav-en's approval, is the highest guerdon woman can ever win."[41] Here the ide-ology of nurture was wedded to Christian service. The woman who served both would win not only public esteem but also a place in heaven. Another proponent defended military domesticity as woman's province: "The right of women to the sphere which includes housekeeping, cooking, and nursing has never been disputed. The proper administration of these three depart-ments makes the internal arrangements of a hospital complete."[42] By 1863 Northern approval took the form of a paean to spartan mothers delivered by

Popular illustrations, such as this two-page spread entitled "The Influence of Women" in *Harper's Weekly* of September 6, 1862, characterized women in domestic work for the soldiers and challenged the early belief that military hospitals were no place for women. (Courtesy of Indiana Historical Society)

a hospital inspector at Cairo, Illinois, where the city's position at the confluence of the Ohio and Mississippi Rivers made it a crucial medical installation: "When warworn, wounded, or disabled by disease, we retire a moment from the contest, [the women] welcome us home with the sunshine of warm hearts and console and strengthen us; and when recuperated through their care, they ever encourage us to return to duty. They visit our hospitals and nurse and fan and lave the temples of our poor wounded, banished from homes of love, ease and comfort, to cheer us when disabled, either in the hospitals or swamps of Dixie."[43] By midwar, women considering service could find ample public support—evidence that Northern opinion had waxed gentler.

Once decided, women sought positions in a variety of ways. As many as half who served during the war never made application. They presented themselves after battles and were swept up to help with feeding and washing the wounded. Compelling need encouraged them to stay on.[44] Others were dispatched by local aid organizations to convey supplies and found reasons to remain at the front.[45] Contrabands who fled into Union lines and were put to work in hospitals and camps also never went through a formal application process.[46]

Still others traveled to war as regimental cooks, matrons, and laundresses. States in both sections had allotted six domestic service positions to each regiment, easing the way for wives who could not subsist without husbands. Sarah Sampson of Bath went armed with a letter of introduction from Maine's surgeon general when she accompanied her husband, a ship's carver, with the 3rd Maine to Washington in June 1861. As it turned out, her husband's permission was her primary obstacle.[47] One historian has suggested that regimental women were not vulnerable to social disapproval because they could rely on the rhetoric of wifely duty to provide domestic comfort for their mates.[48] But if they were less vulnerable, it is more likely that middle-class arbiters did not hold them to the same standard of conduct that it did middle-class women.

The transience of life on the march was a hardship for regimental women. Some stayed with husbands when units were ordered to move to the front; others were barred from continuing and asked to return home. A soldier from Coffeeville, Alabama, observed in 1862 that regimental officers permitted indigent kin to remain only if they agreed to do laundry—an unappealing offer that involved carrying two 35-pound washtubs, buckets, scrub boards, and the like.[49] Orders to send such women away usually stranded them. A Union soldier wrote of a woman and child thus abandoned in Washington:

I overtook a young Irish woman that had come away here from Pennsylvania at Pitsburg [sic] to see her husband willing to follow him as he fought for his country but when his regiment came to embark at Alexandria to go farther South they would not let her go any farther[,] drove her back[;] she was but poorly thinly clad she & an infant some nine or ten months old in her arms, both mother & child shivering & crying with the cold. . . . She had nothing but the charities of the soldiers and warm womans love to cheer and sustain her passage back to her desolate home, such cases are not rare I know of many of [sic] Irish women that have shared the privations and hardships of a winter in camp with their husbands that are now drove back alone to their homes.[50]

Regimental women were usually married to soldiers in the ranks, but widows without support also sought these posts. The destitute were not beyond stowing away on transports bound for the front to reach regiments.[51] Runaway slaves valued regimental positions for sustenance as well as the freedom they conferred, although freedom was ambiguous when Union troops moved south.[52] Georgia's Susie King Taylor escaped to Union-held Fort Pulaski in 1862, married Edward King, and moved to the Sea Islands with his regiment later that year. Despite being labeled "regimental laundress," Taylor learned to shoot, dismantle, and clean guns; taught soldiers to read and write; and nursed smallpox victims during four years of service.[53] For Fanny Wright, a laundress who worked alongside Taylor in Thomas Wentworth Higginson's 33rd U.S. Colored Infantry, freedom had a great price. As she and her husband escaped into Union lines, one of her two children was picked off by a sniper.[54]

Midwestern women, free blacks, and Irish immigrants found a ready path into regimental work, which was shunned by the white urban middle class because of its rough conditions and the fear of social contamination. Women working in regiments were sometimes loosely referred to as "camp followers," a term that military authorities used euphemistically for prostitutes, but which was obviously misleading. In 1861 the eminently respectable Mary Newcomb joined the 11th Illinois at Bird's Point, Missouri, where her husband died of measles several months later. In need of a livelihood, Newcomb remained with the regiment until it was dissolved in 1864.[55] As the wife of the chaplain of the 1st U.S. Colored Troops, Eliza Preacher Turner found herself a de facto nurse. So too for Mary A. Ellis, who in helping her husband organize the 1st Missouri Cavalry, traded a ceremonial role for one as nurse: she attended men with the measles and assisted surgeons after the battle of Pea Ridge in March 1862.[56] When Eunice Norton Godfrey joined the 11th Kansas at Camp Aubrey, her husband William, ashamed of her menial status as laundress, insisted that she be "promoted" to cook.[57]

Working women were also active in Confederate regiments, especially in the more socially relaxed western theater. Soldiers revered the 1st Tennessee's Betsy "Mother" Sullivan, who "shared every hardship endured by the men," including imprisonment with her husband after he was wounded at Perryville, Kentucky, in October 1862. Thirty-one-year-old Bettie Taylor Philips went to her husband at Bowling Green with the 4th Kentucky and remained for four years with only one short furlough. Lucinda Horne was forty-six when she joined her husband and son in the 14th South Carolina. Always on hand to nurse, cook, and do laundry, Horne stayed with the regiment through the battles around Richmond in 1862, Second Manassas, Antietam, Fredericksburg, and the siege of Petersburg in 1864.[58]

Long-term service won women their units' loyalty and affection. Some rose to mythic stature in the ranks for their martial demeanor—endurance and fortitude granting immunity from questioned virtue.[59] Members of the

Susie King Taylor escaped slavery at Fort Pulaski near Savannah, married Union soldier Edward King, and went to work as a nurse and laundress in King's regiment, the 33rd U.S. Colored Troops, within several months during 1862. (From the frontispiece to *Reminiscences of My Life in Camp* [1903])

Regimental women did duty as laundresses, but also as cooks and nurses when the need arose. Empty wash tubs weighed as much as thirty-five pounds, not including the boilers and scrub boards that rounded out the laundress's equipage. (Courtesy of U.S. Army Military History Institute, Carlisle Barracks, Pa.)

3rd Maryland Cavalry gladly testified in behalf of Catherine Oliphant's post-war pension claim: "Mrs. Oliphant is universally respected and esteemed by the officers and soldiers of this regiment," one wrote of her three years' service, "and is worthy of all respect and confidence which our people at home can give her."[60]

Hundreds of others found their way to the front when sons, brothers, and husbands became casualties. Concerned that their menfolk might not receive proper nursing, civilian women traveled great distances to find them. Some of these women became nuisances, but many proved their worth and were hired to stay on. Julia Wheelock traveled from Michigan in 1862 to find her brother at Antietam. Deeply moved by the suffering she witnessed in Washington, she dedicated herself to hospital work after his death.[61] Common among survivors was the maternal sentiment that caring for other women's kin was the most fitting tribute to a dead soldier—that one might "soften [one's] grief by assisting in the work."[62] When a Union woman went to Tennessee in search of her sick husband during the battle of Shiloh, she performed tirelessly:

> As soon as the surrender, the Boat was ordered to the Fort, where [Mary] had a chance of using herself in taking care of the wounded & Dying, she stood by & helped day & night dressing wounds & helping amputate limbs for 3 or 4 days & gained the respect of all the *Staff Officers* in her efforts to relieve the wounded of their pains. They insisted on her going to Mound City with the Boats but she could not think of going away & leaving myself & Bela, so she came to Ft Henry & cooked for all the Staff Officers until this last Expedition.[63]

Confederate women who went to loved ones after Shiloh had difficulty finding them among the twelve square miles of terrain where nearly ten thousand had fallen. Searching for her son and husband, Susan Smith traveled ninety miles before spotting them amid Confederate evacuees in Corinth, Mississippi. There she witnessed a scene not unlike the one at the Atlanta depot in *Gone with the Wind*, where wounded bodies littered the ground in every direction.[64]

Women who traveled to kin behind enemy lines provided care under the most extenuating circumstances. In attempting to reach her son James after the battle of Missionary Ridge in 1863, Hannah Lide Coker covered 402 miles from Darlington, South Carolina, into Union lines near Chattanooga only to live as a prisoner of war for the next six months.[65] The Union's Fanny Ricketts, who sought wounded husband James after First Manassas, found herself in similar straits. For five months she shared his prison cell while Confederate women gawked at her. But the early taste of incarceration— including a stint at Richmond's Libby Prison—did not discourage her from offering to nurse on two later occasions.[66]

While Ricketts and women who followed regiments became de facto workers, many middle-class women sought positions more conventionally. Nursing hopefuls contacted prominent citizens to enlist their support and public connections in the application process. If she found an ambassador or agency to help her, the applicant might write a series of letters before receiving any response. Sometimes she addressed the surgeon general; other times, hospital directors or female nurses already on duty.[67] If a more formal introduction was necessary, a clergyman, mayor, or male relative could testify to her hardihood and good intentions.[68]

Prospective nurses asked about the nature of the work and the accommodations, presumably to prepare themselves for the worst. "Please inform me," wrote Mary J. Jordan of Dowagiac, Michigan, "if it be true what so many tell me that a woman is more in the way than can profit them in a hospital?"[69] "Is it requisite to be an accepted nurse by the chief surgeons," asked a young Southerner, "before one can have the privilege of nursing in the Army? Are [the nurses] subject to orders? to be sent without their option to any point—and is each one expected to defray her own expenses?" Another Southerner begged leave to ask "plain questions": "Will you not tell me exactly what is expected of a nurse? and if they are all, irrespective of age, expected to perform the same duties. . . . If a soldier should have his leg amputated or be wounded in his stomach would it be expected of a *young lady* to dress those wounds?"[70] Without public endorsement, applicants expressed anxiety about the propriety of nursing and wondered if hospitals would attend to matters of feminine modesty. The prospect of male nudity was, for a young lady, unthinkable. Indeed, it was this scenario that made their guardians anxious as well.

Even veteran nurses were expected to present letters of reference whenever they sought new posts, as a courtesy and a concession to potentially hostile hospital administrators. Men wrote such letters as a matter of course; it was unseemly for refined women to contact male strangers directly.[71] When surgeons of the 12th Illinois vacated Fannie Oslin Jackson's home near Resaca, Georgia, they presented her with letters of reference testifying to her fidelity as nurse, which Jackson then used to obtain a position in the Department of the Cumberland—an extraordinary accomplishment for a woman whose husband was a soldier in the Confederate army.[72]

Referees emphasized the moral character of applicants and sometimes conceded economic need. Surgeon N. McGowan wrote from Chattanooga in behalf of Mrs. Halsted, a matron widowed early in the war with two children to support: "Of her amiabilities & Christian Deportment, she has testimonials sufficiently ample and is now seeking a more remunerative position."[73] "As to Education, disposition, habits of neatness, order, sobriety, and industry," wrote another about Ophelia Miller of East Pharsalia, New York, "[I] should say she was all that could be desired. She is of excellent moral character, a woman of integrity."[74] Another wrote from Trumball County,

Ohio, that his charge was "a lady of high standing in this community, possessed of good moral, intellectual, and religious qualities."[75] Frequent reference to moral and religious attributes testified to their centrality as prerequisites. The best nurses, these letters implied, were beyond reproach and would summon the resoluteness of will learned through Christian training. The attention paid to virtue and reputation also revealed public anxiety about the sexual accessibility of women in military hospitals.

Women without references at the ready wrote in their own behalf to nurses already established in the service. Juliet Opie Hopkins fielded a battalion of letters early in the war from fervent Confederate petitioners hoping to do something for the Cause. Union nurse Jane Swisshelm was shocked at the number of strangers who begged her help in securing them positions: "It is perfectly surprising the number of people, generally women, who write to *me* even, to get them places, people I never saw, never heard of, will refer me to people I never saw, never heard of and ask as confidently as they would ask for a glass of water . . . bidding me get their places immediately and drop them a line when they will come on at once."[76] More than audacity, Swisshelm observed job seekers' institutional naïveté. Few hospital administrators had time to read the barrage of letters they received, much less answer them. But many would-be nurses started right at the top, such as the woman from Red Wing, Minnesota, who wrote to President Abraham Lincoln asking him for influence with a medical director.[77] Mrs. Nathan Tinkham, of Springfield, Massachusetts, had no idea whom to contact, so she wrote to the pastor of the First Congregational Church, the president of the state sanitary organization, the president of the "Ladies' Christian Commission," and even the president of the Third National Bank before directing a letter to Dorothea Dix.[78]

Others wrote directly to surgeons from their home states. In August 1861 Amy Morris Bradley contacted two in the 3rd Maine, stationed at Fairfax, Virginia. Though public perceptions of women's hospital work improved every year, women's institutional acceptance by medical men was frequently rocky, even late in the war. Both surgeons replied to Bradley, but neither one encouraged her. "I am fearful that you would be deprived of many comforts and even necessities of life," wrote the first, "and that you would be sorry that you had left those comforts for the rough life of the camp." The other assumed that Bradley would work only for pay: "The Army Regulations are very strict about nurses and it will be doubtful whether you can draw any adequate compensation." Despite the chilly response, Bradley joined them before the end of the year and made herself indispensable. But many other applicants never heard back.[79]

If it came at all, the reply might read like a form letter. The secretary of the Michigan Soldiers' Relief Association wrote one applicant that "we are daily in receipt of similar applications . . . and we are obliged to say to you as we do to all others, that we will place all such applications on file, and procure positions for them as fast as possible." He added wearily, "While we commend the patriotism of these ladies . . . we must remind them that there are many thousands of their sex scattered over the whole Union who are offering to make the same sacrifice."[80] Such correspondence bespoke a greater supply than demand for Northern women and a hospital infrastructure not ready to handle them.


**Whether a woman pursued** the formal path to a position or gained one by default, she was obliged to make domestic arrangements before leaving home. Married women had to secure their homesteads and decide whether children would accompany them or be sent to relatives. Contraband women had to take their households with them, which resulted in a more chaotic transition. Southerners made these decisions less often, as they cared for soldiers in their own homes, but those who left plantations had much to do. Mary Smith Reid, the forty-nine-year-old widow of Florida's former territorial governor, helped establish a state hospital in Richmond. Before leaving Lake City in 1861, she drew up a will in the expectation that she would not survive the war.[81] Bereft of two young children and her husband by age twenty-eight, Ada Bacot of South Carolina was anxious for a change. As she planned her departure—a move her father strongly opposed—concerns about the operation of Arnmore, her Florence County estate, led her to conclude that she ought to sell her six slaves. But disaster was averted when a one-eyed neighbor, who could not be drafted, agreed to look after the place.[82] Like the genteel Bacot, twenty-four-year-old Ella Newsom was widowed and childless when she left her plantation home in 1861 for Memphis, but Newsom's slaves accompanied her to the city.[83]

That white middle-class women left their children with others suggests that nineteenth-century maternal prescriptions might be waived for the sake of patriotism: the call of the wounded soldier was enough to excuse women, at least for the time being, from mothering their own children. Those with infants and toddlers frequently took them along, whereas older children were dispatched to relatives or friends—their mothers confident that friends and family could mother them just as well. Mary Ann "Mother" Bickerdyke of Illinois sent her sons to a boardinghouse run by a Chicago minister and his wife. When they closed their house in late 1863, Bickerdyke asked Mary Livermore to find the boys a new situation. They landed in Beloit, Wisconsin, for the war's last two years, where they complained of their mother's epistolary neglect.[84] Livermore herself was hesitant when offered a job with the Northwestern Sanitary Commission for fear it would "take me altogether too much from my husband and children. But," she reasoned, "the need of relief work for the sick and wounded men of the army became more and more imperative. . . . And I felt compelled to withdraw all objections and obey the call of my country." Daniel Livermore supported his wife's patriotic absence by hiring a housekeeper and a governess.[85]

Once settled in positions, domestic emergencies might intervene. Dorothea Dix frequently wrote the surgeon general requesting furloughs for her nurses. In April 1865, for example, she ordered transportation from Washington to Bangor, Maine, for Mrs. Spaulding, who had lost two sons in battle and was taking the third home wounded.[86] Class prejudice made it more difficult for working-class women to bring children with them, even though necessity often compelled it. Nurses at Columbia College Hospital in Washington were so concerned that surgeons would object to the presence of Caty, the three-year-old daughter of their cook, that they kept her hidden away. Several laundresses from Mobile, anticipating a ban on their children, gave false testimony to Kate Cumming's father, David, who was overseeing the arrangements. After they arrived in Chattanooga with their children, much to Kate's surprise, David Cumming explained that he had been betrayed: "I was very particular in hiring them as washerwomen, & on no account was any of them to take children, indeed I was told that none had children, but Mrs C[arpenter] & *she* had a boy of about nine, which she was to leave with a friend."[87] In an era when child labor was common, working alongside their mothers in military hospitals may have been preferable to long hours in mills or factories. Soldiers whose own children were absent lavished attention on them, making their mothers' decisions to bring them decidedly beneficial.[88]

For a runaway slave from Memphis, becoming a laundress in St. Louis hinged on being permitted to bring her toddler with her. When a white relief worker interceded with hospital officials to make the allowance, the slave "looked as if she would like to go down at the doctor's feet"—a scene all too

Wives who brought their children to camp had little time to look after them in the face of cooking and washing clothes, like this woman in the 31st Pennsylvania Infantry. Soldiers said that children's presence made military camps more homelike. (Courtesy of U.S. Army Military History Institute, Carlisle Barracks, Pa.)

reminiscent of the bondage she had just left.[89] Elite Southerner Fannie Oslin Jackson had an easier time persuading Union surgeons to allow her to bring her daughters Josie and Emma to the field hospital in Resaca, Georgia, which suggests more tolerance on the part of surgeons for women of their own class and race, despite the sectional difference.[90]

In the chaos of camps and hospitals, mothers had little time to monitor children. For black women, who looked after white workers and their children in addition to doing custodial chores, there was even less time. Occasionally a child died in an accident, like the son of Benton Barracks nurse Rebecca Otis, killed by a falling log. Disease was even more virulent: Diphtheria claimed Caty before her mother had served a year at Columbia College; the young son of Christian Commission workers Hannah and Edward Smith died of typhoid shortly after their arrival in Nashville.[91]

With or without children, traveling to the front presented many challenges. For a lucky few, home was near and travel connections were made on time. For many others, however, travel proved hazardous, prohibitively expensive, and inconvenient. In the mid-nineteenth century, expanding rail travel made Americans more mobile. Although travel had traditionally been the province of men, women's mobility increased. Still it was unusual for them to travel alone, even after the advent of "ladies' cars" insulated them from male undesirables.[92] Southern society continued to expect women to travel with men, although, as George Rable has noted, the war eased travel prohibitions.[93]

The differences between Northern and Southern women's perceptions of travel are striking: Northerners said little about it, except to announce departures and arrivals or to complain about its dangers. Southerners, who were more concerned about the propriety of travel, mentioned chaperones and traveling companions. Phoebe Pember consoled herself for having to travel without escort back to Chimborazo after a furlough by rationalizing that everyone seemed to be doing it: "General advice was unanimously given to 'go alone' on the grounds that women had become entirely independent at this time."[94] Although this may have overstated the case, as the testimony of others suggests, Pember did give voice to independent action undertaken in the name of necessity.[95] On her first trip home from the Shiloh front in June 1862, Kate Cumming observed that women were crowded in the cars because Confederate soldiers were given priority. "I could not help wondering," she sniffed, "what had become of our boasted *Southern chivalry.*" Later in the war Cumming noted the frequency with which women and children were traveling by rail to sick and wounded kinfolk.[96]

Northerners also mentioned escorts but did not automatically seek protectors when traveling alone. They reported having made chance acquaintances with men who graciously delivered them to the next points in their journeys. Some were so sanguine about the ease of travel that they mocked the convention of escorts altogether. As she returned to Armory Square in Washington after a furlough, New York's Amanda Akin Stearns noted matter-of-factly that she had met a man on the train who conveyed her from the station to the trolley.[97] Escorts seem to have appeared magically for Louisa May Alcott as well. As she first set off from Concord, she met a man who later helped her get from the Boston depot to New London, Connecticut, where she was to sail for Washington. Aboard the *City of Boston* she met another stranger who delivered her to Union Hotel Hospital in Georgetown. Alcott exploited the double stroke of luck by satirizing chance encounters between solitary female and male travelers:

> Having heard complaints of the absurd way in which American women become images of petrified propriety, if addressed by strangers, when traveling alone, the inborn perversity of my nature causes me to assume an entirely opposite style of deportment; finding my companion hails from Little Athens, is acquainted with several of my three hundred and sixty-five cousins, and in every way a respectable and respectful member of society, I put my bashfulness in my pocket, and plunge into a long conversation on the war, the weather, music, Carlyle, skating, genius, hoops, and the immortality of the soul.[98]

Though Alcott's humor may have masked some anxiety in setting out alone on a 500-mile journey, she showed little of the deference to male protection more common among Southerners.

Far from appearing deferential and vulnerable, Elvira Powers also communicated that women could take care of themselves when she traveled to a Nashville hospital from Buffalo. At Louisville, she noted wryly that it was civilian men who wanted to attach themselves to ladies in order to secure precious seats on overcrowded trains: "An elderly . . . man . . . asked if we each had a gentleman traveling with us. We hesitated and evaded the question. This was being in too great demand altogether." Another "gentleman . . . could get no admission to the cars, no lady would take him under her care."[99] Tongue in cheek, Powers reversed the conventions: it was women who guided men's travel. After a trip of almost a thousand miles, she felt confident and even giddy about the liberty.

Throughout most of the war, the Union and Confederate governments expected service workers to furnish their own transportation. Vermont's Lydia Pierce ran into trouble when she accepted a position at Finlay Hospital in Washington. Assured by the Quartermaster's Office that she would be reimbursed on her arrival, she was shocked when it declined on the grounds that she had not been appointed under "proper authority." Pierce next appealed to Dorothea Dix, writing in anger that "our salary is so small I feel that we ought to have our transportation paid." But Dix could not help because she had not appointed Pierce. After a year-long struggle, Pierce was finally reimbursed by the quartermaster, but officials never conceded to having misled her.[100]

By 1862 Northerners working for Dorothea Dix were routinely provided travel expenses, but those working independently had to come up with travel money on their own.[101] Laura Haviland left Michigan in 1863 to carry clothing to contrabands in Cairo, Illinois, with only five dollars for food, travel, and accommodations. Having nothing left by the time she reached Chicago, she prevailed on local sanitary commissioners for the balance of her fare.[102] State and local relief agencies covered workers' expenses if they could. The aid society of Galesburg, Illinois, paid Mary Ann Bickerdyke's way to hospitals in Memphis and Nashville until the U.S. Sanitary Commission, recognizing her genius for relief work, gave her carte blanche to pass throughout the western theater for the duration of the war. When Fannie Oslin Jackson was ready to return to Georgia in 1865, the commission covered expenses for her *and* her two daughters—an allowance she could not have expected from the Confederate hospital service.[103] State and local relief committees chipped in for Mary Smith Reid's transportation from Florida to Richmond in July 1862, but the trip home was less auspicious: she fled Richmond with the Davis cabinet from which she parted in Abbeville, South Carolina; traveled into Georgia with the retreating forces of the Trans-Mississippi; and returned to Florida alone and penniless.[104] Although her church had paid for her trip to Shiloh in 1862, Kate Cumming had a similarly arduous trek back to Mobile in 1865: after leaving her post in Griffin, Georgia, she spent ten days traveling the 445 miles—by train, wagon, steamer, rowboat, and on foot—the last 250 with only a dime in her pocket.[105] With Confederate rails and roads in disarray by war's end, travelers expected protracted journeys.

The record of institutional difficulties associated with travel gives us little insight into the personal experience of travel: By what means and how far did women travel? Of what duration were their trips? How did they arrange overnight stays en route? Women who could furnish their own transportation usually went by rail unless a water route was more practical. New Englanders appointed to the Sea Islands after Union forces besieged them in 1862 made the weeklong trip by ocean vessel. On her way from Buffalo to Nashville, Elvira Powers took "the cars" to Chicago, journeyed by wagon to the Mississippi, and floated her way down to the Ohio River, where she disembarked at Louisville for the remaining 175 miles overland. Going both by land and water was common for those traveling great distances.

Long trips like Powers's and the voyage from New England to the Sea Islands were not unusual. Administrators kept distance in mind when assigning workers to new posts. But if a hospital in Memphis needed female atten-

State relief agents often traveled hundreds of miles to serve soldiers in the field. The Michigan Relief Association was one of several benevolent organizations to distribute supplies in the eastern theater. (Courtesy of Library of Congress)

dants and a nurse had just finished a stint in Washington, she might get the assignment regardless of the trip's length or cost. Records of the Union surgeon general document numerous trips of over a thousand miles.[106] One of the lengthier sojourns was that of "Mother" Elnora Ransom, who in early 1865 was sent from her post in New Orleans to New York and thence to Washington, where she was given travel back home to Memphis—a trip of over 2,400 miles to travel a distance of only 400 miles. Only three months earlier, Ransom had boarded a hospital steamer in Florida that sank en route to Virginia when another ship accidentally broadsided it.[107]

Workers in the field became veteran travelers since their service depended on the quick supply and relief of mobile armies. Those afloat on the Mississippi and Ohio in the West and the Potomac and James in the East became experienced water travelers. When the object was to get as quickly as possible to soldiers in need, workers took any available conveyance, giving little heed to comfort. Sometimes they rode in ambulances or boxcars, or went on horseback.[108] Mary Newcomb recalled a miserable trip from Corinth to Shiloh in the pouring rain on top of a baggage wagon. A boxcar filled with lice, fleas, and drunken soldiers provided overnight accommodation for Mary

Phinney von Olnhausen from Beaufort, South Carolina, to Smithville, North Carolina.[109] Contraband women were knowledgeable travelers long before most whites, having found their way to Union camps on foot without the help of male kin. Once encamped, they did not remain in one place for long: when troops marched to a new location, so did they.[110]

As an independent worker, Clara Barton executed ambitious travel plans. Leaving for Antietam and Fredericksburg while the battles still raged, Barton got to fallen soldiers more quickly than slower-moving relief organizations. She stockpiled supplies for months in her modest Washington flat, then secured wagons from the Quartermaster's Office. On the morning of October 14, 1862, Barton headed for Harpers Ferry, unaware of the precise location of the fighting. As teamsters drove up to her door on Seventh Street just off of Pennsylvania Avenue, Washingtonians on their way to church saw the diminutive Barton climbing up to the buckboard. Camping in the wagon while the four men slept on the ground, Barton spent four days on the road to Antietam and later recorded the mishaps of the trip:

> Left Washington for Harper's Ferry expecting to meet a battle there. . . . Traveled and camped as usual reaching Harper's Ferry the third day and found that the troops had passed over the Bridge at Berlin[;] after some deliberation we followed, at the first end of the pontoon bridge one of Peters mules ran off and we delayed the progress of the Army for 20 minutes till it could be extricated. Then we passed over and followed on, in the afternoon York had changed work with my ambulance driver James and he was run off an embankment of five feet upsetting the heaviest wagon breaking the bows.[111]

Even a well-prepared worker like Barton had difficulty tracking armies in the field. For neophytes, the uncertainty of wartime conveyances and accommodations might be overwhelming. In October 1862 Harriet Eaton sailed without incident from Boston to Washington for $12.25. Getting from the capital to the Maine regiments she was to supply in rural Virginia was another matter. Unable to find transportation, she made her way on foot and spent the night in tiny Bolivar Heights, where she was "coolly informed" by a woman who agreed to board her that "she supposed I would not mind sleeping in same room with herself and husband. I found I was in for that and more too. With the man and his wife, lay their youngest child and to my horror, when they were about to retire, there came also their dirty grown up daughters, and camped down on the floor, just at my back—I don't know how many *live inhabitants* they brought with them, but one thing is certain, sleep departed from my eyes and rest from my body."[112] The middle-class Eaton found the last miles of her walk anticlimactic compared to her overnight adventure, determining thereafter to ride coal boats and freight trains to and fro.[113]

**Getting to the hospital** involved a series of hurdles that tested the tenacity of aspiring workers. Southerners encountered more resistance than Northerners, but voices of disapproval derailed women from both sections and cast the determination of others in an unfavorable light. What Alcott's Tribulation Periwinkle confronted on her way to Hurly-Burly House (Georgetown's Union Hotel) served allegorically as an induction to the service. Red tape haunted her at every portal as she planned and executed her travel, until she sensed something immanent impeding her progress. Initially, bureaucracy thwarted her, but she came to perceive the enemy as her femaleness amid a male-centered military. The adversity she encountered in securing a pass became an initiation rite: only those who persisted would get to serve.[114] And only the persistent would survive once they arrived at the place where men fought and died.

## CHAPTER THREE

# Adjusting to Hospital Life

It is an odd life, living so entirely among men.
—Emily Parsons to her mother, December 7, 1862

My tent was not ready as I expected, but before night my
stove was up and I began to make myself at home.
—Amy Morris Bradley, December 31, 1862

**As she waited** aboard a hospital steamer for wounded from the Seven Days battles in June 1862, Amy Morris Bradley waxed philosophical: "My life is full of interest and I am happy beyond expression to know that I am here. . . . My labors are arduous but I enjoy the work much! I am doing good— living a life of usefulness! And I thank God for it!"[1] Bradley's confidence resulted from knowing that her work had been appreciated. Ella Wolcott was sorry not to have gone sooner when she saw how much good women could do in hospitals: "I have been a 'female nurse' since a year ago last October and only regret that I did not go in the beginning when a mistaken humility was all that withheld me. . . . I went with many misgivings—but now I *know* what women are worth in the hospitals. It is no light thing to hear a man say he owes you his life and then to know that mother, wife, sister, or child bless you in their prayers."[2]

As novices in the military-medical arena, hospital workers lacked confidence in the worth of their work. But as time passed and they inured themselves to the physical and emotional hardships, they began to believe that they were indispensable to the men they served. "I am hearing too many blessings now-a-days from sick and dying men," wrote Elvira Powers six months into service, "to be in doubt any longer whether or not I am doing good."[3] So much of her identity had Clara Barton invested in ministering to soldiers that when removed from the daily round of military emergencies on the Sea Islands in 1863, her self-respect began to erode. "All things conspire to give me an impression that this is not a sphere of usefulness for me," she wrote. "I cannot feel settled to remain here. . . . I feel out of place."[4]

It took time for new workers to develop the emotional fortitude central to their jobs. Although most had encountered sickness before, none was prepared for the carnage that filled military hospitals. Adjusting to hospital life required the interior and often isolated journey of an individual who, after grappling with the physical and psychological signs of death, might achieve the respect of superiors and stay on or decide that the rigors were too much to endure. The personal challenges were considerable; what most had not expected to find, however, was a contentious arena for women across class and racial lines. The sheer variety of jobs meted out to them, not to mention their steep learning curve in matters of military conduct, created friction among women made manifest in elite enmity and mistrust of the lower class and in white dismissal and even hatred of black women. When one considers the competitive model that structured reality for surgeons and officers more generally, it is not surprising that female workers, unsure of their place

Standing in the doorway of a U.S. Sanitary Commission outpost, Amy Morris Bradley was best known for whipping Camp Misery, the convalescent camp in Alexandria, Virginia, into shape. (Courtesy of Library of Congress)

and with more ground to lose than soldiers who might enlist without raising eyebrows, were subject to gendered infighting.

Still, the first battle women encountered was with the self. For many, only strong religious faith steeled them against the sickening sights of disease and infection, and they remembered the period of initiation as one of emotional vulnerability. The Union's Anna Morris Holstein confessed that she was of little use until she overcame her constant urge to cry. Even later, when she had learned how to suppress the tears, the "earnest thanks" of soldiers was enough to destroy her composure.[5] Although she spoke enthusiastically about her work as she waited for the wounded of Fair Oaks to arrive, Amy Morris Bradley later admitted to breaking down at the sight of the war-torn bodies. Unable to master her feelings until a surgeon reminded her that the only way she could help was to stop crying, she "realized that tears must be choked back. . . . *Action* was the watchword of the hour!"[6]

Sheltered Southerners were especially mortified to recount their earliest experience of work at the front. Cornelia McDonald reeled on her first day at a local Winchester hospital when a surgeon asked her to wash a soldier's face wound and she stumbled over a pile of amputated limbs. Unprepared for such sights, Virginia's Sarah Pryor passed out even while insisting that she was up to it. "I . . . had to fight hard to keep down the emotion," wrote

Fannie Beers in her first few weeks.[7] Genteel Confederates may also have faltered at the class inferiority of their charges when pressed into close quarters.

Although at pains to control themselves, women learned to rein in their feelings until they could vent them in private. Many believed in the catharsis of tears, but not in front of soldiers. The "luxury" of crying after bottling up her emotions permitted Amanda Akin Stearns to take up her work at Armory Square "with renewed spirit and energy."[8] So too for Louisa May Alcott, who felt herself "refreshed by the shower" after a long cry with a bereaved visitor. To Alcott's mind, tears were not a weakness but "a receipt proved and approved, for the use of any nurse who may find herself called upon to minister to these wounds of the heart. They will find it more efficacious than cups of tea, smelling-bottles, psalms, or sermons; for a friendly touch and a companionable cry unite the consolations of all the rest for womankind; and, if genuine, will be found a sovereign cure for the first sharp pang so many suffer in these heavy times."[9] Whereas tears eased bereavement for some, others became so adept at stifling emotion that they "could run or sit or wash wounds all day and talk like a politician the day before election."[10]

The devotional context in which many women acted eased an otherwise harrowing initiation. They attended church at every opportunity and participated in impromptu prayer gatherings in the wards.[11] Praying with soldiers was comforting, even if it did not prepare them fully for the suffering they witnessed. Emotional resilience and longevity in the service were frequently tied to piety. "How could I do what I am called to," wondered Rebecca Pomroy, "if I was not strengthened by an unseen hand and fed daily and hourly with the bread of heaven?" Maine's Harriet Eaton characterized the early months of her service as a time "in which I think I have been led more into the *depths* of Christian experience than any hitherto . . . my own will swallowed up, and I purified, this poor sinful body made a meet temple for the Master's use." After a year of service in the West, Iowa's Mary Shelton still resisted entering wards full of sick men but reasoned, "When duty calls and so much can be done for the Master I must not waiver."[12] Such testimonials characterized service as the fulfillment of a divine contract.

Women of all religious persuasions believed strongly in attending patients at the deathbed and participating in last rites. Ritual lent welcome structure to chaotic schedules; it helped workers endure the emotional turbulence. Many thought that soldiers could find consolation in impending death only by giving themselves over to God and worked to aid conversions. Nurses believed that patients' redemption hallowed their work. A Confederate implied that her own spirit had been redeemed when she watched at the bedside of a dying man:

> He said he was quite resigned to God's will concerning him, and that he was not afraid to die. . . . Well was it for him that he had strength from on High and that the everlasting arms of God's love were about him, for in a few hours from the time of our conversation it was found that amputation of his arm would be necessary, from which he suffered excruciatingly until death came to his relief. But all the time of his mortal agony his faith remained firm and unshaken, and he pillowed his sinking head on the bosom of Jesus and "breathed his life out sweetly there," while to all around witnessing a good confession of Christ's power to save to the uttermost all who put their trust in Him.[13]

A virtual batallion of female soldiers for Christ helped the dying "[enter] upon [their] last sleep," reading them the Bible and sometimes administering last rites.[14] Some went as far as proselytizing. With the zeal of missionaries, they reported trading soldiers Bibles for packs of cards and performing "hundreds of baptisms." So adept were Amy Morris Bradley and Rebecca Pomroy that each claimed to have converted Rebels to Unionism, winning victories for both Jesus and Old Abe.[15]

With a field ripe for religious conversion, evangelism bolstered the more temporal aid women rendered. Harriet Eaton believed that her worth as a nurse rested on her success as an instrument of the Lord. Initially, she lamented her failure to "point [a dying soldier] to Jesus." But success with another thrilled her: "It seems as if my soul must burst this clayey tenement and soar away," she mused in December 1864. "My dear J. has found Jesus. Last night my agony was so great, that I rose to pray for him. I felt that God alone could do the work and I gave it up to him, just as much as I gave myself to him at my conversion."[16] Even nuns—not known for self-promotion —were proud of the errant souls they converted. Maryland's Sister Camilla O'Keefe reported that her Emmitsburg order baptized sixty Confederates during the three weeks they languished in tents at Gettysburg. "To witness the change in those men," she beamed, "was evidently the mercy of God over His redeemed creatures."[17]

Just as the power of redemption gave meaning to their work, female workers made sense of death by invoking the retributive power of the Almighty. "Our sins must have been great," wrote Kate Cumming of the slaughter at Shiloh, where twenty thousand men were killed in four days, "to have deserved such punishment." The Union's Eliza Chappell Porter, who believed that the war was "God's scourge" against whites for enslaving Africans, concurred. Harriet Foote Hawley believed that only a "baptism of blood" could "purify this country & cleanse it of greed & selfish ambition, as well as of Heresy."[18] The God who forgave and redeemed thus seemed to have undergone His own conversion to the righteous militancy of Julia Ward Howe's "Battle Hymn."

If religious devotion aided women's adjustment to the military, it sometimes deserted them when asked to nurse the enemy. Though workers promoted themselves as Good Samaritans, they had trouble following through. Those for whom religion transcended all other concerns were generally amenable to nursing enemy soldiers, whereas those with greater investment in the sectional strife were more resistant. Union women at Gettysburg complained that hospitalized Rebel prisoners were whiners; at Vicksburg, they were "saucy."[19] Mary Phinney von Olnhausen was blunter: "How I hate my Rebel wounded," she declared at Fredericksburg. "I don't think I can dress their wounds anymore."[20] Confederate women were also reluctant. Embittered toward "invaders" hospitalized at Newnan, Georgia, Fannie Beers "could *not* meet them,— could not nurse them" until a surgeon asked her not to think of them as Yankees but as "God's creatures and helpless prisoners." Others were not as charitable and tendered their resignations.[21]

Few Southerners were enthusiastic about succoring enemies but relented once involved with them on an individual basis. Evalina Dulaney was hesitant to nurse two wounded Yankees after the battle of Blountville (Tennessee) but became attached to them as their condition worsened. When her house was impressed by Union surgeons, Georgia's Fannie Oslin Jackson had no choice but to care for Yankees wounded at Resaca during William T. Sherman's relentless Atlanta campaign in 1864; to her surprise, she found the assignment compelling. Virginia's Annie Johns was so distraught when wounded Union prisoners were abandoned at Danville that she elected to stay behind while the Confederate hospital entourage moved on to Richmond in the autumn of 1863.[22]

Though occasionally barred from entering wards where enemy soldiers lay, some nurses insisted that enemies be treated humanely. "If thine enemy hunger, feed him" was Julia Wheelock's exhortation at Fredericksburg.[23] Amy Morris Bradley also quoted scripture when a surgeon advised her not to help a wounded Alabamian. "Doctor," she protested, "that poor boy is wounded[,] suffering intensely—he was my enemy, but now he needs my

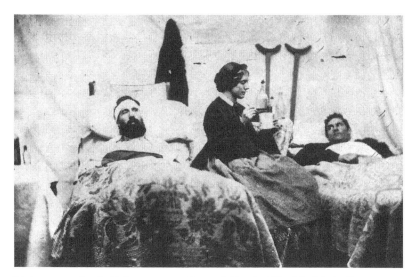

Union nurse Annie Bell, matron at General Hospital No. 8 in Nashville, prepares to feed an amputee. Bell also served in the field after Gettysburg. (Courtesy of U.S. Army Military History Institute, Carlisle Barracks, Pa.)

aid, if I obey not the teachings of the Saviour I am not a true disciple."[24] A Northerner boasted that she knew Southern parents who wished their sons to convalesce in Northern hospitals, where they believed they would receive better treatment.[25] Southerners, like Kate Cumming, dismissed such charges and insisted that they treated enemy soldiers no differently from their own.[26] The defensiveness of women on both sides undoubtedly masked occasional abuses and suggests that they may have felt less goodwill toward enemy soldiers than their Christian rhetoric indicated.

Sisters of Charity, who made a point of observing no political allegiances and of ministering to any soldier needing help, were sometimes thwarted in their work. When in 1863 a Union surgeon inveighed with the sisters not to treat four hundred Rebels in Frederick, Maryland, they ceased their labors, but they were not always so compliant. On another occasion, they refused to obey orders that compromised their Christian obligation and aided Confederate soldiers in defiance of a commanding Union officer.[27]

Hospital and camp accommodations varied widely, especially early in the war before either section had amassed an adequate number of hospital beds.

Thus from First Bull Run in 1861 through the 1862 battles at Shiloh, Antietam, and Fredericksburg, few soldiers or hospital staff were quartered in structures that had been built for medical purposes. Sometimes women stayed in private housing as many as three miles from work sites, but when it was unavailable, they might sleep in hospital closets or packed into a room.[28] By the second half of the war, however, both sections built large general hospitals with the needs of male and female staff in mind. In spite of early rumors that female workers would find no creature comforts, some were surprised that hospital living exceeded their expectations.[29]

Newer hospitals provided more ample accommodations but were not always sturdily constructed. In the fall of 1862, as soldiers wounded at Antietam were shipped to general hospitals along the eastern seaboard, Emily Parsons complained that there were so many cracks in the "unfinished" barracks at Fort Schuyler that "a regiment of stoves could hardly make them really warm."[30] Though older buildings, like Washington's Armory Square, had been fitted to quarter women, some were beyond sanitary habitation. The hotel-cum-hospital in Georgetown where Louisa May Alcott, Hannah Ropes, and free black Matilda Cleaver John served was maligned for its narrow hallways, poor ventilation and drainage, decaying woodwork, inadequate bathing facilities, and latrines contiguous with the kitchen.[31]

Hospital administrators could not always hire female staff or dispatch those already in service if there was no place to put them. After the battle of Chickamauga in September 1863, Kate Cumming and the band of women at work with her in Newnan, Georgia, were barred from traveling to hospitals in Ringgold because there was no place for "the ladies" to stay. In July Cumming had assured Surgeon Benjamin W. Avent in Kingston, who "did not approve of ladies in hospitals" when accommodations were unsuitable, that she and her coworkers "were all good *soldiers*, and had been accustomed to hardships."[32] Sometimes a dearth of building supplies thwarted women's work. From camp in Yorktown, Virginia, Colonel B. O. Fry of the 13th Alabama complained that he could not finish building quarters for a matron until he could obtain the lumber. Six weeks later when the cabin, "a rough affair," had been completed, the regiment—still matronless—received orders to retreat, whereupon its surgeon asked Juliet Opie Hopkins to send instead "a negro man and woman." A white woman could not apparently labor in such a field, though a black couple could.[33]

Female workers regularly reported on the quality of hospital fare. The ration allotted to Union workers was no different from soldiers', and few

The surgical staff at Seminary Hospital in Washington, D.C., accompanied by a steward (with sash, at right) and a teenage bugler. The child in the foreground probably belonged to one of the women at left. Harriet Eaton wrote in her diary that the surgeons at Seminary had more toothsome fare than their underlings. (Courtesy of U.S. Army Military History Institute, Carlisle Barracks, Pa.)

found it palatable. Elvira Powers tired of the endless round of mule meat, bread, coffee, gravy, and applesauce. A coworker she encountered at Clay Hospital in Louisville left after two days because of the tedious diet. Emily Parsons enjoyed greater variety at Benton Barracks—bread and milk for breakfast and supper; soup, bread, rice, and fruit for the noontime meal—but complained that her duties as chief matron made her miss too many meals.[34] Culinary inequities beset Louisa May Alcott's Union Hotel Hospital: cooks reserved more tasty food for surgeons, while patients, nurses, and staff dined on "prison fare." Down the street at Seminary Hospital, Harriet Eaton noted a similar disparity: at one mid-October meal, surgeons ate roast chicken and ducks, sweet and white potatoes, peas, tomatoes, and apple pie, while nurses subsisted on hard tack.[35]

Although food aroused complaint, some were surprised by its abundance and variety and looked forward to the social outlet meals provided. In the spring of 1863, Clara Barton was amazed to find white linen and silver on the tables of Sea Island military staff—probably pilfered from nearby plantations.[36] Amy Morris Bradley found soldiers saying grace at mealtime. "Is this the rough life of camp," she wondered, "which has so often been pictured to me?"[37] The Medical Purveyor's Office at Richmond sent Juliet Opie Hopkins a coop of chickens and dozens of eggs for her Alabama soldiers during the summer of 1861, but by midwar the effects of the Northern blockade and of fewer acres under cultivation were beginning to be felt all over the Confederacy. Two months after soldiers at Chimborazo had consumed twenty-four gallons of eggnog, a dozen turkeys, and "gallons of oysters" for Christmas dinner, Phoebe Yates Pember complained that the $1.25 spent daily on each soldier was inadequate to feed a hungry man.[38] Another noted in 1865 that peas, cornmeal, and bacon had become staples, while flour, tea, coffee, and sugar were luxuries. The dearth of coffee, more than any other comestible, lowered hospital morale—soldiers in the field felt the lack so keenly that they made temporary truces to swap tobacco, abundant only in the Confederacy, for Union java.[39]

Exposure to the elements challenged workers in the field as often as food shortages. Women reported floods, tornadoes, and hailstorms so fierce that they shattered hospital windows. Clara Barton had to sleep on the ground in the rain at Antietam, where, after three days of round-the-clock work, she crawled into her tent, propped up her head to avoid drowning, and lost consciousness. Similarly soaked at Chancellorsville, Harriet Eaton—used to strange bedfellows after her night in the hinterlands six months earlier— found herself quartered with wounded men: "The streams were so swollen that the bridges were carried away . . . and drenched to my skin, I rode up to a house, found it crammed full of wounded soldiers. . . . There was not even standing room, but the doctor managed to find me a corner long enough to lie down, in an old attic, full of old rubbish & wounded soldiers [where] I rolled myself up in a corner, after one o clock and lay in the dark, with our poor boys, not one of whose faces I had ever seen until morning."[40] Nurses in the West were no better off. If one had the misfortune to be quartered in Memphis in the spring, then "you [ate], [drank], and [slept] in the mud and [were] phlebotomized by the musquitoes [sic]." Maria Mann, raised in eastern luxury, had never seen anything like the mud at the freedmen's camp in Helena, Arkansas: "The streets are almost impassable," she wrote in the winter of 1863, "except for heavy mule teams . . . [that] fall in the holes in the mire, often lie there & die. . . . Pedestrians sink to their boot tops . . . in depths unknown."[41]

If mud and mosquitoes were not bad enough, workers also complained of vermin in their quarters. Mann admitted to having contracted lice, as did Emma Crutcher of Mississippi. The house secured for Mary Phinney von Olnhausen near Smithville, North Carolina, was full of such unwelcome guests. Esther Hill Hawks spent her first night in the Sea Islands fending off rats. Veterans reported that the intruders could be deterred by submerging bed legs in cans of water.[42]

Workers found the transience of life in military hospitals disconcerting because most (excluding slaves) had resided in one place before the war and were unaccustomed to the constant rumbling of wagons, nocturnal cannonading, and sounds of human suffering. Field mobilization involved striking tents, gathering and loading supplies, harnessing animals, and readying patients for travel. "I cannot tell you," complained Clara Barton to a cousin, "how many times I have moved, with my whole family of a thousand or fifteen hundred and with a half hours notice in the night perhaps—sometimes under the guns & no time to waste."[43] Cornelia Hancock recorded the toll of heat, dust, and Rebel ambushes as she retreated on foot from Fredericksburg to White House Landing with eight thousand troops after the battles of the Wilderness in 1864—a distance of sixty miles covered in six days. When camps were struck, relief workers looked closely to supplies and personal belongings, which had a way of disappearing when men and matériel were in transition.[44]

Transience and exposure were facts of hospital life, as were a host of other dangers. Fires were a hazard everywhere, burning workers out of their tents, singeing the clothing of workers at soup kettles, and worse. In 1864 a fire that started in a cotton warehouse in Americus, Georgia, spread to the hospital where Kate Cumming worked and leveled two city blocks.[45] Many female workers were trained to evacuate when fire or bombardment threatened by carrying patients and supplies to safety. Workers in border states had to be vigilant of enemy raids. Rookie nurse Jennie Fyfe wrote from Paducah, Kentucky, that workers were instructed to hide valuables and run to the cellar if the hospital were fired upon—but only after helping patients take cover under their cots. The efficacy of this latterday duck-and-cover exercise was tested when Nathan Bedford Forrest's troops surrounded the facility in the spring campaigns of 1864. Although "we were powerless and of course could do nothing but surrender and allow them to plunder," such maneuvers taught Fyfe and her peers to be "ready for any emergency."[46]

Workers in the field reported numerous incidents in which they had nearly been hit by stray bullets and shells. Harriet Eaton made ambulance

Surgeon Bernard Vanderkieft took charge of the naval hospital at Annapolis in 1863. Section Five consisted of tents where over thirty women cared for prisoners of war returned from Andersonville, Libby, Salisbury, and other Confederate facilities. Maine's Adeline Walker and New York's M. A. B. Young both died of typhoid there. (Courtesy of Patrick Schroeder Collection, U.S. Army Military History Institute, Carlisle Barracks, Pa.; Vanderkieft courtesy of U.S. Army Military History Institute, Carlisle Barracks, Pa.)

runs to within one-half mile of the fighting at Fredericksburg, noting that "the noise of the musketry and the cannon's roar and flash was perfectly terrific"; two shells hit the house-hospital that was her destination, although she was not harmed. A Louisiana encampment of contrabands protected by black Union troops was not as lucky: the Confederate shelling of Goodrich's Landing in 1863 made "charred remains" of the women and children.[47] Mary Newcomb and Clara Barton narrowly escaped bullets at Shiloh and Antietam. Newcomb was moving a typhoid patient whose tent was in the line of fire when a ball struck and killed him; balls that passed through the sleeve of Barton's dress as she slaked the thirst of another soldier killed him on the spot. Even bullets that hit home did not deter workers from continuing: Juliet Opie Hopkins took two in the leg at Seven Pines; Michigan's Annie Etheridge was shot in the hand at Chancellorsville and New York's Elmina Spencer, through the sciatic nerve at City Point, Virginia. Though wounded, none of these women left the service.[48]

All manner of accidents unrelated to combat befell women as well. Maine's Isabella Fogg, a coworker of Harriet Eaton's, fell through a hatchway on a hospital transport and sustained life-threatening injuries. Drowning was also a danger to transport workers, who had to climb steep ladders when changing ships. Others reported nearly being swept away when fording swollen rivers. A pontoon bridge over the Tennessee River at Decatur Junction, Georgia, made Wisconsin's Eliza Chappell Porter nervous: "The river is very broad at this point, but the bridge is narrow and only admits of one in the line, a bell is suspended at each end to announce the crossing and the team which rings first is first across. . . . Those on the opposite side must wait."[49] Over rough terrain, driving accidents were commonplace. Amy Morris Bradley wondered at the irony of a near-death accident on her last day of service, when a train whistle spooked the horse conveying her carriage, leaving her to the mercy of the frightened animal: "My driver dropped the reins and jumped out. . . . I knew it was useless to attempt to jump. . . . Still when I saw the horse rushing on towards the bank some 40 feet high I . . . was on the point of jumping when I saw the right rein had caught in the dasher." Ten feet from the precipice, Bradley caught the rein and averted disaster. "How strange," she wrote, "that I should live through four years of hard labor in camp and hospital [only] to be killed on the last day of my sojourn in the Army."[50]

The more likely killer among relief workers, as among soldiers, was disease. Hospitals were breeding pits for germs before antisepsis was widely

Women in the field became accustomed to travel by land and water. Here two workers at Antietam Bridge prepare to board an ambulance in September 1862. (From William A. Frassanito, *Antietam: The Photographic Legacy of America's Bloodiest Day* [New York: Scribner, 1978], 89)

practiced, and few who had regular contact with soldiers escaped infection. "Going through the hospital today," wrote Sarah Gregg from Camp Stebbins, Illinois, "I ascertain the diseases prevalent among the patients are small pox, measles, pneumonia, erysipales [*sic*], flu, diorrhea [*sic*], and consumption."[51] Hannah Ropes, Louisa May Alcott's supervisor, died of typhoid at Union Hotel; when Alcott was stricken several weeks later, surgeons shipped her home rather than risk another woman's life. U.S. Sanitary Commission (USSC) nurse Sarah Beck begged to be released from a Washington-area hospital when she contracted typhoid. On a mattress on the floor of a baggage car "in the dust, & sun & excessive heat," she returned to Philadelphia.[52] But, as Dorothea Dix acknowledged, many never saw home again. Amanda Kimble emerged in good health after a year at Chester Hospital south of Philadelphia, but thirty-five days after she was transferred to care for prisoners returning from Andersonville, she died of typhoid.[53]

When they could, nurses avoided contagion by keeping their distance from smallpox wards. The neglect of patients shunned by others drew nuns in particular and at least one Confederate woman who praised patients' gratitude. Two nuns from Goshen, Indiana, Asinae Martin and Hannah Powell, traveled to a Memphis hospital where they caught smallpox and died. Because they had less status than white workers, nursing smallpox patients often fell to black women, like fifteen-year-old Malinda McFarland Jackson, assigned to Knoxville's Asylum General in 1864.[54] Of course, no worker had immunity, as the deaths of Confederate women at Institute Hospital in Culpeper and at Warren Springs Hospital near Front Royal will attest. Disease also took the lives of Daughters of Charity in Philadelphia, Sisters of Mercy in Washington, a Sister of Charity of Nazareth in Paducah, and Consolata Conlan, a twenty-year-old nun from Emmitsburg, Maryland, at Point Lookout—some of whom had to be buried on site because their orders could not afford to retrieve them.[55]

**Women at the front** came to understand that relief work offered little sanctuary and that war, even in its most philanthropic guises, was a risky business. What bothered them more than hazards, however, was their isolation from others doing the same work. Emily Parsons noted: "It is an odd life, living so entirely among men. Only once in a while when we nurses have time we see each other for a few minutes." Another moaned, "How lonely I am in this great concourse of men."[56] Relatively few worked with more than two other women, and many did not see coworkers for months at a time. "Nothing can better convey the idea of the entire isolation of the various parts of the army," wrote Jane Hoge of transport work on the Mississippi, "than the fact, that women engaged in the same work, should have been in the same fleet for weeks without suspicion of such contiguity."[57] Women's perception that they were alone in a vast sea of men—even if they were not alone—bore witness to the extent of their isolation.[58] Unlike soldiers in the field, they had no instant source of camaraderie. Esther Hill Hawks, one of only six white women on Hilton Head in October 1862 and the only white woman on site after the battle of Olustee (Florida) in February 1864, felt relief whenever white company came to call: "It is a real pleasure to *see folks* once in a while!" But Hawks was also content to bide her time alone, which raised the eyebrows of a U.S. Christian Commission agent: Mr. Henry "expressed his surprise at my having the courage to live here all alone—and departed, no doubt, with the idea that I must be a 'strong-minded' female!"[59]

In Confederate hospitals, where much of the kitchen work and ward labor was done by slaves or working-class whites, elite women hungered for the company of social equals. Fannie Beers lived for the after-dinner society of the Buckner Hospital linen room; she was crushed when transferred to a remote tent hospital near Omega, Mississippi: "The loneliness of my cabin was almost insupportable. Sometimes I longed to flee . . . from the dismal monotony. Often I sat upon my doorstep almost ready to scream."[60] Though Phoebe Yates Pember scrupulously avoided fraternizing with hospital staff at Chimborazo ("In an exposed position where Argus eyes were always watching, a woman could not be too careful"), she took an active part in Richmond society whenever she could. After a party where local belles visited Rebel fortifications at Drewry's Bluff, Pember wrote her sister, "I suppose that you are surprised at my seeing so much company, but if I did not make an effort to be agreeable and encourage people to come to me, I should be very isolated and lonely." Three months later Pember lamented the departure of friends to Charleston: "I have spent every evening with them for five months, and shall have no place to go now."[61]

Elite Northerners also sought out social peers. Maria Mann wrote from Helena that she was "the only female in a mess of twelve," with only two "intelligent" men and "the rest common privates." To Mann, an urban easterner adrift in rural Arkansas, regional displacement was as disturbing as the lack of white faces. In the absence of peers, however, she was willing to settle for the society of other female nurses: "If a boat comes in with volunteer nurses on it," she wrote, "I go & see them if I can get there."[62] Class differences seem not to have dampened Mann's enthusiasm for simple contact with other white women. Mary Phinney von Olnhausen, on the other hand, felt slighted that middle-class nurses were expected to eat with cooks and kitchen help. She noted derisively, "To appreciate them, you must once see and hear them," indicating that where women were more plentiful, class snobbery could divide them. Harriet Foote Hawley similarly eschewed the company of Walt Whitman at Armory Square, where both served.[63]

This was nowhere more true than after battles, when family members would descend on hospitals to search for loved ones. The job of accommodating visitors fell to female staff, who resented the drain on their time. Tennessee's Susan Smith made arrangements for a family of five whose house had been destroyed in the Confederate victory at Chickamauga. They were still at the hospital several weeks later—much to the surgeons' dismay. "Sorely beset were we at times," lamented Confederate matron Annie Johns from Danville, Virginia, "to know what to do with them." At Paducah, Jennie Fyfe counted visitors from Maine to Minnesota during one month of 1864.[64]

With staff and resources stretched to the limit, anxious relatives became nuisances. The surgeons at Kate Cumming's Chattanooga hospital "[did] not like the wives of the men to come and nurse them" because "they invariably kill[ed] them with kindness," paying no heed to dietary regulations.[65] A woman at Lincoln General in Washington proved such "a constant source of annoyance" that nuns scattered whenever they saw her coming and the surgeon in charge requested aid from the surgeon general to banish her. At Union Hotel Hospital, where space was at a premium, one "indomitable" mother slept on the floor through her son's convalescence; despite her constant scolding, pecking, and cackling, none of the staff "had the heart to oust her from her post." A male coworker teased and commiserated with Amy Morris Bradley about civilian charges in their cramped quarters, asking whether "any more fat desponding mothers [had] kindly volunteered to share your bed with you so as to avoid giving you trouble."[66]

If some scorned the comic demeanor of squatters, others found them tragic. A nurse in the western theater maintained that indigence drove wives to seek their husbands in hospitals; if nurses had not fed them, they would have gone hungry.[67] Such was the experience of fleeing slaves, who depended on the Union army for food and shelter but were often rebuffed despite their willingness to work. After the government authorized the mustering of black troops in 1862, slaves with little more than the clothes on their backs threw themselves at the mercy of enlisted relatives—including one matriarch who sought her grandsons with twenty-two children and grandchildren in tow.[68] Confederate and Union nurses alike recounted the stories of soldiers' wives and lovers delivering babies on the premises. Sarah Gregg reported the death of a Mrs. Shrum two days after giving birth to a daughter; just as desperate was the case of Mrs. Daniells, who delivered her baby at Chimborazo and then abandoned it at the depot on her way home.[69]

People in crisis added to the burden that hospital personnel already carried. Surgeons regularly left female workers to inform soldiers' relatives of bad news, which in turn left them vulnerable when visitors arrived too late to see their kin alive. Harriet Eaton described "one of the most painful sights I ever witnessed" in the wife of a wounded New Yorker who had traveled to find him in Virginia only to learn that he had died the night before her arrival. Matron Gertrude Thomas reported the same sad spectacle of a woman arriving at the Millen Wayside Home in Augusta with three children, including a six-week-old infant. One wife was so distraught, noted a Union nurse, that she began, barehanded, scraping dirt away from her husband's grave.

Another managed to persuade Confederate hospital officials to disinter and embalm her husband's remains so that she could take them home for a proper Christian burial.[70] Assignments of this magnitude took their emotional toll on female workers.

Some sought solace by distancing themselves from the hospital. Amanda Akin Stearns's favorite refuge was the nearby Smithsonian Museum; Clara Barton took off on horseback.[71] Unlike those who craved sisterhood, Harriet Eaton wanted more privacy and considered it a "*luxury*" to be left alone. Pursued for two weeks by Captain Thomas of the 2nd Maine Battery, the retiring Eaton, unaccustomed to the social whirl, finally let him show her the entrenchments at Petersburg. By evening she had still not extricated herself from the battery's colonel, major, or surgeon and protested, "I am weary with this continual beau hunting, lady seeking, joking, laughing community."[72] Whereas others found it easy to be sociable, the harried Eaton did not.

The suggestion that men and women away from home were preoccupied with one another was not idle. Cornelia Hancock wrote her niece from Gettysburg that "there are many good-looking women here who galavant around in the evening" and that people back home believed that she had entered the service to find a husband. "It is a capital place for that," she quipped, "as there are very many nice men here."[73] Families were anxious where nubile, white, middle-class women were concerned: they worried that socially inferior men in the ranks might treat their daughters rudely or, even worse, make love to them. When a surgeon urged Fannie Beers to leave her ward before dark lest her virtue be assailed, she ignored him. "I can truly say," she wrote later, "that *never* during the whole four years of the war was that trust disturbed by even the roughest man of them all."[74] At a distance of thirty years from the war, Beers may have sugarcoated the experience of mingling with soldiers. But that women on both sides emphasized their safety suggests that they were more anxious about doubters than predators. Like Beers, other elite women pooh-poohed the notion that they were at risk with working-class men. Clarissa Gear Hobbs was certain that "not one of those men . . . would . . . ever lay a finger on me. I was safe as though I had been at home."[75] Emphasizing military gallantry to offset the rumor mill at home, Anna Morris Holstein used superlatives to characterize soldiers' conduct: "I have been for weeks the only lady in a camp of seven hundred men, and have never been treated with more deference, respect, and kindness than when [here]." Emily Parsons marveled at her freedom to haunt the hospital grounds at night without the slightest concern for her safety.[76]

Abby Hopper Gibbons pictured with 7 of the 160 men she cared for in Fredericksburg after the battles of the Wilderness in 1864. In one small room of her makeshift hospital lay 23 men, 14 of whom were amputees. Gibbons wrote, "The filth exceeded anything you ever dreamed of—stench terrific." (Courtesy of U.S. Army Military History Institute, Carlisle Barracks, Pa.)

Loath to look at soldiers in an unfavorable light, workers extolled the gentility of even the humblest, convinced that women in the masculine multitude exerted moral suasion. Their presence acted symbolically to remind soldiers of the civilizing influence of home and hearth.[77] Whether bidding soldiers to stifle profanity, interceding in disputes, or distributing tracts, women saw themselves as peacemakers. Abby Hopper Gibbons's charges told her that they were "better men when women [were] about." Charlotte McKay attributed her success in breaking up soldiers' fights "solely to the fact of my being a woman, and believe that it was not so much my personal presence as the suggestion of some mother, wife, or sister, far away, that tamed their ferocity, and shamed them out of their bloody purpose."[78]

Others observed soldiers who used good manners selectively, noting that

A contraband laundress at her washtub at Hilton Head Island near Savannah. Esther Hill Hawks sought justice to no avail for black women assaulted by Union officers on the Sea Islands. (Courtesy of National Archives)

female recipients of politesse may have shut their eyes to more graphic lapses of etiquette. Of Tennessee Yankees, Iowa's Amanda Shelton wrote: "It is remarkable with what respect a lady from the North is treated by the soldiers. Let one of the 'natives' or a negro woman pass them and they seldom fail to say something annoying. A Northern lady is recognized and respected immediately." In other words, "Niggers" and "Secesh" did not merit ladylike treatment, no matter what their social standing. Ironically, at the very moment Shelton was criticizing regional and racial prejudices, the surgeon in charge of her Nashville hospital—a Northern middle-class white man—was entangling her in an inappropriate alliance.[79] Expecting bad manners from soldiers in Helena, Arkansas, Maria Mann wanted nothing left to chance: she secured papers from the regional commandant that specified "that I was not only not to be molested, but protected & assisted" and "that they should feel obliged to do it courteously."[80] Inexperienced workers assumed that social pedigree entitled them to courtesy but would soon learn that many male peers felt differently.

In "this great concourse of men," white middle-class daughters might depend on safety of person if not courtesy; women of color could count on neither. While whites attested to their freedom of movement no matter where they went, blacks had cause to be vigilant. Union commanders saw contraband women as nuisances who distracted soldiers, subverted military order, and used up precious supplies. The extent to which such women were arbitrarily stereotyped can be seen in white officers' characterization of them as prostitutes, despite the protests of their soldier-husbands.[81] The pervasive view among whites that black women were morally lax prompted officers to expel them and their children from camp, or worse. Some presumed sexual access to contraband women like their owners had. Though they might at first have regarded Union soldiers as liberators, contrabands were to discover that theirs was a perilous freedom, fraught with personal insult. In some cases, black regiments extended protection to contraband families, as in the case of a young Kentucky woman whose former owner was barred from bringing her back into bondage. But as workers from Susie King Taylor to Abby Hopper Gibbons attested, white military officials and their lackeys could abuse ex-slaves with impunity.[82]

Esther Hill Hawks was outraged by the brazen conduct of white soldiers as soon as the Sea Islands fell into Union hands:

No colored woman or girl was safe from the brutal lusts of the soldiers—and by soldiers I mean both officers and men. . . . The Col. [of the 55th Pennsylvania Infantry] for a long time, kept colored women for his especial needs—and officers and men were not backward in illustrations of his example. Mothers were brutally treated for trying to protect their daughters, and there are now several women in our little hospital who have been shot by soldiers for resisting their vile demands. One poor old woman but a few months since, for trying to protect her daughter against one of these men, was caught by her hair and as she still struggled, shot through the shoulder. She is still in Hospital. No one is punished for these offences for the officers are as bad as the men. Many such instances have come to my knowledge.[83]

Amid such lawlessness, Hawks despaired that she could do little, either to help the women or to intercede with officials, to bring malefactors to justice. Though white women were rarely objects of assault and rape, Hawks's testimony suggests that the same conclusion should not be drawn about black women. One historian has suggested that slaves became stand-ins for white Southern women whom soldiers reviled but could not assault lest they compromise the obligations of manliness. Because soldiers considered white women their enemies and black women their enemies' property, they could transfer their "impulse" to rape whites onto blacks.[84] In spite of their precarious position, black women continued to serve: slave or contraband, they had little choice when their sustenance depended on it. Free blacks, like Union

Hotel's Matilda Cleaver John, and slaves, like those at Sally Tompkins's Robertson Hospital in Richmond, may have fared slightly better; the former less likely to be regarded as easy targets and the latter under the watchful eye of the matron.

Mutually sanctioned relationships took place, despite workers' professed view that convalescent soldiers were in no position to court them. They did not publicize their own flirtations but were sometimes inclined to speak of others'. Ada Bacot and Amy Morris Bradley confessed to their diaries their crushes on doctors; Jenny Fyfe used a letter to her sister to praise the good looks of Paducah surgeons.[85] One Sea Islands nurse was so solicitous of male company that the surgeon in charge dismissed her, noting that "Miss Nye" received "quite a number of visits from officers"—some of them lasting until 2 A.M.—and was found in "an entirely nude condition" when another doctor attempted to treat her for an internal inflammation.[86] Yet seduction was not wholly the province of women. Sarah Palmer noted that married patients courted eligible women in her hospital under false pretenses. Some exchanged passionate letters with them after they had returned to the field. Others were more direct, as the horrified Phoebe Yates Pember concluded about the Rebel who disrobed whenever she entered his ward.[87]

A number of hospital romances resulted in more permanent bonds. Dorothea Dix expressed alarm at the number of nurses marrying soldiers, surgeons, and coworkers lest the charge that women entered the service to find husbands prove true. Nurses sometimes acted as matchmakers, arranging for the minister, wedding party, and cake when a couple wanted to tie the knot in camp. Sophronia Bucklin did so for a contraband couple whose marriage took place in the candle-lit linen room at Point of Rocks Hospital. Other ex-slaves took advantage of the opportunity to marry that had been denied them earlier: in 1863 Minerva Trigg and Henry Dillard—both kitchen help at Asylum General—said their vows.[88] Amanda Akin Stearns, Georgeanna Woolsey, and Annie Bell all married doctors they met in the service. Though she was deeply attached to a surgeon with whom she worked, Ada Bacot married a former patient from Midway Hospital in Charlottesville once she learned that the surgeon had a fiancée back home.[89] A Sister of Charity was so smitten with a soldier she had nursed at Satterlee Hospital in Philadelphia that she left the order to marry him.[90]

Though few women openly admitted romantic attachments, a number obliquely acknowledged the sexual energy that infused their work. Louisa

May Alcott's description of Virginia blacksmith John Suhre's death (her "manliest" patient) invoked maternal imagery, but was full of grasping, clutching, and other sexual cues.[91] Fannie Beers experienced a tense moment with a charge who shrank from her attempts to make him more comfortable: "He submitted . . . at first unwillingly, but just as I turned to leave him, he suddenly seized my hand, kissed it, and laid his burning cheek upon it."[92] Using the language of conquest, Beers ironically cast herself in the role of pursuer.

Phillip Shaw Paludan has suggested that hospital workers "avoide[d] their sexual feelings" by burying them in the maternal.[93] Although women concerned about respectability were guarded in acknowledging their sexuality, their role as maternal caregivers did not preclude sexual expression. They could, in fact, admit the affection they felt for soldiers through the mask of the maternal without jeopardizing reputation. Like kinfolk, they called patients "boys" and were themselves called "Mother"—a soldierly gesture that desexualized intimate contacts.[94] Unmarried thirty-eight-year-old Amy Morris Bradley invoked this rhetoric of family relations by announcing, "*I love them as if they were my own children!*" Chicagoan Mary Newcomb was not sure if she wanted to be called Mother: "It sounded a little harshly on my ears at first . . . I was then only forty-four years old, and felt as young as a girl of twenty . . . [I] felt a little reluctant to be called 'Mother' by men as old as I was."[95] However hesitant some might have been to wear the maternal badge, all came to recognize the reverence and respect it held for soldiers.

Couched in the language of familial relations, nurses' sympathy rested on the mutual devotion they witnessed soldiers expressing for one another—cases in which badly wounded men deferred to others who were in greater need of assistance.[96] Workers described soldiers' solicitousness of one another in highly effeminized language. Soldiers who bade John Suhre farewell in Alcott's *Hospital Sketches* "kissed each other tenderly as women" and cried themselves to sleep for comrades left behind. Emily Parsons remembered the sentimental parting of two comrades on a hospital ship at Cairo: they "put their arms round each other, and with the tears running down their cheeks kissed a goodby as tenderly as two children."[97] Workers who compared hospitalized soldiers to women and children had no intention of compromising traditionally received definitions of manhood, however. Several weeks after her initial observations about comrades literally "in arms," Parsons began to notice that the prolonged effects of suffering brought soldiers into a more infantile state: "The peculiar sort of submissiveness it causes is like that of a poor tired child who wants somebody to take care of him, and is too weak to do for himself." Distinguishing between the sick and the wounded, Mary Livermore noted that those who wasted away with disease became so "despondent" that they behaved like children.[98] The infantilization of the soldier resulted from nurses' perception that soldiers were helpless, which in turn fed nurses' own need to be maternal.

Though female workers saw themselves as surrogates for absent wives, sisters, and mothers, this alone does not account for the evolution of familial rhetoric in military hospitals. If we think of the hospital as a place with a sexually charged atmosphere—especially where only men were patients and a handful of women (in addition to other male medical staff) took care of them—then familial language can be said to have developed as a counter to candid talk of sexuality. By conceptualizing the hospital as a home, both patients and workers offset the public concern that wolfish military men preyed on sexually vulnerable women there. The adoption of familial language also evolved out of contemporary evangelical rhetoric. Those who slipped easily into familial usage were often those whose missionary zeal had impelled them to serve. It is no coincidence that the language of Christian homecoming happily commingled with domestic parlance in the military hospital.

As they got to know soldiers better individually and collectively, female workers began to think of them as comrades. Like veteran soldiers, they felt battle hardened: they fought disease, infection, and a system that too often ignored the sufferer's humanity. Even as they tired of the bitter fruit of war, their loyalty to and admiration for soldiers grew. In the first summer of the war Mary Foushée wrote from Institute Hospital in Culpeper, Virginia, that despite the "amputated limbs and ghastly wounds" everywhere in evidence, "a groan has rarely reached my ears and that the heroism of our men has developed itself more strongly & beautifully in enduring bodily suffering." Blue-blooded New Yorker Jane Stuart Woolsey also bore witness: "How nobly the men behave! I *must* testify to their patience and sweet humor through everything, dying in a torment with a smile in their eyes and grateful thanks on their tongues; praying for their country and *their nurses* in their last delirium." Similarly struck by soldiers' courage in the face of protracted illness, Mary Livermore intoned, "To lie suffering in a hospital bed for months . . . with no companionship, no affection, . . . utterly alone in the midst of hundreds; sick, in pain, sore-hearted, and depressed—I declare this requires more courage to endure than to face the most tragic death."[99]

There was more to the link between workers and soldiers than the dependence of recovering patients on their caregivers. As civilian workers, women were aware of their low status relative to male employees, ranking below the surgical staff, ward masters, and stewards. Similarly, sick soldiers ranked at the bottom of a vast military hierarchy. Notwithstanding hospitalized officers, who generally received better food, lodging, and treatment than the rank and file, patients got little attention from overburdened surgeons.[100] The only soldier with a lower rank than private was a sick private because he was of no use in battle *and* drew on limited medical resources. Female workers had little influence with surgeons to improve patient care and were often at odds with them, seeing themselves as promoters of more humane care.[101] As the medium between surgeons and patients, they more often took the soldier's part because they understood his compromised military status.

The bonding of workers and incapacitated soldiers resulted not only from a parallel status, but from an unspoken willingness to look beyond class differences. Elite nurses, like Phoebe Yates Pember, expected that elite surgeons would defer to them but were surprised when the conventional civilities maintained outside the hospital were not maintained within.[102] Instead of forming alliances with their class equals (surgeons, who snubbed them on gender grounds), nurses bonded with class inferiors (soldiers) by waiving the prescriptions that defined their differences. The war was nothing if not a class leveler for workers like Livermore, who wrote, "If there had ever been a time in my life, when I regarded the lowest tier of human beings with indifference or aversion, I outgrew it during the war."[103] Clara Barton's bond with the soldier grew stronger when she perceived that medical administrators on the Sea Islands neglected ailing privates. Another worker inveighed at the hierarchalization of patient care, "feel[ing] all due deference for Major Generals and Brigadier-Generals, but my heart goes warmly and gratefully out to the 'brave boys' without whom high officers are powerless." Even Pember—that doyenne of class consciousness—disparaged elite officers at Chimborazo, who were "in all . . . cases . . . rougher than the men."[104]

Middle-class women, who would have eschewed contact with laboring men at home, now had an opportunity to celebrate their nobility. Alcott labeled her patients "docile," "respectful," "affectionate," "lovable," and "manly"; Pember called them "patient, enduring and brave"—adjectives that elites did not often apply to the working class.[105] For Jennie Fyfe, manliness outweighed less desirable qualities: "Rough, coarse, and ignorant [the soldiers] may be, but as we watch over them in their pain and suffering, can but see something to admire in the bravery, manliness and gratitude they exhibit." Two weeks later she was still trying to make sense of their appeal: "They feel we are their friends, and it would seem a little strange to you perhaps to know how much we come to think of those we have cared for even if they are ignorant and of such a different class from those we mingle with at home."[106] Workers' acknowledgment of their patients' humanity helped erode class barriers.

White Union nurses' praise of African American soldiers offers evidence that their democratic attitudes about class extended to race inside the hospital. Their solicitousness of black patients, even of Native Americans, is particularly striking against the backdrop of midcentury race relations, which dictated that white women not speak to racial others unless addressing them as servants.[107] The extent to which racial conventions had been suspended during the war is evident in white women's willingness to work in integrated and all-black hospitals. Sanitary Commission agent Helen Gilson took charge of the black hospital at City Point, Virginia, managing a black and white nursing staff and caring for soldiers as well as contraband men and women. Emily Parsons, head nurse at Benton Barracks in St. Louis, segregated black soldiers into special wards but insisted that they be as comfortable as those of white soldiers. When white nurses began teaching convalescent soldiers to read and write, Parsons called the recipients' gratitude "touching."[108] Abby Hopper Gibbons became a one-woman benevolence committee at Point Lookout, Maryland, by serving as advocate, counselor, and judge to blacks who found themselves objects of racist scorn. Gibbons helped restore order in the contraband encampment after it was sacked by the 2nd Maryland Infantry in June 1863. For her intercession in this and other incidents where black civil rights were ignored, Gibbons became the target of hate mail.[109]

Other white nurses were impressed by the soldierly bearing of their black patients. Late in the war Mary Phinney von Olnhausen reported that the Union hospital in Smithville, North Carolina, admitted five hundred black soldiers, the first she had ever seen: "They are a splendid set of men and are so much better disciplined than the white soldiers who are here."[110] Physician Esther Hill Hawks took the liberty of practicing medicine on black soldiers in Beaufort, South Carolina—a position she could not have sought with white troops—because she believed that military officials in Washington, uninterested in Negro regiments, would look the other way. One patient, a twenty-year-old ex-slave named Charley Reason, was "noble looking" and "uncomplaining," even after his arm was amputated. In terms reminiscent of Alcott's tribute to John Suhre, Hawks described Reason's last moments: "The majesty and the mistery [sic] of death stole over his face, fading the eager look from his great mournful eyes, and clinging close to my hand, with a whispered 'pray with me,' he sank into unconsciousness, to be roused no more by the loud roar of the cannon or the low voice of sympathy—and kissing his *white* forehead I went to minister to other sufferers needing me more."[111] Whether Hawks meant that her patient had light skin or she used "white" as a metaphor for purity is not clear. But her expression of sentiment suggests that the death of this slave-soldier was no different from those of the white soldiers she had attended. Hawks's paean to "my black heroes" is even more effusive than von Olnhausen's: "Hardly one, out of the seventy under our care but won golden opinions from us all by their patience in bearing the petty annoyances and deprivations to which all must be subjected—and during the two months that I went in and out among them no difficulties occurred which my presence and word could not settle. I endeavored with my whole heart, to make this dreary hospital life, as home-like as possible—and I was richly rewarded by their grateful thanks."[112]

Although white women and black soldiers achieved more egalitarian relations within than outside the hospital, white and black women had more difficulty. White women could not look beyond the race and class differences of their coworkers, even though many had made this allowance for soldiers. It must be conceded that those who served black soldiers were not likely to censure black coworkers and that those who disdained black coworkers left little evidence of their attitudes toward black soldiers. In other words, racist workers would have avoided working at black hospitals and those with abolitionist views would not have maligned coworkers. That said, the fact remains that it was easier for white workers to be severe upon their own sex than upon soldiers, whatever their race.

Relationships between workers illumine class and racial distinctions. When women interacted in hospitals, they summoned whatever weapons of socially prescribed superiority they could. White workers of the same social class found it easier to get along with one another than with women from other classes. Invoking the familial rhetoric of the nurse-patient relationship, middle-class white nurses referred to their peers as sisters.[113] Upper-crust New Yorker Katharine Prescott Wormeley embraced the elite women who joined her in hospital transport work: "They are just what they should be," she wrote, "efficient, wise, active as cats, merry, light-hearted, thoroughbred, and without the fearful tone of self-devotion which sad experience makes one expect in benevolent women." USSC agent Jane Hoge, not nearly as fashionable as Wormeley and her set, started out from Chicago for Memphis's Gayoso Hospital with a group of women "as true, tender, and competent as the sun ever shone on." Fannie Beers had similar praise for Mrs. Lee and Mrs. Thornton, both surgeons' wives, in service at Ringgold, Georgia.[114] Hoge's and Beers's characterizations suggest that regional homogeneity may have influenced nursing bonds as much as class homogeneity.

But women of different social classes, whose differences were made more visible by the military's practice of assigning lower-class women to lower-status jobs, found reason to clash with one another. The well heeled, who were in a position to donate their services, were critical of women obliged to accept pay and transformed their economic advantage into exalted virtue. Even Amy Morris Bradley, who made it a point to tell surgeons that she was no "contract nurse" but a volunteer, was resentful when she sensed that she was being exploited to clean hospital ships on the James River, while "*the Aristocracy of the Commission*"—women like Wormeley or the wife of USSC officer George Templeton Strong—had more agreeable work to do and were the darlings of the press.[115] Bradley felt cheated of the privilege of those whose social status was perceived, at least in Sanitary Commission circles, to be higher than hers. But more often, the disparities of social class were enumerated by the privileged, not the dispossessed. Charleston-born Phoebe Pember, whose family moved in an elite orbit, noted with derision the pipe-smoking female relatives of her more humble patients and took satisfaction in dismissing a nurse of questionable background who showed up for work drunk. Although Fannie Beers was partial to doctors' wives, she resented the "jauntily dressed" nurses she met in Gainesville who sneered at her as a "fine lady."[116] At the other end of the lens, Iowa's Amanda Shelton criticized "ladies" who skipped their duties to go sight-seeing and "live[d] off the Sanitary." Cornelia Hancock's wish that such "ladies" be barred from hospitals also bespoke her more modest social pedigree.[117] Significantly, those who criticized commoners were Southern, whereas Northerners were more likely to censure those who put on airs.

The religious differences between women also bred trouble. Protestant nurses were disgusted to see Catholic sisters receive what they considered special treatment when it came to daily devotions. National anti-Catholic prejudice, which had become virulent in the 1840s and 1850s with the rise of Irish immigration, did little to raise the sisters in the esteem of lay-

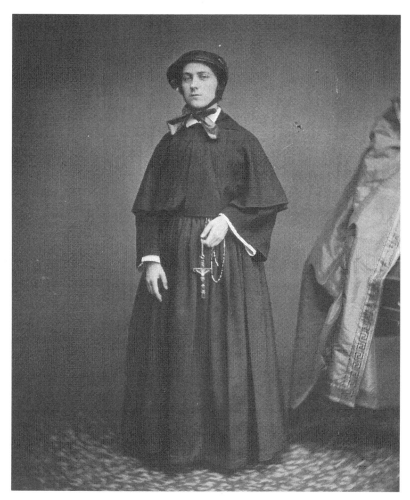

Sister Verona was one of several hundred nuns who cared for Union and Confederate soldiers during the war. As a rule, lay workers kept their distance from women of the Catholic orders. (Courtesy of National Archives)

women. It was a matter of pride to Protestant women that so many surgeons had gone on the record preferring the nursing services of nuns—many of whom were immigrants—to the native-born. Laywomen like Rebecca Pomroy rationalized their nativism by insisting that the Catholic clergy were more interested in proselytizing than in healing and that nuns were merely the conduits for an impersonal series of rituals that finally neglected the soldier's spiritual well-being.[118]

Class conflict was not reserved for whites only. Free blacks, slaves, and former slaves also clashed over issues of social standing. Many free blacks considered themselves better than ex-slaves. Slave workers believed that their position in wealthy white families gave them an edge over modest free blacks. Contrabands and ex-slaves in the North resented the pretensions of free blacks, which resulted from arbitrary and erroneous distinctions, as far as the formerly bonded were concerned. From her white Southern vantage point, Kate Cumming observed class tensions among free and slave workers at Dalton, Georgia. Shamed by the haughty behavior of free blacks there, slaves had nothing but "contempt" for them, believing themselves more exalted by virtue of their proximity to whites.[119] Though Cumming only glimpsed the outer layer of black social interaction, she was able to observe the extent to which intraracial sparring animated Southern hospital culture.

That tolerance and intolerance shared a seat in military hospitals made them socially complex places to work. Class differences were, of course, relative. The ease with which elite workers embraced "the poor boys" shows their reverence for the defenders of family and nation. The bond also reflects the pleasure women took in displaying the maternal ideal of nurture. That they did not similarly revere officers and surgeons speaks to their conflict with the upholders of hierarchy (for whom they could feel little sympathy) rather than a lack of patriotism. At the same time, their troubled commerce with coworkers suggests that within the gender group, parties competed for dominance through class. Furthermore, that workers had ostensibly little to gain by embracing peers but much by exhibiting obedience and reserve before military superiors reveals the saturating influence of military authority: though they did not necessarily revere it, they were bound by it, and being bound by such authority drove a wedge into their relations with peers. Thus their reticence with surgeons and peers, unlike their devotion to soldiers, suggests that they did not directly challenge the terms of sexual hegemony that ordered their social world.

If gender and class differences complicated female work relationships, racial difference compromised them even more. Hospital administrators, supporting a cultural belief in white superiority, put white workers in charge of black, even when all performed chores that were domestic and custodial. Whites' characterizations of black women ranged from polite, self-congratulatory tolerance to violent and mean-spirited dismissal—nothing new for a nation where race was the great divide. White women reminded black coworkers of their inferiority as often as possible, perhaps to deny the harsh truth of their own precarious status relative to male officials. Interracial friendships, like that between Sojourner Truth and Laura Haviland of the Freed-men's Relief Association of New England, were exceptional. More often, the relationship was one of servitude; administrators almost always put white women in charge of black. Both Southerners and Northerners mention that black women aided them by taking on heavier and more distasteful labor. While white women were busy caring for soldiers, they detailed black women as chambermaids, cooks, and their own personal servants.[120]

For New England nurses, who had had little contact with them, the presence of contrabands who would work in exchange for domestic comforts was a novelty. Even though the story chronicles a white nurse's admiration for a black soldier, the image of ownership conveyed in Alcott's "My Contraband" (1869) indicates that standard usage was marked by prejudicial constructions. Maine's Amy Morris Bradley resorted to dehumanization when she wrote her sister in 1861 about contrabands at Camp Franklin, Virginia: "We have one very nice nigger gal that I shall try and send home to you if possible—Do you want her?" A year later Bradley reported from Fortress Monroe, "I brought a capital contraband that I have had since last May. I am going to carry her home when I go." The rhetoric of possession was also evident with Clara Barton and Mary Phinney von Olnhausen of Massachusetts. Barton's diary entry of June 16, 1863, reads: "Taught my contraband to wash"; von Olnhausen wrote a friend: "I am sometimes tempted to send you a nigger; I know such a nice servant and she wants to go North. I have a little one to take care of my room and run my errands."[121] The extent to which Northern whites, pressed into intimacy with blacks, adopted the speech patterns of the master race is remarkable, as Harriet Beecher Stowe had recognized a decade earlier when she described Aunt Ophelia's disgust at Topsy in *Uncle Tom's Cabin*. It is a striking demonstration of systemic racism that women who believed slavery was a moral evil could so easily absorb its linguistic resonances.

Many Northerners assumed the role of parental enforcer, charging contrabands with laziness, slovenliness, and misbehavior. When eastern abolitionist Maria Mann traveled to Helena, Arkansas, she could not imagine why contrabands there did not better their condition, even when provided with material goods. "It is discouraging," she wrote, "to see their wastefulness & the want of tact or ambition in the large majority of them." Von Olnhausen threatened corporal punishment when her harsh words brought tears to the eyes of recalcitrant laundresses: "If I'd been big enough and strong enough," she proclaimed, "I would have slapped them all."[122] Such punitive zeal contrasts with von Olnhausen's praise of black soldiers—another demonstration of the relative inconsistency of racial ideologies when coupled with assumptions about gender.

Despite their demonstrations of racial superiority, a number of workers considered themselves champions of equality. This apparent contradiction reveals how deeply embedded constructions of race were in mid-nineteenth-century discourse. Although abolitionists who muttered racial slurs would appear to be hypocrites, we must also consider that what looks like racism to modern readers may have passed as a liberal view in the nineteenth century.[123] Louisa May Alcott became a crusader for black rights because she was scandalized by the way white workers treated blacks at Union Hotel. Expecting to be chastised by racially sophisticated coworkers when she arrived fresh from the New England countryside, Alcott was "surprised to find things just the other way, and daily shocked some neighbor by treating the blacks as I did the whites. The men *would* swear at the 'darkies,' would put two *g*s into negro, and scoff at the idea of any good coming from such trash. The nurses were willing to be served by the colored people, but seldom thanked them, never praised, and scarcely recognized them in the street; whereat the blood of two generations of abolitionists waxed hot in my veins."[124] Like Alcott, Emily Parsons was distressed by the racial prejudice she observed at Benton Barracks, despite her own adoption of the master/slave dialogic in letters home. As long as she equated blacks with cats or dogs, nobody minded. "But if you carry out before their eyes the fact of their being *freedmen*, by treating them on an equality, there is no end of the opposition." Incensed that members of the Colored Ladies Union Aid Society of St. Louis were allowed to ride streetcars to the hospital only once a week, Parsons noted wearily, "This is the state of things here."[125] Even though they bore the stigmata of racial superiority, both women set in motion a dialogue between races that otherwise might not have occurred—Parsons through the training of black nurses and Alcott through the conviction to "take some care for these black souls" whom white workers kept at arm's length.[126] For both races to have begun that dialogue during Emancipation took gumption.

**Women who went to work** in military hospitals were quickly educated in the rigors of war. Those who had never worked away from home would learn that hospitals offered few comforts, in spite of the familial rhetoric that characterized relations between caregivers and patients. Those who had worked outside the home would nonetheless find hospital work different from the agricultural, industrial, commercial, or cottage labor they had performed before the war. The primitive accommodations and the press of ravaged bodies tried even the stouthearted. Worn down by the physical and emotional challenges, hundreds of women lasted little more than a month in service. But for those who could get beyond the psychic cost of witnessing human suffering, relief work became a gratifying vocation and a Christian mission. Hospital veterans valued their work with patients above any other aspect of service; they believed that one-on-one interactions helped patients better endure pain and protracted hospital stays.

Workers shared with soldiers a low status relative to the medical and military officials who directed their work. Women of both sections held such reverence for the men under their care that they sometimes transcended the class barriers that separated them elsewhere. In Union hospitals, white women also developed bonds with black soldiers—an extraordinary suspension of social custom that suggests the extent to which at least Northern women at the front sought to replicate peacetime patterns of male leadership and female partnership, even when the men were African Americans and they might have played the card of racial superiority. That elite whites enjoyed greater workplace privileges than black or working-class women similarly employed may help to explain the lack of self-consciousness that surrounded their kindness to black infantrymen. The conditions that placed them on a level with soldiers were oddly also those that strained their relations with coworkers. They reenacted the dismissive behavior toward black women that they themselves experienced at the hands of superior officers. Gender seems to have been the litmus test that policed white women's obedience, whereas black women's world was ordered by a racial hegemony. Thus even though female workers recognized that they had little authority relative to surgeons or hospital administrators, this commonality was not strong enough to galvanize them when class and racial variables came into play.

At the center of this web of relations were the hospital worker's assumptions about power: what constituted it, who had it, and how to use it. As workers gained confidence in their abilities, they began to believe that they could ameliorate conditions for hospitalized soldiers. Patient care crystallized as the locus of struggle between female workers and their superiors—another irony when one considers that both groups shared the goal of returning healthy men to the field. Workers who rankled at patient abuse or neglect were willing to sacrifice everything to bring an errant officer to justice. Though the great majority did as they were told, those who chose to stretch the system learned a tactical lesson that put them in the line of fire but also opened the field for progressive action.

CHAPTER FOUR

# Coming into Their Own

The only fault that they find is "that I have too much sympathy for the sick"!
—Amy Morris Bradley, April 16, 1862

Mercy! what do the women at home know of work? *We never* stopped till the whole house were pronounced doing well.
—Hannah Ropes, January 11, 1863

I can't let them die—If they do a piece of my life goes too.
—Harriet Foote Hawley, May 31, 1864

**Ten months into** her service Cornelia Hancock wrote to her sister from a field hospital near Fredericksburg: "We have scarcely anything to eat. I have had nothing but hard-tack and tea since I came: The wounded also are suffering for food as the trains are all taken up carrying forage and ammunition to the front. I never was better in my life: certain I am in my right place."[1] Hancock would remain, working for the U.S. Sanitary Commission (USSC) and the Army of the Potomac, until the end of the war when, under the auspices of a Philadelphia Quaker organization, she traveled to Pleasantville, South Carolina, to open a school for freedpeople. The harder the life and the greater the privation, the more animated and diligent in her labors Hancock became. Esther Hill Hawks, assigned to rude quarters and spartan conditions on the Sea Islands, also rose to the challenge: "It is wonderful, this power of adaptation, possessed by nature! People living in comfortable homes, surrounded by all the luxuries of life would hardly believe they could live amidst the privations and discomforts, which we soon accustom ourselves to!"[2] Emily Mason, who had ministered to Yankees on the docks and Rebels in private homes and field hospitals, summarized her war nursing as "the life of my life."[3] Hancock, Hawks, and Mason were transformed: their experience at the front—with disease and death, soldiers and surgeons, politics and protocol—had hardened them. They began to see themselves as veterans.

Hundreds of Union hospital workers stayed at their jobs for several years. Although we lack comparable Confederate data, narratives like Mason's suggest that many Southern women achieved similar longevity.[4] Women's staying power is curious in light of domestic discomfort, less-than-cordial relations with hospital administrators, and frequent physical isolation from other women. If for some the promise of regular pay contributed to longevity, a religious commitment kept others at their posts. Money and devotion aside, many began to substitute early patriotic ardor with vocation. Feeling that they were an integral part of the staff, previously inexperienced women gained personal confidence as they grew into positions of responsibility.

For those who had seldom left home and its environs before the war, the hospital away from home was a new world. For those more accustomed to travel but with no knowledge of work outside the home, the workplace demanded a cooperation and allegiance little glimpsed. For Southerners whose homes became hospitals, the transformation of private space into public, of personal and domestic work into work for the state, also brought change. Women at the front understood the change in a variety of ways. Some felt that their perception quickened, others experienced alienation from their past lives, still others began to take a proprietary interest in hospital policy. As veterans, their object was less to do as they were told than to improve patient care through manipulating the system. In her first year of service Kate Cumming had observed, "Like a true soldier, I obey orders and *try* to *ask* no questions." But seasoned nurses took greater risks. After two years of hard service Sophronia Bucklin saw beyond the routine of military discipline into a complex world of power relations: "Nurses and soldiers were supposed, by many of the officers," she protested, "to be mere machines, incapable of thought, and unworthy of any attention beyond requiring them to be obedient, without questioning, whenever their rights were infringed upon."[5] Though some lost their naive optimism before a month of service had elapsed and others never outgrew it, most came to see themselves as players on a political field.

As novices, hospital women thought that they and the male staff were working together for soldiers' well-being, and they embraced the opportunity to serve by becoming part of a medical team. But once they believed that they had mastered the systems of authority and hierarchy that undergirded military etiquette, they were not content to fulfill old assignments; they sought new frontiers. It was no longer enough to see that soldiers got meals and medicine on time and the linen room its daily supply of clean sheets. Workers now wanted to enhance the menu, make suggestions about treatment, and innovate bed making. Inevitably those who rose to positions of responsibility had much to say about hospital systems and patient care. Just as inevitably they confronted the makers and implementers of hospital policy.

As workers became more adept in their assignments, their insistence on humane care put them in conflict with surgeons and ward masters. They had little patience with military officials who, in following orders, neglected patients' needs. They saw themselves as advocates, especially as it became clear that hospital potentates had scant time to manage patients *or* nurses. Indeed, because the medical elite had defined women's hospital work as domestic and ancillary, women meticulously guarded their piece of legitimacy by becoming local experts—a quality that irked more than a few surgeons. Despite conditions that set surgeons and their subordinates at odds, many women still worked harmoniously with their superiors. Those unable to settle their differences transferred frequently or left the service entirely.

Discord resulted from the hierarchical structure of hospital jobs. Though some women may have desired powerful positions, all understood that their sphere of action was limited. The patient's body thus became a site of conflict between workers and their superiors. Not only did workers hold surgeons responsible for their inability to carry out duties that would alleviate patient suffering, but also they held one another responsible: lacking the larger view that would have shown them the flaws inherent in the military administration of medical care, they blamed their peers before those whose authority gave the system its raison d'être. If workers were molded by the subordinate status assigned them, then surgeons were also molded by the dominant status granted them. The hegemony that positioned hospital staff in adversarial relations often trapped them in communications that emphasized disparities in status and hid from them the growing pains of nineteenth-century medicine.

We cannot well understand working relationships in Civil War hospitals without knowledge of the history of nineteenth-century medical professionalism. Military surgeons' lukewarm reception of female attendants was complicated by an internecine struggle over the standardization of medical training and practice. In an age when homeopaths and other exponents of natural healing found a popular forum for less intrusive methods, traditionally trained physicians felt threatened by the apparent eclipse of their elite status. The formation of medical societies in the 1840s had helped them consolidate their power, but the American Medical Association's decision to grant membership to a wider base of practitioners in 1859 alarmed its more conservative members. This emergence of dissenting medical sects founded on alternative therapeutic philosophies—in which debate over the use of anesthetics played a significant role—prompted additional professional insecurity.[6]

Professional insecurity and the inability to handle every medical problem they encountered disposed physicians to rely too often on their rank. Able to ascend only to major early in the war, army surgeons found themselves taking orders in their own hospitals from nonmedical officers whom they felt they should outrank.[7] Like a bullet in the gut, these inequities prompted infighting, creating conditions where nepotism, corruption, and graft thrived. Some surgeons sought promotion to avoid having to negotiate with nonmedical officers; others had neither the poise nor the political connections to pursue such a course. Thus authority over subordinates and responsibility for hospital operations were areas of ambiguity and struggle. Hospitalized soldiers and the lower tier of hospital workers—including nurses, cooks, and orderlies—got caught in the crossfire, especially when surgical ambition took precedence over patient care.

Contributing to the melee over rank in Northern hospitals was the controversial appointment of William Hammond as Union surgeon general in 1862. Hammond was a proponent of the newer therapeutics in contrast to doctors trained in heroic medicine. The old guard of the Army Medical Department, most of whom were trained in the heroic tradition, resented Hammond not only on medical grounds but also because military authorities had passed them over for a younger, more progressive practitioner. As surgeon general, Hammond initially supported USSC plans to reform the Medical Department, but not the appointment of civilian women. Indeed, War Department insiders believed that the sanitary project would be short-lived, "the folly of weak enthusiasts and of well-meaning but silly women." In a political tug-of-war, the surgeon general alienated army elders and women, and this lack of support compromised his tenure.[8]

At the helm of the Confederate Medical Department was Samuel Preston Moore, a surgeon known and feared for his authoritarian demeanor but also respected for his organizational zeal. As in the Union, Moore and his medical directors saw a need to institute standards for the selection of surgeons, but the examining board was wracked with nepotism that sometimes excluded the deserving and favored the inept.[9] The greatest challenge during Moore's tenure as surgeon general was to centralize a far-flung network of hospitals. In the war's first year, aid societies had eased the burden of caring for the sick and wounded by establishing state hospitals near the eastern front. Although much of the action was concentrated in Virginia, western fighting was more diffuse, necessitating constant mobilization and restationing of hospital units. Transience discouraged the construction of more permanent hospitals, a condition that vexed surgeons and subordinate staff alike.[10]

When the Confederate Surgeon General's Office authorized the use of female hospital workers in September 1862, women had already been working in prominent administrative capacities for over a year. Though medical leaders tolerated women in their midst, the government's move to standardize workers eroded women's sphere of action. Ironically, women like Ella Newsom, Emily Mason, and Juliet Opie Hopkins, who served as chief executives of hospitals they established in 1861, saw their power subside as they confronted a more centralized bureaucracy.[11] George Rable has argued that Confederate white women's hospital service tacitly acknowledged women's

William A. Hammond was appointed Union surgeon general in the spring of 1862, much to the consternation of more senior medical officers who coveted the promotion. Secretary of War Edwin Stanton's dislike of Hammond, despite Hammond's backing by the U.S. Sanitary Commission, made it difficult for him to be an effective administrator. During his tenure an ambulance corps, a medical inspection system, and pavilion-style hospitals were established. Despite these innovations, he was unenthusiastic about female workers. (Courtesy of U.S. Army Military History Institute, Carlisle Barracks, Pa.)

willingness to be subsumed in an order that validated and enshrined traditionally understood gender identities in Southern society.[12] Although there is credence in this notion, the dynamic of gender relations made women more *re*actors to male-driven centralization than actors in their own right. Southerners may have appeared acquiescent to their superiors, but in public deed and private writing they proved themselves worthy of self-assertion.

Women North and South entered a divisive military-medical arena armed with little more than common sense. Few had the training their superiors desired, notwithstanding attempts by the Woman's Central Relief Association in New York and several Confederate hospitals to orient women to the rigors of the battlefront, as well as the expertise of several Roman Catholic orders.[13] A status-anxious and poorly supplied corps of surgeons wondered why the untrained and militarily naive had been foisted on them, even when some had had little medical education themselves and could have been considered novices like the majority of women.[14] If they were anxious about their own abilities, surgeons' deficiencies contributed to their lukewarm reception of women.

In addition to the educational profiles of medical workers, other factors affected the evolution of work relationships in military hospitals: the ratio of medical staff to patients, nurses to surgeons, male nurses to female nurses; the duration of workers' commissions; and the size, location, and funding of facilities. At smaller hospitals, these variables intersected more easily than in larger establishments, which resulted in better patient care. The unparalleled recovery rate of men at Sally Tompkins's Robertson Hospital prompted Surgeon General Moore to grant a stay of operation long after other Richmond inmates had been transferred to Chimborazo and Winder hospitals.[15]

At Chimborazo and large Northern hospitals, like Philadelphia's Satterlee, more complex chains of command did not always ensure expeditious treatment of patients. Workers from surgeons and stewards to cooks and nurses could more impersonally confront one another and more easily duck responsibility. Despite rigid protocol in larger institutions, their very size made obedience to orders and claims to power more ambiguous. Phoebe Pember was frustrated in her first month at Chimborazo because no one informed her how to request supplies. In time, however, she caught on and "learned to make requisitions and to use my power."[16] Others, frustrated with the bureaucracy, circumvented it. Mary Phinney von Olnhausen quickly saw that obtaining supplies from stingy ward masters would require special efforts. "I've learned enough to know that all who make complaints to head-

Interior of Armory Square Hospital in Washington, D.C., festooned with garlands and flags. Nurse Amanda Akin Stearns observed Walt Whitman visiting soldiers there in 1863. (Courtesy of Library of Congress)

quarters are not only unpopular there but are pitched into by all the house; so I just speak to nobody, get what I can, and buy the rest." Ultimately she drew supplies directly from the quartermaster, bypassing the ward master altogether.[17] At giant Armory Square, Amanda Akin Stearns took matters into her own hands by ordering a special diet for thirty men when the surgeon was too busy to do it and, on one occasion when he was absent, by prescribing and obtaining medicine for a delirious patient. Invoking the wisdom of the red tape cutter, Stearns confided, "I have been in the army *long enough not to ask questions.*"[18]

It was this circumvention of surgeons' authority that fanned resistance to the idea that women could be of any real help in military hospitals. Throughout the war surgeons on both sides persisted in the view that women were meddlers unwilling to play by the rules of military etiquette. Nurses manifested similar prejudice, observing that hospitals run by surgeons who opposed the use of women were "without exception" chilly places for new appointees and comfortless for patients. Amanda Shelton and Sophronia Bucklin, at work in Tennessee and Virginia early in the war, believed that female workers were being scared off by surgeons bent on "a systematic course of ill-treatment."[19] Georgeanna Woolsey claimed that she had "known surgeons who purposely and ingeniously arranged . . . inconveniences with the avowed intention of driving away all women from their hospitals." She insisted that nurses in such straits understood the utility of staying put: "These annoyances," she continued, "could not have been endured by the nurses but for the knowledge that they were pioneers, who were, if possible, to gain standing ground for others—who must create the position they wished to occupy."[20] Even the powerful Dorothea Dix lost ground when surgeons began to hire nurses without her sanction in April 1862.[21] Dix would not be stripped of her full power to appoint nurses until October 1863 but felt frustrated in the intervening eighteen months as she tried to consolidate her authority without any encouragement from the likes of the surgeon general or the Sanitary Commission. In February 1863 she even attempted to bring the by-now famous Mother Bickerdyke under her wing, but Bickerdyke never wrote back.[22]

Early in the war, Fannie Beers, Kate Cumming, and Felicia Grundy Porter observed similar conflict in Confederate hospitals. Surgeons opposed Beers at first because they believed her too young to endure the stressful work, though she proved to be a resilient and hardy nurse. When surgeons barred women from helping after Shiloh, Cumming responded that "the doctors, one and all, are getting terrible characters from the ladies." Several months later, the ladies triumphed: "It is useless to say the surgeons will not allow us. We have our rights, and if asserted properly will get them. [To nurse] is our right, and ours alone."[23] In the fall of 1862, when rumors circulated that women were still to be banished from the western theater, Porter—who had started the first hospitals in Nashville—traveled to Richmond to represent the Nashville ladies "in high places." Porter's sister, Mrs. M. C. Bass, wrote Juliet Opie Hopkins that "our Western & Southern boys *cannot get along without us.*"[24] What Cumming and Porter perceived initially as a denial of access translated, with more experience on the job, to standing their ground. Certain that the Confederate medical service could not do without the help of competent female nurses at Shiloh, both women negotiated the sexual politics of relief work by asserting themselves "properly" in Cumming's words —behavior unconventional by any Southern standard of femininity. Mother Bickerdyke also learned the wisdom of holding firm in her first encounter with the Union medical service. After several days at a brigade hospital in Belmont, Missouri, following the 1861 battle there, she was told to pack up: "Dr. Buck informed me that he didn't wish a woman in his military hospital, that it was no place for a woman." Unwilling to abandon thirty amputees, Bickerdyke decided to demonstrate her value to the soldiers by putting the decision in their hands; they voted unanimously to let her stay.[25] Since the rank and file also elected its officers, the doctor wisely conceded the point.

What gave women like Cumming and Bickerdyke the confidence to challenge superiors whose authority they also readily acknowledged? The longer a worker stayed at the job, the more likely she was to prove her mettle with surgeons and suppliers. Positive working relations sometimes led to added responsibility, which brought women a richer appreciation of the compromises inherent in hospital administration. Those who had risen to managerial positions were less likely to simplify the struggles of surgeons and nurses and were shrewder about manipulating procedure to exert greater control of patients without overtly challenging those more powerful than themselves.

Emily Parsons was offered the position of head nurse at the 2,000-bed Benton Barracks in April 1863 by earning the trust of surgeons in an earlier assignment. Three months' service aboard the *City of Alton* had transformed Parsons from a civilian into a combatant ready to take the reins of responsibility: "I feel now as if I had really entered into the inner spirit of the times, the feeling which courts danger as nothing, but works straight on. . . . I do not mean that I am anything heroic, but I am understanding what it is to be in the army. . . . Self has to be put down more and more."[26] Parsons supervised not only multiracial female and male nurses, but also the women hired to manage cooks and laundresses. Temperamentally reserved and conscientious to a fault, Parsons won laurels for what Chief Surgeon Ira Russell described as a "rare combination of zeal and executive ability." James Yeatman, head of the Western Sanitary Commission, told Dorothea Dix that Parsons was "earnest, just and discriminating."[27] Similar terms were used to describe Sister Mary Gonzaga at Satterlee General, who oversaw fifty thousand cases from June 1862 to August 1865. Known for their medical knowledge and silent obedience, nuns were regarded by medical practitioners as ideal attendants in contrast to more opinionated laywomen.[28]

That surgeons prized the obedient and retiring did not prevent more outspoken workers from rising to prominence, however. After little more than two months with the 5th Maine, Amy Morris Bradley was appointed matron of the 2nd Brigade Hospital, which served soldiers of the Army of the Potomac. During the Peninsula campaign of 1862, Bradley managed the cleaning of hospital ships, using transport work—thought to be a conduit into service for the socially privileged—as a vocational stepping stone. Her

Emily Parsons impressed hospital administrators with her executive talents and versatility. Though a blue-blooded New Englander, she did not hesitate to scrub floors or to join the fleet of boats serving western soldiers on the Mississippi. At Benton Barracks outside St. Louis, she established a nurse training program for African American women. (Courtesy of U.S. Army Military History Institute, Carlisle Barracks, Pa.)

service led to managerial positions at the first soldiers' home established in Washington in September 1862 and a year later at the huge Convalescent Camp in Alexandria, where she would assist 2,200 men in obtaining back pay.[29]

Women like Bradley and the western theater's Bickerdyke were rewarded for their tenacity despite their lack of class privilege. Others landed in executive positions because of their status in society, not their diligence. In the Confederacy, where staffing hospitals with white women met resistance, only those beyond social reproach could work without fear of compromised virtue. Women at the other end of the social spectrum—slaves, whose reputations were irrelevant to those in charge of hospitals—could also work with impunity. In the North, where racial stigma dogged black workers, the ability to earn the trust of white administrators was nothing short of miraculous. After passing numerous hurdles at the New England offices of the Freedmen's Bureau, the aristocratic Charlotte Forten ultimately taught and nursed in the Sea Islands and became secretary of the Boston branch. Sallie Daffin of Philadelphia gained teaching and nursing positions in Norfolk, Virginia, and Wilmington, North Carolina, through similar means; she later became an officer of black soldiers' relief organizations and a correspondent. Runaway slave Maria Bear Toliver was so adept a nurse at the Washington contraband hospital that superiors transferred her to a smallpox hospital where the need of nurses was greater.[30] Sojourner Truth—lionized by the African American community in wartime Washington—worked tirelessly at the District's Freedmen's Hospital and the nearby Freedmen's Village in Arlington, not to mention earning a legendary status as a charismatic speaker for women's rights.[31] Harriet Tubman, widely known for escorting blacks out of slavery on the underground railroad, was so skilled in surveillance and reconnaissance that she was assigned to intelligence work as she cooked and nursed in a Sea Islands hospital in 1862.[32]

Less luminary black women continued to perform work that they had always done but gained more recognition from whites for their skill. They took charge of delivering babies born on Edisto Island (in the Sea Islands) and at the freedmen's camp in Helena, Arkansas, much to the delight of white observers who had expected that midwifery duties would fall to them.[33] And black women, seldom recognized as nurses, cared for sick white nurses, as Matilda Cleaver John did when Hannah Ropes and Louisa May Alcott contracted typhoid at Union Hotel in 1862.[34]

No matter how well connected in the African American community, black women had to make their own way through the hospital service, while whites routinely depended on family clout. Family prestige was especially pertinent in the South, where the plantation economy revolved around familial paradigms. Juliet Opie Hopkins, Ella Newsom, and Phoebe Yates Pember created jobs for themselves in which they directed the work of others primarily because of family position. All were from slaveholding families, and all married well. Newsom and Pember had both been widowed shortly before the war and initially regarded their service as an economic necessity. But in spite of the perceived self-sacrifice, each fell into a position of great responsibility—Newsom as the superintendent of hospitals at Bowling Green (Kentucky) and later as head matron in Nashville, Memphis, Chattanooga, Corinth, Marietta, and Atlanta hospitals; and Pember as the highest-ranking woman in the Confederacy's medical flagship, the Chimborazo. Hopkins, more socially prominent than Newsom or Pember because her husband was the governor of Alabama, had the political and economic resources to establish hospitals in the first months of the war. As superintendent of hospitals for Alabama soldiers in Virginia, Hopkins had final say about hiring and firing; even male administrators would not act without her sanction.[35]

Positions of responsibility required a tacit agreement to abide by hospital regulations and to maintain a public face before superiors and subordinates. As she assumed wider duties, Emily Parsons learned to "keep clear of all cliques and intimacies,—it is lonesome, but necessary." So it was with Phoebe Pember, who spoke of her time away from the care of patients as "exclusive, from habit, inclination and prudence. Living a great part of my time away from all intercourse with my own sex, in a solitude that was unbroken after dark, it was better that no intimacies should be formed and no preferences shown."[36] Pember expressed vulnerability by virtue of gender—not uncommon among women who sensed that work at the front challenged Southern society's prescriptions for femininity. By contrast, Parsons's circumspection was a conscious choice to give the appearance of fairness to those she managed. Both women acknowledged that they had to discharge their duties conscientiously, that others were watching them, and that they were the objects of an authoritarian gaze that could remove them at the first misstep.

As willing as Parsons and Pember were to abide by the rules, others were less compliant. Women who had already made names for themselves could protest more vigorously, whereas the newly hired were at greater risk of dismissal.[37] Unwilling to let patients suffer under any circumstances that she could remedy, Mary Ann Bickerdyke constantly locked horns with military authorities. She derived much of her power from her sterling reputation among USSC officials and the rank and file, which led to her consulting in the building of Memphis hospitals in 1863 and her accompanying Sherman's troops on the March to the Sea in 1864.[38] Clara Barton, who also saw herself as a champion of the common soldier, recognized that anyone who dedicated herself to that cause could not easily work within the system. Barton felt silenced during her 1863 sojourn on Morris Island when a civilian begged her to do something to improve the miserable conditions of the men there. "What can I do," she wailed, citing a chain of command that did not acknowledge her: "I feel that *my* guns are effectively silenced—My *sympathy* is not destroyed, by any means, but my *confidence* in my ability to accomplish anything of an alleviating character in *this* Dept. is completely annihilated. I went with all I had, to work where I thought I saw greatest need . . . and after six weeks of unremitting toil I was driven from my own tent by the selfish cupidity or stupidity of a pompous staff surgeon with a little accidental temporary authority."[39] After such a confrontation, Barton was loath to take on a new assignment—especially when other women were in charge. Fearful that she would be subsumed under the rule of Dorothea Dix or the Sanitary Commission, Barton saw a dead end:

> Each hospital is labeled *No admittance*—and its surgeons bristling like porcupines at the bare sight of a proposed visitor—How in reason's name was I "to labor there," should I prepare my food and thrust it against [the] outer walls, in the hope it might strengthen the patients inside, should I tie up my bundle of clothing and creep up and deposit it on the door step and slink away like a guilty mother. . . . I *might* have been *expected* to watch my opportunity some *dark night* and storm them.[40]

Invoking the disastrous assault on Fort Wagner the previous July, Barton made it clear—complete with military metaphor—that she would not labor where another system had precluded her. When given charge the next summer of nursing at the 10th Army Corps hospital in Point of Rocks, Maryland, Barton again fought with staff well schooled in hospital regulations.[41]

Workers rose to positions of responsibility when authority was handed to them or, occasionally, when they resisted authority. Whatever the route to a more prominent post, workers passed through a hardening process to get there. In fact, any worker who remained at the front for more than a few weeks became hardened of necessity. All witnessed lingering death. Those who began work after battles were in for an experience not unlike the soldier's first combat. The darker side of hardening manifested itself in becoming desensitized to brutality—a state that some feared and others ignored. As ex-slave Susie King Taylor put it, "It seems strange how our aversion to seeing suffering is overcome in war."[42] However quickly the physical realities of hospital life became apparent, it was a challenge for workers to maintain self-control in the face of so much suffering. Once they had mastered self-possession, they confronted the deeper psychological pit of despair. It was one thing to become accustomed to the sight of blood, but quite another to cope day after day with mortality. Thus the hardening process entailed becoming habituated to the physical *and* psychological aspects of death.

Scores of nurses reported that during the war they became competent wound dressers—a task that lost some of its horror through repetition.[43] But developing the skill took an act of will. When Elvira Powers arrived at Indiana's Jefferson General in 1864, she had already been in the service for several months but had not yet dressed a wound. Asked to hold a soldier's gangrenous arm while a surgeon dressed it, Powers behaved like a novice: "It will be necessary," she admitted, "to imbibe a little more of the heroic, before I can be of much help during an operation. . . . All laughed at me, even to the patient; but it isn't expected that a Yankee school-ma'am can be transformed into a dissecting surgeon in a minute."[44]

One of the chief tests of a worker's powers of endurance came in witnessing amputations. It took Amanda Akin Stearns fourteen months at Armory Square before she worked up the nerve to watch one; even then, at the moment when the surgeons were tying the arteries, "I thought it prudent to leave."[45] Mary Newcomb was atypical, priding herself on her stoutheartedness after amputating a soldier's finger when a surgeon could not be found to do it: "I had occasion many times afterward to assist in operations, until I believe I could have taken off an arm or a leg without flinching."[46] Surgeons came to prize women who could stand firm during amputations, but such fortitude was rare.

A few days after arriving at Gettysburg Cornelia Hancock noted that she did not mind the gory sights, but two weeks passed—a relatively short time compared to other workers—before she began to understand the hardening process as a form of distancing oneself from one's past. "You will think," she told her mother, "it is a short time for me to get used to things, but it seems to me as if all my past life was a myth, and as if I had been away from home for seventeen years." Another observed, "It is as if my former life lay away back, out of my reach, and this was my real life."[47] After a year in Paducah Jennie Fyfe explained her transformation in similar terms: "I sometimes feel I hardly know myself, what effect this army life is having upon me. . . . We become familiar with sorrow suffering & even death—it changes us somewhat—it cannot be otherwise. . . . We feel a change some way has passed over us & that we shall never be *just* as before, you do not understand me quite—it's hard for one to who has not been in such a place."[48] Nurse after nurse described acclimating to the work as a process of distancing the self from the past. "I can now write of scenes from which I should once have run with closed eyes," claimed one. "How naturally we accept this strange daily life! And yet, how unnatural it would have seemed two years ago," wrote another.[49]

Workers' alienation from the familiar past allowed them to forge new, tougher selves, but also made them vulnerable to periods of doubt. Low morale was a problem for caregivers who established close bonds with patients only to see them die or return to the killing fields. Despondent over the seeming neglect of government toward soldiers no longer able to fight, Harriet Eaton protested from Windmill Point Hospital near Aquia Creek: "Poor Grinell died this morning and was already dead, yes, starved to death, nothing but hard tack and salt pork for 4000 poor sick men! Just like all the army movements, *No Kettles* to cook with, not even wash basins for washing, nothing, nothing, nothing, but indifference. When a man is sick, no longer effective as a soldier, what does government care for him!" Eaton sank lower as her malaise produced claustrophobia: "What shall I do? It seems as if I could endure it no longer. To stay in this room and look at those decripid [*sic*] men as they come to this new Division Hos. so many of them must suffer on, growing more and more feeble, till they feel as one told me yesterday 'it is better to be laid away in a box and be covered up.'"[50] The interminable cycle of illness and death brought many to the brink of quitting. Wrote one about the deaths of her two favorite soldiers on successive days: "Cruel fate of war. . . . It seems to me at times that I cannot endure these scenes much longer."[51]

Frustration ran high when workers lacked emotional outlets. Kate Cumming noted that she was "completely *demoralized*" working in isolation at Macon in 1865 and began to question her sticking power: "Left wholly to myself, I felt that all my boasted determination to remain in the hospital till the war was over, or as long as I could be of service to the suffering, would now be put to the test."[52] Also in isolation, but not for lack of female company, Clara Barton searched in vain for a quartermaster to restock her medical supplies after her return from the Sea Islands in 1864: "I felt," she fumed, "as if I had to accomplish pretty nearly alone all that I did. . . . I cannot read a single instance where any person from my state of Massachusetts has ever lent me the aid of a straws strength to help me on in my purpose of attempting to care for her soldiers." Anger dissolved into depression three weeks later as Barton, still without commitments from the state or federal government, languished: "Have been sad all day. I cannot raise my spirits, the old temptation to go from all the world. I think it will come to that some day. It is a struggle for me to keep in society at all. I want to leave all."[53] Barton succumbed to depression when she felt isolated—feelings that led to flight as well as hardening.

Hospital workers needed to look beyond misery in order to work effectively without becoming desensitized to the human beings in their midst. Inevitably some did depersonalize patients, renouncing their role as advocate and sparing themselves the emotional grief. Amanda Akin Stearns, not entirely sure what to make of the new self she saw emerging, became "quite automaton-like" in serving patients whom she referred to by bed number instead of name. Others avoided dying patients in the expectation that somebody else would attend to them.[54] Remaining on guard lest the process of desensitization alter them could only be accomplished at great cost.

Ultimately the experience of hospital work itself—negotiating with soldiers and surgeons, serving in an unfamiliar setting, and laboring perhaps for the first time—was transforming. Veteran workers became attached to place and spoke of coming "back home" when they returned from furloughs. When convalescent soldiers returned to their regiments, workers complained that they disliked the "breakings-up of [their] little household."[55] That women used the imagery of home in describing their work is significant: the notion of home place had shifted as they settled into hospitals.

Popular resistance to women's hospital work was manifest in a culturally based concern for the compromised delicacy of unmarried women exposed to male nudity, profanity, and lechery. Professional medical resistance, on the other hand, had a different source: because the management of untrained workers had been left to surgeons, many perceived women's arrival as an intrusion. John Brinton, who became a medical director in the western theater after arriving in Mound City, Illinois, in 1861, wanted nothing to do with the Union nurses that Dorothea Dix sent him. "Can you fancy," he wrote, "half a dozen or a dozen old hags, for *that* is what they were . . . surrounding a bewildered army surgeon, each one clamoring for her little wants?"[56] Another declared that "the members of the profession" were "egregiously victimized by such dilapidated & shriveled up old maids," and that any woman interested in military nursing must be looking for a husband.

Elite surgeon John Brinton, cousin of General George McClellan, felt slighted when assigned to Mound City, Illinois, in 1861, but was soon made curator of the Army Medical Museum—a position that allowed him to collect and document all manner of gunshot wound specimens. Pictured with his staff at Petersburg in October 1864, Brinton (front row, center, with full beard) tolerated nuns as nurses but disparaged fussier laywomen. (Courtesy of U.S. Army Military History Institute, Carlisle Barracks, Pa.)

"My Dear General," he addressed William Hammond in May 1863, "in behalf of modesty do I beseech you to issue an order prohibiting Feminine Nurses—throwing themselves into the Arms of Sick & wounded Soldiers and Lasciviously Exciting their Animal passions." A milder commentator observed that "even good men have opposed [the introduction of female nurses] on the score of so few being trained to nurse."[57] Though lack of training was a sticking point with surgeons, some would not hire women simply because they were women.

Others welcomed women and acknowledged their skill as morale boosters. When women were present, surgeons could leave the domestic details to them and devote themselves more fully to the business of diagnosis and treatment. When women were present, hospitals were cleaner and soldiers' hygiene was taken more seriously. To smooth the transition for surgeons who were encountering female attendants for the first time, the Union Surgeon General's Office conducted a survey in October 1862. The cover letter asked surgeons to evaluate the "practical workings" of the system employing women and to "communicate freely" about them; it also asked surgeons to "state 1st whether in your opinion it is desirable to continue them in force, 2nd whether in your opinion the introduction of female nurses has been advantageous to the hospital service, [and] 3rd whether their utility could be increased by any system of management."[58] Hammond's letter anticipated surgeons' dissatisfaction and bespoke his own anxiety; at the same time it communicated that female attendants would not necessarily become a permanent fixture of hospital life. The questionnaire also formalized nurses' status as objects of surgical scrutiny.

Many surgeons responded. Thomas F. Azpell, stationed in St. Louis, replied in November that his five female attendants were serving satisfactorily in the hospital linen room and kitchen. "But Females as nurses proper," he stated, "I candidly believe to be unnecessary and in some instances productive of decidedly pernicious effects. . . . The moral effect of the presence of a few women in a military Hospital seems to be worthy of attention in restraining and rendering the inmates more amenable to control, but when employed as general and actual nurses laying aside the natural delicacy of the sex, the proper respect for them is lost or forgotten and they become worse than useless."[59] To Azpell's mind, women could be of use to the military as moral prompters. But service that bordered on medical practice was unacceptable. Surgeon J. H. Baxter of Campbell Hospital in Washington chose not to use women at all: "Having had charge of Hospitals in which female nurses were employed, and also having conducted this Hospital . . . without the aid of female nurses, I give it as my honest opinion that I can conduct this Hospital in a much better manner, and with greater justice towards my patients without female nurses."[60]

Whether they wished to retain female workers or not, surgeons sometimes used a woman's virtue as a pretext for dismissing her. In response to some complaints about the "improper characters" of Miss Mollie Davis and Mrs. Maggie Messeroll employed in a Memphis hospital, James E. Yeatman of the Western Sanitary Commission wrote: "If there is the least reason for suspecting the chastity of a nurse she should be at once dismissed. . . . If they were once so spoken of even if satisfied of their innocence, I would advise them to return to their [plans?], where they would be removed from the evil thoughts & suspicions of those around them—in fact no truly virtuous woman would remain where her virtue was talked about or suspected."[61] In other words, merely the suggestion that a woman's modesty had been compromised was enough to send her packing.

Though such conditions made nurses residents in a fish bowl, most eventually performed to surgeons' satisfaction. Surgeons cited nurses for bravery: "When the Rebels were approaching [Winchester] I put the question to her, whether she wished to leave. . . . Her answer was 'I came to give my services to the sick and wounded, and if the Rebels come my services will be needed by those in the Hospital, just as much as now, therefore I will stay'— and she did and was a faithful nurse";[62] for competency: "The female nurses thus far have been essential to the working of the hospital";[63] for versatility: "It will require a man to take her place";[64] for loyal service: "The day that would witness Miss Morrison's departure from the ward would carry sadness to the hearts of the brave sick and wounded entrusted to my care";[65] and even for medical expertise: Almira Fifield of the 9th Indiana was "capable, zealous, worthy, robust & has withal a good knowledge of medicine."[66] Surgeon J. M. Palmer was so certain that Mary Phinney von Olnhausen had been maligned in his absence by acting Assistant Surgeon Mudie that he wrote to Dorothea Dix defending von Olnhausen's unsullied record ("A more sincere worker, or more faithful, untiring, & intelligent nurse I have not known in the Army—And if Asst Surg Mudie has written you anything to the contrary he deserves exposure & censure")—an extraordinary gesture in light of most surgeons' reluctance to take the part of a subordinate over a professional colleague.[67]

Once they learned that quiet, competent duty won them laurels, nurses found surgeons praiseworthy. Amy Morris Bradley credited Surgeon Sanford Hunt and his assistant with bringing order out of the chaos of the Convalescent Camp in Alexandria: "Under their judicious management, rapid improvements were made. . . . And here let me say I have been treated with the utmost kindness by these officers." Surgeon Hunt responded in kind, calling Bradley "actively and unobtrusively useful," one who "has never interfered with duties belonging to others"—praise that confirmed his desire for obedience over enterprise.[68] When Surgeon D. W. Bliss singled out Ward E of Armory Square as the "cleanest" in the hospital, Amanda Akin Stearns took "pleasure" in announcing the fact to coworkers. The more Bliss praised her, the harder she worked to impress him.[69] The same psychology worked on Clara Barton—but only with men in charge. She could not get along with female nurses in the 10th Army Corps Hospital, but Barton spoke of the surgeons in glowing terms: the doctor in charge was "a young man of uncommon good nature and ability, enterprising and humane." Of the executive officer, she wrote that "no better could have been desired, every thread

Surgeon D. W. Bliss fostered competition between his nurses for keeping their wards tidy at Armory Square Hospital in Washington, D.C. Here Bliss (seated third from left) is pictured with his staff and the facility's chaplain (seated second from left) on the hospital grounds. (Courtesy of U.S. Army Military History Institute, Carlisle Barracks, Pa.)

of him was common sense"; even the ward master was "by nature one of her nobles—clear, true, warm hearted & dignified."[70] Such glowing accounts were rare in Barton's diary.

These examples of mutual respect did not exist between equals, however. By virtue of their medical authority and military rank, surgeons could urge nurses to obey or threaten to fire them. Surgical authority, acknowledged or not, placed the burden of adaptation on women and other subordinate workers. At the same time, women's marginal status did not deter them from disagreeing with surgeons when they saw fit, and sometimes surgeons left them a wide berth. Writing that she would never have gone to Helena if she had had "the least conception of what was involved," Maria Mann wilted under the scrutiny of her superiors, which "destroy[ed] the little self confidence I ever possessed."[71] Emily Parsons shared cordial relations with the chief surgeon at Fort Schuyler ("a thorough gentleman") but was no less vulnerable to his unremitting gaze. Describing "the Doctor" as "fearfully particular," she was "much afraid of failing at some point."[72] When they perceived that surgeons arbitrarily limited their sphere of action, nurses turned the tables, questioning surgeons' authority. The Union's Ella Wolcott was so incensed that Union surgeons barred female attendants from ministering to Rebel soldiers at Point Lookout that she went to Dorothea Dix to complain. Permission granted to nurse the soldiers, Wolcott took a step back to reaffirm her cooperation: "In all things I am thoroughly amenable and I hope acceptable to the authorities of the Hospital."[73] Having been dismissed with several others from Hammond General two years earlier for "noncompliance with [the] rules of the hosptl," Wolcott was anxious to live down her reputation as a troublemaker.[74] Her negotiation with superior authority must be seen as an attempt to assert her own authority, however. She was willing to comply only after she had won her point.

Such concessions were sometimes the result of being handed authority they had not expected. Susan Smith called surgeons at Tunnel Hill, Georgia, "gentlemen [who] treated me with reverence and kindness due a mother." The source of Smith's admiration was the freedom to "administer to the wants of the patients as I thought best."[75] In other words, where superiors acknowledged the autonomy of subordinates, where they were willing to share a little of their own authority, all worked more harmoniously. Although it may have veiled nurses' own anxiety about reputation, their emphasis on surgeons' gentility also suggests that their good opinion had conditions: surgeons earned class respect only when they allowed nurses some control over their own turf.

Beneath the surface of comments that praised surgeons or acceded to their authority, hospital workers revealed a multiplicity of tensions that paralleled the complex balance of power on which hospital relations rested. Some of their accounts damned surgeons with faint praise. Wishing to contradict the popular impression of surgeons as inebriated, insensitive butchers, nurse-memoirists recounted the good deeds of the men under whom they had served. Jane Hoge was willing to "testify to the devotion and efficiency of a large number of army surgeons" but added that "unfortunately" and "inevitably" they were "not perfect." Elvira Powers allowed that at least as many "wise and noble" surgeons "rightly appreciate[d] woman's influence in a hospital" as dismissed them for interfering.[76] Though Fannie Beers thought of Dr. Gore as one of "Nature's Noblemen" and other surgeons as "self-sacrificing," she was quick to add that "with only two exceptions, they were devoted to their patients, and as attentive as the immense number of sick allowed them to be"—a qualification that apologized for their being only human.[77] Judicious in their summaries of the surgical corps, these nurses disputed unfair characterizations, but they also qualified their praise.

Under wartime conditions, where surgeons and administrators could not attend all who needed their help, female workers wrestled with conflicts between obedience and conscience. Should they respect medical officers' adherence to military regulations when the patient's well-being might be compromised? Or should they breach protocol if they could alleviate suffering and risk incurring medical practitioners' displeasure? Phoebe Yates Pember chose to observe professional etiquette and resign herself to the outcome: "No temptation could induce me to interfere in any way with medical treatment, not even to offering the slightest alleviation to suffering men."[78] Coming from a Confederate woman, whose military participation was not enthusiastically endorsed, such paeans to obedience might have indicated sincere deference to male authority, but they also might have reflected a more rhetorically acquiescent strategy to mask other forms of disobedience. Although Pember's public silence had costs, she was fearless in her journal and private correspondence, where she uncovered a conspiracy among surgeons and male nurses at Chimborazo who "doctored" reports for one another to conceal unscheduled absences. Pember could report neither their disappearance nor their intoxicated return to duty out of fear that she would be dismissed. In fact, it was easier for her to censure an inebriated female nurse than to "unsex" herself by implicating male coworkers.[79]

Workers who more directly challenged superiors believed that they were ameliorating conditions for patients. They questioned matters of diet and treatment and, if they observed corruption, might carry their complaints beyond the hospital—particularly galling to administrators who balked at having the workings of their houses subjected to public scrutiny. The most fearless of combatants were white middle-class nurses, who shared racial and class status with surgeons and thus felt more secure in their resistance, unlike those who had more to lose if dismissed for insubordination. For African Americans whose work gave them subsistence, it would have been folly to air grievances.

Surgeons and stewards often oversaw the distribution of food and medical supplies in their hospitals, which put them at odds with workers who felt that they should govern these areas. Early in the war Confederate women without the resources of Juliet Opie Hopkins or Ella Newsom begged surgeons to establish "regular hospital arrangements" so that they could furnish domestic labor, but their pleas fell on deaf ears. Isabella Stuart reported that wounded soldiers in Chantilly, Virginia, were "*entirely* destitute of propper [*sic*] nourishment" due in part to surgical neglect. "Appeals have been made to the surgeons & officers to effect some plan for the relief of the suffering," she wrote, "but they seem to have become hardened to the sight & to regard it as a necessity without taking any means to remedy it."[80]

Esther Hill Hawks and Harriet Eaton expressed shock at Union supply men who made no attempt to hide their swindling. Policing hospitals was difficult where women were sparse, as Hawks had learned when no punitive measures were taken against the white officers who molested black women in the Sea Islands. She sat by in mortification as chickens she had procured for the sick found their way to the officers' table. A steward's foul play became apparent in a second incident when Hawks spotted him in new garb the day after a box had arrived from a Boston aid society.[81] As a state relief agent in the field, Harriet Eaton also worked in relative isolation. On the job for only two months, she shrank from lodging a complaint against a corrupt quartermaster but had no trouble venting her rage privately:

> That Quarter Master Litchfield of Rockland, is in my opinion a great rascal, a man void entirely of principle, he buried a man to day before the body was cold, detailed some poor sick men to dig the grave with threats of putting them into a similar hole and then boasted to Mr. Hays that he hustled him into the ground—quick. He asked Capt. S. the other day to draw a pair of pants for some one connected with him and charge it to one of the dead men. He orders the sick seargents [*sic*] to do guard duty threatening to tie them to a cart wheel. Are our sons to be under the tyranny of such an awful man? I wish I had power.[82]

Without officers willing to prosecute offenses that some among them saw as harmless pranks, nurses felt stymied.

What Hawks and Eaton encountered as a power vacuum, Jane Stuart Woolsey understood as an opportunity to galvanize female workers in a moral cause. Woolsey was surprised that the moral imperative with which she had always credited women broke down at Bedloe's Island Hospital, where nobody would report a corrupt steward. Manifesting the view that women were inherently more humane than men, she resolved to launch a crusade: "We are determined, we 'females,' to make the place much too hot for him if we can *prove* anything. But how many weak-minded sisters there are! I never realized before now . . . very few are capable of 'taking the responsibility.'"[83] Woolsey was disappointed in coworkers because she expected, rather naively, that they would join her in exercising their highly evolved moral organs. She found instead women reluctant to blow the whistle, whose moral indignation was not nearly as well developed as their fear of the consequences.

Conflicts involving food impelled women to action more than any other cause. Surgeons regarded home-prepared foods as harmful to convalescents, but nurses who believed that they knew better insisted that patients should enjoy them.[84] The U.S. Christian Commission tried to head off trouble by reminding workers in special diet kitchens of their obligation "to assist the surgeon" and that "the wish of the surgeon must control the preparation and distribution of all food issued from your kitchen."[85] Appeals to obedience were effective, especially among God-fearing souls, but inevitably some subordinates took matters into their own hands. At a Chattanooga hospital, Surgeon Roberts Barthalow delivered an injunction to women who overstepped their bounds: "Ladies," he addressed them, "Your province in this hospital is the special and extra diet kitchen, and you are ordered to confine your operations, herein to the discharging of your duties in this kitchen. You are ordered also to discontinue your visits of interferences to the Laundry and other Departments of this Hospital." Invoking the adage that too many cooks spoil the broth, Barthalow moved to limit workers' ever-widening sphere of action. Those perceived as meddlers were let go and sometimes even court-martialed.[86]

But nurses were just as willing to expose medical staff whose theft of food and supplies blossomed into corruption — even under pain of retribution. At general hospitals in Washington, Nashville, and Madison, Indiana, nurses accused quartermasters of serving substandard food to convalescents and selling palatable food on the side.[87] From Nashville, Mary Newcomb observed that the surgeon in charge had three female nurses so cowed that "they were afraid to speak out." After reporting the graft, Newcomb boasted that "it does a great deal of good sometimes to let the doctors know that you are not afraid to give them a little wholesome advice."[88] Always ready for a fight, Newcomb seldom reported on her rate of success, despite her imperious tone.

Disagreement about medical treatment was especially divisive. The nurse may have wished to give the surgeon "a little wholesome advice," but he regarded it as interference. Set upon by up to thirty women daily, Surgeon Harvey E. Brown of Fort Wood in New York Harbor was so intent on en-

The U.S. Christian Commission, here at White House Landing in Virginia, required its female employees to defer to surgeons. (Courtesy of Library of Congress)

forcing a standard of treatment for his patients that he limited the number of nurses who visited his hospital to two, then further restricted the days of visitation to two weekly.[89] Surgeons were vexed by nurses' use of home remedies, and nurses were vexed by surgeons' dependence on whiskey—used in lieu of chloroform to anesthetize patients and to intoxicate themselves.[90] Phoebe Yates Pember waged a veritable war with Chimborazo surgeons over control of the cabinet in which liquor was kept; others complained that the abuse of alcohol "brutalized" members of the surgical staff and led to botched operations.[91] Nurses refused to let patients go under the knife if they felt an amputation was unwarranted. Mary Edwards Walker, an upstate New York physician who peeved army medical officers, conspired with soldiers to forestall the surgery. Sister Anthony of an Ohio religious order deftly persuaded surgeons to let her care for afflicted limbs instead of amputating them.[92] Despite her successful intercession with some patients, Clara Barton was unable to reverse the fatal effects of hourly dosing with whiskey punch, quinine, ammonia, and opium prescribed for one man by a meddlesome post surgeon.[93]

Such conflicts represented the contrast in approaches to patient care. Overburdened with dying soldiers after battles, surgeons proceeded with dispatch, seldom devoting more than minutes to individual cases. Nurses, on the other hand, were loath to think in terms of cases and individualized patients' suffering. It was nothing for nurses to throw themselves wholeheartedly into cases that surgeons had pronounced hopeless and take pride in announcing their triumph over the grim reaper.[94] When soldiers died, nurses indulged in detailed descriptions of the deathbed—another channel for individualizing suffering.[95]

Surgeons were by contrast more likely to refer to patients in the abstract or to the clinical details of a treatment. Surgeon William Watson, writing home from Gettysburg, mentioned only the kind of operations he performed and said little about individual patients. "I have lost but one case from disease," he noted before the fighting began. "That was a case of pernicious fever and died before anything could be done." Two weeks later he wrote with enthusiasm about the practical experience he had gained: "I have performed the greatest number and variety of operations. Have ligated the Carotid Femoral and Brachial Arteries and resected and amputated every bone in the body. . . . Our secondary operations have been unfavorable. Most of the cases die."[96] Watson often referred to patients as "cases"—language not uncommon in medical prose of the time but unexpected in correspondence with family members of the recently deceased.

Not only were surgeons more likely to think of patients in the abstract, on occasion they recorded details of practice without referring at all to their human subjects. Of a patient who shot off his own hand in an attempt to be discharged, Iowa surgeon Seneca Thrall wrote, "I took of[f] the thumb & metacarpal bone of thumb & made quite a decent hand out of it."[97] Michigan surgeon Cyrus Bacon wrote from Gettysburg, "Whitingham helps me put a thigh in splints—anterior-splint—at which he is an adept having been a pupil of Nathan R. Smith the inventor of the splint."[98] Bacon's satisfaction in performing a difficult procedure overshadowed any acknowledgment of the soldier's response to treatment. Louisa May Alcott observed this remote lens in "Dr. P.," who "seemed to regard a dilapidated body" with pleasure. "The more intricate the wound, the better he liked it. A poor private, with both legs off, and shot through the lungs, possessed more attractions for him than a dozen generals, slightly scratched in some 'masterly retreat'; and had any one appeared in small pieces, requesting to be put together again, he would have considered it a special dispensation."[99] To quote Watson, Thrall, and Bacon is not to expose them as inhumane but to illustrate their mode of discourse: trained at elite institutions, their clinical, detached, and professional tone spilled over into their private accounts. Medical officers without elite training, like New York's Daniel M. Holt, were less likely to put the patient at such a distance.[100] But for many surgeons, the human being was principally a medical specimen, not some "poor mother's son," as nurses might have viewed him.

Nurses' emphasis on individuals left them without the bureaucratic wherewithal to battle hospital administrators. An Illinois nurse was dismissed for lodging formal complaints with her governor about the meager subsistence given to recuperating soldiers at Quincy. Mrs. S. A. M. Blackford reported to surgeons that the men under her care frequently complained of hunger. Unheeded, she circulated a petition among the men, which she later presented to state officials. Incurring the wrath of military officials by taking her case to a civil authority, she wrote in defense of her actions that she had been "ignorant of military rules," but that her "intentions were good[.] I did not want to wrong any one but all I wanted was to get our sick & wounded enough to eat." Nevertheless, her appeal to President Abraham Lincoln for reinstatement was denied.[101] For taking the moral high road, Blackford found herself without a job.

Hannah Ropes had more success, but it came at great cost. In the six months she served at Union Hotel before contracting typhoid, Ropes leveled serious charges against Surgeon A. M. Clark and the hospital steward, leading to their arrest and imprisonment.[102] When earlier that autumn the steward suggested that Ropes join him in reselling hospital clothing, soap, and food, she reported him to Clark, who neither reprimanded nor dismissed him. Clark's apathy enraged Ropes, who fielded soldiers' complaints about the dearth of supplies. Long a student of reform movements, she brought charges directly to Surgeon General Hammond, whom she described as more interested in "protocol" than human welfare.[103] When Clark demanded to know why Ropes had gone over his head, she responded in a letter: "In regard to the course I have taken in uttering such grave charges I have but one *personal rule*, and that is never to speak in self defense. Among my own people, 50 years of my life is on record, the time left to anyone after that is very short at best. I am here doing my Master's work. The poor privates are my

Hannah Ropes, a Massachusetts native with abolitionist leanings, complained to the secretary of war about the cruelty of the surgeon and steward at Union Hotel Hospital. Afterward, the hospital staff shunned her. Ropes died of typhoid in Union Hotel in January 1863. (Courtesy of U.S. Army Military History Institute, Carlisle Barracks, Pa.)

children for the time being."[104] By stating that she would not defend her actions and invoking her pious mission, she placed her motives beyond reproach—a self-defense unknown to Mrs. Blackford.

When the Union Hotel steward struck a boy with a chisel and imprisoned him in the vermin-infested hospital cellar, Ropes paid a call to the surgeon general, where she sought redress in the "joy and satisfaction over the thing that is right."[105] Hammond would not see her. Because he had not acted on

Ropes's earlier letter, she took her complaint to Secretary of War Edwin Stanton. At odds himself with Hammond, Stanton acted with dispatch to send a delegation from the Provost Marshal's Office to Union Hotel. The steward and Surgeon Clark were hauled off to Old Capitol Prison, and Stanton delivered an order—anticipating reprisals—that Ropes be allowed to keep her job. Hypothesizing that the entire surgical staff had trivialized her complaints, Ropes suspected collusion. "Why do the surgeons, from the general to his humblest aides, feel so sensitive about this matter?"[106] Ropes was puzzled that the surgeons were more concerned about protecting themselves than preventing the misdeeds of colleagues. However, she never lost sight of her purpose—to shield the physically vulnerable from suffering. That the surgeon had lost sight of these ends illustrates the extent to which the patient's body became the site of conflict between male and female staff.

Ropes observed a gendered pattern in the actions of the staff: "I think through all this troubled water the men have been much less clear in the sense of right than the women have. Is it that they hate to give up one of their club to the law?"[107] Ascribing to women a simpler route to moral truth, Ropes speculated that for men the demands of workplace loyalty had beclouded ethics. Better to protect a professional equal than to come forward with damning testimony. Her exchange with military officials represented professional etiquette as an amoral, fraternal, authority-based system. Far from feeling the triumph that Mary Newcomb described after having evildoers removed from responsible positions, Ropes found meager satisfaction. Conditions improved only slightly, and she still had to work with Dr. Clark's cronies.

Although nurses felt obliged to expose corruption and graft, nothing aroused their indignation like the brutal handling of convalescent soldiers. Both nurses and patients reported hospital officials striking men under their care; African American soldiers were particularly vulnerable to the violent whims of racist hospital employees. An ailing member of the 36th U.S. Colored Troops was so miffed at the repeated beatings he received from a medical officer for saying that he was too weak to perform guard duty at Fortress Monroe that he wrote the Union surgeon general to ask "if it ar allowed . . . to Beat a Patient in hospital."[108] Abby Hopper Gibbons took the part of another African American sentenced to a beating on a trumped-up charge. When Gibbons appealed the man's case to higher authority, the incensed surgeon promised to dismiss her for having "transgressed a military rule." After Gibbons had pleaded her case successfully, she observed that the surgeon "knew he had gone too far. . . . His position was in peril. He knew I had power and would use it."[109] Though Gibbons may have been referring to woman's perceived power of moral suasion, it is just as likely that her social standing as a politically well-connected elite white was her instrument of power. Maria Mann reported similar behavior on the part of hospital staff members in Helena, Arkansas, who whipped black patients suffering from diarrhea when they fouled their beds.[110] Although Mann was not much of an abolitionist when she entered the service, her growing sense of racial injustice sent her back to Washington with a long list of grievances.

Nurses were no less protective of white soldiers. When Mary Ann Bickerdyke observed a soldier made to march on the "double quick" with his shoulders lashed to a beam and then strung up all night until his hands turned black from want of circulation—all for missing roll call—she fired off a letter to "the proper authorities!" Not afraid to name names, Bickerdyke insisted that she was "here to look after the interests of soldiers . . . in health as well as those who [were] sick," and that she would not tolerate Union officers' "uncalled for *harshness*."[111] Again female workers pitted themselves against surgeons and officers through the medium of the soldier's body.

Like Mrs. Blackford and Hannah Ropes, New York's Sophronia Bucklin had a chance to bring about better patient care by exposing hospital negligence and corruption. From September 1862 to the end of the war, Dorothea Dix assigned Bucklin to work in hospitals of the Army of the Potomac. No stranger to the raw comforts of tent life or the exigencies of triage, Bucklin understood the importance of medical teamwork, especially after her experience at Gettysburg, where wounded soldiers lay in the streets up to two weeks after the battle. *In Hospital and Camp* (1869), her narrative of three years' service, returns again and again to strained exchanges between surgical staff and attendants over food, accommodations, and supplies. Like so many others, Bucklin saw herself as a maternal advocate for hungry soldiers, few of whom "dared to brave the punishments sure to follow any declaration as to the insufficient, or ill-cooked food." In her first post at Wolf-Street Hospital in Alexandria, Bucklin had recognized the extent to which nurses were silenced: "*We* were not cowered from any fear of corporeal punishment being inflicted; no thought of bearing a load of wood on our backs, and being marched around by a guard for hours, deterred us from speaking of the wrongs we endured; but rather thoughts of usefulness cut off, of the disgrace of dismissal, of being shut out where our hands could not minister unto the brave wounded—those considerations argued against all complaints, and kept sentinel over our tongues to their every utterance."[112] A spirit of rebellion clothed in military metaphors pervades these thoughts. Bucklin was happy to submit to physical pain if it meant that soldiers would get more to eat. But complaining might also result in her discharge from service—an interruption of her charitable mission without any substantial improvement for the men. Thus Bucklin initially kept her concerns to herself.

But six months later she lost her post. Surgeon General's Office records indicate that Bucklin and five other nurses (including Ella Wolcott) were dismissed from Hammond Hospital in Point Lookout by Assistant Surgeon C. Wagner in March 1863. In a letter to William Hammond, dated March 2, 1863, Dix requested information about the dismissal. How could this have happened with "no previous notice given—no present cause of offence or dereliction assigned"? Indeed, Dix bristled, she had visited Hammond Hospital on February 21, "at which time Dr. Wagner distinctly expressed his satisfaction with the entire corps of nurses then on duty, and added that their services would still be required." Wagner responded four days later that Bucklin and three others were "discharged for inefficiency."[113] Though we are left to speculate about what really happened, the incident's absence from Bucklin's memoirs is conspicuous: Did she want to conceal her ouster for fear of being misjudged, or had Dix imposed a gag order?

By the spring of 1864, serving in a tent hospital at Camp Stoneman, Virginia, Bucklin had become a seasoned field nurse with a sophisticated understanding of how to negotiate hospital bureaucracy. Lyde Sizer has suggested that Bucklin's ability to work the system resulted from her manipulation of "the conventions of manhood."[114] This time an instance of sexual harassment put Bucklin at odds with medical officials. She reported that a Mrs. Boiler had traveled five hundred miles to care for her dying husband. After her arrival, the surgeon in charge informed Boiler that the case was hopeless and in the next breath stunned her with "infamous proposals." A shocked Bucklin escorted the bereaved woman to the depot and later learned that the surgeon had reported her (Bucklin) for being absent. More outraged by the surgeon's lewdness than by any action against her, Bucklin decided to conceal her case against him instead of confronting him directly—an approach that had backfired at Point Lookout.[115]

In a separate incident, Dix had cautioned Bucklin on her arrival at Stoneman about "the suspicious nurse, who had no duties to perform in the hospital."[116] Surmising that the nurse was the surgeon's mistress, Bucklin believed that he intended Mrs. Boiler or herself for new conquests. By communicating with Dix's office instead of the surgeon's superiors, Bucklin

Union physicians at Hammond Hospital in Point Lookout, Maryland, dismissed Sophronia Bucklin, Ella Wolcott, and four other women for "inefficiency" in 1863. Nurses complained that military brass barred them from caring for Rebel wounded and promoted a culture of racism there. (Courtesy of National Archives)

succeeded in having him fired, obtaining a transfer for herself and the other women employed, and securing an official order that no more female attendants would be assigned to Camp Stoneman—lest any surgical hard feelings remain. Though Bucklin's actions did not produce improvements for soldiers—and she regretted this deeply—she had learned how to exploit the system without inspiring retaliatory wrath. Still more troubling is the suggestion that surgeons strategically harassed women to force their departure from the hospital corps.

Bucklin arrived at City Point in June 1864, as hundreds of wounded were pouring in from the siege of Petersburg. As at Alexandria and Gettysburg, she protested the army's mismanagement of supplies and the inadequate number of medical personnel to look after patients: "Dead and dying lay," she observed, "like the logs on a corduroy road. The condition of those for whom shelter could not be obtained was pitiable in the extreme. Worms soon bred in the fresh wounds; the sun burned their faces till the skin pealed [*sic*] away, and in the agony of thirst and fever it seemed like a merciful relief when their spirits rid themselves of the mortal and mutilated bodies."[117] In charge of three hundred wounded men, Bucklin despaired of being able to nourish them, for only wormy and moldy food was on hand, and she had no stove. When appeals to the head surgeon went unheeded—he was at work around the clock dealing with casualties—she attempted to find the officer responsible for this "most culpable neglect of duty," this "crime."[118] Even though she identified the culprit, she could do nothing to improve conditions. It had been easier to expose moral turpitude than to counter neglect.

This incident caused Bucklin to reflect on the attitudes of superiors toward subordinates. "Nurses and soldiers were supposed, by many of the officers, to be mere machines, incapable of thought, and unworthy of any attention beyond requiring them to be obedient whenever their rights were infringed upon."[119] Clara Barton had used similar language to convey her disgust of medical operations in the Sea Islands: "I have no doubt but the patients lack many luxuries which the country at large endeavor to supply them with and suppose they have—no doubt but men suffer and die for the lack of the nursing and provisions of the loved ones at home, no doubt but the stately, stupendous and magnificent indolence of the officers in charge embitters the days of the poor sufferers who have become mere machines in the hands of the Government to be ruled and oppressed by puffed up, conceited, and self sufficient superiors in position."[120] Both nurses bespoke their hierarchical affinity with soldiers by characterizing them as "mere machines" —language that assailed the lack of humanity in mechanized interactions.

Kate Cumming also criticized surgeons' neglect of soldiers. In the hospital at Kingston, Georgia, Dr. Avent refused Cumming's requests to improve sanitary conditions, responding so rudely that she did not "wonder that so few ladies of refinement enter[ed]" the service. Certain that the surgeon would not have spoken thus to medical assistants, Cumming resisted self-pity and refocused her attention on the lowly soldier: "All this has made me feel more for our proud-spirited men, who I know have to endure insults from the petty officers over them."[121] Thus she too identified with the soldier as an object of contempt; she felt closer to the soldier because of that contempt.

All three women recognized that their bond with soldiers rested in part on the common source of their oppression. The hospital hierarchy under which nurses labored was analogous to soldiers' position in the broader military arena. Able to perceive the force that devalued her service along with that of the infantryman, Bucklin came as close as any Civil War hospital worker to understanding that her problems with hospital authorities were located in gendered relationships.

As Sophronia Bucklin and others looked beyond their unique circumstances, they came to see that hospital conflicts were not isolated. They also began to realize the professional implications of gender difference—the ways in which being women barred them from the peer respect and camaraderie that surgeons shared with other surgeons, set them apart as intruders in a male-defined arena, and cast them into roles as moral watchdogs. Because they were not considered medical professionals like surgeons, they were expected to behave in ways that surgeons had themselves prescribed. They observed that surgeons' peer allegiance, demonstrated through insistence on hospital protocol, sometimes resulted in poor patient care. If the authority granted to surgeons permitted lapses in standards—through corruption, moral transgression, and depersonalization—then veteran nurses saw themselves as a stopgap. When surgeons chose professional loyalty over patient welfare, nurses brought the physical evidence of the patient's body to bear, even if it meant devaluing the etiquette that surgeons wished to institutionalize.

Professional interests constituted hospital hierarchy, kept the least powerful workers silent, and led more privileged subordinates to resist the iron countenance of the status quo. Although it might have been their shared class and racial status that armed white middle-class nurses to take on surgeons, class and race allegiances ultimately could not transcend the defining—and limiting—characteristics of gender in the hospital culture. Hospital officials expected women's obedience, just as they expected cooperation from black and working-class attendants. Most subordinates did not publicly question the distribution of power in hospitals. But that so many did shows us the extent to which the system's rigid configuration of roles could not hold up when thousands of lives were at stake.

# PART TWO

# The Legacy of War Work

Give her the soldier's rite!
She fought the hardest fight
. . . . . . . . . . . . . . . . . .
She faced the last of foes,
The worst of mortal woes.
—Rose Terry Cooke,
   "The Army Nurse," ca. 1890

## CHAPTER FIVE

# After the War

I wonder what I shall do with myself when the war is over. I never can sit down and do nothing.... I never expect to *live* at home again, I shall always be working somewhere or other, I hope. Work is my life. I cannot be happy doing nothing.
—Emily Parsons to her mother, July 19, 1863

At the close of those four fateful years, she returned to her home in Uniontown, and devoted the few remaining years of her life to the cause of the South, and was instrumental in erecting the soldiers' monument at Morganfield.
—Matthew Page Andrews on Kentucky regimental nurse
   Bettie Taylor Philips, 1920

After getting settled, I opened a school for Negro children. I had twenty children at my school, and received one dollar a month for each pupil.... [Later] I went to work for a very wealthy lady, Mrs. Charles Green, as laundress.
—Susie King Taylor, *Reminiscences of My Life in Camp*, 1902

For most civilians, the Civil War ended with Robert E. Lee's surrender to Ulysses S. Grant on April 9, 1865. For medical corps and hospital staff, however, the war was far from over. Thousands of soldiers languished in hospitals, the victims of chronic winter illnesses or the previous summer's intense fighting in the eastern theater.[1] Female hospital workers were as anxious to be mustered out of service as the sick and wounded men they still tended. Like them, they were battle hardened, war weary, and ready to seek the comforts of home.

For those who returned to homes intact, life might continue as the steady advance toward material reward, the war having but temporarily interrupted that progress. The postwar economy favored middle-class and elite Northerners lucky enough to emerge from war without familial loss. Even for the newly widowed, there were expanding professional, clerical, and industrial opportunities, provided individuals could get beyond the social stigma commonly attached to waged labor. For the majority of former hospital workers, however—white Southerners, ex-slaves, and the Northern working class— peacetime meant struggle. With the closing of military hospitals, many lost jobs; finding new work was not easy. Southerners were particularly hard hit: African Americans continued to farm, but those who fled plantations were obliged to start from scratch. Despite the efforts of freedmen's relief organizations to ameliorate their conditions, most former slaves were mired into lives where even benevolent gestures did little more than reproduce social and economic power imbalances apparent in the peculiar institution. White Southerners might expect more, especially if they had genteel connections. But for those whose family fortunes had been destroyed, labor passed from choice to necessity. Kate Cumming's family had never been wealthy, yet the sight of her sister at the stove and her brother washing dishes on her return to Mobile—tasks performed by servants in the past—suggested in *tableaux vivants* the changes that many elite homesteads could not forestall.[2]

Hospital relief work changed individual lives after the war. Middle-class whites believed that the confidence government had bestowed in them by allowing, however reluctantly, their entry into the military should not founder. Hardened veterans, who had spent at least two years learning military etiquette and watching men suffer and die, saw an opportunity to build on the social advocacy the war had served up to them. In a stroke similar to the one they would use when appealing for a nurse's military pension in the 1890s, they reasoned that war work had involved their partnership in a military objective that had both conferred on them an honored place in the polity and fitted them to do other public work. For the few women who had acquired medical degrees before the war and for those inspired to become physicians after it, public sanction blunted the fury of disapproval surrounding the medical education of women. Despite small numbers, female physicians were able to put their war work in the service of professional advancement. That rare alignment of racial, class, and regional privilege made for an optimism not necessarily shared by those whose social coordinates strayed from white, elite, or Northern, although the variables of temperament and will were enough to mobilize some of lesser advantage to find satisfying work after the war.

If individuals found the public world of work more accessible after the war, it is not clear why. Women's military relief services may have changed public opinion, opening the way for middle-class whites to work, but whether employers sought to accommodate more women in the workforce remains uncertain. Historians believed at one time that women's movement into work outside the home gradually increased throughout the nineteenth century and that the war behaved like a dynamo in speeding their entry. But we now understand that a linear progression does not accurately reflect the periods of retrogression and retrenchment that have often followed wars.[3] The experience gained by women confident enough to write about their war service did not necessarily translate into workplace achievement. Nor was such confidence pervasive, given that two-thirds of relief workers were not elite and thus not well positioned to challenge voices trumpeting progress. Though they believed that their service gave them the potential to lay claim to a larger share of work outside the home, elite women as a whole did not seize the chance —a point amplified by how few former relief workers sought training as nurses or physicians in the postwar period. A discussion of women in nursing and medicine late in this chapter will show that despite the success of individuals in the health professions, there was little group momentum: Elite women did not for the most part press for equality of opportunity, though they did promote their own interest. Their conviction that their pleas for recognition were made in behalf of all women ran roughshod over humbler relief workers whose expanded industrial opportunities did not apparently increase their social status.

A wish to restore the domestic order by sending women home characterized much postwar rhetoric. Celebrants of female relief work insisted that after four years of intensive labor, women anonymously resumed the rhythms of domestic life.[4] If they were enjoined to seek shelter, what of the men who had spent long years subjected to bullets and exposure? Traditional conceptions of manliness, amply demonstrated during the war, precluded veterans from the language of domestic comfort. Instead, postwar rhetoric focused on men's resumption of roles as breadwinners and protectors of women and children. When we consider that few Americans could turn the clock back to 1860, such insistence is suspect: Public endorsements of middle-class torpor may have arisen precisely to discourage women from remaining in the workforce and to counter the anxiety of those who feared employment competition. In this light, postwar injunctions become an instructive propaganda that tell us more about instability in gender roles than women's actual work in the public domain.

The belief that women would return to a domesticity that antedated the war had other ideological implications. Home place values were consistent with the ethos of hospital work, where women cared for other people's children and husbands. If hospital work had merely extended feminine prescriptions, women could take up domestic work on an even more public playing field after the war. That so many relief workers moved into teaching and social service scarcely departed from the prewar script of helping others. Linus Brockett and Mary Vaughan, authors of *Woman's Work in the Civil War* (1867), were among those who believed that the war had not altered women's domestic bent. These "heroines," they proclaimed, could participate in a "higher and holier future" by delivering "vagrant and wayward childhood from the paths of ruin; the universal diffusion of education and culture; the succor and elevation of the poor, the weak, and the down-trodden; the rescue and reformation of the fallen sisterhood; the improvement of hospitals and the care of the sick; the reclamation of prisoners, especially in female prisons; and in general, the genial ministrations of refined and cultured womanhood, wherever these ministrations can bring calmness, peace and comfort."[5] Brockett and Vaughan touted womanhood's readiness to embrace a host of reform causes. In the center of their vision were middle-class women who, as doers of good deeds, would ransom those in less respectable circumstances. As long as what such women intended to do away from home was ideologically compatible with what they did in it, there was no immediate cause for alarm.[6]

In the spirit of noblesse oblige, wealthy Northerners translated their war experience into high-profile charity work—an avocation expected of women with time on their hands. Patrician duty and social obligation were manifest in the actions of women like the Woolsey sisters and Maria Mann. A niece of Horace Mann—educator, lawyer, politician, and reform activist—Maria followed in the family footsteps by spending 1863 in a freedmen's camp in Helena, Arkansas, and by devoting herself to orphanage work on her post-war return to Washington.[7] Among those who had staffed the elite corps of transport ship nurses of the U.S. Sanitary Commission (USSC) was Katharine Prescott Wormeley, a native of Suffolk, England, with homes in New York, Boston, and Newport. With the resources to organize others, Wormeley had mobilized soldiers' struggling dependents to produce military clothing in 1861. Her active war service, which lasted little more than a year before she returned exhausted to Newport, consisted of ferrying boatloads of wounded soldiers during the Peninsula campaign and directing female staff at a general hospital in Rhode Island. Immediately after the war, Wormeley published a history of the USSC; later in life she would translate French classics by Balzac, Daudet, and Molière into English. In 1879 she established the Newport Charity Organization Society, a project that led her in 1887 to found an industrial training school for working-class girls.[8] Independently wealthy, Wormeley never married, and unlike women whose postwar lives were shaped by family or the need to earn wages, she published a war memoir in 1889.

Cornelia Hancock, the daughter of New Jersey Quakers, had more modest expectations. In the field for twenty-two months without a break, Hancock was with the Union army's 2nd Corps hospitals in City Point in the spring of 1865. On May 3, she wrote her sister that "the last lot of sick I hope ever to see" had arrived the night before, and that she "[could not] leave here until this hospt is done and no one can say how long that will be . . . the days seem long to me now."[9] Hancock would muster out with the 12th New Jersey by summer's end, happy to bid farewell to relief work. She returned home but did not remain long. Convinced like other middle-class whites that much humanitarian work remained to be done, she traveled to South Carolina under the auspices of a Quaker group promoting the advancement of freedmen and, with Laura Towne, established in 1866 the Laing School in Mount Pleasant. Building on the legacy of Freedmen's Bureau and American Missionary Association schools established during the war, Hancock taught ex-slaves for a decade. Late in the 1870s she helped found societies for children's aid in Pennsylvania and by the 1880s had become a settlement worker on the outskirts of Philadelphia. When Frank Moore approached her in 1866 about writing a brief summary of her war activities, she demurred, explaining that "to put upon paper the scenes I have witnessed is beyond my powers of description."[10] For Wormeley and Hancock, war work had proved that others needed them. Though both dedicated themselves to helping others in the postwar years, their class backgrounds made for different trajectories. Whereas Hancock created a life for herself as an educator, Wormeley took up literary pursuits. Both took part in the vocational training of working-class people, but Wormeley became a manager and author, whereas Hancock performed the labor of social work, eschewing any public recognition. After the war elite Northerners could devote themselves to charity work without much concern for their economic well-being, whereas middle-class spinsters and widows without familial support had to seek wages.

What women did before the war may have influenced their postwar choices as much as class status. Abby Hopper Gibbons, Mary Livermore, and Jane Hoge were Northern women of genteel respectability but not aristocratic means, who had affiliated themselves with abolition, temperance, and social welfare in the 1840s and 1850s. Not as sheltered as patricians for whom reform carried the taint of controversy, their activism was nevertheless rooted in class and racial privilege. White, married, and middle class, they engaged in work consistent with the domestic ideals on which their class position rested. In her study of nineteenth-century philanthropy, Lori Ginzberg posits a generational split in organizational loyalties among relief workers. Those active in antebellum benevolent work aspired to a "virtuous femininity" that fueled their war work with religious conviction.[11] As teachers, moral reformers, and abolitionists, the older generation understood war work as work-in-progress. A more youthful cadre, represented by women like Wormeley, cut its reform teeth on the model of scientific order embraced by leaders of the Sanitary Commission. These younger relief workers looked askance at what they believed to be the outmoded practices of the older group. More recent scholarship has suggested that despite their commitment to streamline relief operations, they grew skeptical of sanitary commissioners who placed the consolidation of their own power ahead of humanitarian objectives.[12] Their disaffection with institutional philanthropy may have led to postwar malaise and fragmentation on the reform front. Such women may also have taken the rhetoric of domestic comfort to heart if further struggle in the corridors of organized benevolence did not appeal to them.

It would be hasty to assume that all who returned to domestic life devoted themselves exclusively to it. Women who married and raised families after 1865 still found ways to extend social interests that the war had kindled. Having served at Jefferson General in southern Indiana, Rena Littlefield Miner was assigned to Jefferson Barracks near St. Louis in the spring of 1865, as Union prisoners of war returned north. Discharged in October, Miner went home to Michigan and considered her options. A teacher and factory operative before the war, she could expect to labor on unless she married well. Before the year was out, she married a returning veteran of modest means. Busy with three children in the 1870s and 1880s, Miner took up freelance writing and cofounded the *Sociologic News*. There and in the *Western Rural*, the *Chicago Courant*, and the *Industrial News*, she wrote articles advocating the dignity of labor for women and challenging the middle-class ethos of genteel lassitude. By 1895 she was living in St. Charles, Missouri, where she published the *Army Nurse Reveille* and helped build an organization dedicated to preserving the memory of hospital workers.[13] Like Hancock, Miner would not have considered herself a philanthropist, but her war work provided a platform for later interests in social welfare.

As whites, Hancock and Miner reentered peacetime society with relative ease. This was not so for ex-slave Maria Bear Toliver, who gained neither citizenship nor personhood through her war labor. Born in 1839 on a Williamsburg plantation and sold into King William's County, Toliver fled to Washington in 1862—the destination of some 40,000 contrabands between 1861 and 1863. She found work caring for other former slaves at Camp Barker (now the site of Howard University), where she later married Henry Toliver, who was engaged in the same work. When Henry contracted smallpox and Maria varioloid (a milder form), both were quarantined. When able to return to work, they nursed the multiracial staff at Freedman's Hospital— still open in 1895, when Maria applied for a pension. At age fifty-eight, she was in ill health and "not able to work much."[14]

What Toliver and others like her did after the war has been obscured by the heavy dust of history. With few exceptions, former slaves did not write personal accounts of the conflict. Pensions, hospital correspondence, and coached narratives provide clues, but personal voice is compromised by examiners' scripted questions and clerks' written answers. Despite scant evidence, ex-slaves who had worked for the hospital service had little choice but to work after the war. When they were lucky, they found manual labor —agricultural and domestic in the South, domestic and industrial in the North.[15] Though the Reconstruction years may have afforded moderately good opportunities for the racially stigmatized, growing segregation made it difficult for black women to enter the same labor markets as whites.[16] If they got work at all, it was low-prestige, low-end labor, like it had been during the war.

Regional identity also bore crucially on postwar lives. Economic prospects were not bright for Southerners. The wartime destruction of Confederate capital and the ruin of great fortunes adversely affected the development of commerce and industry, so that even women ready and willing to work could not always find jobs.[17] The task of rebuilding communities ravaged by shot, shell, and depredation was itself considerable; the impediments of Reconstruction policy on the defeated population even greater. Caught between the need to work and the stigma attached to it, genteel women were at an ironic disadvantage not shared by Northerners. Unschooled in shifting for themselves, except what a protracted war had taught, many failed to find paid work. Even the executive acumen of Sally Tompkins could not forestall poverty: she spent the last decade of her life in a home for indigent women, having depleted her entire fortune in church charity work.[18]

The fortunes of Kate Cumming, who like Tompkins never married, were only slightly better due to a large network of family and friends. Getting home to Mobile was no easy task in May 1865. It took ten days from Griffin, Georgia—a distance of 445 miles—in a wagon, small boat, and on foot. Servants gone, Cumming set to work. A family friend advanced her four hundred dollars to publish the diary she had kept during her service, but hopes of profit were dashed when her Louisville publisher reneged on his promise to distribute the book.[19] In the wish to help out at home—the collapse of the Confederate economy ruined Cumming's father David, a commercial trader—Cumming worked as a governess and Sunday school teacher for a time. By the early 1870s the family moved to the growing city of Birmingham. There at forty-five, Cumming became a schoolteacher and tried her hand at writing novels. Though none was ever published, she did come out with a sanitized version of her diary in 1895. Always an ardent Confederate, she took part in charitable initiatives like the fund-raising effort of the United Daughters of the Confederacy (UDC) on behalf of Ella Newsom Trader, who by the mid-1880s was "homeless, in bad health, [and without any] visible means of support."[20] But the line between helping others and being the object of philanthropy oneself seemed narrow indeed. Cumming's own modest background, compared to the likes of Trader, may have better prepared her for the toil ahead.

Born in Mississippi and educated in Arkansas, Newsom was widowed just before the war. Left a substantial legacy by her physician husband, she contributed most of it to outfitting Confederate hospitals in Memphis, Belmont (Missouri), Bowling Green (Kentucky), Corinth, Chattanooga, and Marietta (Georgia). A second marriage after the war did not improve Trader's fortunes; her Tennessee property had been confiscated during the war, and she was widowed again in 1885. In 1886, after she had come to the attention of the UDC, she secured work in the General Land Office in Washington—the favor of a Southern legislator who remembered her war service. For the next thirty years, until her late seventies, she supported her family through clerical work in the land, patent, and pension offices—a fate, according to Mary Boykin Chesnut, that would have made starvation a welcome alternative.[21]

Southern women poised to play philanthropic roles before the war thus had little opportunity to do so after it. The end of the plantation economy ruined the fortunes of many who had financed medical and hospital relief for Confederate soldiers. Juliet Opie Hopkins, arguably the richest woman in Alabama by 1861 (her father owned two thousand slaves and her second husband was a state supreme court justice and railroad magnate), met Kate Cumming on her way home to Alabama in 1865 and reported that she and her husband were now reduced to eating corn bread and bacon.[22] Things would get worse. Widowed in 1866, Hopkins moved to New York with a niece and took in sewing. In 1880 the niece married a former federal officer thirty-seven years her senior and Hopkins moved in with them. After the death of her own husband, Hopkins's niece attempted to raise money by selling parcels of Hopkins's letters to the Alabama state archives. She confessed that she had agreed at age seventeen to marry a man of fifty-four so that she and her aunt could have a home. Despite her impassioned letters to archives officials, Hopkins's niece had little luck in resurrecting her aunt's memory or mitigating her own need. Hopkins died in obscurity and poverty in 1890.[23]

In *Civil Wars: Women and the Crisis of Southern Nationalism* (1989), George Rable has argued persuasively that well-connected Southern women did not exploit their administrative expertise in the postwar labor force. Pundits and politicians regarded elite women's war work as the temporary response to a crisis; when it subsided, women could again seek shelter.[24] As they had encountered familial resistance when embarking on relief work, so too the prospect of postwar work threatened to disrupt the return to order scripted by Southern leaders. Whether compelled by the rhetoric of domestic renewal or reluctant to put themselves forward, former relief workers shrank

Juliet Opie Hopkins and Ella Newsom used large fortunes to establish Confederate hospitals in Virginia and Tennessee. Both outlived their husbands and were reduced to poverty by the 1890s. (Hopkins courtesy of Alabama Department of Archives and History, Montgomery, Alabama; Newsom from the cover of *Confederate Veteran*, February 1919)

from earning money despite straitened circumstances. The foregoing examples would surely lead us to conclude that they *could not* exploit their administrative know-how. That they tried and frequently failed to find adequate work suggests more systemic problems. Kate Cumming's difficulty finding work as an educator, despite the social acceptability of teaching for middle-class Southerners, provides a case in point. Teaching jobs were scarce as Southern institutions scrambled to reorganize.[25] And once women found places in the labor force, there was no guarantee of longevity.

If genteel war workers were slow to enter the lists initially, the availability of clerical work to those who had fallen on hard times made them less reticent. Some had stepped into jobs as local postmistresses and treasury note signers during the war, which is thought to have expanded their opportunities afterward.[26] Southerners and Northerners living in and around Washington avidly sought government posts because wages were comparatively good, notwithstanding women's earning only one-half of what men were paid for the same work. By 1865 note signers earned $720 annually, an amount increased to $900 before 1870. By comparison, women working as teachers were averaging $400 to $600 annually; hospital matrons, $150; and custodial workers, only about $70.[27] Genteel job seekers used their political connections—one indication of how valued such work was—while many who needed the money more desperately could not get a foot in the door. Another marker of the desirability of such work was that once women landed these jobs, they were loath to part with them.[28] New Hampshire regimental nurse Harriet Patience Dame supported herself for twenty-eight years working in the Treasury Department, even after she began to receive a pension in 1884. She retired in 1895 at age seventy-seven, which suggests that she needed both the job and the pension income.[29] Mary Morris Husband of Philadelphia sought clerical work after her husband died in 1881. A sixty-year-old veteran of Antietam, Gettysburg, and City Point hospitals, she jumped at the chance to work in the Pension Office.[30] These and other Northern examples imply that accepting government work may have been a tacit condition for receiving a nurse's pension, or that clerical jobs were meant to supplement the meager income derived from pensions.

With their infrastructure intact, people in the North could more easily find work than Southerners. Not only did they enjoy wider economic opportunity during Reconstruction, but women traveled in a wider orbit—a freedom enhanced by wartime travel and frequent absences from home. Their public example of independence paved the way for women who had not been directly involved in war work but chose to enter waged labor after the war. In New England, whose regiments had sustained heavy losses, women moved easily into factory jobs formerly held by men. With the Northern emphasis on commercial and industrial work, over 100,000 industrial jobs alone had opened to women during the war, most of which remained available after 1865. The antebellum record of women in New England mills had accustomed genteel citizens to the idea of women's paid industrial work, so the rhetoric of postwar domesticity was not finally as corrosive on Northern women's determination to work.[31]

In some cases, a woman's war achievement catapulted her beyond her working-class roots. Mary Ann Bickerdyke, who spent most of her childhood being passed around to relatives and whose twelve-year marriage to a house painter ended with his death in 1859, is perhaps the best-known war worker who, by dint of hard work, achieved recognition and launched a postwar career helping the needy. Less well known was Annie Etheridge, the daugh-

A working-class widow from New Hampshire, forty-nine-year-old Harriet Patience Dame obtained a clerical position at the Treasury Department in 1867 and remained employed there for twenty-eight years. (Courtesy of U.S. Army Military History Institute, Carlisle Barracks, Pa.)

ter of a blacksmith, who served in the field with a Michigan regiment as nurse, cook, water bearer, and factotum. At twenty-two, she joined the 2nd Michigan with her husband; he deserted within the first year, but she had found her calling. The only woman to remain with the regiment throughout the war and on site for thirty-two battles, Etheridge was revered for her hardihood and virtue. Coworker Mary Morris Husband observed in 1866 that Etheridge "was much more respected than the ordinary vivandier" and "very prudent, unobtrusive & modest in demeanor." So many testified to her good character that she landed Patent Office and Treasury Department posts after the war. In 1878, when Treasury officials fired her to make the position available to a male worker, incensed veterans demanded her reinstatement. Congress pensioned her in 1887 at twenty-five dollars per month —twice the amount nurses would receive under the Pension Act of 1892.[32] A spotless reputation had opened the door to greater wealth and respectability.

Occasionally, a former slave was able to achieve greater social status, like Susie King Taylor, who sought an education and became a teacher. Still, as Taylor noted in her 1902 memoir, racial stigma always threatened to derail African Americans whose prospects were on the rise. By the late 1860s Taylor lost her husband and her school was closed; she was forced to work as a nursemaid and laundress while her mother tended her own children.[33] Although there were exceptions, most of the working-class women who had washed clothes and worked in hospital kitchens were likely to remain in some form of domestic labor after the war. Nancy Dodson Carter, a runaway from Mississippi, served at a Union hospital for African Americans in Milliken's Bend, Louisiana, and continued to do domestic work for the next half century. Similarly, ex-slave Rachael Anderson performed "manual labor" for three decades after leaving her cooking job at Asylum General in Knoxville, Tennessee.[34]

What awaited former black workers was of little concern to middle-class whites who sought posts in teaching, writing, and reform work after the war. The feminization of teaching that had begun in the antebellum years included many who went on to work in military hospitals. Some former teachers were drawn to the burgeoning field of social welfare in the 1870s and 1880s and did not return to the classroom. War work was not nearly as fruitful for returning teachers as it was for those headed into reform work; the latter could count their hospital duty as a training ground where the efficacy of teamwork, management of resources, distribution of supplies, and military etiquette had been imprinted. Still others sought work in the health

Annie Etheridge, awarded the Kearney Cross for bravery, managed to escape the censure of respectable society despite her service as the only woman in the field with the 2nd Michigan Infantry during four years of war. In the 1870s friends helped her secure positions in the U.S. Patent Office and Treasury Department, though she had received no pay during the war. (Courtesy of U.S. Army Military History Institute, Carlisle Barracks, Pa.)

professions—a logical step for women who had assisted in medical procedures and found that they liked the work. Whether teachers, writers, reformers, or healers, these women carried a nuanced understanding of the social and political stakes of the workplace into their postwar careers.

Eliza Chappell Porter had been a teacher for almost forty years when the war began. By 1835, when she married Presbyterian minister Jeremiah Porter, she had taught in a New York City religious school, a Michigan school catering to Native Americans, and a Chicago school run out of a log cabin—the city by the lake still a frontier town at that date. The Porters next were called to Green Bay, Wisconsin, where Eliza established a seminary school after the eastern model of Mary Lyons. When the Civil War began, they were back in Chicago, deputized by the Sanitary Commission (he as a chaplain, she as an agent) to oversee hospital relief all over the western theater. Never far from her desk, Porter helped establish a contraband school at Fort Pickering convalescent camp near Memphis in 1862, and for the next eighteen years she opened schools as Reverend Porter spread the gospel in Texas, Oklahoma, and Wyoming.[35]

Among schoolmistresses who made names for themselves during the war was Clara Barton, who began teaching in 1839. By 1852 she was superintendent of a successful free school in Bordentown, New Jersey. When the local school board discussed replacing her with a man whose credentials compared unfavorably, she quit in protest and moved to Washington, where she began a clerkship at the Patent Office, one of few offered to women at that time. Barton's postwar endeavors—running a clearinghouse for missing soldiers and later founding the American Red Cross—superseded teaching, but early exposure to educational struggle helped her build a prominent public life after the war. Like Barton, Amy Morris Bradley used prewar teaching as a stepping stone to public postwar work. As the eighth child of a shoemaker from rural Maine, she also outstripped her modest beginnings by compiling a résumé that included organizing a brigade hospital, superintending a hospital transport, and cleaning up Alexandria's Camp Misery for convalescent soldiers. As a teacher and principal in New England schools from the late 1830s, Bradley earned an opportunity to travel to Costa Rica in the 1850s. Becoming fluent in Spanish, she established an English school in San José and taught there for three years. On her return to Boston in the late 1850s, several businesses used her as a translator. Testimonials written on the occasion of her departure from the hospital service stress the administrative acumen she acquired during the war—talents she put to good use in the next phase of her teaching life. After the war, Bradley attempted to open a free school in impoverished Wilmington, North Carolina. With the help of a Boston philanthropist who knew of her wartime work, she founded two schools that became models for Wilmington's public school system in the late 1860s. Convinced that a school to train teachers locally was needed, Bradley organized the Tileston Normal School in 1872 from which she retired in 1891 at age sixty-eight.[36]

Efforts to improve the South through establishing schools were alive and well among women involved in freedmen's relief. So certain were they that the state would not look after its own that Michigan nurses Hannah Carlisle and Jennie Fyfe remained in Kentucky in 1865 to teach former slaves. Charlotte Forten, Susie King Taylor, Esther Hill Hawks, Laura Towne, and Laura Haviland all taught freedmen in conjunction with their relief work. African Americans Forten and Taylor, as well as Hawks and Towne, worked among soldiers and civilians in the Sea Islands; Haviland, with destitute freedmen in Mound City, Illinois. After the war, Hawks and Taylor opened schools for blacks in Florida and Georgia. Ever devoted to the uplift of African America, Haviland promoted the value of education at black schools and churches, while establishing orphanages with the American Home Missionary Society.[37] The thirty-six-year-old Towne divided her time on St. Helena Island between teaching and doctoring, having been trained in homeopathy. By September 1862 she started the Penn School, which for many years was the only source of secondary education for Sea Islands blacks. Towne was to spend the rest of her forty years there, developing the school as a site for teacher training, temperance activity, and agricultural and industrial instruction.[38] In addition to teaching literacy skills, Forten was called on to nurse and counsel Sea Islands slaves as part of the Port Royal "experiment," a Northern abolitionist scheme to demonstrate that bonded African Americans were educable. Overtaxed by the difficulty of the work and the alienation of the slaves, she returned home after a year and a half and meditated on the power of class divisions to undermine racial solidarity. In the early 1870s she moved to Washington, where she helped black educators establish secondary schools. In 1873 she was one of a handful of African Americans to land a clerkship in the Treasury Department. Although Forten's marriage in 1878 to the nephew of Angelina and Sarah Grimké preempted her life as a paid worker, she had seen firsthand the internecine effects of sustained racial oppression, something that her elite status as a fifth-generation free black had not prepared her for.[39]

Veteran of Second Manassas, Antietam, and Fredericksburg, Clarissa "Clara" Harlowe Barton ferried supplies to the Virginia and Maryland fronts with the help of teamsters. Her steely determination, visible in this 1865 photograph by Matthew Brady, drove her to create an unofficial bureau for missing soldiers after the war and eventually establish the American Red Cross. (Courtesy of National Archives)

**Women of more modest** ambition, anxious to elude the class implications of toil, could stay home and write. Anonymity and privacy set this group apart from the teachers and reformers called upon to bare themselves in public. The Northern author of *Notes of Hospital Life* (1864) never revealed her identity, and retiring Southerners kept out of the public eye by publishing their unsigned narratives in collections whose editors concurred that "publication was the auction block."[40] Scores of women helped support themselves by publishing accounts of wartime work, but few would have admitted they were writing for living expenses.

Some had more professional ambitions. Fannie Beers, a wartime nurse in Richmond and with the Confederate Army of Tennessee, was one of several Southerners to profit from writing. In the 1870s she published children's stories and poems, following Louisa May Alcott's lead though never attaining her celebrity.[41] Augusta Evans Wilson, known to Southern audiences after publishing *Beulah* in 1859 (her 1855 novel *Inez* had not done well), obtained the public endorsement she had been seeking. While she cared for Rebel sick and wounded near her Mobile home, she penned opinion pieces for Southern journals and produced the wildly popular *Macaria*. Published in 1864 by Richmond's West and Johnson, the novel navigated the treacherous channel between wedded self-sacrifice and female independence. By war's end, it had sold twenty-five thousand copies—a fifth of those pirated in the North. At least seven more imprints appeared after 1865, the latest in 1903. The publication of *St. Elmo* in 1866 put Wilson permanently on the map. So popular was it that twentieth-century audiences were treated to dramatic and cinematic versions; for thirty years after its publication, Wilson's royalties amounted to more than ten thousand dollars annually.[42] Drew Faust has noted the regressive implications of *St. Elmo*'s stunning success. Unlike the wartime heroines of *Macaria*, who cherish the life of "single blessedness," Edna Earl marries conventionally, thereby ending a progressive chapter in the Southern imagination. A purveyor of dreams, Wilson was herself no dreamer. She labored on and delivered what more privileged belles could not: a fortune built on modest means and a relentless self-discipline.[43]

Though Constance Cary made her literary debut during the war with letters about refugee life as she cared for soldiers hospitalized in Richmond, she had few pretensions to a career in writing; as the daughter of wealthy Virginians, she could expect a life of ease. After the war she traveled with other Southern exiles to France, where for more than a year she exchanged passionate letters with Burton Harrison, a former Confederate cabinet member who had been imprisoned at the end of the war. On Burton's release in 1866, Cary joined him in New York where they married and started a family. As "Confederate carpetbaggers," the Harrisons were outsiders but part of a growing coterie of Southerners in the North who hoped to parlay their misfortunes into new opportunities. In time, Burton built a flourishing law practice and Constance could claim the discerning George Templeton Strong as a social conquest.[44] By the mid-1870s, with three sons out of infancy, full-time help, and a desire to revisit the scenes of her youth, Constance began churning out fiction. Her timing was fortuitous: Northern publishers were more receptive to Southern authors a decade after the war than in 1865, and Northern readers were anxious to consume novels about Virginia aristocrats.[45] She produced on average over the next thirty years one book annually, not to mention scores of articles and short stories. Best known for *Flower de Hundred* (1890) and *The Carlyles* (1905) in which Northerners and Southerners respect one another even at war and symbolically reconcile their sections through marriage, Constance numbered eastern literati like William Dean Howells and Elizabeth Stoddard among her correspondents. Before she died in 1920 at seventy-seven, she had published a satire on New York society, a book on the decorative arts, an etiquette manual, and a memoir —an output resembling that of fellow New Yorker and contemporary, Edith Wharton.[46]

Some former caregivers who established writing careers began as journalists. One Southerner inherited her writing badge when her husband died midwar, leaving her the editorship of the *North Carolina Whig*.[47] Northerners too found their way into the periodical press. An experienced journalist and reformer, Jane Grey Swisshelm traveled to Washington in 1863 on a crusade against the Sioux Nation and was swept up into nursing. From Campbell, Carver, Judiciary Square, and Lincoln Hospitals, she sent a stream of articles to Minnesota papers documenting the misery and medical abuse she witnessed. No stranger to work or to controversy, Swisshelm had started as a teacher in the 1830s, spent time in the family corset-making business, and directed a female seminary near Pittsburgh. Here she began contributing poetry and fiction to Philadelphia papers, as well as opinion pieces on slavery, women's rights, and capital punishment. In 1848 she began publishing the *Saturday Visitor*—a forum for abolition, temperance, and married women's property rights. By the 1850s she had moved to Minnesota, where she resurrected the *Visitor* and started up a second paper, the *St. Cloud Dem-*

*ocrat.* An object of wrath for her critiques of patriarchy, politicians, and moral turpitude, Swisshelm was put out of business when thugs destroyed her printing equipment. Forty-nine by war's end, she inaugurated another paper in December 1865, the *Reconstructionist*, which was shut down after a year for criticism of the Johnson administration. She worked part-time at the War Department until she went on the lecture circuit for woman suffrage in the 1870s. Ultimately more interested in moral reform than in the press, Swisshelm retired from newspaper work and published her memoirs in 1880.[48]

**Women who went to war** with teaching or writing experience were part of a larger network of reformers in antebellum America. As surely as their religious convictions led them to care for the sick and wounded during the war, so too their postwar work was characterized by notions of *caritas*. Southerners may have promoted reform in less public ways than Northerners, given their antebellum tradition of community philanthropy sponsored by church organizations.[49] But beyond differences of region, race, and class, some former hospital workers felt morally compelled to continue work they had begun before or during the war. Those with backgrounds in reform understood the power of individualized care and were thus inclined to recreate its model of face-to-face communication in postwar work. The generational tendencies that Lori Ginzberg points to may not finally have been as compelling a predictor of postwar reform work as the transformation wrought in individuals *through* their relief services. It is difficult to say how those already ensconced in reform work by 1860 were changed by the war or whether their postwar work was the result of what occurred between 1861 and 1865. For the Mary Ann Bickerdykes and Annie Turner Wittenmyers, whose war work catapulted them into public recognition, such an argument is more persuasive. However, the extent to which the older generation was influenced by war experience may merely be a matter of degree. Surely an Abby Hopper Gibbons, who devoted her time to prison reform and abolition before the war, was sensitized to the urgency of racial equality through her wartime contact with runaway slaves. Similarly, the war became a testing ground for Mary Livermore's developing ideas about women's rights as she worked with the male elite of the Northwest Sanitary Commission and wrote dispatches about soldiers and surgeons for newsletters on the home front.[50] If it cannot be said that the war initiated the older generation of women into the postwar world of reform work, it must certainly be said that war work gave them new perspectives on what could be achieved socially, politically, and institutionally after it.

The social welfare projects in which this diverse group of women took part centered on mopping up the human misery left by war. They created benevolent institutions for soldiers' widows and children, governed asylums, organized vocational schools, and served African Americans rendered indigent by the transition from slavery to sharecropping or urban industrial life. Linus Brockett observed to Clara Barton in 1877 that many of the war's hardest workers were still at it—patricians like the Woolseys, Ellen Collins, and Louisa Lee Schuyler, who, after driving the Women's Central Relief Association, founded the New York State Charities Aid Association in 1872, and women of lesser social stature like Emily Parsons, Harriet Eaton, and Isabella Fogg, marvels of reform energy despite their physical limitations. Brockett continued: "Not one of these noble women has reverted. Not one . . . has felt any disposition to console herself with the frivolities and gaieties of fashionable life. The scenes they witnessed, the dread realities, the heroic self-sacrifice, the spirit of self-denial they then felt—All these have remained with them and have lifted them so far above the petty trifles of fashion that they could not again descend to them."[51] To Brockett's mind, the war had liberated these highly capable women from lives of genteel idleness to which they would never return. In the celebratory mode that had characterized *Woman's Work*, he regarded the war as having been the catalyst for elite women to realize their "better natures." Though the politics of class and gender privilege are suspect here (Was Brockett trying to retain a foothold in high society through heroine worship? or advocating the maintenance of traditional domestic roles for women?), the sense that the *war* had made a difference to these women, had persuaded them to fund humane initiatives on behalf of those they regarded as less fortunate, was evident in his words. Unlike the "snare of preparation" that would besiege Jane Addams and her college-educated peers a generation later, this group had found a ready channel for its will in a great and terrible war.

Abolitionism had from the 1830s been an issue around which Northern female reform interest coalesced. Several who went on to establish careers in military hospitals had received public recognition for their antislavery work before the war. Harriet Tubman, who had escaped from a plantation in eastern Maryland in 1849, became perhaps the most eloquent spokesperson for abolition as she conducted scores of slaves north before 1861. Tubman went to work on the Sea Islands as a scout and spy during the war, later camouflaging her intelligence work with a nursing post at the freedmen's hospital in Fortress Monroe. Dedicated to advancing the cause of freedmen, she spent the postwar years helping build schools in the South, establishing a home for the elderly on her Auburn, New York, farm, and speaking on behalf of woman suffrage.[52]

In common with many antebellum reformers, Abby Hopper Gibbons worked on behalf of a wide range of social ills, not just abolitionism. A teacher at Quaker schools in Philadelphia and New York in the 1820s and 1830s, she joined the Manhattan Anti-Slavery Society in 1833 and later gave her attention to prison reform, capital punishment, and vocational schools for disadvantaged children. With a lifetime of benevolent work already behind her, the sixty-year-old traveled to Washington in 1861 and became a relief agent and advocate in contraband camps near Point Lookout, Maryland. In 1864 Gibbons and daughter Sally worked on hospital ships at Belle Plain and Alexandria as wounded were removed from the battles of the Wilderness. Later that year she took charge of the 3,000-bed general hospital at Beverly, New Jersey.[53] After the war Gibbons resumed her welfare and prison reform work. One program that she established in the 1860s aided veterans, war widows, and orphans in finding employment. In 1873 she started the New York Diet Kitchen Association for the poor, elderly, and infirm—a nineteenth-century equivalent of meals-on-wheels. Gibbons made frequent appearances before legislative and political bodies, lobbying for all of these causes well into her nineties.[54]

Mary Livermore was the most accomplished of reform-minded war workers who went on to establish major careers in the social movements that defined the second half of the nineteenth century. Active in temperance and antislavery before the war, she and husband Daniel, a minister, moved to Chicago from Boston in the late 1850s, believing that their antislavery gospel could best take root in western soil. Here in 1858 she met Jane Hoge, with whom she took part in initiatives ranging from homes for destitute women to a hospital for women and children organized by future war nurse and physician Chloe Annette Buckel in 1859.[55] This work prepared both women to lead the northwestern branch of the Sanitary Commission in 1862—a project that was to take them to military hospitals throughout the western theater and put them in touch with over three thousand aid societies in the five-state Great Lakes area. Among their administrative duties was to raise private money for the commission's hospital ventures. Together they planned the Chicago Sanitary Fair of October 1863, so successful that it became the standard for subsequent fund-raising efforts. In the same year Livermore wrote to General Ulysses S. Grant to secure the discharges of a score of gravely ill soldiers, then accompanied them from Vicksburg to their Northern homes. During this flurry of activity, Livermore also managed to write articles about her work for several magazines, including Daniel's *New Covenant*, and edit a local commission bulletin.[56]

After the war Livermore's reform horizons expanded with interest in the woman suffrage movement. She ran state and national organizations, and moved back to Boston in 1869 on behalf of the cause. By the 1890s she had served as president of the Illinois and Massachusetts state suffrage societies and as vice president and president of the American Woman Suffrage Association (later called the National American Woman Suffrage Association when it merged with another national group). Throughout these decades Livermore continued as a journalist: she edited suffrage papers (the *Agitator* and the *Woman's Journal*) and spoke on the lyceum circuit from the 1870s onward, publishing her lectures in the *North American Review*. In addition to pitching woman suffrage, Livermore advocated higher education for women (a position also embraced by old friend Jane Hoge after the war), dress reform, temperance, and spiritualism. For ten years she served as president of the Massachusetts branch of the Woman's Christian Temperance Union (WCTU).[57] With lifelong support from an enabling husband, Livermore enjoyed more freedom of movement than many of her peers, using her Civil War pulpit as entrée to a host of reform issues. The war experience had convinced her that reform initiatives could best be realized through the formalization of women's political rights—a stance that she elaborated on in an 1887 memoir and an 1897 autobiography.

Whereas women like Abby Hopper Gibbons and Mary Livermore encountered the war as a way station in their reform work, the energies of Mary Ann Bickerdyke and Annie Turner Wittenmyer were unleashed by the war. Having gained a wealth of managerial experience, returning to private life held little appeal for them. After bullying countless petty officials into submission and moving herds of cows, vegetables, and washing machines down the Mississippi, Bickerdyke took on the war's homeless and indigent. Just as she had found the chaotic aftermath of the battles at Fort Donelson and Shiloh ripe for domestic organization, the welfare of soldiers, widows, and orphans presented a new and welcoming field of endeavor. After nursing soldiers released from Andersonville and participating in the mustering out of

Illinois troops, she helped establish and administer a Chicago home for struggling women and children. By 1867 she was working to settle unemployed veterans on farms in Kansas—a project that took her for a decade to the Sunflower State, where she tended a boardinghouse, worked as a missionary, and joined her sons on their farms. In 1876 she moved to San Francisco for the milder climate and worked for the Salvation Army. Military connections from the war helped her secure a clerical position at the San Francisco mint. Before her death in 1901, she had gone to bat for soldiers applying for pensions, publicly supported woman suffrage, helped organize the Woman's Relief Corps in California, and appeared as a regular feature of national Grand Army of the Republic (GAR) reunions.[58] Ever a favorite with the Union rank and file, Bickerdyke corresponded for almost forty years with veterans whom she had nursed from Belmont, Missouri, to Resaca, Georgia. Although her postwar career never matched the glorious reputation she had earned for her war work—by 1886, for example, a biography was "published for the benefit of M. A. Bickerdyke" who was having difficulty supporting herself—Bickerdyke's motto of helping those less fortunate, sealed during the war, was confirmed after it.[59]

Annie Turner Wittenmyer had married well in the 1840s and was living in Keokuk, Iowa, when the war began. As Elizabeth Leonard has observed in *Yankee Women* (1994), the war gave Wittenmyer the chance to wrest control of woman-sponsored relief efforts from men who wished to head up relief organizations without performing any of the labor. Resisting the male leadership of an Iowa state sanitary agency by maintaining her own aid society in Keokuk as the primary Iowa conduit to the U.S. Sanitary and Christian Commissions, Wittenmyer created, promoted, and administered a system of special diet kitchens for use in Union general hospitals. Although she encouraged her workers to accede to the model of submissive cooperation touted by the national benevolent groups, she quietly insisted on autonomous direction of the facilities she established.[60] By 1864 she had already begun to establish homes in Iowa for children orphaned by the war; the first opened in 1864 in Farmington and the second in 1865 in Davenport, where she was on-site matron until 1867. By the late 1860s she attached herself to more explicitly religious endeavors, first as a promoter and an organizer of a civilian-clerical visiting society to aid the needy and later as publisher of a Christian periodical. In 1874 she became the first president of the Woman's Christian Temperance Union, until her own view that the WCTU should not endorse woman suffrage disenchanted her followers. In the late

1880s Wittenmyer was elected president of the national Woman's Relief Corps (WRC)—an organization dedicated to providing old-age support for former Union hospital workers—and she presided over the establishment of homes for former Union army nurses, veterans, and their widows.[61] As leader of the WRC in the early 1890s, Wittenmyer also helped secure a military pension for female hospital workers.

The paths of women who achieved a national celebrity through their war work are easier to trace than those who did not. Rebecca Pomroy of Chelsea, Massachusetts, who had been widowed, like Bickerdyke and Wittenmyer, before the war, went to Washington to find work in the hospitals after seeing an ad in a local paper. She spent most of the war tending the rank and file at Columbia College Hospital but agreed to accept a special assignment arranged by Dorothea Dix in 1862 to become private nurse to the First Family. Periodically leaving her work at Columbia to minister to Tad and Mary Lincoln, Pomroy believed that she had become a valued family servant, receiving assurances that she should never want for support during her lifetime. But with Lincoln's death, she later wrote, "all the generous promises of ample remuneration and support which he guaranteed . . . were rendered void," forcing her again to shift for herself.[62] Drawing on her relief experience, Pomroy found work in Massachusetts as matron of a girls' reformatory in Newton—a job she still held twenty years later when, in her sixties, she published her memoirs. The Confederacy's Rose Rooney, a widowed Irish immigrant who served with the 15th Louisiana throughout the war, similarly spent her waning days as matron of Camp Nichols, the Louisiana state home for Confederate veterans in New Orleans. Cherished by the inmates and drawing a monthly stipend of six dollars, the working-class Rooney was better off than former aristocrats who had to depend on relatives for housing or ended up jobless, destitute, and forgotten.[63]

In the 1870s nurses' training schools sprang up in several cities; war had crystallized the demand for skilled surgical and domestic help in hospitals. Medical officials agreed that it was no longer desirable for untrained civilians to assist physicians, prompting the American Medical Association in 1868 to recommend that schools to train nurses be attached to hospitals.[64] Even Sarah Josepha Hale, arbiter of bourgeois convention, argued in the pages of *Godey's* in 1871 that nurses' training was as essential to women as surgical training was to men.[65] The nursing curriculum established by Florence Nightingale in England after the Crimean War had considerable influence in postwar America. Nightingale opened her first school in 1860, and by 1876 twenty-two nursing schools were in operation in London alone. Her *Notes on Nursing*, published in 1860, had encouraged some to become wartime nurses, but the impact of the book was more widely felt after the war, when the American medical community acknowledged that it must take part in educating medical attendants.[66] The English example convinced well-positioned women, like New York's Abby Howland Woolsey and Louisa Lee Schuyler, that nursing merited the status of a profession. By 1873 the first nurses' training programs appeared in New York, Boston, and New Haven, but few former workers were among those who matriculated.[67]

One might have expected that workers in their teens, twenties, and thirties at the time of the war would have exchanged recent experience for formal training, but there were obstacles. American nursing leaders adopted Nightingale's model of admitting only young, white middle-class women for training—those whom leaders believed were most susceptible and receptive to their disciplinary and educational standards. This excluded two-thirds of the war's relief workers, neither white nor middle class, who had staffed hospital kitchens and laundries during the war. This exclusionary mentality was doubly punitive: the "undesirables" could have used the steady work that nursing offered, and, unlike nursing neophytes, they had the advantage of prior experience.[68] Age and pay also seem to have been deterrents. Whereas nursing educators hoped to attract young, malleable women, war nurses were middle-aged or elderly by the 1870s and 1880s. Moreover, educators' insistence that nursing be paid work must have scared off some in the "desirable" pool of middle-class women who thought wages a working-class necessity.[69]

Even though few workers enrolled in nurses' training schools after the war, several took part in launching the profession. In 1873 and 1874 a "Mrs." Billings and Mary Phinney von Olnhausen became the first superintendents of nursing at Boston's Massachusetts General Hospital—the institution where Emily Parsons had received informal training in 1861 before setting out for New York and points west.[70] Both Billings and von Olnhausen used their wartime positions to advantage by securing administrative jobs in the new field. When Parsons returned to Cambridge from Benton Barracks in 1865, she began making plans to start a charity hospital. Located initially in a private residence, the hospital opened in 1867 with Parsons as nurse-administrator and two physicians to see patients. Thirteen years later, when she was fifty-six, a fatal stroke cut short Parson's good works, but by 1886 the hospital reopened and continued successfully in a new building on the endowment she had raised.[71]

Catholic religious orders were in the vanguard of postwar hospital development. When the war began nuns had more nursing experience than any other group; several orders had established hospitals in the 1840s and 1850s and continued to do so in the 1860s. Sister Anthony O'Connell of the Sisters of Charity in Cincinnati had led her order in establishing St. John's Hotel (Hospital) for Invalids in 1852 and implemented a visiting nurse service there in 1854. From an 1861 measles epidemic at Camp Dennison, Ohio, to transport work in the Army of the Cumberland after the battle of Shiloh, to treatment of contrabands with smallpox in Nashville, O'Connell had been one of few to arrive at the front with practical nursing experience. Building on her knowledge of acute care, she founded two new hospitals in the postwar decade with an emphasis on nursing education.[72] Lacking a prewar tradition, two Indiana orders, the Sisters of Providence in St. Mary of the Woods and the Sisters of the Holy Cross in South Bend, established hospitals on the strength of their wartime service. Eleven of the St. Mary's sisters had started their nursing careers in 1861, when medical authorities called on them to help staff the new City Hospital in Indianapolis; thirty-six Holy Cross sisters split their time among ten different institutions.[73]

Several of the Woolsey sisters of New York devoted time and financial resources to nursing education. Jane and Abby were instrumental in the founding of New York's Presbyterian Hospital in the early 1870s. As its director, Jane supervised the training of nurses, although no formal nursing education program was established there. Abby served as clerk, helping Jane organize drug, kitchen, and supply departments and standing in for Jane when she was absent. During this time, both sisters worked with the New York State Charities Aid Association on other hospital projects. Abby was a key player in the founding of Bellvue Hospital Training School for Nurses in 1873 and sat on its board.[74] Georgeanna had nursed alongside Jane at Portsmouth Grove in Rhode Island and on her own at Hammond General and Fairfax Seminary Hospitals; had served on transports with sister Eliza at Gettysburg, Belle Plain, and Fredericksburg; had established triage stations for wounded from the battles of the Wilderness; and by war's end had helped organize the general hospital at Beverly, New Jersey, with sister Caroline and fellow New Yorker Abby Hopper Gibbons. "Georgy" (as her sisters and friends were fond of calling her) married surgeon Frank Bacon a year after

Though appointed as a nurse, Esther Hill Hawks was able to practice medicine in a contraband hospital in the Sea Islands. Among her patients were African American soldiers wounded in the July 1863 assault on Fort Wagner. (Courtesy of Library of Congress)

the war but did not settle back into private life. In 1873 she was a founder of the Connecticut Training School for Nurses at the New Haven Hospital, and in 1879 she authored a popular nursing manual. In the 1880s and 1890s she engaged in more general charity work—befitting women of her upper-class background—and like others before her, made children's welfare a priority.[75]

Few female hospital workers participated in the professionalization of nursing in the postwar years, but even fewer went into medicine. As historians from Regina Morantz-Sanchez to Mary Roth Walsh have observed, American women encountered educational roadblocks and the petty tyranny of anxious male physicians in their attempts to be doctors.[76] Among hospital workers, I have identified only thirteen Northern and three Southern women who sought medical training.[77] Seven got their start in the 1850s at women's medical colleges and the few schools that did not systematically exclude them. Finding few officials in the military establishment to acknowledge their professional status, female doctors worked as nurses, sometimes alongside surgeons with more questionable training. New Hampshire's Esther Hill Hawks was trained by European wunderkind Marie Zakrzewska at the New England Female Medical College in Boston before the eminent doctor left Samuel Gregory's establishment to start her own clinic.[78] New York's Chloe Annette Buckel, who had held teaching and factory jobs, was an 1858 graduate of the Women's Medical College of Pennsylvania, as was the Confederacy's Orrie R. Moon of Albemarle County, Virginia. Moon married a physician during the war, but because the historian who recorded her service disapproved of careers for women, he wrote virtually nothing about the length or terms of her service.[79]

After having borrowed on a life insurance policy to put herself through medical school, Buckel practiced at the New York Infirmary for Women and Children—an experience that led her to start a similar clinic in Chicago in 1859.[80] By midwar the thirty-year-old spinster was working for the state of Indiana, placing Hoosiers in Vicksburg, Louisville, and Memphis hospitals, and superintending female workers in Jeffersonville (Indiana), Nashville, Chattanooga, and Huntsville. Buckel practiced briefly in Evansville after the war and then secured a more permanent appointment as a resident physician at the New England Hospital for Women and Children. Following a trip to Europe in the 1870s to observe surgical techniques, she moved to Oakland, California, opened a practice, and became a consulting physician at the Pacific Dispensary for Women and Children. By the time of her death in 1912, Buckel had become a crusader for children's health issues and had lent her hand to a variety of reform causes.[81]

Esther Hill Hawks, whose practice among African American regiments in the Sea Islands was never officially sanctioned, had learned so much from her husband's medical books that in 1854 and 1855 she gave lectures on physiology in St. Louis and Vicksburg. Despite Milton Hawks's growing resistance to Esther's medical ambitions, Esther enrolled at the New England Female Medical College in Boston in 1855 and completed her degree. A decade later, when Milton was stationed at Morris Island and Esther was on furlough in New Hampshire, he still regretted his wife's vocation, remembering the lecture tour as "a sacrifice" that "broke up our little home." "At this moment," he wrote in 1864, "I wish Ette had never seen a medical book, or heard a lecture. It is not a businessman-like worker that a husband needs—It is a loving woman."[82] Milton's views softened for a time, but Esther continued her practice only intermittently. Settling in Florida after the war—Milton hoped to make a commercial success there during Reconstruction—Esther opened a school at New Smyrna for black children and became active in the Woman's National Loyal League (WNLL)—a group formed during the war to promote abolition and women's rights.[83] With her husband still in Florida, she moved back to New England in 1870 to join the medical practice of Lizzie Breed Welch in Lynn, Massachusetts. Dealing primarily with gynecological cases, Hawks built a flourishing practice. In later years she was active in medical and charity organizations, supported children's educational initiatives, and, like Chloe Annette Buckel and Mary Livermore, promoted woman suffrage.[84]

Several of those who earned prewar degrees got them from eclectic and homeopathic schools of medicine, including Mary Edwards Walker, who graduated from Syracuse Medical College in 1855. The Confederacy's Ella Cooper had taken a full course of study at the Medical College of Cincinnati but was not granted a degree because women were ineligible. Cooper managed to secure a nursing position during the war, but what she did afterward remains unknown.[85] Susan Edson and Caroline Brown Winslow also pursued medical studies in the West: Edson graduated from Cleveland Homeopathic College in 1854 and Brown from the Western College of Homeopathy in 1856. Edson and Brown met as nurses in Washington during the war, where both practiced medicine through the end of the century, helping to organize the Homeopathic Free Dispensary, the National Homeopathic Hospital, and the Washington chapter of the American Institute of Homeopathy. Edson, who started a training program for nurses in New York in 1862 with financial support from the Masons after the surgeon general had vetoed the idea, was named family physician to the Garfields and supported various GAR auxiliary projects in her remaining years.[86]

Others in the midst of formal medical training when the war began postponed it as long as military hospitals were surfeited with the sick and dying —a four-year-long clinic for any aspiring doctor. The war interrupted the medical studies of Michigan's Mary Blackmar, who went to City Point when a nursing opportunity beckoned. A personal friend of Rena Littlefield Miner, Blackmar graduated from the Women's Medical College of Pennsylvania in 1866 and started work at Elizabeth Blackwell's New York clinic, as Chloe Annette Buckel had done before the war. She ultimately married and was still practicing in 1911.[87]

At least six nurses were so transformed by hospital work that they sought careers in medicine after the war. Nancy Maria Hill of Massachusetts served at Washington's Armory Square Hospital under Surgeon D. W. Bliss, who encouraged her to study medicine when the war ended. Under the tutelage of Marie Zakrzewska in Boston and later at the University of Michigan Medical School, Hill earned her degree in 1874 and opened up shop in Dubuque, Iowa, where she was still practicing at the turn of the century.[88] Another Massachusetts native, Caroline Burghardt, had taught school in Vermont and served as governess to the children of schoolroom poet William Cullen Bryant before she took the Woman's Central Relief Association course in nursing on her way to Washington in 1861. A Dix nurse and veteran of Antietam and Gettysburg, Burghardt also served at Fortress Monroe, Winchester, Wilmington, and Alexandria. She remained in Washington for a decade after the war, employed by the government and ensconced in social activism. In 1876, at the age of forty-two, Burghardt graduated from Howard Medical School and began to practice homeopathic medicine. It is likely that she knew Susan Edson and Caroline Brown Winslow professionally, since both worked in the postwar years to make Washington a center for homeopathic medicine.[89]

Harriet Dada Emens, a nursing veteran of both military theaters during four years of service, also used her war experience as a springboard to a career in medicine. Before the war the New York native had taught school among the Choctaw in the Southwest. In 1868 Harriet Dada graduated from the Women's Medical College of New York and settled in Syracuse. Five years later, at age thirty-eight, she married Peter Emens, who also became a physician, but medicine outlasted the marriage. Harriet was still seeing patients when well into her sixties.[90] Frances M. Nye, who worked with Adelaide Smith at City Point in 1864, studied homeopathy in New York after the war. Her marriage—to a Confederate veteran serendipitously named Francis M. Nye—was much happier than Emens's. Nye and Nye met in medical school and after graduation practiced together for many years.[91]

Mary Jane Safford, born in Vermont and raised in Illinois, worked briefly as a teacher before the war, like several others who later became physicians. Known as the "Cairo Angel" for her gentle ministrations to Illinois soldiers, Safford was one of the earliest female volunteers in the western theater, where she worked closely with Mary Ann Bickerdyke at the battles of Belmont, Fort Donelson, and Shiloh. After earning a degree from the Women's Medical College of New York in 1869, she traveled to Europe to study surgery in Vienna and several German cities because no American medical school would admit a female surgical student. Safford moved to Chicago in 1872 to open a practice but relocated a year later to take a faculty position at the newly opened Boston University (BU) School of Medicine. In addition to appointments at BU and Massachusetts Homeopathic Hospital, this able angel conducted a flourishing private practice. Like others for whom reform was a locus of professional life, Safford took an interest in women's hygiene and dress reform, and before her retirement in 1886 attempted to better conditions for working women.[92] Vesta Ward Swarts, a high school principal in Auburn, Indiana, before the war, worked for the Christian Commission in and around Louisville from 1864 to 1865. After the war she studied medicine at Fort Wayne Medical College and the University of Michigan. She practiced in Auburn from 1882 until 1898, when she was too ill to continue. In 1862 Vesta had married David Swarts, assistant surgeon of the 100th Indiana Volunteers, who encouraged her postwar study and career in medicine. Working together—a road not taken by John and Esther Hawks—the Swartses' marriage and practices flourished; their son also became a physician.[93]

The most celebrated and notorious female medical practitioner of the war years was Mary Edwards Walker of Oswego, New York. After graduating from medical school, she practiced briefly in Columbus, Ohio, before returning to upstate New York, where she married medical student Albert Miller. Though the marriage was short-lived—Miller's infidelities and Walker's eccentricities created fractures—the two practiced for about four years in Rome, New York. During this time she became interested in dress reform, adopting bloomers and eventually the trousers that became her trademark. Walker went to Washington in search of a medical commission when the war began, the only practicing female physician to have done so. Unlike Elizabeth Blackwell who stayed in New York to train Washington-bound nurses for the Woman's Central Relief Association, Walker went right to the capital and volunteered at the Patent Office and field hospitals near Warrenton and Fredericksburg. Finding little enthusiasm for her proffered medical service among military surgeons, she was back in New York taking a new round of medical courses at Hygeia Therapeutic College by early 1862.[94]

It took Walker more than two years to obtain a surgical post; she used unofficial service under General Ambrose Burnside in Virginia during the summer of 1862 to conjure an appointment as a contract surgeon in the Army of the Cumberland in 1864. Her flamboyance was no asset in an anxious, mistrustful, and officious medical establishment. Staff surgeons immediately questioned her credentials and opposed commissioning her as much for personal as for professional reasons.[95] Surviving an inquest at the hands of hostile examiners, Walker traveled to Tennessee, where she became acting assistant surgeon with the 52nd Ohio, lately returned from the battle of Chickamauga. The regiment paid her $80 per month—$20 to $50 less than male assistants but a fortune compared to other women in the service. In April 1864, as she foraged outside of Union lines, Walker was arrested by Confederate scouts who suspected her of espionage and extradited her to Richmond's Castle Thunder, where she remained for four months.[96] Dressed in trousers and a surgeon's uniform, the twenty-five-year-old made such a sensation when she rode into camp that several Confederate soldiers and visiting wives mentioned the incident in their letters and diaries.[97] After her release, Walker was appointed surgeon at the Louisville women's prison in an attempt, on the part of Union medical officials, to deny her a post in the field. After several unhappy months there, Walker became superintendent of a refugee home in Clarksville, Tennessee, in early 1865, but this new endeavor was equally unsatisfying.

She left the service before the end of the war, never to reestablish her former medical practice.[98] For the next fifty years she would immerse herself in a variety of causes, stumping for woman suffrage, dress reform, and reform of the workplace. In 1866 Walker launched a European lecture tour to promote her war service—not unlike the U.S. tour undertaken by Clara Barton in the same year to generate income on the rising tide of war senti-

Matthew Brady photographed Dr. Mary Edwards Walker wearing her customary pants beneath a shortened skirt and her Congressional Medal of Honor in
1865; the same clock appears in Clara Barton's portrait. Walker's spunk made
her a thorn in the side of army medical officials, who attempted to discredit her
medical expertise, though she was one of only a few women recognized as surgeons during the war. (Courtesy of National Archives)

ment.[99] Like other women who had worked for the hospital service, Walker secured a clerkship with the U.S. Pension Office in the 1880s but was fired several years later in what appears to have been a sexual harassment scandal. Walker's supervisor dismissed her for being a troublemaker—after which she publicly accused him of carrying on an illicit affair with one of the young women on his staff. Her attempts to win back her job and obtain lost salary and benefits were fruitless.[100] In 1865, despite her ill-starred history with the military medical elite, she was the first woman awarded the Congressional Medal of Honor, a tribute that did little to discourage her radical views. But in 1917, when Congress voted retroactively to exclude noncombatants from eligibility, the medal was revoked. Not one to take lightly what she perceived as the government's move to discredit her, Walker went to work to protest the slight—made all the more shameful because she had held the medal for half a century. She died fighting for its reinstatement when, at age eighty-seven, she fell down a flight of steps at the capitol.[101]

Those who chose medical careers were aware of the prestige accorded to medicine in the postwar period—a time when professionalization had already taken place. By contrast, nursing was in its professional infancy, and because of the gendered division that already characterized the two fields, nursing would never be on a professional par with medicine.[102] Lacking letters and diaries from women who chose medicine during the war, we cannot know whether they ever considered becoming nurses afterward. But they surely learned from their wartime hospital service that surgeons were powerful actors in the military medical arena and, accordingly, chose work that would give them greater autonomy and financial reward. War workers who determined to pursue careers in the health services may have decided against nursing because of the institutionalized inferiority that had already been their lot.

**What became of the** working-class women who performed the manual and custodial labor in Civil War hospitals? Because they did not write narratives of the war, because historians have not remembered them individually for outstanding contributions, because most were ineligible to apply for the pensions that might have provided clues about their postwar lives, we know little about them. Many undoubtedly returned to their prewar agricultural, domestic, and industrial work. Southerners who had tilled the soil in men's absence, whether as slaves or yeomen, would till the soil again—albeit on different terms with landowners. Institutions of higher learning opened their doors to women anxious to study horticulture after the war, evidence that female-headed agricultural households were on the rise. Factory jobs and government work were prized but difficult to come by.[103] Domestic work was more readily available but paid poorly. Rather than work for others, some Southerners chose to employ themselves. Lucinda Horne, of Edgefield County, South Carolina, accompanied her husband and son, along with the 14th South Carolina, to war as regimental nurse, cook, and laundress. Both men sustained wounds but survived the war, and all three Hornes returned home in 1865. In the 1880s Lucinda and her husband went to work as peddlers, traveling between Augusta and Edgefield, selling pottery.[104] Not so different from belles who had served Confederate troops, Lucinda Horne faded into obscurity in the immediate postwar years. Southern women and men had to go about the business of repairing lives and homesteads damaged by invasion—work that took place in private and that registered memory as another of the war's casualties.

As a group, African American women fared worse than Southern whites, despite liberal postwar policies and the passage of the Fourteenth and Fifteenth Amendments. Ideally designed to give ex-slaves access to educational and economic opportunities, temporarily constructed civil rights did not improve social status for most African Americans, whether they had been enslaved or not, and after Reconstruction, their situations worsened. Even if they found higher-paying industrial jobs, they were paid less and given more tedious work than whites. As former slave and teacher Susie King Taylor had discovered after losing her school, it was hard for any African American woman to find steady work commensurate with her educational attainments. And as many others were to learn a generation after the war, their service diminished in public memory in inverse proportion to that of middle-class whites who enshrined themselves at the side of veterans—an enduring connection facilitated by literacy and greater social privilege. Both the assignment of low-prestige war work to black women and the burial of their record of service compounded their fate as Congress celebrated white women's war achievements with pensions.

Notwithstanding the differences of place and condition that figured in the postwar lives of former hospital workers, the example of thousands of women working away from the home place during the war encouraged a reunited U.S. labor force to receive them more readily after 1865. That labor force had always included working-class women and women of color, but it now made way for middle-class whites who had seldom worked outside the home but whose war service compelled a reappraisal of the appropriateness of their work. Northern whites not economically obliged to seek work were perhaps the most happily situated of war workers when it came to postwar opportunities. Because their domestic lives had not been as profoundly disrupted as Southerners', they did not cling as tenaciously to prewar roles. With the Northern economy expanding, little deterred them from what seemed an inexorable expansion of their public roles.

Many war workers did resume their private domestic routines. But others had found a forum for activism in their war work and intended to seek out new channels for its expression. Whether or not they had taken an active part in the war, women could secure postwar work and contribute to the public life of the nation with greater impunity than they had before the conflict. Still, the pervasiveness of conservative rhetoric between 1865 and 1870 may have been more than propaganda aimed at getting women to return to private prewar roles and out of the public work many had chosen for themselves. The magnitude of the public reaction may have been the very sign that women North and South had already succeeded in initiating a revised domestic agenda.

## CHAPTER SIX

# Pensioning Women

Are we not all soldiers?
—Anna L. Beers to Mary Ann Bickerdyke, October 22, 1886

She sought no soft place, but wherever her regiment went she
went, often marching on foot and camping without tent on the
field. She was always present where most needed, and to the suffering, whether "Yank" or "Grayback," it made no difference. . . .
I have seen her face a battery without flinching, while a man took
refuge behind her to avoid the flying fragments of bursting shells.
Of all the men and women who volunteered to serve their country
during the late war, not one is more deserving of reward.
—Testimony of Gilman Marston on behalf of
    Harriet Patience Dame, March 15, 1884

When I worked in Arm[or]y Square hospital D.C. I was quite young.
. . . My stepfather also worked there. His name was Samuel Taylor.
He looked after me and I suppose my name was registered as
Martha Taylor or Martha Lewis as they use [sic] to call me by Tay-
lor and sometimes Lewis. I lived with a family by the name of
Lewis before I went to the hospital to work but my mo[t]her [sic]
name was Smith.
—Pension affidavit of Martha Smith Reed, June 30, 1896

Three months before the armistice at Appomattox, Maine's Isabella Fogg —a widowed seamstress and Union nurse since 1861—was serving aboard the *Jacob Strader* on the Ohio River near Louisville. At dusk she inadvertently stepped into an open hatchway as she carried a drink to a soldier and fell into the hold below. Forty-one at the time, Fogg was laid up for the next few years with a spinal injury. She was still hospitalized in April 1866 when she began drawing a pension of $8 per month—the first female worker to earn compensation because of injury sustained in the line of duty. Nearly destitute by 1870, she sought and won an increase to $20, raised to $30 only a year later. With the help of Generals Joshua Chamberlain of Gettysburg fame (and governor of Maine from 1866 to 1871) and Oliver Otis Howard, another Mainer of sterling repute, Fogg secured a Pension Bureau job and relocated to Washington in 1871. Like other nurses aided by special acts of Congress in the 1860s, 1870s, and 1880s, she was able to augment the living provided by the pension with government work, but her tenure was brief: within two years, she died of complications arising from her 1865 plummet.[1]

Without powerful advocates, Martha Spicer and Elizabeth Martin Handy had a tougher time convincing pension officials that they were worthy candidates. From October 1861 through October 1864, Spicer, who was African American, had worked as a matron in Rolla (Missouri), Helena, and Little Rock hospitals. Detailed to wash clothes and carry water, she assumed a wider range of duties as thousands of contrabands fled to Union army installations. Spicer applied for a pension in 1882 when she no longer was able to work, a decade before the passage of the Army Nurses Pension Act and eight years before the Pension Bureau would generate its master list of female hospital attendants from the Civil War. Having granted claims thus far only to nurses who could coordinate passage of a special act of Congress, pension officials rejected the claim outright.[2] Spicer's three years of service counted for nought. Handy fared little better. Having joined the 21st New York Light Artillery with her husband in 1862, she served as laundress until she landed nursing assignments in Memphis and Baton Rouge. In 1892, twenty-seven years after the end of her government service, she applied for a pension. In a deposition filed from a poorhouse and taken by a notary public, the illiterate former nurse testified that she had been in service for three years (the Carded Service Records listed only one month). A surviving officer of the 21st corroborated Handy's length of service, but her attempt to file witness testimonials was fruitless: because she could not satisfy pension officials that she had served the requisite six months, she was ineligible for a pension.[3]

By the end of Reconstruction, a time in which cultural rhetoric mitigated regional differences, the U.S. government was celebrating its military ascendancy among the nations through an unprecedented expansion of veterans' and dependents' pensions. By the mid-1880s the Grand Army of the Republic (GAR) had grown to 295,000 members and would reach 409,000 by 1890—more than a tenfold increase in only twelve years.[4] The GAR attracted thousands of women, including veterans' daughters and wives and groups like the Woman's Relief Corps (WRC). WRC membership alone was estimated at nearly 100,000 by 1890.[5] In addition to valorizing the republican ideals on which Union victory had been founded, female auxiliaries took up the task of honoring war nurses, many of whom were now elderly. Comparable Southern groups invested their energies in monument and asylum building but took no formal political action to relieve Confederate nurses in need. Indeed, Northern ignorance and dismissal of Southern claims constricted the political voice of Southern women in the 1880s. Workers who had the ill fortune to be on the losing side had no access to pensions. The closest they came to postwar government sanction and recognition was in securing civil service jobs in Washington or the local post office. Ex-Confederates were required to take an oath of allegiance before their work could be authorized—a symbolic surrender that fueled resentment and sectional separatism. Nina Silber has astutely observed the "romance of reunion" in which Northerners engaged Southerners in the 1870s and 1880s.[6] But as much as a new nationalist rhetoric may have taken hold, government had no intention of wooing former Rebels with pensions. Against this rhetorical backdrop of sectional reunion, Northerners first conceived of a pension for Union nurses only.

The legislative history of the Army Nurses Pension Act of 1892 and the special acts of Congress that pensioned former workers from 1866 to 1892 were the trademark of a liberal bureaucracy ready to honor military workers of every stripe. However, the Union surgeon general's classification of female hospital workers on the basis of race and social class when they entered the service jeopardized their success in the pension process. In practice, exclusionary language undergirded the claims process, and access to the pension bureaucracy was linked to literacy. Moreover, workers' social status encouraged the valuing and devaluing of specific forms of domestic work on which pension eligibility would be judged.

Soldiers had received military pensions from the time of the Revolutionary War; soldiers' widows became eligible for pensions after the War of 1812. By July 1862 Congress drafted a pension bill that expanded benefits to widows and orphans and included soldiers' mothers and sisters as beneficiaries for the first time with a view toward assuring reluctant recruits that their families would be compensated if they died. By 1866 fathers and brothers of dead servicemen had been added to the rolls.[7] By 1879 new legislation promised payment in arrears to dependents who had lost male kin in the war but had not been granted pensions until later. With the prospect of collecting years of "back pay"—an average of $1,200 for the first payment—surviving family members rushed to file claims. In the year after the passage of the Arrears Act, more than 110,000 new claims were filed—three times the 36,900 claims registered the previous year.[8] In 1890 government opened its arms even wider by declaring any disabled veteran eligible for a pension as long as he had served ninety days, regardless of whether his disability had been incurred in the line of duty. Public response was overwhelming: In one year, 655,000 claims were filed by first-time applicants and those wishing to increase their allotments. Although only 17 percent of the claims were approved at this time, the draw on government coffers was substantial. By 1890 the annual pension budget was $106 million, and it would get larger. Between 1890 and 1892 more than 338,000 new claims were allowed, which required an army of more than 2,000 clerks in Washington and 3,800 examining physicians nationally. By 1893, 41.6 percent of the federal budget went to pay pensions; by the end of the century, almost a million people, or 1.3 percent of the nation's population, were on the government dole.[9]

Historians have suggested that the goal of welfare policy after the war was to shore up manhood and keep widowed pensioners dependent—a gendered model that army nurses challenged.[10] Asking for pensions required government sanction of female independence—not easily granted when, after the Dependent Pension Act of 1890, huge numbers of soldiers' family members were being added to the rolls.[11] Theda Skocpol and Megan McClintock have shown how pension officials monitored widowed beneficiaries in the hope of snaring those living in sin—those who had chosen to forego marriage rather than renounce their monthly allotments. In a single stroke, the bureau donned the mantle of moral prescription by putting widows on notice that cohabitors would be stricken from the rolls.[12] Former army nurses —many of whom were widows and mothers eligible for relief under other headings—had their work cut out for them: In both lobbying for legislation and assembling individual pension claims, they would need to prove that they were morally deserving of pensions.

With the social welfare of veterans and their kin a national concern, former Union nurses began asking questions about the meaning of their work as early as the 1870s. If soldiers' dependents were pensioned, they reasoned, why not war workers who fought the battles of disease and infection? Though the promise of regular monthly income was attractive, those who labored for a pension bill—primarily white middle-class women—were motivated as much by principle as by need. Simply put, they wanted their war work to be evaluated alongside the soldier's. Having based their camaraderie with soldiers on their mutual military subordination, former nurses wanted the government to signify that hospital work had been as important as combat in winning the war. Few workers could claim that they daily risked their lives (nor could most soldiers), but helping the sick and wounded return to the field should, they argued, entitle them to pensions and thus government acknowledgment of their citizenship.

By legislating the Army Nurses Pension Act of 1892, which made monthly pensions of twelve dollars available to nurses who had served for at least six months, Congress tacitly acknowledged that women's war work *had been* roughly equivalent to soldiers', a remarkable concession in light of the bureaucratic inclination to keep military and civilian work separate. The legislation favored, not surprisingly, the white middle class—not black and working-class women who had constituted two-thirds of the female hospital workforce.[13] Anxious to quell public resistance to middle-class women's labor during the war, Dorothea Dix had enforced these distinctions by channeling "respectable"—or white and middle-class—women into nursing jobs and "common"—or black and working-class—women into laundry and kitchen jobs. In a related move to shield white elites from doing unsavory custodial chores, the Surgeon General's Office circulated an order by midwar stipulating that hospitals hire only blacks as cooks and laundresses.[14] Though it had difficulty enforcing such an injunction since "respectable" whites had to cook and wash after all, medical officers promoted this hierarchy of job classifications based on race and class. Hospital administrators and their female deputies thus made explicit the link between social status and the perceived value of work by handing devalued custodial jobs to black and working-class women, a process that set in motion the system of privilege that excluded many of them from pensions a generation later.

In 1890, when the Carded Service Records were compiled to identify female hospital workers for pension eligibility, Surgeon General John Moore produced a scheme that again linked social status with job classification by differentiating among the several classes of nurses but lumping together all other workers into one category. The list of nurses included those hired by Dorothea Dix or the War Department; "white female nurses" hired directly by surgeons, including those deputized by the Sanitary Commission (USSC) or Christian Commission (USCC); "colored persons employed as cooks and nurses under authority from the War Department"; unpaid volunteers, such as Sisters of Charity; and independent workers, like Clara Barton, who administered their own relief programs. The surgeon general described "another class of females known indifferently, as Hospital Matrons, Laundresses, and Washer Women . . .; the legal definition of this class of employé is 'Hospital Matron' and must not be mistaken for the word 'laundress' which legally means, 'women allowed to accompany the troops.'"[15] The legal definitions show that women who went off to war with regiments were classed as laundresses, which led in the 1890s to misconceptions about the work they had done during the war. Regimental workers thus encountered greater obstacles when making application to the Pension Bureau because the burden of proving that they had done the work of nurses—in addition to washing clothes—fell entirely on them.

Approximately one in nine Union female hospital attendants applied for pensions after 1892. For about forty more years—long enough for workers who were teenagers in the 1860s to still be alive—the Pension Bureau processed claims from 2,448 women, some of whom were already receiving pensions as soldiers' widows.[16] Because there was great variation in the amount paid veterans and widows, depending on the soldier's disability and the number of dependents he had, it might be in the best interests of widows, if they also had been hospital workers, to refile with the bureau for a more lucrative nurse's pension.[17] Indeed, some filed in the hope of adding to their monthly allotment with a second pension, unaware of the ban on such practice.

In the twenty-seven years between 1865 and 1892, a select group of nurses won pensions through special acts of Congress, designed for those who had achieved distinction in their positions but had been unable to earn a postwar living.[18] Texts of the bills provided hagiographies of workers' deeds that reinforced notions of feminine self-sacrifice. One New Hampshire nurse was described as "faithful and untiring in the discharge of her duties," "truly an angel of mercy," and "always willing to give up everything to the sick and wounded." Another from Massachusetts, whose "superior fidelity and skill required her assignment at the most difficult and responsible stations," was "exemplary in conduct and competent through good judgment."[19] Narratives varied from several sentences in support of the applicant to weightier documents, like the six-page, 5,000-word paean to Harriet Patience Dame, appended to which were depositions from two soldiers she had tended. Testimony often included mention of the hundreds of dollars workers had spent on soldiers—more material evidence of personal sacrifice.[20]

Stipends varied widely. Whereas Isabella Fogg received $8 per month in 1866, only two years later Congress authorized a $17 monthly pension for Maine's Harriet Stinson Pond, who not only was captured by Rebel soldiers during her tour of duty, but also was disabled by smashing her leg in a wagon accident as she removed wounded from the field at Antietam.[21] After 1880 Congress authorized payments of $25 per month to women it deemed had performed extraordinary service, like Harriet Dame and Mary Ann Bickerdyke. This was more than twice the amount the bureau would allot to women under the act of August 5, 1892, and some chafed at the discrepancy. Caroline Burghardt, who in 1891 was awarded only $12 per month by special act, wondered why she had been stinted: "If I am entitled to receive $25.00 per month, $75.00 per quarter as I am informed that the other Army Nurses do," she wrote, "I would like to have the matter adjusted as soon as possible." But she assumed too much. Applications made in the several years before the act of August 5, 1892, were routinely approved for $12—a result of negotiations between ex-nurses and legislators toward the passage of the 1892 bill.[22] In 1919, having drawn $12 per month for almost thirty years, Burghardt wanted a cost-of-living increase, despite the fact that she had been earning income as a physician for more than forty years. Rather than appealing to the Pension Bureau on the basis of ill health and indigence in the spirit of earlier pensioners, she regarded the increase as her due for loyal service to the nation.

Caroline Burghardt was not the only nurse-pensioner to wonder why her monthly allotment had not increased in thirty years. Fanny Titus-Hazen, a nursing veteran active in the National Association of Army Nurses (NAAN), began drawing $12 per month in 1893. Her husband Charles had received a veteran's pension (for service as a sergeant in the 19th Massachusetts Volunteers) since 1882. Fanny watched Charles's pension grow from $4 to $30 per month by 1912, while her own pension remained unchanged at $12. When Charles died shortly after their fiftieth wedding anniversary in 1916, Fanny qualified for a widow's pension of $40 per month, provided she relinquish the nurse's pension. It was an easy choice: she drew the widow's portion until, in 1926, Congress authorized a long-overdue increase in nursing pensions to $50 per month. Again, Titus-Hazen manipulated the bureaucracy in her own pecuniary interest. She applied for reinstatement of the nursing pension, canceled the widow's pension, and for four more years until her death at age ninety received a monthly check for $50.[23]

Physician Vesta Swarts used similar reasoning in 1913 with less success. While working on behalf of ex-army nurses for an increase in the twelve-dollar pension, Swarts was also examining Pension Bureau policy for loopholes that would entitle her to more money in the interim. She explained to Pension Commissioner James F. Davenport: "As I believe the army nurses to be entitled to an increase for old age similar to that awarded the veterans whose hardships and dangers they shared, besides working more hours per day than the soldier for the greater part of their service, I am writing to you for information which I need in order to be able to work to advantage in an endeavor to secure a consideration of recent bills introduced in Congress looking toward better pensions for the army nurse."[24] Drawing on arguments used by nursing advocates prior to 1892 and venturing the controversial opinion that her tribe had worked longer hours than soldiers, Swarts next employed a bait-and-switch strategy. In an attempt to win a more lucrative widow's pension, she claimed that her husband David's death in 1905 from chronic diarrhea had been the result of a wartime affliction, pleading her case as the examining physician. She submitted a corroborating diagnosis from their son, also a physician, calling into question not only her professional objectivity, but also her judgment. Such grandstanding did little to reverse the bureau's view that the former army nurse "was not in extreme want, nor totally disabled."[25] Still, Swarts tried to cover every contingency, asking the commissioner in March 1913 "if in the future the Army Nurses are granted an increase over and above what I would get as a widow, could I be again placed on the Army Nurse pension list?"[26] Swarts's clinical diagnoses and her shrewd navigation of murky pension policy backwaters may have put off bureau officials in light of Titus-Hazen's smoother sailing.

Nurses critical of those who had worked for money during the war were prominent among proponents and beneficiaries of postwar pension reform.[27]

Though they had once viewed toiling for wages as unseemly, the prospect of public assistance in old age was welcome. As early as the 1880s, pension advocates believed that all former nurses ought to be eligible because of the work they had done—remunerated or voluntary—a generation earlier. Formed in 1883 to provide assistance to veterans, the Woman's Relief Corps dedicated itself "to cherish[ing] and emulat[ing] the deeds of the army nurses, and of all loyal women who rendered loving service" during the war.[28] The WRC's insistence on honoring female as well as male veterans translated into an organized political effort to secure a pension for nurses. Lobbying by such groups had not only enhanced soldiers' pension opportunities but also had fueled an elaborate system of soldiers' homes for disabled veterans.[29] In the late 1880s the WRC's Pension and Relief Committee (PRC) circulated a petition that garnered over 160,000 signatures; it argued that nurses ought to be paid $25 per month in keeping with standards first set by special acts of Congress. By 1890, however, the PRC conceded that "'half a loaf [wa]s better than none,'" scaling back its request to $12 per month when legislators balked at the prospect of paying out sums that doubled the amount usually granted to veterans' widows.[30] It was also the year of the Dependent Pension Act, which flooded the bureau with new applicants, increased its backlog of cases, and thus dampened its enthusiasm for a whole new army of pension hopefuls.[31]

Banking on the fact that Congress in 1890 was in no position to ignore the service of female nurses after opening the door to unprecedented numbers of soldiers' relatives, WRC leaders went to work building their case. Sarah E. Fuller, secretary of the PRC, went right to the top, asking Clara Barton, whose name was synonymous with war relief, to support the blanket bill in 1890: "From all over the country comes the cry of these aged needy women—who when our country was in its darkest hours of need, the men of its glorious army and navy were suffering from wounds or disease—these noble patriotic women, with souls fired with the same zeal that inspired the men, gave of their time and strength in a service which saved thousands of precious lives."[32] After all, argued pension advocate Kate Scott in the same vein, nurses' work was often as demanding and dangerous as that of soldiers. As an officer of the National Association of Army Nurses—an incarnation of the Ex-Nurse's Association of the District of Columbia established by Dorothea Dix in 1881—Scott noted that the organization's raison d'être was "to seek out and aid unfortunate and needy nurses and assist in procuring pensions" for them.[33] With a two-tiered effort on the part of WRC auxiliaries as well as the NAAN, the effort to pension former nurses gained credibility.

In appealing to congressional leaders, ex-nurses represented themselves as soldiers of care who had fought foes as deadly as those on the front lines. Given that over two-thirds of the war's casualties were from disease, they might well have argued that hospital work put them at the mercy of an even deadlier foe. Such heroic military imagery was enhanced by the pleading that many were single women who could no longer sustain themselves. By the 1890s many who had married before the war or been widowed in the intervening years could not apply for widows' pensions if their husbands had been civilians.[34] Why, they wondered, should widows who had done nothing to serve relief efforts and won stipends by virtue of marriage be entitled to pensions, but not they who had actively served? Appeals based on the rhetoric of self-sacrifice, enlisted to urge middle-class women to work without pay during the war, were by the 1890s transformed into a rhetoric of financial reward for services rendered. Cornelia Hancock, who drew a monthly stipend from 1895 until her death in 1927, exploited the new rhetorical angle by stating that the only pay she had received for two and a half years of service was $9.25, and that she was now owed compensation.[35]

As Americans became increasingly sentimental about the war in the 1890s, nurses (and their supporters on Capitol Hill, many of whom were former soldiers themselves) had little trouble persuading legislators to make them eligible for pensions. Compared to thousands of veterans' widows already on the rolls, the names of 6,284 nurses culled from hospital records by the Pension Bureau in 1890 seemed an insignificant number. It would appear that advocates did not consider the nearly 15,000 matrons, cooks, and laundresses, which the records also turned up, as pensioners-in-waiting. But the pool of potential new applicants—whether 6,000 or 21,000—would barely be noticed in the ocean of 876,000 pensioners to whom the bureau was already beholden in 1892.[36]

The Army Nurses Pension Act went through several readings before it was passed on August 5, 1892. A Senate bill in February of that year had proposed a graduated scale of payments based on length of service and sanctioned "double dipping" (the practice of drawing two pensions at the same time), but neither proposal survived a March reading of the bill.[37] As legislated in 1892, the act promised twelve dollars per month to those who could prove six months' service as nurses and who were not already drawing widows' pensions.[38] By 1893 the act was already in need of amendment because of the narrow way in which pension authorities were applying the label of "nurse" and because hundreds of claims had been filed by nurses who had not been appointed by the Surgeon General's Office but who could still prove service commensurate with those so appointed. The bureau also noted a need to expand the range of eligible witnesses.[39]

Once nurses could apply for pensions, those who had worked gratis—the very group advocates believed most deserving—had difficulty proving their service. Because hospital registers were not always accurate even when available, the Pension Bureau used payroll records to corroborate applicants' claims. Payroll records routinely included a worker's place and dates of service, but the names of those who had not been paid did not appear. Though Mary Smith Frush labored for three years in Maryland and Pennsylvania hospitals and on site at Antietam and Gettysburg, the bureau found no official record of her service and rejected her 1893 claim.[40] The institutional quagmire that beset the Surgeon General's Office regarding pay meant that even those who wished to draw wages were not always listed on payrolls. Such conditions created a double penalty for workers who not only failed to receive wartime pay, but also could not ultimately prove length of service in the pension era. In 1906 the WRC's Pension and Relief Committee introduced an amendment that would have placed nursing volunteers on the rolls, in addition to any nurse who could prove that she had been paid. Though bureau rulings at the turn of the century took an ever greater number of civilians and war workers into consideration, pension officials did not look favorably upon the amendment because the WRC could not provide a reliable estimate of those who had gone without pay. Unwilling to absorb an unknown quantity of potential new applicants, the Pension Bureau rejected the proposal.[41]

Regimental workers may have endured the toughest conditions of any female workers, but they were often overlooked at pension time because their names were not listed on hospital registers. The case of Elizabeth Nichols illustrates the ease with which some applicants fell through the institutional cracks. Nichols served two years with the 111th New York Infantry at Centreville, Virginia, and Chicago's Camp Douglass. Her 1892 petition assured the bureau that "I would not ask for a pension if I did not need it[.] I onely received 19 dollars for serveces from govrment[.] I volunteered to take care of the sick soldires not looking for any pay but I had to sign the pay scale and signed it onely on[c]e while I was out in the field it was through some mistake." Indeed, the War Department documented Nichols's pay as matron for the period from December 31, 1862, to February 16, 1863, but not the six months required to establish a claim under the 1892 act.[42] Over the next six years, Nichols locked horns with pension officials in an attempt to prove length of service ("again & again word comes back that nothing has ever been received by the government from me. Until I have concluded they do not mean to admit I was ever in the government employ"). Neither testimony from a soldier she had nursed nor help with her written English proved persuasive, however, and her claim was denied.[43] Ultimately her decision to forgo pay at the time of her service had been costly.

Pension officials spent over a decade trying to sort out the details of Sarah Chadwick Clapp's unusual claim, which raised the question of how to pay a regimental worker who had entered the service as a doctor, not a nurse. Having spent nine months as assistant surgeon and surgeon to the 7th Illinois Cavalry, Clapp first petitioned the bureau in February 1892, six months before the Pension Act went into effect. Because women had not been acknowledged as medical practitioners at the war front, Clapp expected that officials would dismiss evidence of her surgical work. Hoping to head off their doubts, she got surviving members of the 7th to "show conclusively" that "she served successfully in the capacity indicated . . . but that owing to the refusal of the State medical examining board to examine for this service one of her sex, she could not be commissioned or paid. . . . Testimony that the services were faithfully and intelligently rendered under trying circumstances and resulting in the saving of valuable lives is ample and apparently of a thoroughly reliable character."[44] In a unique determination, the bureau agreed in 1895 to pay her a pension commensurate with the "allowances of a surgeon of volunteer cavalry," conceding her unofficial medical status. But because of the problematic classification of her war work and resulting bureaucratic confusion, Clapp had to wait until 1906, when she was eighty-two, for the first payment of $8.50. Aware that other pensioners were receiving larger stipends, she soon appealed for an increase from her home in Lee Centre, Illinois. Having no standard procedure for former regimental surgeons, the bureau replied that Clapp would have to refile as an army nurse to secure the $12 amount.[45]

Lavinia Payne's case also befuddled pension officials. With her own funds and with the blessing of Secretary of War Stanton, Payne had established an independent homeopathic hospital near her Virginia home in 1862, but Surgeon General Hammond, frequently at odds with Stanton, shut down the operation before its first patient arrived. "If homeopathy is introduced into the military hospital," he wrote, "it will cause incessant and unnecessary confusion and trouble of every sort. . . . If the door is opened to homeopathy, the same facilities should be extended to the admission of Thompsonianism, eclecticism, hydropathy, and every other 'ism' and 'pathy' that has a name or an advocate." Undaunted, Payne secured work at the Patent Office Hospital, scarcely anticipating the bureaucratic snare that awaited her thirty years down the road. While on duty in Washington, Payne had nursed soldiers of the 19th Indiana Infantry—a fact she included in her 1894 pension application that led case workers erroneously to conclude that the Patent Office had been a regimental hospital and its staff therefore not pensionable. Even though it had been among the most prominent hospitals established in the capital to accommodate soldiers while other area hospitals were under construction, bureau officials stonewalled. Why the form of hospital should have made any difference is a mystery, especially when it was clear that Payne was not a regimental worker. Finally, after several months of bureaucratic hairsplitting, Payne won on appeal when authorities, aided by the testimony of a former assistant surgeon, conceded that the Patent Office had indeed been a general hospital.[46]

The cases of Payne, Clapp, and others demonstrate the ambiguous military status of independent workers who deviated from the standard of general hospital service. But they also suggest the Pension Bureau's willingness to adjudicate anomalous claims with outcomes that pension applicants found satisfactory. The bureau's flexibility in granting pensions to unusual applicants was borne out in the question over "competent authority." After the passage of the 1892 act, many former cooks and laundresses petitioned the bureau in the belief that their work had been no different from nurses'. But unless they could prove by competent authority—by which the bureau meant the testimony of surgeons, ward masters, hospital stewards, or Dorothea Dix —that they had done nurses' work, their pension requests were denied. In response to unhappy applicants denied pensions on the basis of ineligible job classifications, the bureau established an amendment in 1893 by which former workers could prove with other testimony that they had "superintended and prepared the diet of the sick and wounded in hospitals under the direction of those in charge" and were "not merely cooks, or other persons performing the usual and ordinary duties of kitchen employés."[47] The expansion of witnesses also signified the bureau's recognition that thirty years after the war pension applicants could not always locate or even remember the medical officials under whom they had served. The amended definition of competent authority allowed applicants to submit the testimony of soldiers they had nursed or of female coworkers, two groups with whom they were more likely to be in contact in the postwar years.[48] To maintain some form of control, the Pension Bureau still reserved the right to determine the credibility of the applicant's witnesses. Holding this power would prove to be essential in the bureau's handling of cases brought by former slaves.

The competent authority amendment became the saving grace for Ruth Danforth, an unpaid USCC worker from Chicago, who drafted a soldier she had nursed in Louisville to testify on her behalf. Because she had volunteered, Danforth's name did not appear on hospital payrolls. Even worse, her USCC paperwork had been destroyed in the Great Chicago Fire of 1871.[49] Danforth's only hope was to secure other testimony, so she turned to Annie Turner Wittenmyer, prominent in the Christian Commission.[50] Despite Wittenmyer's extensive record of service, bureau claims agents nearly balked because "a report from the Surgeon General's Office states that there is no record in that office of any authority given to Mrs. Annie Wittenmyer to employ nurses. In the absence of any record showing that the person who employed the claimant had authority to do so, she cannot be recognized by this Department as having had authority to employ her."[51] Ultimately the bureau accepted Wittenmyer's testimony on Danforth's behalf, conceding that the absence of military directives empowering her to hire employees could contradict neither the fact that she had hired them nor that they had served.

By the late 1890s Wittenmyer herself ran short of funds and legislative energy. Although she was proud to have helped raise $87,000 for army nurse pensioners, she was tired. In June 1897, while the sixty-nine-year-old ex-president of the Woman's Christian Temperance Union was in Washington lobbying for a more liberal interpretation of the pension laws, she injured her knee when a "rickety chair" in which she had been sitting collapsed. Two months later Wittenmyer's friends threw her a seventieth birthday gala during which they presented her $3,000. Relieved that she was "now free from financial embarrassment," Wittenmyer soon changed her tune: having devoted herself to hundreds of other applicants since 1892, she decided that it was "about time" to mount her own case.[52] Though once comfortably situated, like others who had fought for pension legislation, her high-profile reform work had not paid her bills. In another two months, a bill recommending that Wittenmyer be pensioned at $25 per month—more than the

Annie Turner Wittenmyer was best known during the war for establishing a system of diet kitchens sponsored by the U.S. Christian Commission. Her post-war work as head of the Woman's Christian Temperance Union and as an advo-cate for relief workers in pursuit of pensions demonstrated the political acumen she had gained in military hospitals. (Courtesy of U.S. Army Military History Institute, Carlisle Barracks, Pa.)

now-standard $12 allotted by the Pension Act—was introduced in the House. Five months later, checks began to arrive.[53]

Rebecca Usher, of Maine, not nearly as well connected as Wittenmyer, was less fortunate. Having secured depositions from five female coworkers, she later learned that their testimony was invalid. The Pension Bureau explained that since the surgeons for whom she had worked were all dead, she must next gather supporting documents from the soldiers she had nursed.[54] Although Usher was finally approved for a pension five years later on the basis of her original evidence, her correspondence with the bureau illuminated a pecking order of acceptable witnesses, with surgeons at the top followed by soldiers and finally female workers. The racial identity of witnesses further complicated the pecking order—apparent when black women used witness depositions to file claims, as we shall see shortly.

Though the bureau had accepted testimony from coworkers and soldiers since 1893, pension applicants' ignorance of the change disadvantaged them in later years. In a particularly painful instance because of her helplessness, Jane Hoge Patton was denied a pension in 1913 because she could not prove by competent authority cumulative service of six months.[55] Eighty-seven at the time, Patton could not remember in which Nashville hospitals she had volunteered. Proud of the fact that she had "never received one cent" for her services, her hospital record could not be exhumed. Any papers she might have produced as evidence had been destroyed in a house fire. Because she knew nothing about the 1893 addendum, she did not supply names of the surgeons or officers with whom she had served, and her request was denied.[56] Ex-slave Nancy Dodson Carter knew enough to seek witnesses when she applied for a pension in 1914, but finding them a half century after the war presented problems. Carter served in a Union hospital for black soldiers and civilian workers in Milliken's Bend, Louisiana, during 1862 and 1863, but could find no one from the hospital to corroborate her claim. She remembered the name of the surgeon in charge but was informed that Surgeon Smith had died in the 1890s. Without witnesses or any reference to her in the hospital register, she could not establish a case.[57] Still active on behalf of surviving army nurses in the early twentieth century, the Woman's Relief Corps set aside monies to help women who had been turned down but were in need of public assistance.[58] The WRC also supplied applicants with up-to-date information about pension laws so that predicaments like Patton's could be averted.

The cases of Catherine Oliphant and Margaret O'Donnell, white working-class women whose claims were ultimately funded by the bureau, show the extent to which job classification and the search for competent authority initially hindered but later helped pension hopefuls. O'Donnell, a laundress with the 22nd New York Artillery, found the road more treacherous in 1892, when the pension act was new, than Oliphant would in 1904. Less than a month after its passage, O'Donnell filed a claim based on having nursed soldiers with smallpox at Camp Bayard, Virginia, in 1863: "I been the onley woman with the Battry[.] I was called on to Perform the dutis of Nurse in most capasity and done it cheerfully . . . I done all that any one woman could Do in the way of Nurseing."[59] An affidavit produced by Private George Avery corroborated that O'Donnell had attended the sick "night and day," and a testimonial letter presented to her by six officers in October 1865 served as additional evidence.[60] Five months later pension examiners rejected her application because "it appear[ed] she acted as laundress."[61] Determined to persuade officials that despite her title, she had performed nursing work, O'Donnell appealed. Commissioner William Lochren, still inundated in the backlog of cases surrounding the Dependent Pension Act, took more than a year to respond. In May 1894 he deemed that "the fact that [O'Donnell] was carried on the rolls or drew rations and transportation as laundress, will not defeat her right to pension as an army nurse . . . if the evidence discloses she performed the actual services of a nurse in attendance upon the sick or wounded . . . and is now unable to earn a support."[62] The bureau thus acknowledged that some laundresses might have performed the full gamut of nursing services outside of hospitals and that they should not be disqualified simply because of the job label they had received on entering the service.

The precedent established by O'Donnell's case led to the bureau's consideration of petitions it formerly would have dismissed. This was true for German-born laundress Catherine Oliphant, who in 1863 had joined with her husband Company K of the 3rd Maryland Cavalry. On the move during two years in the Red River and Mobile campaigns, her name never appeared on a hospital register. Because the Surgeon General's Office could not verify her service dates, it fell to Oliphant to prove that she had performed as a nurse. Using a testimonial letter signed by the regiment's officers in 1865, as Margaret O'Donnell had done, Oliphant was granted a pension six months after she applied. The document endorsed her length of service and stated that she had "endured hardship and privation with the stoutest soldier and [was] ever ready to be useful to all who needed the gentle care of a woman."[63] Major Junius Turner wrote that "while she was enrolled as a laundress, she served, in fact, as an army nurse" and "rendered . . . arduous and unstinted attendance upon the sick and wounded."[64] By 1904, ten years after Lochren's precedent-setting clarification, the settlement of pension requests by regimental women who could produce officer testimony in support of their nursing claims was almost assured.

Earlier rulings by the Pension Bureau—the expansion of competent authority and the broader application of the definition of nurse—indicated its willingness to do justice to women of diverse social backgrounds. But when faced with claims from African Americans who argued that they too had worked as nurses, the bureau reverted to narrower standards. Because it routinely denied pensions to blacks with the title of cook and laundress, its more positive judgments on behalf of similar white petitioners raised the specter of racism. Bureau practice rested on the tentative equation of literacy with credibility, so that speakers of nonstandard dialects, who might also lack literacy skills, appeared less credible. Black applicants strained to overcome bureaucratic prejudice with varying degrees of success, but they encountered many obstacles; even their witnesses were treated less seriously if they were speakers of nonstandard dialects. Thirty, forty, even fifty years after the war, the discriminatory practices that had led the Surgeon General's Office to define job classifications on the basis of race had a profound impact on who would and would not be awarded pensions.

It is difficult to know how many of the 2,448 women who applied under the 1892 act were black because of incomplete record keeping.[65] The Pension Bureau never tabulated how many applications it funded, which has made systemic racism more difficult to trace.[66] In spite of statistical uncertainty, it is likely that a lower percentage of African American women, relative to their numbers in the total group of workers, applied for pensions after the war. There are many reasons why this might be so, including the cost of hiring pension attorneys, limited access to institutions, illiteracy, and racial prejudice in wartime hospitals.[67] White notions of black credibility compromised the deposition process, so that former slaves, many of whom were illiterate, were poised to fail in their pension negotiations. Although many learned to read and write in freedmen's schools during and after the war, literacy was a luxury that took a back seat to the more immediate need to subsist.[68] The inability of these workers to communicate with the bureau except through third-party correspondence was another disadvantage; women who could argue their own cases reduced the possibility of miscommunication. We can only guess at the number who never learned that pension leg-

African American contraband workers in a contraband hospital in Nashville. The wartime job assignment of laundress disadvantaged black women in the pensioning process. (Courtesy of National Archives)

islation had been enacted, a circumstance that applied to illiterate whites as well.

The deposition process had the potential to compromise African American voices by altering meaning and the rhetorical intention of spoken language. Recent work has shown the extent to which white interviewers and editors revised slave narratives taken on behalf of the Federal Writer's Project in the 1930s to conform with their own sense of slavery's paternalism. To make the narratives more authentic and readable to federal officials, state employees sought a scripted text that expunged personal trauma and mollified the violence of slavery.[69] Similar mediation occurred when white notaries and pension officers deposed black subjects. Just as telling as linguistic hazards were bureaucratic doubts about black credibility. If the issue of credibility posed challenges for white applicants, then it presented even greater challenges for black applicants, whose presentation of witnesses to corroborate claims was routinely undermined by racist perceptions of what constituted credibility. Applicants could not easily solicit the testimony of former surgeons and military officials because black women and the white men in charge of hospitals had had little contact with one another. Officials who had had the opportunity to observe black women at work tended to regard them as a faceless group rather than as individuals.[70] As the case of Malinda McFarland Jackson indicates, surgeons called upon to testify had poor recall of the names of their black employees, which contributed to making them less credible in the eyes of pension bureaucrats. William H. Mullins, chief surgeon at Knoxville General Hospital No. 2 where Jackson served, stated that "some negro women were employed for the laundry—but what were their names—the terms or length of their service I am unable to recall."[71] The races may have mingled more freely in Union military hospitals than in society at large, but it was unlikely that overtaxed surgeons would have paid much attention to black women in whose work they had little interest.

White female supervisors were not much help, either. Even though Iowa's Annie Turner Wittenmyer had testified on behalf of 618 female pension applicants by 1897, none was African American.[72] Neither white nurse Emily Parsons, who trained black women to nurse at Benton Barracks, nor Amy Morris Bradley, who took charge of relief services at the convalescent camp outside Washington, D.C., from 1862 to 1863—positions that required directing civilian-contracted black workers—was ever called upon to testify in a black applicant's claim.[73] Ironically, supervisors were able to use their management of black workers in building their own pension cases. Chloe Annette Buckel brought testimony "that the colored women who swarmed about the hospital" were put in her charge. As a white nurse responsible for the female staff at the pavilion hospital in Jeffersonville, Indiana, Buckel sought to prove her superiority by deploying insect imagery, which rendered her black employees less human and less autonomous.[74] One need only consider that women's comparatively low status relative to other workers in military hospitals made for uneasy racial relations. During the war, few white nurses were willing to acknowledge that black laundresses bore similar responsibilities when the white nurses themselves were fighting for status and recognition.[75] After the war, intent on procuring pensions, white nurses had even less incentive to support black workers' claims lest pension judges deny their own claims on the basis of unholy alliances with alleged racial inferiors.

White manipulation of legal language hurt black petitioners when it might have helped them. When ex-slave Rachel Anderson, formerly of Asylum General in Knoxville, applied for a pension in 1896, white matron Margaret Haynes, who had known Anderson since childhood and whose aunt had owned Anderson, testified that even though Anderson "was subject to orders to assist in handling the sick," she had been hired and paid as a cook.[76] Rather than recognizing that "handling the sick" might have been called nursing in other hospitals, Haynes emphasized Anderson's job classification. It is not surprising that she was unwilling to testify that a former slave held a rank similar to her own. Because Haynes was white and had been Anderson's supervisor during the war, the bureau received her testimony as more credible than that of the applicant herself, and Anderson was not pensioned.

Few black applicants experienced the ease of Matilda Cleaver John's passage through the pension bureaucracy. John was a literate free black who served in Washington area hospitals for a total of eight months between 1863 and 1865. Among her assignments, she had cared for ill nurses at Union Hotel Hospital in the winter of 1863, including Louisa May Alcott and hospital matron Hannah Ropes.[77] In a handwritten note to the Pension Bureau, John also claimed that Dorothea Dix had sent her to hospitals at Fortress Monroe, City Point, and Alexandria—an exception to the nursing superintendent's practice of appointing only white women.[78] John was listed as a nurse on the muster rolls of all three institutions, which meant that her length of service and job classification both could be verified, and she began drawing twelve dollars per month in 1893.[79] John's case pointed to an order in the pool of black applicants based coaxially on region and education: Literate Northern workers could more easily persuade pension examiners that they had done the work of nurses than Southern-born workers like Rachel Anderson. Appointment to higher-status jobs during the war, also a consequence of their verbal mastery, thus helped the highly literate twice. By contrast, the slave-born and illiterate bore lower-status wartime titles and loss of credibility with pension examiners a generation later.

Black applicants who needed witnesses to corroborate their claim of nursing had greater difficulty establishing cases than those who did not. Sarah Thompson Gammon served in Knoxville hospitals in 1863 and 1864 as "laundress and kitchen servant" but could not satisfy the Pension Bureau, despite ample testimony from witnesses, that she had also nursed. Special Examiner Webster Davis, appointed to the case when Gammon appealed an unfavorable decision in 1897, noted that she had "filed affidavits from several colored persons who say that she was employed as nurse."[80] Davis's characterization of Gammon's coworkers in Knoxville as "several colored persons" was misleading in that their status as workers of equal rank was not acknowledged. One coworker's report that Gammon "done a general line of duty. . . . in clearing up" persuaded Davis to disqualify the appeal on the

Matilda Cleaver John, one of the few African American women pensioned after 1892, nursed Hannah Ropes and Louisa May Alcott when they became ill with typhoid at Union Hotel Hospital in Washington's Georgetown. In her *Hospital Sketches* of 1863, Alcott dubbed the facility "Hurly-Burly House" because of the chaotic working conditions. (Courtesy of National Archives)

basis of her having performed char work. Other witnesses alluded to her nursing work, but its juxtaposition with chamber services was enough to pollute her claim. The special examiner concluded that "the records of the hospital furnish the best evidence as to the capacity in which she was employed."[81] In other words, if the hospital classified Gammon as a laundress, she could not by definition have nursed, and nothing in the testimony of racially stigmatized speakers could alter that perception.

**Maria Bear Toliver** was the only ex-slave pensioner I found whose testimony was corroborated by black coworkers and accepted as credible by the Pension Bureau. Like Gammon, it fell to Toliver to prove that she had performed nursing work despite her classification as laundress. After having escaped from her master's King William County (Virginia) plantation in 1862, the twenty-four-year-old made her way to Washington and found work nursing contrabands at Camp Barker. While caring for black soldiers and their families, she later testified, "I got my orders from the doctors, I would wait on the patients, give them medicine and had full control of [them]."[82] Toliver subsequently found work at the local smallpox hospital, where she took care of both blacks and whites. Louisa Frazer, an ex-slave employed there as cook, remembered seeing Toliver "come to the dispensary and get medicine for [her patients] and also to the soup house," suggesting that like many other hospital workers black and white, she delivered food and medicine to her charges.[83] Another ex-slave, Betsey Lawson, who had nursed Toliver at Camp Barker when she contracted varioloid, before moving on to the smallpox hospital, corroborated Toliver's testimony. Two other witnesses, black soldiers whom Toliver had nursed at Camp Barker, also testified on her behalf.[84]

In what appears to be an instance of a racial double standard, Toliver's pension was funded because no bureau official could dispute that she had nursed other blacks. Her four black witnesses could not be discredited because they spoke specifically enough about the services Toliver performed and because bureau officials knew that black hospitals seldom were staffed by white workers. As long as blacks did not claim to nurse white patients in hospitals established for white patients, they stood a better chance of being awarded pensions.

The cases of Minerva Trigg Dillard Washington and Amanda Jones illustrate more clearly how racial stigma created doubt among pension examiners. In 1863 ex-slave Minerva Trigg had married Henry Dillard at Asylum General Hospital in Knoxville, where both were employed—she as the officers' dining room attendant and he as a special diet cook. From the beginning of her service hospital registers listed Minerva as "Dillard," not "Trigg," which gave rise to suspicion that she was concealing the date of her marriage or not legally married at all. The Pension Bureau required widows and other female dependents to produce marriage certificates and carried over this practice into its hearing of army nurse pension cases, because a woman who had remarried after the war could not obtain a pension if her husband was supporting her.[85] Even if she was petitioning as an army nurse, a widowed woman would also need to show her husband's death certificate to prove that she had no other means of support. Former slaves who married during and just after the war had difficulty producing certificates. The uncertainty of shelter for those making the transition from slavery to freedom made official documents hard to preserve. Amanda Jones noted that her own marriage certificate was destroyed when it got soaked in her husband's pocket; a second certificate, carried in the same fashion, met the same fate.[86]

Dillard (now Washington by a later marriage) was asked to sign an oath of allegiance to the United States in 1905, the year that she first filed a claim. It was common practice during Reconstruction for government to require the oath of Southerners offered civil service jobs, but that a former Union hospital worker who was also an ex-slave was required to take the oath was highly unusual. Her integrity was again called into question when pension officials challenged the veracity of her nursing claim: how, the bureau wondered, could a woman assigned to wait on tables also have ministered to the sick and wounded? Because some applicants were tempted to exaggerate their duties or length of service to win pensions, the bureau was always on the lookout for fraud. Washington explained that she regularly carried the special diet and medicine to patients in the wards as Maria Bear Toliver had, but did not actually administer them.[87] Although the bureau did not consider her transport of food a nursing activity, it had done so in the cases of white women like Ruth Danforth and the USCC workers appointed by Annie Turner Wittenmyer to special diet kitchens. Minerva Washington's complicated marital history did little to bolster her credibility among white officials when certification of marriage was central to successful applications from widows and wives. Through Sarah Gammon, the bureau sent the message that even if they carried out the same tasks as white women, there was little black women could do to make pension officials recognize their work as equivalent.

Five witnesses, including Henry Dillard from whom she was divorced, corroborated Washington's testimony that, in addition to serving in the officers' mess, she had waited on the sick with special diets. Two of the five witnesses—Cynthia Franklin Shields and Annie Ragan Carmickles who appeared on the hospital register as nurses—claimed that Washington had had responsibilities similar to their own.[88] Special Examiner N. H. Nicholson reported of all deponents that they were "very ignorant but apparently try to tell the truth."[89] This concession was still too tentative, however, to convince the bureau that Washington ought to receive a pension, and she was denied on grounds that she "did not render service as a nurse."[90] After calling into question her loyalty as a citizen, insinuating that her marital vows had not been authentic (a problem that plagued many ex-slaves), and assailing the credibility of her witnesses, the bureau fell back on its narrow definition of what constituted a nurse and rejected Washington's claim.

The bureau also challenged the honesty of ex-slave Amanda Jones because of inconsistencies in her testimony. Jones, who had worked for two years in Union hospitals at Port Hudson and Baton Rouge, Louisiana, first applied for a pension in October 1892. Within several months, the bureau rejected her application on the grounds that the hospital had classified her as a laundress—an action consistent with the denial of other laundresses before the case of Margaret O'Donnell established a precedent in 1894 for pensioning women with job titles other than nurse. Two letters of appeal by Henry W. Brown, late surgeon of the 76th U.S. Colored Troops, for whom Jones worked in Port Hudson, were not enough to reopen the case. In his letters, Brown referred to Jones as having performed nursing duties in addition to cooking and doing laundry, but he could not "fix the dates and places" of her service.[91] Even though Jones had performed these functions in a hospital for black soldiers, her own testimony, supported by that of the white surgeon who employed her, did not satisfy the bureau because the dates and duration of service could not be confirmed.

The case was reopened ten years later when Jones's husband Henry died. Henry's veteran's pension would have reverted to a widow's pension, but Amanda determined to reopen the case when she realized that she would draw only $8 per month on a widow's pension compared to $12 on a nurse's pension. In addition to refusing to reopen the nurse's claim (Jones's 1892 testimony that she had been hired as a laundress disqualified her), the bureau now questioned her right to a widow's pension based on inconclusive evidence that she had ever legally married Henry Jones. Although the Union army offered ex-slaves an early opportunity to make their marriages legal, many were not as fastidious about the law as pension authorities would have liked, which made women such as Jones appear ignorant or disdainful.[92] As Special Examiner E. D. Narrington put it, "[Jones] exhibited so much lack of the necessity of telling things as they really were as to raise a question as to the validity of any statement she might make, though her neighbors regard her as one of those reliable old aunties."[93] Documents in the possession of the chaplain who had married Henry and Amanda in 1864 reported Amanda's surname as "Parker," even though she went by the name of her former master, James Pritchard—a detail suggesting that even white chaplains may not have been as fastidious as black pension applicants might have liked.[94] Over the next two years the bureau probed Jones's life in slavery to determine the legality of her marriage to Henry Jones. No one ever questioned whether or not the chaplain had entered Amanda's surname incorrectly. P. J. McCall, the second special examiner assigned to the case, speculated that "it may be that the word[s] Pritchard and Parker were confounded at the time of the marriage. But the two names are so different that is not likely."[95]

The bureau put Jones—well into her seventies by 1902—through rigorous questioning, which verged on baiting. When the examiner asked her under what name she had married Henry Jones, he added, "now be careful how you answer this question."[96] In the same deposition, Jones was asked for information about her parentage, her liaisons with other slaves before her marriage to Jones, and the children she gave birth to through those liaisons—information largely irrelevant to establishing the legality of her marriage to Jones. Special Examiner Narrington even conceded that "the fact that . . . [Jones] had a consort in slavery would cut no figure in the case." However, when he determined that "it [was] unquestionably wise to get all the information that we can in regard to such matters," it was clear that Jones's privacy would not be spared.[97]

Jones's responses to the questions revealed her mortification. She had to make a matter of public record that she had never known her father, quite possibly her first owner, George Brasier of Kentucky, who sold her to Pritchard of Louisiana while she was still a child; that she had been forced to live with a slave on the Pritchard plantation whom she did not care for and by whom she had been forced to bear a son; and that before meeting Henry Jones at the hospital in Port Hudson, she had had another child by a man whose last name she never knew. Jones made it clear that she dreaded being coerced to divulge information that she had chosen not even to share with her husband and had never shared with the father of her second child, who died in infancy. She testified that "Henry Jones never knew anything about this child, nor anybody but myself and the Lord."[98] Special Examiner McCall's report to the bureau on this question revealed, "I must confess that I am not posted on these slave marriages," but he finally conceded that the Joneses' marriage ought to be considered valid and that Amanda could receive a widow's pension.[99] Jones might well have considered herself lucky: though the nursing claim had been dismissed, a bureau official's admission of ignorance about slave marriages and the petitioner's willingness to make private confidence a matter of public record together resulted in a widow's pension for Jones.

During the two years it took to process the case, the Pension Bureau displayed a sense of satisfaction that its procedures had been scrupulous. Special Examiner Narrington was certain that his conduct in questioning Jones had been beyond reproach. As he explained to the pension commissioner in 1903, "I brought the old woman up with a round turn and tried to impress upon her the necessity of telling things straight and giving me all the information. . . . If," he concluded, "from the data furnished, the case fails to be established, certainly the bureau will not be to blame."[100] Though such administrative perspicacity is not unique in the annals of bureaucratic correspondence, the special examiner's disdain for the applicant's privacy was the singular result of his own ignorance of African American marital customs.

**The first legislation** to grant pensions to women on the basis of their own wartime service was enacted to acknowledge their relief efforts on behalf of Union soldiers during the Civil War. Granting women pensions for their own work rather than through their relationship to male pensioners had important implications for social welfare policy in the United States at the end of the nineteenth century. Government would reward women's work by pensioning women directly and thus sanction not only the work performed but also a model of female economic independence. Against the backdrop of a generous expansion of veterans' benefits, the Pension Bureau authorized the work of nurses, but not of women who had entered the service under other job classifications, despite their performance of work equivalent to nursing. As thousands of nonelite women had been assigned to lower-status work, so pension officials determined eligibility on the basis of what were often titular distinctions. Reproducing a system based on social inequities disadvantaged those who, due to advanced age or illiteracy, could not convince examiners that their cook, matron, or laundress jobs had consisted of taking care of sick soldiers on the march or of delivering food and medicine to them in hospitals.

Two years after Congress legislated the Army Nurses Pension Act, the bureau acknowledged that some who had entered the service as cooks, matrons, and laundresses might have done nursing work and were therefore eligible for pensions if they could prove by the "competent authority" of hospital officials, soldiers, or coworkers that they had been detailed as nurses. Despite the liberal intent of the policy, many former workers could not establish claims because of incomplete hospital and payroll records. Ironically, the middle-class women who had taken pride in working for free during the war were at pains to produce evidence of six months' service when their names did not appear on any payroll. The black women who managed to escape slavery and find work in Union hospitals found the pension process inaccessible and inhospitable to their linguistic and cultural differences, although some still managed to persuade the bureau to pension them. Their experience illustrates how policies of racial exclusion were challenged and at the same time, paradoxically, institutionalized. Ultimately workers' battles with the pension bureaucracy illustrate the contested definitions of their war work a generation later. Whether they were motivated by a sense of entitlement or desperate need, women at the front were determined not to be forgotten.

## CHAPTER SEVEN

# Memory and the Triumphal Narrative

I am as willing to do my part with the pen as I was with Body &
soul, to complete the history of the war.
—Mrs. Steven Barker to Frank Moore, March 21, 1866

They live in history, . . . but who shall rehearse the story of those
lives offered as a sacrifice on the altar of their country, when this
generation shall have passed away?
—Anna L. Boyden, 1884

It is the project of the Division to collect and have printed in book
form such narratives as illustrate the people of Confederate
years. . . . I would respectfully recommend that the names of
those who figure in the narratives . . . shall be given without
reserve.
—Mrs. Thomas Taylor, President, South Carolina Division
    of the United Daughters of the Confederacy, 1907

Under the guns our love grew up, under the sod it shall remain.
—Clara Barton, July 13, 1911

In 1866 Frank Moore asked Dr. Mary Edwards Walker if she would write a narrative of her wartime exploits for a volume on the achievement of "American" (he meant Northern) women during the late war. Never at a loss for words, Walker responded: "I had contemplated publishing a work on the same subject and have correct histories of a number of ladies who have served our Cause, besides a very *thrilling* one of my own which is 'stranger than fiction.'"[1] Walker's sense that her story was unusual resulted from the government's ambiguous acknowledgment of her wartime services. Her 1865 request for a surgical commission had perplexed army officials. Though some had noted her early medical service to the Union, others considered her a charlatan. Her case was referred to Judge Advocate General Joseph Holt, who determined that no legal precedent had established the status of a female military surgeon.[2] No one doubted Walker's service as a surgeon, but no one was willing officially to confirm that she had been one. In a mysterious gesture, legislators awarded Walker the Congressional Medal of Honor in November 1865 for "meritorious service"—whether to acknowledge her war work or to send her off quietly from the capital is uncertain.[3] The thirty-three-year-old returned to New York hoping to reestablish her medical practice but embarked instead on a European lecture tour. Preoccupied with traveling, Walker never wrote her book. Whether because he supposed she might or simply felt her story to be too outlandish, Moore did not include her in his 1866 *Women of the War: Their Heroism and Self-Sacrifice*.

In 1865, when Mary Walker considered telling her story, Northerners were faring better than Southerners. Northern property and fortunes were largely intact, industrial development proceeded at a healthy pace—particularly the publishing industry, which sat poised to transform recollection into profit —and military triumph fed a regional wellspring of confidence. By contrast, the Confederate infrastructure from Virginia to Louisiana was tattered, the economy was in need of a capital infusion, and the ethos of loss and defeat dampened hopes to rebuild. Materially advantaged, Northerners seized the opportunity to write the first histories of the war and set the political agenda for the reuniting states. Few Southerners produced accounts right after the war; many waited until their versions could be absorbed into the stream of sentimentality that fueled sectional reunion in the 1880s and 1890s. In reversing the silence to which early Northern accounts had consigned them, Southern writers took up memory like a cudgel, to insist on its unique place in the mind of a vanquished population and to undergird the values of the Lost Cause.[4]

Mnemosyne, the classical muse of memory, is depicted as a Southerner with Confederate artifacts in the frontispiece of Fannie Beers's 1888 nursing narrative, *Memories*.

In 1888, after contributing war sketches to the *Southern Bivouac* and *The South Illustrated*, Fannie Beers of Louisiana published her *Memories*, an account of Confederate hospital life with the Armies of Northern Virginia and the Tennessee. Five years earlier, surviving soldiers of the latter had given Beers an "entertainment" where they honored her wartime service by taking up a collection. In 1885 Beers had attended a Rebel reunion in Dallas, where she "walked hand in hand with memory, turning again and again to clasp her closely and to feel the throbbing of her sad heart upon my own."[5] Beers also personified memory in the frontispiece of *Memories*, which depicted Mnemosyne as an elite Southerner draping the Stars and Bars over a stone monument. At her feet were the armaments of war as well as a broken wagon wheel, a drum, and a corncob pipe. Abutting the prone nose of a piece of artillery was a satchel embossed with the letters "W.A." for women's auxiliary—a reminder that Confederate women had not only aided the war effort but also were now the chief repositories of its legacy.[6]

The representation of the goddess of memory as a Confederate woman is telling: Mnemosyne signaled to readers that remembering the war was both a Southern and a feminine duty. Situated on the national margins by virtue of region and gender, Southern women came to terms with the politics and poetics of memory; those who laid claim to it might influence the larger narrative of war. A defeated population could assuage the pain of loss by rehearsing its triumphs, and who were better suited to the task than women, who, as survivors, were memory's living emissaries? By aligning themselves with memory, Southern women resisted the Union characterization of them and their kin as "spiteful women" and "intemperate men."[7] They countered unflattering portraits with heroic ones rooted in the past and participated in what David Blight has termed a national act of forgetting in which a model of "reconciled conflict" vanquished the "resurgent, unresolved legacy" of war.[8]

Northern editors discredited Southern relief efforts in the first postwar commemoratives, labeling Rebel women as heartless and bloodthirsty. "Indeed it would be difficult to find in history," offered Linus Brockett and Mary Vaughan in *Woman's Work in the Civil War* (1866),

> even among the fierce brutal women of the French revolution, any record of conduct more absolutely fiendish than that of some of the women of the South during the war. They insisted on the murder of helpless prisoners; in some instances shot them in cold blood themselves, besought their lovers and husbands to bring them Yankee skulls, scalps and bones, for ornaments, betrayed innocent men to death, engaged in intrigues and schemes of all kinds to obtain information of the movements of Union troops, to convey it to the enemy, and in every manifestation of malice, petty spite and diabolical hatred against the flag under which they had been reared, and its defenders, they attained a bad preeminence over the evil spirits of their sex since the world began.[9]

Writers of early monographs were no more charitable. Elvira Powers's narrative of 1866 vilified "the ladies (?)" [*sic*] of Nashville who had nothing but "contempt" for Northerners. Even the mild-mannered Jane Hoge wrote in 1868 that former Confederates "should be severely condemned" for the destruction they had wrought.[10]

Such attacks served as a rallying point for Southerners, who were all the more determined to create their own versions of Civil War history. Although the first Confederate commemoratives did not appear until a second generation of Union volumes was under way, the Charleston News and Courier's *Our Women in the War: The Lives They Lived, the Deaths They Died* (1885) launched a series of works aimed at retrieving a past that Northern writers, like so many carpetbaggers, had attempted to bury.[11] Far from participating in the restoration of the Union engineered by Northerners, contributors to *Our Women in the War* declared their sectional independence, thrashing Yankees and ex-slaves alike in domestic accounts of life in Dixie. Rose W. Fry of

Bowling Green, Kentucky, took pains to differentiate the experiences of Northern women from those of her more unfortunate countrywomen: "The contrast between Southern women and their Northern sisters was striking. The Northern woman was never called upon to endure. She lived far from the seat of war and carnage; the sword did not cross her threshold—the smoke of battle did not dim her sight—the foe did not trample her heritage, burn her barns, rob her orchards, devastate her firesides, pillage her altars, and drive her forth a homeless wanderer on the face of mother earth."[12] Challenging Brockett and Vaughan's vitriolic attack of twenty years earlier, Fry's account, and others like it, established a Southern sensibility resistant to the blanket characterizations of Union pundits. Only in the twentieth century did editors make a concerted effort to retrieve the story of Confederate women's hospital work, with John Underwood's *The Women of the Confederacy* (1906), Francis Simkins and James Patton's collection also titled *The Women of the Confederacy* (1936), and Matthew Page Andrews's *Women of the South in War Times* (1920).

A change in the character of Northern commemoratives was also apparent by the 1890s. Whereas early accounts bluntly vilified Southerners, later books whipped them chiefly through exclusion. In a nationalist sleight of hand that purported to represent "Our Army Nurses," Mary Gardner Holland's 1895 tome excluded all but Northern white women. African Americans, like Susie King Taylor, had to fend for themselves. Despite Northerners' belief that they spoke for the nation, works commemorating women's war achievements, even at the turn of the century, reproduced the sectional divide and obliterated the memory of people of color.[13]

While commemorative editors engaged in an exclusive celebration of white women, former relief workers joined in a triumphal narrative whose self-congratulatory tone shrouded the deep disappointment and domestic need that were the inevitable results of war. The restoration of the Union had left the North in a more favorable economic position, but widowed and single relief workers did not return to lives of comfort and wealth. In need of income, they approached publishers with tales of middle-class rectitude and persistence. Tapping a cultural vein still rich in patriotic fervor, they praised the heroism of common soldiers and their own supporting role in holding at bay the body's natural enemies. While Southerners engaged in revising the script of Confederate loss with stories of endurance and religious ecstasy, Northern custodians of what Robert Penn Warren would later call "the treasury of virtue"—the righteous sense that they had won a moral victory—emphasized their charity, diligence, and moral superiority. In heroic narratives, workers presented themselves as tireless crusaders inspired by soldiers' selflessness. Many were the patients they returned from the brink of death. Satisfied that they had done as much to save souls as bodies, they remembered victories more readily than defeats and created triumphant personae to divert attention from the economic exigency that their writing represented.

Relief workers in both sections used their recollections to remind the nation that they too had taken part in the war—a fact that might have escaped popular notice in an era where the grand army encampment enshrined manhood like the military version of a great awakening. In establishing their own war record, they contributed to a foundational narrative on which claims to citizenship and political reward might be built. Though their professed goal was to demonstrate their partnership with men in negotiating the outcome of a civil war, their written record betrayed more volatility and uncertainty. Their willingness to criticize individual surgeons and, more important, the models of organized benevolence that structured their work contradicted the partnership message. In sum, they utilized a patriotic discourse already audible in soldiers' narratives to gain acceptance in the marketplace but then rerouted that discourse through representations of conflict.

Studies by David Blight, Carol Reardon, and Kirk Savage have characterized war memorialization as a regressive process susceptible to erasure and invention.[14] Women at the front were no more immune to historical elisions than men: they too were blind to the racial and class privilege that put their memories of war at the center of the triumphal narrative. Since women's place in military memory was less secure than men's (whose participation in combat gave them automatic entry), they had to work harder to achieve recognition—an impetus confirmed by their coalition to pass the nursing pension act in the 1890s. With an arguably more conservative agenda than men —to gain a national foothold in the chronicle of war—their critique struck a discordant note but did so gently as they swaddled recrimination in a rhetoric of military praise. Had they enjoyed a more central place in the making of war memory, they might have been more frank and direct.

**Memorialization of** hospital work in the postwar era had two distinct but related engines: monument building and personal narrative. Both forms of memory became nationalistic shrines to human endeavor. Recent scholarship reminds us that monuments bear the signature of their time, reflecting a calculus between shifting public ideals and memory.[15] Early war statuary graphically depicted loss of life, whereas later memorials represented death more abstractly and promoted national restoration.[16] Such changes illustrate how Northerners and Southerners wanted to remember the war at intervals in their trajectory away from it. As chronicles of memory that mediated between present and past, narratives also did this work.

Civil War monuments and narratives made martial values their foundation. They honored the decency of the rank and file in the face of harsh conditions. Grouped with traditionally male qualities like courage and stoicism was the feminine virtue of self-sacrifice. Hospital workers were quick to recognize self-sacrificial gestures—at the ideological heart of midcentury domesticity—among the men they nursed.[17] They characterized soldiers as patient sufferers whose bodies were effeminized through affective displays of sympathy. Such narratives contributed to the larger constellation of war stories a renegotiation of the meaning of self-sacrifice through the domestication of a world perceived as exclusively male. In bringing the stuff of domesticity to the seat of war, female chroniclers authorized a model of conduct in which men could give vent to qualities associated with women without compromising their manhood, and women could represent themselves as soldiers of care without surrendering their femininity.

Postwar monuments built to commemorate relief work provided physical symbols of this transformation. Women in the act of succoring soldiers are represented in statues from Galesburg, Illinois, to Rome, Georgia. In Galesburg, Mother Bickerdyke–in-stone towers maternally over a soldier whom she helps to a drink of water; in Rome, a Confederate Everywoman performs the same service.[18] Monuments commemorating Confederate workers at Little Rock, Baltimore, Jackson, and Columbia were built later than Union ones but play on similar themes of woman as maternal protector and partner in shouldering affliction. Dedicated in 1911 by the United Confederate Veterans, the statehouse monument in Columbia "Testif[ied] to the Sublime Devotion of the Women of South Carolina" whose "Tender Care Was Solace to the Stricken" and who were "Unwearied in Their Ministrations."[19] A bas-relief in Washington depicting maternal nuns of the battlefield touts the nonpartisan service for which Roman Catholic orders were known.[20] Though rendered as maternal, these images reflect the hybridity of relief workers as props to manhood but also experienced pillars of strength.

Public memorialization of the war was nowhere more apparent than in groups dedicated to veterans' welfare. In addition to monument building, these groups launched initiatives to win pension, housing, and medical relief for veterans. By contributing to a dialogue that inaugurated a new model of social welfare policy in the United States, the Woman's Relief Corps (WRC), the Ladies Memorial Association (LMA), the United Daughters of the Confederacy (UDC), and the Daughters of Union Veterans (DUV) played leading roles in the institutionalization of war memory. The work of such groups, whose intent was to secure benefits and preserve cemeteries and battlefields, bespoke their reverence for former soldiers as well as the sacralization of war deeds in the national memory. Northern groups like the National Association of Army Nurses (NAAN) dedicated themselves to female war workers. Southern groups focused initially on burial and other bereavement rituals, but with the growth of the UDC in the 1890s, they made the education of the rising generation of Southerners their central focus.[21] Men were often the founders and donors behind these organizations but deferred to the female membership to carry out plans, reflecting the shared belief that memorial work was women's work.[22]

Southern women who recognized the importance of pooling human resources in the face of diminished capital began organizing as early as 1866. Sophie Bibb established the LMA of Montgomery in April, which funded the tending of Richmond's Oakwood Cemetery, burial site of 800 hundred Alabama soldiers.[23] The 278 women of the Petersburg LMA raised money to secure the remains of hometown boys scattered around the Confederacy and annually restaged their city's siege as a living history lesson to local youth. Having restored a church as a Rebel shrine, the ladies insisted "that the women who worked and suffered through that terrible war deserve to be called heroes and veterans as much as the men who stood behind the guns" —a position articulated by the Union's NAAN as well.[24] Augusta's LMA, reincarnated from its Ladies' Hospital and Relief Association in 1868, was, like other memorial groups, invested in the "rehabilitation" and "reconstruction" of Southern manhood.[25] Their completion of a soldiers' monument in 1875 drew an unparalleled crowd of ten thousand—evidence of broad support behind initiatives that resurrected Confederate legacies of honor and military prowess.

Northern women also formed memorial societies derived from wartime associations. One of the earliest was organized in 1869 at Portland, Maine —a state that counted Amy Morris Bradley, Harriet Eaton, Isabella Fogg, and Rebecca Usher among its army of female relief workers.[26] Groups that aspired to a national following, like the Ladies of the Grand Army and the Loyal Ladies' League, became forerunners of the Woman's Relief Corps, established at the height of war sentimentalization in 1883. This ostensibly national emphasis, in reality a regional phenomenon, excluded Southern groups, which neither won Federal support nor went gently under the Federal umbrella after the war.

Later memorial organizations branched out beyond the welfare of veterans into projects concerning how the war would be remembered. Engaging in civic initiatives to build public libraries and archives, groups like the Sons and Daughters of Confederate Veterans carried the values of the Lost Cause into the modern era through elaborate reunions such as the one Fannie Beers attended in 1885 and the Dallas reunion of 1902, which amassed a crowd of 140,000. Confederate monument building continued at such a heady pace at the turn of the century that one Georgia marble company regularly visited UDC meetings to solicit business.[27] Instead of enacting the "ceremonial bereavement" of the 1860s and 1870s, later groups rallied around educational projects—a transformation symbolized by moving monument sites from graveyards to public spaces.[28] The UDC lobbied for the adoption and promoted the republication of classic Confederate texts, introduced war heroes into school curricula, paid for mass-produced portraits of Robert E. Lee and Jefferson Davis, and funded college scholarships for veterans' relatives.[29] By 1912 more than 800 chapters were active with a head count of 45,000, but the mostly white middle-class members, who had grown up in the midst of Jim Crow segregation, found themselves increasingly at odds over the memorial representation of slavery.[30]

At the turn of the century, WRC members paid tribute to Union veterans at GAR encampments where army nurses marched in parade. "We always gather," touted an advertisement for the 1899 meeting in Philadelphia, "to participate in their pleasures, as we did in the sixties to gather beside the cots of pain and anguish." Once there, former nurses passed out souvenir badges donated by Strawbridge and Clothier and other local merchants.[31] In its work to pension former hospital employees in the 1890s, the National Association of Army Nurses was reinvigorated by an increasingly political mandate. While WRC and DUV members attended reunions, the NAAN set its sights on female veterans. Holding business meetings at GAR encampments in 1899 and 1907, it planned strategy regarding bills to increase nurses' pensions from twelve to twenty-five dollars.[32] The NAAN's longevity resulted from work to keep publicly visible the plight of military nurses who, as leaders intoned, had helped the country in its hour of need.

The survival of such auxiliaries into the twenty-first century bears witness to memory's staying power. Since the 1960s the UDC has sponsored a yearly ceremony on Jefferson Davis's birthday in which Southerners may rededicate themselves to Confederate ideals—an opportunity, in Catherine Clinton's words, for Lost Causers to drink at the "well of fond remembrance."[33] In 1990 the UDC publicly criticized the representation of Southern interests in Ken Burns's Civil War documentary—a signal that its opinions still mattered.[34] Union auxiliaries have kept a lower profile; the Confederate mania of recent times has usurped the limelight.[35] Still, Union groups profit from contemporary interest in women and the military, and continue to do their memorial work quietly. The Daughters of Union Veterans, which claims four thousand members, were holding annual conventions throughout the 1990s; in 1996, the Julia Dent Grant Tent No. 16 of the DUV dedicated a monument at Jefferson Barracks National Cemetery in St. Louis "to honor the Union women who fought on the battlefields, nursed and comforted the sick and dying, and sacrificed their own lives to preserve our nation."[36] The ultimate coup of memorial organizations—both Southern and Northern—has been their creation of a narrative fusing women's interests with those of soldiers dead and living. In so doing, these groups have generated a paradigm of remembering that has sustained itself for over a century.

In keeping with the lavish memorialization of the war begun even before Lee met Grant at Appomattox, hospital workers constructed a triumphal narrative of their service that wartime diaries and letters refute. Women left approximately 347 accounts of their war relief work, 69 of which were monographs. The remaining sketches, ranging from one to thirty pages, were collected in commemorative volumes.[37] Of the 69 who wrote monographs, 43 (or 62 percent) sought publication. Fourteen other accounts were published by editors, sometimes without the subject's knowledge, and the remaining 12, including Clara Barton's diary, have never been published.[38] Of the 43 who sought publication, 32 were former citizens of the Union and 11 of the Confederacy—a ratio of three to one.[39] From 1861 to 1880, 16 Northerners and 5 Southerners published war narratives; from 1881 to 1900, 11 Northerners and 3 Southerners did so.[40] Several things, aside from the simple fact that a greater number of Northern women performed relief work, may account for the disparity. Because few elite Southern women experienced the large general hospital phenomenon with which Northerners were so familiar, they may have lacked the perspective and confidence that prompted others to publish. Alabama's Barbara Simmons, who nursed soldiers in her home, observed a narrow slice of hospital life and never attempted to publish her letters, whereas Phoebe Yates Pember, who traveled far to manage scores of soldiers and staff, had every opportunity to see Confederate hospital bureaucracy at work. Access to Southern publishers may also have figured. Because she was "not . . . permitted to pass the lines" to Mobile after the siege of Vicksburg, Mary Loughborough sought a New York publisher for her account. D. Appleton brought out *My Cave Life in Vicksburg* in 1864, urging Loughborough "to dispatch the papers as speedily as possible while public interest in the siege life [is] still vivid."[41] A war on Southern soil meant a virtual publishing blockade, and New York houses seized the day. Whether the smaller number of Southern accounts resulted from limited access to publishers, personal scruples, or the material toll of the war, we should not conclude that Southerners were reluctant to write. The huge Southern archive of unpublished reminiscences and diaries bears witness to their chronicle.

Most caregivers who wrote narratives offered them to editors of commemorative volumes without expecting or receiving pay. Frank Moore's correspondence with workers in 1865 and 1866 as he compiled *Women of the War* (1866) reveals much about women's sense of themselves as public actors in a period of social transition where propriety dictated restraint but also made way for greater self-assertion. Perhaps because they saw themselves as contributors to Moore's project and not as authors in their own right, Moore's subjects downplayed their service: "You flatter me too much," wrote Mrs. J. L. Colt of Milwaukee, "when you speak of any acts of mine being worthy of being made matter of History."[42] "I am no writer," quipped another, "only a worker," while others considered their experience "too trivial to put in print."[43] Unable to imagine why her service should be deemed memorable, Maria Hall —one of the few women in Surgeon Bernard Vanderkieft's Smoketown Hospital at Antietam—insisted: "My own *choice* in the matter is to receive no manner of public notice whatever—I *prefer* that my name should not appear in print—but on the other hand I know your book will be of interest to many readers & a valuable memorial of the noble work done by the women of the country."[44] Appeals to patriotism were apparently enough to ransom the impropriety of public notice; despite her modesty, Hall allowed a sketch

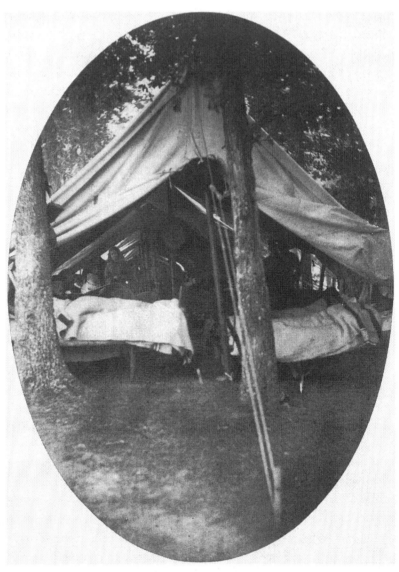

Maria Hall was already an experienced nurse when photographed at Smoke-town Hospital following Antietam, having served at the Patent Office Hospital, aboard the *Daniel Webster*, and later at the naval hospital in Annapolis. Though included in both postwar commemorative tributes to women workers, she de-murred at the prospect of writing a sketch about her tour of duty. (Courtesy of Edward G. Miner Library, University of Rochester School of Medicine)

of her activities to appear in Moore's book, and the following year Brockett and Vaughan also featured a chapter on her.

Creators of the triumphal narrative established a genre that drew on the conventions of fiction as well as nonfiction. In its skeletal form, the genre reproduced the story of an untried woman who had to swallow pride and modesty to carry out her nursing work effectively, then emerged as a champion of the common soldier. The genre had its origins in Alcott's *Hospital Sketches* (1863), which fictionalized location, narrator, and the names of hospital personnel, but otherwise followed Alcott's account of six weeks' service in Washington, where, despite being carried off with typhoid, Nurse Periwinkle rose from uselessness to articulate receptacle for soldiers' woes. Charlotte McKay's *Stories of Hospital and Camp* (1876), which cast the nurse as moral arbiter, were a chronological collection of loosely fictional vignettes. Shifting narration from nurses to army privates, McKay offered another view of the psychic equation that linked nurses with soldiers. Accounts like Kate Cumming's *Journal of Hospital Life* (1866) and Jane Hoge's *Boys in Blue* (1867) adhered more closely to their authors' diaries and less often reflected the fictionalized coming-of-age narrative.

Distinguishing between fiction and nonfiction became harder as the war receded; the more distant the memory, the more subject to embellishment it became. Even those who made a point of announcing that strict historical guidelines governed their narratives were given to straying. The *Campaign of Mrs. Julia Silk* (1892) and Catherine Lawrence's *Autobiography* (1893) walked a generic tightrope of implausible events: Silk told of a chance meeting with an ax-wielding Confederate woman in Maryland whose impertinence unleashed Silk's wrath. Even though she discharged a "first-class seven-shooter" at this she-Rebel, Silk reported that the two "parted good friends" because her assailant admitted that "[she] was wrong in acting the way [she] did."[45] Lawrence's account dripped with sanctimonious justification of dubious military conduct by which she claimed greater authority than her professed experience warranted. Yet potshots at Dorothea Dix and German immigrants bespoke a candor that may ironically have damaged her credibility with readers.[46] The historical integrity of such works was questionable, but published as memoirs, their sins of commission could be forgiven. More significant, racist and nativist remarks scarcely registered with native-born whites whose stake in national reconciliation was sought at the expense of racial and ethnic others.

The reluctance of nurse-authors to admit financial need—from their letters with Frank Moore to the books they published themselves—undergirded the triumphal narrative. Writers employed the halting language of feminine modesty, offering apologies for their acts of authorship. The professional careers of Catharine Maria Sedgwick, Fanny Fern, E. D. E. N. Southworth, and Harriet Beecher Stowe had done little to change this tendency, especially where novices were concerned. The perception that writing women compromised their privacy and should avoid publicity was as widespread after the war as before it. Whereas Mary Livermore and Jane Grey Swisshelm had exploited the press to convey to large audiences the extremity of soldiers' needs, Maria Mann and Harriet Eaton were furious to discover their private correspondence in newspapers from posts in Arkansas and Maryland. Simply the mention of her name in conjunction with the Maine Camp Hospital Association "annoyed" Eaton at first. Later she was "vexed and mortified" that her notes to coworkers found their way into the papers when they had been hurriedly dashed off without an audience in mind.[47] Maria Mann was willing to have letters to her Aunt Mary published as long as her name would not be used. But when her anonymity had been breeched, she fretted over "ingrammatical" sentences written in haste and threatened to "write less & with less freedom in [the] future" if her aunt continued to publish her correspondence.[48] Southerners were apparently no less squeamish.[49]

Anxiety about publicity marked relief workers' replies to Moore in the early postwar years. Some positively shrank from the prospect of writing about themselves, equating public exposure with promiscuity. Sometimes an angry parent or husband fired off a letter. When a Pittsburgh man learned that Moore was gathering information about his daughter and had used her name to publicize the prospective collection, he inveighed against the impropriety: "I write to request that you immediately *erase her name* from your book and from the advertisements in the daily papers. Such an unwarrantable liberty, as to take the name and a sketch of the life of a young lady in private life, without her knowledge or consent is what no gentleman ought to do and can hardly be excused. . . . Please let me know that you have attended to this matter, if you wish no further trouble."[50] Although such ultimatums were rare, they conveyed a more subtle prescription to bourgeois daughters that it was unseemly to voice and thus lay claim to their accomplishments.

There was, of course, a crucial difference between seeing one's private letters in print and willingly entering into the world of authorship. But those putting their work forward needed to tread carefully lest the assertion of authorship place their virtue in question. They were anxious to dispel the perception that their stories had inherent worth and interest because such boldness might compromise their femininity. Conceding financial motives would have eroded credibility further, so writers took every opportunity to mask these and highlight their selflessness. One way to divert attention from the charge of self-promotion was to dedicate one's book to soldiers. In 1866 Kate Cumming, less daunted by the prospect of publication than her compatriots, devoted her journal "to the members of the Confederate Army of the Tennessee, whether living or dead, to whose sufferings and heroism I bear witness."[51] Jane Hoge left no doubt in 1867 that paying tribute to soldiers was also her object: *The Boys in Blue; or, Heroes of the "Rank and File"* was intended "to tell the story of their heroism, long-suffering, and patience, even unto death."[52] The anonymous author of *Notes of Hospital Life* (1864) similarly honored the rank and file. Not only did she succeed in concealing her identity, deflecting publicity at its source, but she asserted that she "regret[ted] the necessity of any mention of self."[53] It is difficult to say whether the desire for anonymity resulted from false modesty, the fear of notoriety, or the need to protect the privacy of those around her. But making it an issue with readers illustrated how women writers might adopt the language of self-effacement without effacing themselves—an act that allowed them to be immodest under the guise of anonymous authorship. Twenty years later Mary Livermore dedicated her story "to the victorious soldiers of the Union Army" and "the honored memory of the heroic dead," convinced that privates of the 1860s were simply too modest to believe that "their experiences were worth narrating"—an echo of the objections raised by some of Moore's correspondents about their own nursing service.[54] Because lionizing themselves would not pass muster with the postwar audience, early diarists transferred their acts of courage onto the soldiery, whereas later memoirists wrote more freely of their own heroism, having chanted the now-conventional mantra of soldierly praise.

Authors also diffused the specter of self-promotion by announcing to readers that they wrote at others' prompting. They distanced themselves from the nether regions of motive by letting associates introduce their books. The anonymous author of *Notes of Hospital Life* enlisted the aid of Alonzo Potter, Episcopal bishop of Pennsylvania, and sought publication "only at the instance [*sic*] of friends."[55] Southerners, too, were eager to announce others' instrumentality in support of their projects. Kate Cumming proclaimed that "a few intelligent, but, perhaps, too partial, friends" induced her to seek publication, just as a St. Louis acquaintance was the impetus behind Mary Loughborough's *My Cave Life in Vicksburg*. A quarter century later Fannie Beers told readers that she had given in to Confederate veterans, who considered the publication of her memoirs a "duty."[56] Though 34 of 55 accounts had been published by 1900, women on the social margins were still hesitant to go on record. Susie King Taylor, who had felt the brunt of racism in "separate but equal" railway cars, stated that nothing could compel her until her regiment's white colonel and a friend of his, who asked for a copy of her book, nerved her to write it.[57]

Memoir writers in particular understood the utility of apology. Aware that distance from the war made memory more selective, they wanted to demonstrate good faith. Confessing their poor recall, they allowed that they were just telling "the facts" and thus created a rhetorical paradox where voicing historical objectives mitigated the impact of faulty memory. Confederate nurse Julia Morgan of Nashville admitted in 1892 that she wrote entirely from memory, and Chicago's Mary Newcomb claimed in 1893 that "no fictitious matter [was] presented" in her reminiscences.[58] Mary Livermore and New York's Adelaide "Ada" Smith circumvented facts altogether by declining any pretensions to history. Livermore assembled "a collection of experiences and reminiscences, more interesting to me in the retrospect than at the time of their occurrence." Smith's claims were more modest inasmuch as she directed readers to think of her memoir as the representation of "sentiments" from a half century earlier, not history.[59]

Others anticipated doubters by enumerating their sources. Amanda Akin Stearns reconstructed *The Lady Nurse of Ward E* (1909) from "long rambling journal letters" to her sister.[60] Rebecca Pomroy had only letters to work from when she produced *Echoes from Hospital and White House* (1884); in 1863 her journal and other valuables had been stolen from a carriage when she was on furlough in Boston. Pomroy saw the loss as a providential punishment: "Perhaps I was planning too much for the future about my journal," she conceded, "for I did mean to give some parts of it to the public."[61] Jane Swisshelm and Mary Livermore made use of their wartime press releases in assembling narratives in the 1880s. Livermore's husband had saved her *New Covenant* dispatches from the trash; Swisshelm used hers from the *New York Tribune* and *St. Cloud Democrat* in lieu of letters and diaries she destroyed during marital disputes.[62]

Writers insistent on the facts meant to differentiate their accounts from works published for artistic or entertainment value. The author of *Notes of*

*Hospital Life*, published the year after Alcott's *Hospital Sketches*, took pains to clarify that her volume was "a simple statement of the facts simply stated," lest readers conclude that the teller was an invention, like Alcott's Tribulation Periwinkle. Jane Hoge made similar claims, arguing as Mary Edwards Walker had done in response to Frank Moore the previous year, that the facts were "more thrilling than fiction." Elvira Powers promised to give "a simple record of scenes and events, just as they occurred from day to day" in her *Hospital Pencillings* (1866).[63] Separating the "factual" from the fictional — a comfortable distinction in the Civil War era — allowed these narrators to claim serious purpose and credibility.

A midwar work that tested the limits of authenticity was Sarah Edmonds's *Nurse and Spy in the Union Army*, published in 1865 by W. S. Williams in Hartford (in 1864 De Wolfe, Fiske in Boston had brought it out as *The Female Spy of the Union Army* and the Philadelphia Publishing Company as *Unsexed; or, The Female Soldier*). Edmonds claimed that she had been a regimental nurse as well as intelligence agent in multiple disguises, including that of soldier. The Canadian-born youth unhinged gender, class, and racial identities, cross-dressing as a white female nurse and Irish immigrant, a male soldier and courier, and male and female ex-slaves. To win readers' goodwill, Edmonds presented herself as a nurse moved by selfless devotion. She dedicated *Nurse and Spy* to "the Sick and Wounded Soldiers of the Army of the Potomac," and her Hartford publisher prefaced the work with a paean to her patriotism: "Should any of her readers object to some of her disguises, it may be sufficient to remind them it was from the purest motives and most praiseworthy patriotism, that she laid aside, for a time, her own costume, and assumed that of the opposite sex, enduring hardships, suffering untold privations, and hazarding her life for her adopted country, in its trying hour of need."[64] Anticipating charges of impropriety, Williams cloaked Edmonds's derring-do in the more suitable garb of self-sacrifice. Edmonds herself later testified that she had donated royalties to the Sanitary and Christian Commissions to dispel the impression that her aim was personal profit.[65] The controversy over the credibility of *Nurse and Spy* assured its success: it sold 175,000 copies, more than any other nursing narrative and roughly three times as many as Mary Livermore's, the next most successful.[66] Williams published subsequent editions in 1865 and 1867, and three more by 1900, including one in German. Although *Nurse and Spy* billed itself as a conventional nursing narrative, it adhered more closely to the "thrilling adventures" genre of Rose O'Neal Greenhow's *My Imprison-*

*ment and the First Year of Abolition Rule at Washington* (1863), Belle Boyd's *In Camp and Prison* (1865), and Loreta Velasquez's picaresque *The Woman in Battle* (1876). None who had written nursing accounts by 1865 publicly acknowledged *Nurse and Spy* in light of its author's compromise of respectability through sexual masquerade. However, their narratives depended less on the triumph of self-promoting female subjects only in degree.


Seventeen former relief workers published narratives between 1863 and 1870. Most were in financial need, especially the four Southerners, all of whom were single. Even the earliest accounts began to sketch out the triumphal narrative of female war work, in which writers represented themselves as soldiers of care battling disease and corruption on behalf of a vulnerable soldiery. Accounts published in 1863 and 1864 helped raise money and labor for the hospitals. On her return from a month in Pennsylvania, Emily Souder explained that she wrote *Leaves from the Battle-field of Gettysburg* (1864) to engage more volunteers in relief work.[67] Louisa May Alcott was more interested in contributing to family income than in altruism. As she turned her diary into *Hospital Sketches* in the spring of 1863, Alcott was surprised to discover publishers eager to vend her wares and a public eager to consume them. James Redpath of Boston published the book after a bidding war with another house, and its quick success encouraged the new author to attempt other projects. Amanda Stearns read it to her patients at Armory Square in 1863, seeing in it a model for her later narrative. There also Walt Whitman saw it and planned his *Memoranda during the War* (1876), which would feature soldiers' suffering, not their caregivers'.[68] Unaccustomed to stardom, Alcott mistrusted the popularity of *Hospital Sketches*: "I don't get used to the thing at all," she confided, "& think it must be all a mistake."[69] Late that summer Georgeanna Woolsey Bacon came out with *Three Weeks at Gettysburg* (1863), and the Sanitary Commission snapped up ten thousand copies of the 24-page pamphlet for distribution to potential donors.[70] Philadelphia's J. B. Lippincott capitalized on the hunger for war stories by publishing *Notes of Hospital Life* in 1864. Not as popular as *Hospital Sketches*, it sold well enough that three years later he brought out a second nursing narrative—Anna Morris Holstein's *Three Years in Field Hospitals of the Army of the Potomac* (1867).

Despite the appearance of Cumming's *Journal of Hospital Life* in 1866, few Confederate women published narratives immediately after the war.

Cornelia Phillips Spencer's *The Last Ninety Days of the War in North Carolina*, published in New York in 1866, and Susan "Grandma" Smith's *The Soldier's Friend*, published in Memphis in 1867, were the only others to appear before 1879, when Phoebe Yates Pember related her years as Chimborazo's head matron in *A Southern Woman's Story*. In 1865 Cumming prepared her diary for publication and took care of her ailing father. She borrowed four hundred dollars from a family friend and contracted with John Morton, a Louisville publisher, to print two thousand copies of *Journal of Hospital Life* in the hope that royalties would allow her to reimburse the debt and to make a modest living. In the spring of 1866 she deputized friends and relatives to sell subscriptions all over the South. She complained in May, when the book had still not been released, that "by not having it soon I am afraid I shall lose the sale of a number of copies [in Mobile] as so many of my friends are leaving for Europe."[71] After publication in late June, Cumming "pray[ed] that I will be able to make some money from my book" and worried that "there is very little money in the South just now" to support sales. By August so few copies had sold that she begged Philadelphia's Lippincott to take them off her hands—"they meet with favor every place in which they are for sale," she reported disingenuously.[72]

Having no other means of support, she took a job as a governess in Louisville in October. The book fared no better later that year, and by winter distributors were mailing back unopened boxes. In February 1867 a friend lamented from Fredericksburg: "I fear, Miss Kate, that the chances for the sale of the book are very poor in this community—Our people are decidedly worse off now than they were at the close of the war. . . . Our people *have not the means* to gratify their literary tastes."[73] By February Cumming was despondent that she had still not earned enough money to discharge her debt: "When I think about the money that I owe on my book, I feel as if I would go crazy. . . . I never had anything distress me like this."[74] In the spring, her strategy changed. "I committed an error," she wrote, "by having my book published in the South, as our Southern publishers do not know how to circulate books. Strong as my Southern proclivities are I regret that I did not go North with it."[75] But a trip to New York that summer met with disappointment when houses like Harper and Brothers wrote that they "would not care to place their imprint on a book containing some of the sentiments herein expressed"—references to the "haughty foe" whose "day of retribution" was imminent and to the blasphemous Union dead at Shiloh whose slouch hats sporting the slogan "To Hell or Corinth" made the devout Alabamian wonder, "Can such a people expect to prosper?"[76] Though she published her diary more than a year after Lincoln's assassination, Cumming did not soften her critique: "Human lives are nothing to him," she wrote of a failed prisoner exchange in 1863. "How long will the people of the North submit to this Moloch[?]" The extent to which writers participated more willingly in gestures of reconciliation after 1880 can be seen in Cumming's revision of this passage in her 1895 *Gleanings from Southland*. Instead of singling out "Moloch" for his inhumanity, she took vaguer aim in observing that "human life seems little worth to those in power at the North."[77] Too partisan to merit the support of Yankee publishers in 1866 and unaffordable by Southern standards, Cumming's work did not sell, despite her persistence. Given the commercial forces arrayed against her "southern proclivities," publication alone was a feat. The tide would not turn until the new century, when writers were urged to "move wisely and discreetly in the publication and sale" of Confederate sketches because they would "find it profitable in every way."[78]

Of the seven Union workers who published accounts between 1866 and 1870, five were spinsters or widows who, like Cumming, sought an income. Elvira Powers tested the waters by asking Frank Moore about his collection but, garnering no promise of pay, sold part of it to the *Chicago Covenant*. In late 1866 she persuaded Edward L. Mitchell of Boston to publish the whole as *Hospital Pencillings*. Just as interested in profit was Sophronia Bucklin, an independent seamstress of modest means, who turned her hospital diary into *In Hospital and Camp* in 1869.[79] Sarah Palmer, the socially humble cook of the 109th New York Infantry, had more to gain through publication of *The Story of Aunt Becky's Army Life* in 1867 than the well-heeled spinster Jane Woolsey, who wrote *Hospital Days* in 1868 while she volunteered as a teacher in Hampton, Virginia. Between 1870 and 1890, only seven more accounts appeared, including widowed Southerner Pember's, reflecting the aging of potential writers and the publishing world's shifting attention.[80] Tribute books, like Margaret Davis Burton's 1886 biography of Mary Ann Bickerdyke—one of six by 1900—were published in this period, but the legendary nurse herself did not enter the literary marketplace.[81] Little time for reflection fell to women like Bickerdyke, who immersed themselves in soldiers' welfare in the 1870s. But the lull may also have resulted from the need to recover from losses, the wish to write from the benefit of hindsight, or hesitancy to leave a record behind them after they had gained it.

Friends urged Mary Livermore to publish a narrative as early as 1865, but political activism on behalf of women kept her from it until 1887.[82] Iowa's Annie Turner Wittenmyer spent thirty years in the reform trenches before writing her memoir of western relief work, *Under the Guns* (1895). Absorbed in orphanage and temperance work, she did not reconsider the war until her election as president of the WRC in the 1890s. This office and her wartime management of special diet kitchens made Wittenmyer chief witness for scores of women bringing pension claims to the Department of the Interior in the 1890s. In a bittersweet addendum, Wittenmyer was to joke two years after the publication of *Under the Guns* that war workers had to resort to publishing their memoirs to sustain themselves in the absence of adequate nursing pensions.[83]

**Those words were** prophetic in light of workers who wrote to supplement meager pensions. Anna Lawrence Platt, a pensioned nurse who had served two years at Armory Square, confided to Mother Bickerdyke in the late 1890s, "I ought to make an income from my *pen*." She briefly considered writing a biography of her correspondent, but Bickerdyke offered no encouragement. Ultimately, Platt's only literary output was "Women of the War," a seventy-two-line poem that detailed nurses' domestication of military hospitals.[84] Catherine Lawrence did what Platt only talked about and published her autobiography in 1893, less than a year after she began to draw a monthly pension of twelve dollars, "hoping that the proceeds . . . [would] supplement this pittance."[85]

Collections commemorating Union hospital life sold well in the postwar North, but relief workers themselves—usually the authors of their biographical sketches—did not reap financial benefits. By 1866 Frank Moore had completed his eight-volume, 596-page *Women of the War*, which went through five editions in less than five years. Linus Brockett and Mary Vaughan's *Woman's Work in the Civil War* (1867), which had four editions and cost a whopping $3.75, was a contemporary entry in a veritable arsenal of popular works that allowed Americans to possess the war through narrative and lavish illustration.[86] In some cases, editors used material prepared by others; Brockett and Vaughan, for example, drew on Harriet Beecher Stowe's sketch of Harriet Foote Hawley.[87] The editors' imprimatur was the hagiographic prose favored by the white, middle-class, Protestant readers they anticipated. Later in the century compilers like Mary Gardner Holland rejected heavy editorializing, marketing *Our Army Nurses* (1895) as an anthology where subjects told their own stories without the interpolations of a Moore or a Brockett.[88]

**Within six months** of the war's end, Frank Moore mailed letters to women and men who might tell him something about Union women's work at the front. Neither Mother Bickerdyke nor Clara Barton wrote him back. The crusty veteran of the war in the West was absorbed by the demobilization of troops in Illinois and in running a shelter for widows and orphans in Chicago. The "angel" of eastern battlefields had left for Andersonville to identify dead prisoners and was making plans to set up a clearinghouse for missing soldiers and their desperate families. Aware of the strong interest in their stories, Moore set out to capture the information. He enlisted the help of Reverend Edward P. Smith, an official of the Christian Commission and American Missionary Association, who knew Bickerdyke. Three months later, after numerous attempts to garner an outline of her activities, she had not responded. Moore applied pressure by telling Smith that he had an engraving of the nurse ready to go to press but no narrative. Another Moore deputy, A. M. Brown, promised to "hunt up" Barton and "all [the women] I can for you," but no sketch of Barton appeared in the 1866 edition.[89]

Over a hundred people did respond, including men who remembered their wartime caregivers. When they heard that a tribute to women was under way, some wrote directly to Moore without asking permission of their female subjects. A Connecticut colonel sent a sketch of his seventy-year-old mother.[90] Ardent in their praise of those who had nursed them back to health and guileless in their wish to spread the word, veterans sometimes appeared unaware of the etiquette governing the privacy of middle-class women. Their enthusiasm caused some women to demur, if only to give the impression that their humility forbade such disclosures. Four soldiers sent word of Mary Morris Husband's work in the eastern theater before the retiring ex-nurse agreed to talk herself. She told Moore, "You must make allowances if the boys talk exaggeratedly of our labors & privations, for naturally they feel warmly towards those who came to them in their need."[91]

Though stalwart matrons like Husband earned their admiration, soldiers were quick to censure women of questionable motive and conduct. Even the most obliging made distinctions among their caregivers. One wrote to Moore as "Dear Friend" with hushed caution: "I do not like to write anything that I am not willing to put my name to, but you will excuse me when you know it only to give you a hint that if you intend issuing another edition of the Women of the War, that you had better make some inquiries about Miss Chase's character before you put her along with true hearted girls like Georgy Willets, Mary Shelton, or Maria Hall. Most any one of an old Round-head Regt except the Col can give you a great deal of information." The woman in question, Nelly M. Chase, was regimental nurse of the 100th Pennsylvania, which saw service at Fredericksburg and later on James Island, South Carolina. A soldier's tale of Chase's saving him from death by exposure formed the basis of the chapter, though Moore's observation that "inquiry has hitherto failed to reveal more concerning the character and services of Miss Chase" revealed his own uncertainty about including her.[92] A woman who was talked about, regardless of her testimony, did not pass the litmus test of virtue. Another soldier told Moore, "If you want to find out about the women that was real good to the soldiers you ought to find some of the boys and get them to tell you because if some of the bad women that were in the army write to you theyl [*sic*] tell you wonderful things about themselves I expect but the boys hated some of them I tell you."[93] What separated "bad" women from "good" was a matter of reputation, but as this soldier implied, self-promoters also exempted themselves from praise.

In a climate where reputation could be challenged at will and where women's acts of self-representation drew suspicion, female caregivers had to be cautious. Speaking about others' accomplishments was safer. Mary Husband initially touted Michigan's Annie Etheridge and New Jersey's Georgiana "Georgy" Willets, explaining that these more diligent and energetic workers deserved mention ahead of herself. "One of my objects," she wrote of the impoverished Etheridge, "is that by bringing her into notice, she may derive some benefit." As for the "very modest" Willets, Husband "[could] not speak too emphatically of [her] conduct, she exercised so much judgement & prudence with untiring zeal in behalf of the soldiers, & was entirely free from 'officer worship,' an uncommon virtue."[94] Like the soldier who differentiated between good and bad women, Husband judged her peers accordingly, reserving blame for sycophants. When contacted directly, Willets confessed her "distaste for, & hesitancy about having what little a kind Providence allowed me to do for our soldiers made public," although she was willing to supply the names, places, and dates of her service.[95]

Moore's less discerning contacts invoked the conventional modesty of

Nelly Chase, seated with members of the 100th Pennsylvania "Roundhead" Infantry at Beaufort, South Carolina, in 1862, lost favor with editor Frank Moore after a soldier advised him to make "inquiries" about her character. (Courtesy of U.S. Army Military History Institute, Carlisle Barracks, Pa.)

self-effacement while directing him to those who could write in their behalf. Mary W. Lee, for example—a veteran of the Peninsula, Antietam, Gettysburg, and the Wilderness—eschewed notice of every kind but did not stop Moore from finding out about her through others. Another sent a message by her sister, explaining "that she would prefer not saying any thing about what she ha[d] done but leave that for others to do."[96] The ease with which some handed over the names and addresses of their cronies suggests that they were more concerned with appearing to behave modestly than with modesty itself. Such a distinction afflicted the fastidious Jane Hoge, who told Moore that she could not offer herself up so publicly, yet, flattered by his proposal, she exchanged three more letters with him in an attempt to decide which personal photograph to submit.[97]

The diffidence of some correspondents betrayed the moral quandary that adulatory publicity inspired. Too candid to feign modesty but too shrewd to admit delight at the prospect of being mentioned, Cornelia Hancock wrote from her freedmen's school in Mount Pleasant, South Carolina, that she had kept no diary during the war. However, if Moore wished to solicit her friends, she had no objection. "I have before been asked to contribute to such a publication," she noted, "but have never felt like making a reply. . . . To attempt to put upon paper the scenes I have witnessed is beyond my powers of description. To shift the responsibility to my friends I do not feel to be very kind but it is all I can do and I do not ask them to furnish any account but you may if you choose."[98] Manufacturing a double indemnity by deferring to others and escaping the obligations incumbent on favor seekers, Hancock maintained the mask of modesty. It was not publicity she hid from, but the burden of having to write, or so she protested.

Another way to appear noble while diverting attention from one's own accomplishments was to characterize the group effort as an unexceptional response to exceptional circumstances. Hannah Stevenson, who earned the title of "general" in *Hospital Sketches* for helping Louisa May Alcott get nursing work in Washington, did not want to see any woman singled out: "Like the privates in the army," she wrote, "they have done their duty to their country & no more. History will care nothing that it was Mrs this or Miss that, who by eloquent tongue or pen roused the enthusiasm & made efficient the patriotism of all other women in her reach."[99] Not only did Stevenson resist "being brought into notice," but also the comparison of nurses to privates showed her internalization of martial values. One put comrades first, scorning individual notice, and viewed extraordinary deeds as ordinary duties — gestures consistent with self-sacrifice.

Katharine Wormeley, who had made a name for herself on hospital ships during the Peninsula campaign and had published a history of the Sanitary Commission in 1863, took a similar view:

> I think the real object of any one giving a history of what American women did during the war should be — not to exalt individuals — but to show the *widespread*, steady character of the work done from a simple sense of duty. I think it would do the country good to know this — but I see no good in making heroines out of a few who chanced to be employed in a conspicuous way. This will not show the country what her women are. Nothing will show it unless the humble patient work which went on all over the land is made to appear in its true proportion. That, I think, *might* be an object worthy of a book about it — and such I hope from your letter is really your object.[100]

Indeed, the one appropriate forum for women's wartime achievement, Wormeley implied, was a collective tribute in which no individual's modesty would be compromised by her being singled out — a prescription that paradoxically defined female heroism through abnegation and stood in contrast to traditions that praised valorous men.

Though the majority of Moore's correspondents resisted recognition, a few envisioned his request as a money-making proposition. The injured Isabella Fogg hoped that Moore would be interested enough in her story to pay for it. Laid up for several years in Cincinnati after her fall through the hatchway of a transport vessel, she was desperate for a payday, as her efforts to secure a military pension had shown. Regretting that she had kept no war journal (her coworker Harriet Eaton had) and imputing that only those who served in the hope of "remuneration or fame" would have done so, Fogg was limited in the "particulars" she could convey. "Much of [my narrative] may be irrelevant to your purpose," she demurred, "but I will send it as it is, and you may make the best use of it you can." Although Fogg cast aspersions on nurses who had earned wages, she saw no contradiction in generating income through the publication of her war story once she was destitute. So anxious was she for payment that, in addition to the sketch of her war activities, she sent Moore several poems "which I am desirous to have criticized in order to ascertain whether they have sufficient poetical merit to warrant their publication."[101]

Elvira Powers of North Oxford, Massachusetts—the same town that produced Clara Barton—did not wait for Moore to contact her. After hearing about the proposed volume from former coworker Chloe Buckel, she wrote Moore: "[Buckel] suggests that you might like to have me write some sketches on the subject. If so, please inform me. I enclose a circular of a work which I am about publishing, which consists of a diary while in the hospital service. If you should desire my services, please inform me as to the kind of sketches you desire. . . . Please also inform me of the terms if you desire me to write."[102] In offering her services to Moore, Powers not only plugged *Hospital Pencillings*, which was published later that year, but made it clear that she expected pay for any contribution. Moore ultimately used Powers's sketch of Buckel in *Women of the War*, but neither gave her a byline nor used her sketch of herself in the volume.[103] Amy Morris Bradley was just as anxious in surrendering three manuscripts and a packet of letters to Moore. "When the proof of the sketch is struck off," she directed him, "please forward a copy to me, as I earnestly wish to have the privilege of reading it before it is published. On no other plan can I give my consent to its publication."[104] Though neither Bradley nor Moore disclosed the financial arrangements, the New

England spinster asserted her right to retain control of her intellectual property.

Others created artificial demand for their stories, hoping to induce Moore to bite. One confidence man—a U.S. Patent Office employee—wrote Moore on behalf of Michigan's favorite regimental daughter, Annie Etheridge, who had also impressed Mary Morris Husband. "She has manuscripts," he asserted, "from which might be compiled a work of considerable merit and of intense interest, for which she has already recd. several liberal offers." Because her war work had been "wholly without compensation," he went on, "she [felt] the need of turning to her own pecuniary benefit. . . . Whether she allows others to so publish will depend upon her decision as to her own work, and *then* upon the liberality of proposals received." Having implied that Etheridge's story would be sought after and that forgoing wartime wages put her in league with the likes of Husband, this "agent" piqued Moore's interest, even though Michigan Annie did not fit the middle-class profile of Moore's typical subject.[105] Judging from the number of books alluded to in such correspondence but never written, merely the mention of a work-in-progress was a bargaining chip meant to entice profit-minded publishers.[106]

Elite women, like Husband and Katharine Wormeley, did not need to employ the arts of persuasion. Having already been approached by Mary Vaughan to submit a piece to *Woman's Work in the Civil War*, Wormeley informed Moore: "I can hardly suppose that *two* books of the kind are undertaken— If yours is the same as Dr. Brockett's, you will find all the information I can give in his hands or Mrs. Vaughan's."[107] In fact, Brockett and Vaughan had themselves joined forces "to avoid conflict" when each became aware that the other was compiling a volume.[108] More concerned about Moore's familiar form of address than the bidding war ("My name is not 'Kate,'" she scolded), Wormeley made other plans. Put off by her haughty tone, Moore neither answered the letter nor published a sketch of her. Not until 1889—twenty-three years later—did Wormeley produce her own account, despite her professions against individual glory and her admonition in the 1860s that Moore should not mention her book in his.

It is important to recognize how the social conventions governing Moore's interaction with the subjects of *Women of the War* helped shape the triumphal narrative of war that relief workers were constructing as early as the 1860s. Moore pursued the stories of women who attached little importance to their

The well-heeled Katharine Prescott Wormeley devoted herself to literary and charity work after the war. In 1866 she took a dim view of postwar paeans to women's relief efforts and failed to submit a sketch to Frank Moore for his *Women of the War*. (Courtesy of U.S. Army Military History Institute, Carlisle Barracks, Pa.)

own achievements and who modeled self-sacrifice. Though it is likely he rewarded women like Isabella Fogg, who was compelled to rely "on the gifts of strangers," he avoided doing business with women anxious to make a buck.[109] His choice of subjects reinforced the narrative's valorization of female heroism but not female subjectivity. Moore's war workers were voiceless objects of admiration who had helped their country in its hour of need and then left the stage of history. They were women, like Fanny Ricketts, who "without a moment's hesitation . . . determined, at all hazards and despite all obstacles, to reach [the] side" of a wounded husband; or like Ellen Orbison Harris, who among "the noble sisterhood" could not have been "more indifferent . . . to all human applause."[110] Moore's sketches were formulaic. They began with the details of parentage, education, and marriage or productive spinsterhood; proceeded to the litany of selfless acts on behalf of suffering soldiers; and finally offered a peroration on the worker's philanthropic virtues, Christian deportment, and anonymous reward. The "genrefication" to which these sketches contributed was animated by a cultural script that represented women as helpers, not initiators, and as instruments of care who put strangers' well-being ahead of their own. They presented women who, in their devotion to the military-medical project, could never upstage the men who made the war. Thus women triumphed, in Moore's idiom, for intuitively adhering to traditional feminine ideals like self-effacement and constancy.

Missing from the triumphal narrative conceived by commemorative editors as well as the authors of monographs were workers' failures. Alice Fahs has observed that popular war literature skipped over the "bad" soldier; it also left little space for portraits of bad nurses. The drunken and disorderly Sairy Gamp of Charles Dickens's imagination had given way to the image of a fiercely loyal and sainted helpmate. Fictional nurses like Alcott's Tribulation Periwinkle and Nurse Dane in "The Brothers," and Rose Terry Cooke's Josephine Addison were idealizations of the diarists and memoirists who, in purporting to tell the history of nurses at war, fed the popular ideal with their fictions of triumphal accomplishment.[111] Their narratives distorted personal conflict and shrouded the competitive urge for recognition in a mist of cooperation. Acts of resistance or disobedience highlighted nurses' executive acumen, not their refusal to adopt military etiquette. Writers depicted themselves as enduring miserable conditions but said little about lapses in temper. Absent from the published record were those who could not adapt to camp life and left in anger, disgrace, or despair. Self-reliance, earned at pains by workers like Phoebe Pember, was represented as a trait consistent with good breeding and common sense, not as the result of a struggle to achieve respect.

Even early accounts, which portrayed disappointment more candidly than those after 1880, depicted women whose perfect moral pitch subdued their male superiors. Sophronia Bucklin's 1869 book trumpeted the success of sympathy over unreasonable surgeons and their female henchmen, and offered lessons in breaking silence. As a "novice" at Hammond General in Point Lookout, Bucklin kept mum about a "drunken, inefficient" quartermaster, whose debauches prevented her from procuring stoves to heat wards; about surgeons who threw "disagreeable things" in nurses' way; and about ward masters who were stealing food.[112] By the time of her transfer to Wolf-Street Hospital in Alexandria several months later, she had conquered the fear of punishment: "No thought of bearing a load of wood on our backs, and being marched around by a guard for hours, deterred us from speaking of the wrongs we endured."[113] A year later, she was not only speaking up, but also addressing surgeons with fighting words. When one wanted to throw her into the guardhouse at Camp Stoneman, "I replied that he could do so . . . if he saw fit, but I rather thought he would stand in some danger of losing his other eye (he had lost one)."[114] From silence to voiced redress, Bucklin portrayed herself as a righteous commando—a soldier willing to take her licks if hospitalized men might suffer less.

Yet Bucklin left out many details of her dismissal for "inefficiencey" from the camp in 1863. When she cooked extra food for soldiers at City Point, a disgruntled tent mate tattled to the surgeon in charge. Insistent that her culinary outlawry had been blessed by the surgeon general, Bucklin appealed to Dorothea Dix for protection. Bucklin narrated the interview in *In Hospital and Camp*, depicting her accuser as a red-faced meddler and her defender as a two-dimensional deity. Through Dix's scripted intercession ("Stop! You shall not talk in that way. Miss Bucklin was relieved from two hospitals for simply doing her duty"), Bucklin's questionable decision-making came off as martyrdom and saved face with readers.[115] The incident also revealed how class tensions bubbled to the surface whenever a representative of middle-class virtue (the tent mate) locked horns with a working-class woman (Bucklin) whose reputation preceded her.

Even though resistance offered satisfaction, the nurse from Auburn, New York, soon saw its limitations. At City Point during the forty-day culmination of the siege of Petersburg, Bucklin dressed maggot-ridden wounds on the field, slept without a tent, and gagged on moldy hardtack. Incensed that soldiers were dying of starvation and not their wounds, and that the deprivations were due to "the most culpable neglect of duty on the part of the officers," Bucklin was stunned when the surgeon in charge solicited her opinion about operations.[116] She used the invitation to secure a new stove, cooking utensils, edible food, and adequate bedding. Earlier expressions of resentment had gone unheeded and even backfired, but when given the chance to abandon the adversarial script, her requests were filled. This event, not without its irony, marked a new understanding in Bucklin's journey from silence to resistance. Unsolicited pleading was as fruitless as silent resentment, whereas redressing grievances with the euphemistic language of cooperation brought success.

Like Bucklin, who dwelled on the ameliorative effects of her initiative instead of the military charges laid at her door, many ex-nurses exploited the drama inherent in their subordination. The nursing narrative was a productive channel for their anger,[117] but casting themselves as heroes—albeit second-class heroes in contrast to fallen men—simplified the complexity of the social tensions that animated military hospitals. Later narratives like Mary Newcomb's *Four Years of Personal Reminiscences* (1893) also sold the image of female subordinates getting even with men who had humiliated them. Prefacing her book with the claim that "no fictitious matter is presented here," Newcomb attempted to gain readers' good faith. Yet her next words ("As you peruse these lines, remember that the half has not been told.") conceded to a selectivity that aroused suspicion. Professing "some knowledge of medicine," Newcomb treated soldiers at Bird's Point, Missouri, with home remedies and escaped discipline, so she tells us, because her interventions were "unknown to the medical dept."[118] In hospital at Mound City, Illinois—the institution where Surgeon John Brinton had "gotten rid" of "complain[ing]," "fault-finding," and "back-biting" lay nurses at roughly the time of Newcomb's service—she again superseded surgical authority by disobeying the lights-out policy. Insisting that she be allowed to bathe a wounded soldier after 9:00 P.M., she enjoined a ward master to "tell that surgeon whoever he is, I will burn just as many lights as I please. I am no hired nurse. I volunteered my services free and there shall be no red tape, but I will break it when humanity demands it."[119] Not one to suffer fools gladly, Newcomb used her class status and the immunity she perceived that working without pay gave her to act out a disregard for hospital rules. On another occasion, she claimed to have told a surgeon about to amputate, "I wear no shoulder-straps, but that boy's arm shall not come off while I am here." Unafraid in retrospect to cross medical men ("It does a great deal of good sometimes to let the doctors know that you are not afraid to give them a little wholesome advice") or even the powerful Miss Dix ("She meant well, but she knew as little of the wants of a hospital as Queen Victoria"),[120] Newcomb believed that her social privilege acted like a magic shield and characterized herself as accountable to no one. Her knack for getting in the last word with superiors without mentioning the consequences dramatized her role as nurse-avenger, but readers are left to wonder whether the Newcomb of the *Reminiscences* eluded the surgical wrath that such conduct would have inspired or simply behaved more deferentially in point of fact.

As scenes of former conflict became more remote, nursing narratives blunted the recollection of contested terrain over the patient's body. Instead of denouncing surgical authority as a cause of patient suffering, writers represented themselves as larger than life and minimized the stature of their former opponents. Caught in self-aggrandizement, they were loath to analyze the structural causes that limited the impact of women's hospital work. The conciliatory mood that infused Civil War narrative and remembrance by the 1890s worked in concert with narrators' focus on themselves to bury a more trenchant analysis.

Still, shadows of discontent are visible in the later works. In 1888 Confederate Fannie Beers remembered the sting of being condescended to by surgeons in Richmond when she first wished to nurse. Later from Buckner Hospital in Gainesville, Alabama, she "could not help feeling that there was a reservation of power and authority, a doubt of my capacity, due to my youthful appearance." Her wording does not directly implicate the surgeons: she employs a passive voice construction which exonerates them. Instead of characterizing interaction with surgeons as combative—what Mary Newcomb felt free to do—she deferred to "angelic . . . Sisters of Charity," who rendered Beers's aid unnecessary.[121] In 1866 Kate Cumming had disparaged this brand of rationalization, noting that Confederate women's standoffishness had led to understaffed hospitals. But by 1895 Cumming too was singing a different tune in her revised diary, *Gleanings from Southland*, which softened references to officious surgeons and ward masters and substituted the euphemistic "servants" for slaves.[122] *Gleanings* allowed Cumming to revisit early sites of frustration with surgeons where she recast verbal abuse as a lesson in tolerance. Dr. Avent, who refused Cumming's requests for laundry facilities and slave attendants, became "a fine old gentleman" in the memoir. Her diary entry for September 13, 1863, criticizing Dr. Bemiss for holding women responsible for the desertion of his men, was expunged from *Gleanings* and replaced by more conciliatory language: "I always made it a rule never to interfere with [surgeons'] prerogatives, knowing that the patients were really under their care and not ours. . . . So we were most deferential to their opinions."[123] Once surgeons became accustomed to her ways, Cumming noted, they conceded their power and authority ("'Do as you please, you know best'"), allowing her to congratulate herself for "diplomacy [which] was wise."[124] Stepping back from direct confrontation in her recollection made Cumming no less triumphant. In fact, not even to enter the lists raised her above demeaning sparring in her own estimation.

The mellowing of perspective is not remarkable in these examples. Indeed, in later decades writers moved beyond the anger that their hospital service had made visceral in the 1860s. Yet their advocacy of the patient ultimately made his body a battleground where a civil war over humane treatment ensued. What bears noting is the change in nurses' self-presentation: over time they distilled their hospital experience into narratives that reconceived the subordinate voice as triumphant. Newcomb represented victories over surgeons who transgressed moral boundaries; Cumming triumphed over her earlier reductive assessments of surgeons. Both forms of remembering required invention on the part of the memoirist inasmuch as she downplayed surgeons' power. Making the foe less formidable allowed her the space to reconstruct her own achievement—greater in recollection than in the immediate chronicle of war.

**As early as 1866** Northern and Southern women, many of whom had to shift for themselves, began to reconsider the war's meaning through published narratives about their relief work. Many writers covered their financial motives with rhetoric that praised the sacrifice and honor of common soldiers. The development of narrative voice depended on a web of social relations that were themselves contested and negotiated. If speaking of their accomplishments was unseemly, then relief workers had to invent selves whose modesty overshadowed any claim to subjectivity or authority. Working-class women like Sophronia Bucklin, Mary Newcomb, and Sarah Palmer were not as worried about the appearance of modesty as elite women like Jane Hoge or Kate Cumming,[125] yet even these were likely to seek shelter in tributes to those whom they had nursed. Regardless of class, however, writers created personae that triumphed over the corrupt in their midst. The moral axis of this constructed voice—vulnerable both to exaggeration and distortion—helped to counteract the bald agency at the heart of such a representation. While Northerners initially lauded a military victory that eclipsed Southern relief work and was thus unwitting of the shared goals and trials that defined women's orbit in military hospitals, Southerners used their work as a corrective to Northern misconceptions about and erasures of their service. The conciliatory mood of later narratives dulled not only sectional differences but the recollection of adversarial relations with surgeons and other nurses. Despite the public and private evidence of troubled hospital sojourns, female relief workers depicted themselves as victorious subjects in a triumphal narrative of war. They molded narrative to their own uses, demonstrating the malleability of memory as they celebrated their religious and domestic work among soldiers and carved a niche for themselves in a hostile arena. The triumphal narrative thus became a projection of desire, a record of the shifting sands of memory. If critics of nineteenth-century American fiction are correct in asserting that women writers created liberating masks for female characters in response to their own social confinement, then their critique has utility for the constructed narratives of relief workers.[126] From the 1860s into the second decade of the twentieth century, accounts of Civil War nursing featured historical actors who diverted attention from their financial motives through stories subject to fictionalizing.

With men as the acknowledged makers of war and thus producers of a history that could be remembered, women logically became the custodians of memory's transmission. Perched as they were between the production and consumption of memory, relief workers and the medical chronicle that is their legacy may inadvertently have nurtured the cycle of war. In tributes to martial glory, they preserved and sustained reverence for fallen soldiers and contributed to a memorial whose ideals lured new generations of young men to look beyond the slaughter. Though their work plainly advertised the glamourless results of military strife, not one of them became an advocate to end war.

If any group of individuals might have parlayed their war work into pacifism, surely it was women, who had witnessed an unprecedented loss of life and saw its impact on the families—especially the wives and mothers—of soldiers. The experience of war had moved many out of a largely private realm into a more public one where access to power mattered. The most astute among them had learned how to manipulate military and medical structures of power to aid suffering soldiers, but these lessons did not translate into momentous progress for women at work or in politics. To be sure, individuals mobilized reform movements that would eventually garner a share of political clout for women; some even changed the complexion of medicine. Yet these advancements were the fruit of personal ambition, not a broadly sustained drive to transform the lives of women. Those who returned to private life did so because their social privilege—their whiteness and elite status —assured a smooth resumption of the domestic ideal. Those whose racial and class identities summoned no privilege were left to the labor and domestic struggle they had always known. For a few moments in a war whose soundings have far outstripped the four years it took to reach a military conclusion, women at the front tested the boundaries of race, of class, and of gender in their interactions with soldiers, coworkers, and medical superiors. These moments of connection could not in the end dismantle social habits whose continuation were the unquestioned prize of peacetime.

# Appendix. A Note on Historiography

In setting out to tell a story of women in hospital and relief work during the American Civil War, I acknowledge the rich foundation Mary Elizabeth Massey laid in the 1960s with *Bonnet Brigades* (1966). Having a wealth of material and wanting to tell as much of the story as that material afforded, Massey wrote a work that was expansive and suggestive. It was nowhere more eloquent than when it invited readers to mine its sources for further study. *Women at the Front* extends one part of Massey's larger examination of gender and the Civil War: that pertaining to the amorphous body of work known as nursing, but which included tasks as various as washing clothes, washing pots, and washing wounds. A central tenet of this project has been to show the limitations of an earlier era's definition of nursing, which eclipsed the vast majority of women who took on relief work during the war and were glad, for the most part, to be paid for it.

Since Elizabeth Cady Stanton, Susan B. Anthony, and Matilda Joslyn Gage published their six-volume text, *The History of Woman Suffrage* (1881–1922), only a handful of writers—Massey and Anne Firor Scott the most prominent among them—took up the question of the war's meaning for women, and even fewer diverged from the consensus that woman's galvanic achievement catapulted women into the polity. Ann Douglas argued in the early 1970s that in their zeal to bring the home front to the battlefront, Union army nurses attempted "to replace the captain with the mother, the doctor with the nurse, and even to outsoldier the soldiers."[1] Douglas presented a model of male-female conflict in which women's exclusion from medical practice gave them incentive to usurp military power. This argument accurately identified the parties to the power struggle but failed to perceive its nuances: female workers did not wish to take the place of medical officials so much as to change the terms of the power struggle. Silenced by their low status within the medical *and* military hierarchies in which they moved, women wanted a greater voice in decision-making that concerned patients

—a process they believed was threatened by unquestioning obedience to military discipline. They wanted surgeons and hospital administrators to take their suggestions seriously and let them treat patients with greater humanity, to engage in discussions about patient care—not be the unwitting machinery of its delivery. Douglas's hypothesis took a first step in glimpsing what we now understand to be a more complex dimension of gender conflict: how class and racial identities, in their intersection with gender, expand motive and agency. The latter version assumed social homogeneity without envisioning how whiteness and class elitism were used to assert privilege within the ranks of subordinate relief workers. The male-female model of struggle also shrouded the resistance of less powerful women to those who held them socially at arm's length. Exploring this dynamic among female workers has been my modus operandi.

In the last twenty years, as Drew Gilpin Faust has observed, the tunnel vision of earlier accounts has given way to a more complex reading of the war. A variety of scholars, from those interested in politics to performance to poetics, has, by raising women's war experiences from the canvas of the new social history, reassessed how gender was no less a contested dynamic than region or race during the war. The "explosion of scholarship" that Faust predicted and indeed helped generate has inaugurated a sea change in how we study women and the war, especially in the sources we use to discover lives that have slipped through the cracks in more traditional analyses.[2] George Rable's *Civil Wars* (1989) and Faust's *Mothers of Invention* (1996) brought an extensive survey of manuscript sources and Confederate imprints to bear on perspectives that questioned not only what gains elite Southern women had made as a result of the war, but whether they had made gains at all in the realms of postwar work and citizenship. Adding to these sources court documents, plantation logs, government records, and the like, Victoria Bynum, LeeAnn Whites, Leslie Schwalm, Catherine Clinton, and Laura Edwards have begun to scrutinize a more diverse population of Southern women whose class and racial allegiances have necessitated a reappraisal of their motives and opportunities.[3] These scholars have carefully articulated the need for regional studies: the Southern agrarian economy gave rise to relations between the sexes, races, and classes that did not mimic the social patterns of a more peripatetic Northern economy.[4]

Several signal studies of Northern women have also appeared since 1990, recasting the gender politics of benevolent work and exploring the instability of gender identity during the war. Elizabeth Leonard's *Yankee Women*

(1994) concludes through its examination of three veteran relief workers that despite women's insistence that they had a place in war, the gender system that structured their domestic lives could not absorb the changes that their hospital work augured.[5] In *Patriotic Toil* (1998), Jeanie Attie ingeniously assesses the U.S. Sanitary Commission as a policing agent of women's charitable labors and posits that the Civil War was the first American conflict in which women expected their labors to translate into expanded political rights.[6] Judith Giesberg is more sanguine in her recent work on the commission, believing that it was "the missing link" between women's antebellum activism and the temperance and suffrage movements. Arguing that the Sanitary Commission was proof of "an evolving women's political culture," Giesberg resists Attie's and Lori Ginzberg's characterization that the consolidation of male power and capital in reform work left slim pickings for women in the postwar political arena.[7] Lyde Cullen Sizer's study of nine "exceptional and representative" Northern women writers has done for the intersection of gender with political culture what Mary Kelley's *Private Woman, Public Stage* did for our understanding of domestic ideology in 1984. By showing how writers from Elizabeth Stuart Phelps to Frances Harper "manipulated" the conventions of womanhood within a publicly acceptable range, Sizer argues that a wartime "rhetoric of unity" engineered a "revolution" in public conceptions about women's political potential. Unfortunately, women's ascendance in the public realm did little to alter their lives in the long term. Here Sizer joins the chorus of scholars who see women reaching out to chance a redefinition of womanhood during the war, but whose hands are slapped in the regressive return to normalcy.[8]

Historians continue to debate whether the Civil War was a political watershed for women in the respective sections, but some have gone at the question from different angles. Catherine Clinton and Nina Silber's collection *Divided Houses* (1993) plays on the metaphor of sectional division, presenting in the whole a multivalent mosaic of women's, men's, and children's experiences of war. Individual contributors explore how social identities could bend or break as war was made away from home and as the war front intruded on the home front.[9] In *The Vacant Chair* (1993), Reid Mitchell has also used gender as an integral category of analysis, arguing that domestic ideals shaped the character of Northern soldiers. Mitchell's work debunks the notion that masculine rearing alone produced men ready for battle and asks readers to refigure their gendered assumptions about male conduct in the midcentury.[10] Ella Forbes has considered the war's meaning by placing black women at the center of the story. *African American Women during the Civil War* (1998) signals an important shift in the field, for even though studies like Elizabeth Fox-Genovese's *Within the Plantation Household* (1988) have brought black-white domestic interactions to our attention, Forbes's work suggests that the portrait of black female experience changes when viewed from sources produced within the contemporary African American community.[11]

Literary and cultural studies of the war have observed the racializing and sectionalizing power of language by directing their attention to the nexus between writers and the production of texts, and readers and the consumption of texts. Among those who have regarded the gendering power of war rhetoric, Nina Silber has shown how a masculinized North enacted a "romance of reunion" with a feminized South to reconcile divisions that were still poignantly felt by Southerners in the 1880s and 1890s.[12] Kathleen Diffley has reminded us, first in *Where My Heart Is Turning Ever* (1992) and more recently in *To Live and Die* (2002), that highbrow writers did not for the most part produce a literature of war; that to find the literature of war, one must look in periodicals whose stories reflected popular tastes and shaped opinion through a melding of "invention and evidence that counted when events were raw."[13] Alice Fahs's *The Imagined Civil War* (2001) takes up Diffley's strand, adding sources like broadsides, songs, imprinted stationery, and advertisements to show how the war was "a people's contest" through which individuals constantly reimagined their relation to the state. Fahs has based her wide-ranging methodology on the notion that despite their political differences, Northerners and Southerners shared a rhetoric about nationhood that was muted as a later generation both racialized and masculinized the war's memory.[14] In her perceptive reading of civil war as a literary framework, Elizabeth Young has produced the border-crossing *Disarming the Nation* (1999) in which she regards women's writing on the Civil War as a logical site for rhetorical struggle. Young posits that postwar writers like Stephen Crane and J. W. Deforest displaced the period's women writers in an attempt to "remasculinize" the war, but that women's writing already bore the metaphorical marks of such incivility. In an analysis of figures of civil war evident on the battlegrounds of race, class, gender, sexuality, and section, Young persuasively shows how women were able "to reinvent their relation to national politics" through powerful cultural tropes.[15]

While literary scholars have regarded the cultural work of Civil War writing, historians have trained their sights on the changing social status of women. Despite the more modest claims of recent work that concedes women's failure to gain real political mileage as a consequence of the war, several historians have adapted the literary scholars' critique of gender as a malleable and permeable form to demonstrate the war's suspension of fixed social identities. Linda Grant De Pauw, Elizabeth Leonard, and DeAnne Blanton and Lauren Cook have followed the trail of women who took on traditionally masculine roles to consider how the war compelled them to feats of heroism. De Pauw's *Battle Cries and Lullabies* (1998) traces the legacy of warrior women throughout human history. Leonard casts a wider net by adding spies, smugglers, scouts, and other paramilitary actors to the list of female soldiers she surveys in *All the Daring of the Soldier* (1999). Culling her evidence from the *Official Records of the War of Rebellion*—a heroic feat in itself—she argues that despite ample pressure to behave conventionally, there have always been women who chose not to and risked censure and ridicule.[16] Blanton and Cook combed contemporary popular accounts of the war in addition to pension and service records at the National Archives to retrieve evidence of female combatants in *They Fought Like Demons* (2002). In positing that nursing was no more the natural province of women than men, they argue that soldiering was not exclusively male work; that there were no essential differences between the military performance of men and women.[17] These studies of women in combat, which have crossed the sectional divide to emphasize the primacy of individual over regional motive, read the war's impact on women more radically than the social and political ethnographies that have dominated the field.

What seems clear from the last decade of scholarship is that the boundaries structuring our thinking about the war—between North and South, war front and home front, soldier and civilian—are too tidy; that the war as Americans lived it did not always reflect the relational oppositions that have come to define and characterize our inquiry. Scrutiny of the war through the lens of gender has yielded a new way to look at events and, perhaps more important, has made visible new classes of spectators. The aggregate narrative of the Civil War is richer for this new field of study because it has forced a reconsideration of how social roles are forged during and after wars as much as it has insisted on the class, racial, and regional differences within gender groups.

# Notes

## Abbreviations

ADAH
  Alabama Department of Archives and History, Montgomery
AGO
  Adjutant General's Office
CSGO
  Confederate Surgeon General's Office
DU
  Manuscript Department, Perkins Library, Duke University, Durham, N.C.
GDAH
  Georgia Department of Archives and History, Atlanta
ISHL
  Illinois State Historical Library, Springfield
LC
  Manuscript Division, Library of Congress, Washington, D.C.
LL-IU
  Lilly Library, Indiana University, Bloomington
LLMVC-LSU
  Louisiana and Lower Mississippi Valley Collection, Louisiana State University, Baton Rouge
MDAH
  Mississippi Department of Archives and History, Jackson
MHC-UM
  Michigan Historical Collections, Bentley Historical Library, University of Michigan, Ann Arbor
NARA
  National Archives and Records Administration, Washington, D.C.
*NAW*
  *Notable American Women*, 3 vols., edited by Edward T. James (Cambridge: Harvard University Press, 1971)
NCDAH
  North Carolina Department of Archives and History, Raleigh

OAGVSB
Office of the Adjutant General Volunteer Service Branch
OIPF
Organization Index to Pension Files, Film Series T289, Pension Files Relating to 2,448 Army Nurses, Veterans Administration, RG 15, National Archives and Records Administration, Washington, D.C.
PSAC
Pensions by Special Acts of Congress, U.S. Bureau of Pensions, Department of the Interior, RG 15, National Archives and Records Administration, Washington, D.C.
RG
Record Group
SCL-USC
South Caroliniana Library, University of South Carolina, Columbia
SC-UI
Special Collections, University of Iowa, Iowa City
SHC-UNC
Southern Historical Collection, Wilson Library, University of North Carolina, Chapel Hill
USAMHI
U.S. Army Military History Institute, Carlisle Barracks, Pa.
USCC
U.S. Christian Commission
USGO
Union Surgeon General's Office
USSC
U.S. Sanitary Commission
VSL
Virginia State Library, Richmond
WSHSC-UA
W. S. Hoole Special Collections, Gorgas Library, University of Alabama, Tuscaloosa

## Introduction

1. *Medical and Surgical History*, 6:958, and Stillé, *United States Sanitary Commission*, 46.

2. In an early power struggle with the USSC over what authority she might claim in relation to the nurses she had trained, Blackwell backed out. See a fuller description of these events in Attie, *Patriotic Toil*, 82–86.

3. See Stanton, Anthony, and Gage, *History of Woman Suffrage*, vol. 2. The set ultimately included six volumes; the first two volumes were published by 1882.

4. Mary Logan (*The Part Taken*, 310) observed in 1912 that women who had lived in hospitals and among soldiers were the real "heroines" of the war. For the

genre of female adventure narrative, or the daring exploits of female spies and soldiers, see Horan, *Desperate Women*; Ross, *Rebel Rose*; Boyd, *In Camp and Prison*; Scarborough, *Belle Boyd*; Velasquez, *Woman in Battle*; and Sizer, "Acting Her Part." The best recent work on the cultural significance of wartime cross-dressing is Elizabeth Young's *Disarming the Nation*.

5. Rable (*Civil Wars*) identifies this backward motion. See also Anne Firor Scott, *Southern Lady*; Faust, "Altars of Sacrifice"; Whites, "Civil War as a Crisis in Gender"; and Elizabeth D. Leonard, *Yankee Women*.

6. Pictorial representations of nursing in the 1860s, such as those in the *Harper's Weekly* of September 6, 1862, depicted women, not men. I thus offer a friendly amendment to Blanton and Cook (*They Fought Like Demons*), who recently observed that nursing was men's work in the Civil War. Though large numbers of men did indeed serve as nurses, the ideology of domesticity in the mid-nineteenth century gendered nursing as female. For antebellum nursing and its gendered implications, see Reverby, *Ordered to Care*, and Kristie R. Ross, "'Women Are Needed Here.'"

7. For a sample of studies that take account of these regional differences, see, for the South, Friedman, *Enclosed Garden*; Lebsock, *Free Women of Petersburg*; and Bynum, *Unruly Women*; and, for the North, Cott, *Bonds of Womanhood*; Ryan, *Cradle of the Middle Class*; Hewitt, *Women's Activism*; and Stansell, *City of Women*.

8. Simkins and Patton, "Work of Southern Women," 485.

9. See Mitchell, *Vacant Chair*, xiii.

## Chapter One

1. The photograph appeared in Culpepper, *Trials and Triumphs*, and in Ken Burns's 1990 PBS television documentary, *The Civil War*.

2. See *New York Illustrated News*, April 23, 1863, p. 404, USSC Papers, LC. For the New York fair (April 4–27, 1864), see Kantor and Kantor, *Sanitary Fairs*, 106–14. The women in the photograph may also have been nurses, but I have not been able to identify them with certainty.

3. Union Army Nursing Superintendent Dorothea Dix advised appointees to dress soberly but never required uniforms. Nuns wore uniforms and headgear, but of their religious orders and not the hospital service. See Matthew Brady photograph of Sister Verona, Sisters of Charity, in Chapter 3.

4. See Moore, *Women of the War* (1866), and Brockett and Vaughan, *Woman's Work*. For postwar domestic rhetoric, see Elizabeth D. Leonard, *Yankee Women*, xiii–xxv.

5. For examples of women who taught before the war, see Hawks, *Woman Doctor's Civil War*; Bradley Diary, DU; Elizabeth Brown Pryor, *Clara Barton*, 49; Haviland, *Woman's Life-Work*; and Grimké, *Journal*. On the prewar teaching of Rebecca S. Smith and Sallie Myers Stewart, see Kate M. Scott, *In Honor of. . . . Army Nurses*. Mary Livermore (*Story of My Life*) served as a plantation governess in the 1830s. Reform activities varied widely, from Jane Hoge's work in orphan

asylums to Laura Haviland's activity on the Underground Railroad. See Ginzberg, *Work of Benevolence*, 159–60, on Jane Hoge, and Haviland, *Woman's Life-Work*. Michigan's Rena Littlefield Miner was a mill operative, seamstress, and compositor before the war. Judging from the nosedive in seamstresses' wages during the war, Miner was much better off as a paid relief worker. See Holland, *Our Army Nurses*, 139, and Paludan, *"People's Contest,"* 182–83.

6. See, e.g., Ada Bacot Diary, SCL-USC; Ex-slave Maria Bear Toliver's pension file (#889647), OIPF; and Pember, *Southern Woman's Story*. For evidence of women joining their husbands in camp to serve as laundresses, see John W. Bell to Nancy Bell, June 15, 1862, Bell Papers, LLMVC-LSU.

7. See Schultz, "Mute Fury," 59; Faust, "Altars of Sacrifice," 1224; Bynum, *Unruly Women*, 142; and Mitchell, *Vacant Chair*, 160–61.

8. Massey, *Bonnet Brigades*, 32. Massey's number may be inflated. Drew Faust (*Mothers of Invention*, 24) estimates that around one thousand groups mobilized in the South.

9. For careful accounting of the relief efforts of aid societies from a single state, see, e.g., Conner et al., *South Carolina Women*, and Anderson, *North Carolina Women*.

10. Lori Ginzberg (*Work of Benevolence*, 134–36) argues that the USSC "masculinized" a formerly feminine ideology of benevolence by promoting a scientific model of operation. Judith Giesberg (*Civil War Sisterhood*, ix, chap. 2) regards male control of the USSC as an attempt by elite men to regain some of the political power they had lost through the broadening of the franchise earlier in the nineteenth century. See also Gallman, *Mastering Wartime*, 134; Stillé, *United States Sanitary Commission*; and Attie, "Warwork" and *Patriotic Toil*. The independent western and northwestern branches of the USSC put women in positions of greater authority. See Kristie R. Ross, "'Women Are Needed Here,'" chap. 3.

11. See Massey, *Bonnet Brigades*, 32, and Bremner, *Public Good*, 54. Bremner reports that the USSC had 450 employees by 1864. According to Mary Livermore (*My Story of the War: The Civil War Memoirs*, 475), the USSC collected and distributed $25 million in goods.

12. Bremner, *Public Good*, 57. Attie (*Patriotic Toil*, chap. 5) argues that public suspicion of the USSC by midwar as an organization devoted to profit prompted many producers of household goods to support the USCC instead.

13. Moss, *Annals of the United States Christian Commission*, 641, 731. Livermore (*My Story of the War: The Civil War Memoirs*, 475) reported $4.5 million. Ralph C. Gordon ("Nashville") estimates that $2.5 million in cash and $3 million in stores and publications were given to the USCC. For distribution statistics on the Christian and Sanitary Commissions, see Paludan, *"People's Contest,"* 352–54.

14. See, e.g., the executive orders of August 26, 1862, and July 15, 1863, from Gov. John G. Shorter to aid societies and the "Appeal to the Ladies of Alabama" from Quartermaster General Duff C. Green, January 25, 1864, Sturdevant-Hall Papers, WSHSC-UA.

15. See, e.g., *Charleston Courier*, July 16, 1863, and *Charleston Mercury*, July 30, 1863.

16. Even in the North, where the efforts of the USSC and USCC threatened to submerge the identity of states, state and local relief agents attached themselves to regiments and hospitals independently of the benevolent giants. The state of Maine, for example, sent Harriet Eaton to minister to its troops stationed in and around Washington. When she first traveled to Virginia in 1862, Eaton spent much of her time trying to locate the regiments from her state and assess their supply needs. See Eaton Diary, SHC-UNC.

17. See Kantor and Kantor, *Sanitary Fairs*, 254, and Simkins and Patton, "Work of Southern Women," 479.

18. Dorothea Dix to Surgeon General Simon Cameron, April 22, 1861, and to Acting Surgeon General R. C. Wood, April 25, 1861, Letters Received, 1818–70, USGO, NARA. For the controversy surrounding Dix's appointment, see Kristie R. Ross, "'Women Are Needed Here,'" chap. 2.

19. See General Order No. 351 of the War Department, issued October 29, 1863, AGO, NARA, and Giesberg, *Civil War Sisterhood*, 47–48.

20. In a document entitled "Remarks on Legislation for the Benefit of Army Nurses," presented on May 23, 1890, as bills to pension female Civil War nurses had been introduced in Congress, Samuel Ramsey, chief clerk in the Surgeon General's Office, estimated that Dix appointed 3,214 women; the Carded Service Records, NARA, list only 594 Dix nurses, however.

21. Circular No. 8, July 14, 1862, Circular and Circular Letters, USGO, NARA.

22. Pomroy, *Echoes*, 26.

23. Quoted in Dannett, *Noble Women*, 47. For examples of other women rejected because of their youth, see the cases of Mary Robert Lacey and Catherine L. Taylor in Kate M. Scott, *In Honor of . . . Army Nurses*. Although initially turned down because they were under thirty-five, Lacey and Taylor served long enough to win nurses' pensions after the war.

24. On the Woolsey family, see Bacon and Howland, *Letters of a Family*, and Kristie R. Ross, "Arranging a Doll's House." For an engaging discussion of "transport women" and their failure to be absorbed by the USSC as "ministering angels," see Giesberg, *Civil War Sisterhood*, chap. 5.

25. Quoted in Holland, *Our Army Nurses*, 467–68.

26. Hancock, *South after Gettysburg*, 3, and Hawks, *Woman Doctor's Civil War*, 15. There was precedent after battles and in chronically understaffed hospitals for engaging women on the premises in paid work. Emily Bliss Souder (*Leaves*, 37–38) noted that women who went to Gettysburg only to learn that they had been widowed were pressed into service. And a surgeon in charge of a Columbus hospital obtained permission from his superiors to hire the wives of his stewards. See Medical Director Charles Trisslar to Surgeon Lincoln R. Stone, September 19, 1864, Letters Received by Stone, USGO, NARA.

27. Grimké, *Journal*, 136–38. For other examples of the obstacles that African American women encountered in seeking teaching positions, see Forbes, *African American Women*, chap. 7.

28. Thirty-two-year-old Matilda Cleaver John of Washington, D.C., performed

custodial work at hospitals in Annapolis and Georgetown. Martha Spicer carried water and washed clothes at post hospitals in Little Rock and Helena, Ark. See John (#1162117) and Spicer (#457620) pension files, OIPF. For the ways in which former slaves were virtually enslaved by the federal government, see Forbes, *African American Women*, 12–16.

29. Constance Cary (Harrison) reminiscence, Harrison Papers, LC. For the prejudice against youthful women in Southern hospitals, see Simkins and Patton, "Work of Southern Women," 484–85.

30. See, e.g., Kate E. Whitebread to Juliet Opie Hopkins, June 10, 1861, Hopkins Papers, ADAH, and Emily Bostick to Gov. Joseph Brown, June 16, 1862, GDAH.

31. When Kate Cumming's coworker, Mrs. Williamson, contracted typhoid, a slave waited on her. See Cumming, *Kate*, 74. While slaves were working as hospital cooks in the Confederacy, ex-slaves found jobs as cooks in Union hospitals. See, e.g., the case of Harriet Jackson in Christie, "'Performing My Plain Duty,'" 220.

32. Bacot Diary, SCL-USC; Newsom, *Florence Nightingale of the Southern Army*; Mason, "Memories," 314. For the wide-ranging mobile hospitals of the Army of the Tennessee, see Schroeder-Lein, *Confederate Hospitals on the Move*.

33. Drew Faust notes that the Baptist Female College of Southwest Georgia was converted into a hospital and that wayside hospitals in Union Point, Ga., and Wilmington, N.C., were tremendously productive. The former, organized by fourteen women in the fall of 1862, served over one million meals to 20,000 soldiers in the next two years; the latter served 6,000 to 8,000 soldiers per month. One wayside hospital in Columbia—run entirely by women—operated for almost three years. See Faust, *Mothers of Invention*, 39, 96, and News and Courier, *Our Women in the War*, 3–5.

34. See Anderson, *North Carolina Women*, 32–33; Conner et al., *South Carolina Women*, 33.

35. Napier, "Montgomery during the Civil War," 114; Balfour Diary, MDAH. See also Cordelia Scales's report of caring for soldiers at Oakland, her plantation home near Holly Springs, Miss., in Cordelia Scales to Loulie, May 15, 1862, Scales Letters, MDAH; Simmons Family Papers, WSHSC-UA; and Whites, *Crisis in Gender*, 91, 114.

36. See Adams, *Doctors in Blue*, 68. For the use of male nurses on hospital ships in the western theater and resistance to using female nurses, see Lauderdale, *Wounded River*. See also Surgeon N. R. Derby to Surgeon General William Hammond, October 3, 1862, Letters Received, 1818–70, USGO, NARA.

37. See Adams, *Doctors in Blue*, 163; Brooks, *Civil War Medicine*, 55, 123; and H. H. Cunningham, *Doctors in Gray*, 73, 267–68.

38. Circular No. 7, July 14, 1862, Circulars and Circular Letters, USGO, NARA. For Hammond's treatment of female nurses and his wish to shelter surgeons, see Kristie R. Ross, "'Women Are Needed Here,'" 108–12. See also Gillett, *Army Medical Department*, 181.

39. John H. Brinton to Medical Director Simons, October 11, 1861, Letters Received, 1818–70, USGO, NARA.

40. See Brinton, *Personal Memoirs*. *Medical and Surgical History*, published from 1875 to 1888, reported, "According to the testimony of all the medical officers who have referred to this point [women's] best service was rendered in connection with extra diets, the linen-room and laundry. Male help was preferred in the wards" (6:958).

41. Surgeon J. P. De Bruler to Gov. Oliver P. Morton, July 15, 1862, Letters Received, 1818–70, USGO, NARA.

42. See Susan E. D. Smith, *Soldier's Friend*, 183; Seigel, "She Went to War," 17; and Newcomb, *Four Years*, 108. For a soldier's account of "incompetent and unworthy" surgeons, see Sam Stafford to Abby E. Stafford, October 2, 1862, Stafford Papers, DU. See also Constant Hanks to Mary Rose, February 16, 1863, Hanks Papers, 1861–65, DU.

43. David Cumming to Kate Cumming, January 10, 14, 1863, Cumming Papers, ADAH. Similar complaints were common in regiments, like the 27th Indiana. See Wilbur D. Jones, *Giants in the Cornfield*, 192.

44. Parsons, *Memoir*, 111, 97. Mitchell (*Vacant Chair*, chap. 5) discusses "the need for femininity in a masculine world." See also Hoge, *Boys in Blue*, 299, and Von Olnhausen, *Adventures*, 87.

45. Moore, *Women of the War*, v; Brockett and Vaughan, *Woman's Work*, 60–61. Later works like Phebe Hanaford's *Daughters of America* (1883) and Mary Gardner Holland's *Our Army Nurses* (1895) maintained the class and racial elitism of the 1860s collections.

46. Emily Mason ("Memories," 309) wrote in 1902 that *Our Women in the War* was "little known" when it was published "and is now quite rare." Several collections celebrated women's contributions to individual state relief efforts, like Mrs. James Conner's *South Carolina Women in the Confederacy* (1907) and H. E. Sterkx's *Partners in Rebellion: Alabama Women in the Civil War* (1970). Simkins and Patton ("Work of Southern Women," 496) noted that "the prevailing conception of feminine propriety prevented the creation of hospital heroines through newspaper publicity."

47. See, e.g., Andrews, *Women of the South*, and Simkins and Patton, *Women of the Confederacy*.

48. See Logan, *The Part Taken*, 306, 308.

49. For cultural histories of American nursing, see Melosh, "Every Woman Is a Nurse" and *The Physician's Hand*, and Reverby, *Ordered to Care*.

50. Locke, *Three Years*, 186.

51. Mary Elizabeth Massey first noted this in *Bonnet Brigades*, 52.

52. Most recently Culpepper (*Trials and Triumphs*, 315) estimated 3,000; Maher (*To Bind Up the Wounds*, 2), "several thousand"; and Kalisch and Kalisch ("Untrained but Undaunted," 25), just under 10,000. Massey (*Bonnet Brigades*, 52) wrote that "at least 3,200 held paying positions"; she seems to have been the only mod-

ern historian to notice racial and class diversity among women in the hospital service of both sections.

53. Soldier quoted in Conklin, *Women at Gettysburg*, 79. For a typical tour of duty for USCC workers, see Ralph C. Gordon, "Nashville." For women's warfront invisibility as it relates to the institutionalization of military support services, see Hacker, "Women and Military Institutions."

54. Italics mine. Note of F. C. Ainsworth, April 10, 1890, Classified Schedule of Female Hospital Employes [*sic*], Record and Pension Division, War Department, NARA.

55. For examples of Confederate soldiers quartered in warehouse hospitals, see Beers, *Memories*, 43; Underwood, *Women of the Confederacy*, 83–92; and W. O. Shepardson to Juliet Opie Hopkins, September 10, 1861, Hopkins Papers, ADAH.

56. Kate Cumming and her father corresponded about white immigrant women looking for positions as laundresses. See David Cumming to Kate Cumming, May 5, 6, 7, 25, 1863, Cumming Papers, ADAH.

57. See, e.g., the narratives of Pember, *Southern Woman's Story*; Cumming, *Kate*; Beers, *Memories*; and Morgan, *How It Was*. George Rable (*Civil Wars*), Jean Friedman (*Enclosed Garden*), and Sally McMillen (*Motherhood in the Old South*) have also argued that elite Southern women were more restricted than their Northern peers.

58. On each index card in NARA's Carded Service Records, a worker's name, her job classification, her hospital and its location, and correspondence dates regarding service are written. African American racial identity is tagged, although it is unclear how systematic the recording of race was. Some cards designate marital status by listing workers as "Miss," "Mrs.," or "Sister" in the case of nuns, but because the vast majority of cards do not include these tags, we are unable to draw statistically significant conclusions about workers' marital status. The cards also note if a worker was appointed by Superintendent Dix or if she was a civilian contracted by another military authority. Because the cards were based on often insubstantial or incomplete hospital records, this body of data provides only an approximate statistical summary of hospital workers.

59. The discrepancy between the Carded Service Records tally of 582 Dix appointees and the tally of 3,200 reported by earlier historians is significant. Samuel Ramsey, chief clerk in the Surgeon General's Office, estimated in 1890 that 3,214 were employed by the Union Army Medical Department but does not specify which of these Dix appointed. Whether the Carded Service Records make a distinction between nurses appointed by Dix or those whose paperwork was processed by her office but may not have been appointed by her is uncertain. However, we can conclude that at least 582 women considered themselves Dix appointees, and as many as 3,214 women entered the service through her office. See Ramsey, "Remarks on Legislation for the Benefit of Army Nurses," May 23, 1890; Adams, *Doctors in Blue*, 178, and Stimson and Thompson, "Women Nurses with the Union Forces," 221–22.

60. Maher (*To Bind Up the Wounds*, 1) estimates that almost 600 nuns nursed; O'Brien (*Forgotten Heroines*, 3), some years earlier, estimated 1,000.

61. Like the statistics for marital status, service dates for the entire body of workers are incomplete. Most of the cards include dates, but what the dates signify is uncertain. It is my guess that the dates, incomplete though they may be, are service dates. If the dates were payroll dates, they more than likely would have included dollar amounts. If these are service rather than payroll dates, we can plot the service of women over time and determine, for example, how many women worked in the first two years of the war compared with the last two. These data also may reveal the number of women at work in various parts of the Union early and late in the war.

62. Adams (*Doctors in Blue*, 153) and Gillett (*Army Medical Department*, 251) report that by the end of the war, 204 general hospitals were in operation, but this figure does not include field hospitals, which, by their very nature, were more transitory. *The Medical and Surgical History of the War of the Rebellion* (1888) lists only 108 Union general hospitals but does not include places like Union Hotel Hospital in Washington, Benton Barracks in St. Louis, Gayoso Hospital in Memphis, regimental or division hospitals in the field, or private hospitals where thousands of soldiers were cared for. H. H. Cunningham's *Doctors in Gray* lists 153 Confederate hospitals, but here too the number is artificially low.

63. Adams, *Doctors in Blue*, 155. Gillett (*Army Medical Department*, 181, 186, 195, 219) reports that by the end of 1862, the Union operated 150 general hospitals, and that New York and Philadelphia, capable of handling about 10,000 hospitalized soldiers by this date, took the overflow of patients from Washington. Though St. Louis could handle 3,700 patients by late 1862 (more than Louisville and Cincinnati combined), by the next summer with the siege of Vicksburg well under way, Memphis became the western city with the largest bed capacity at 5,000. For the Philadelphia statistics, see Gallman, *Mastering Wartime*, 130; for City Point statistics, see Christie, "'Performing My Plain Duty,'" 214.

64. Jeanne Marie Christie's ("'Performing My Plain Duty,'" 214) count of 177 women includes nurses, relief agents, and officers' wives.

65. See Glymph's statistics in "'This Species of Property,'" 58.

66. McKay's narrative, *Stories of Hospital and Camp*, was published in 1876 as a pseudo-fictional account of life in a cavalry camp.

67. Richmond Civil War Centennial Commission, *Confederate Military Hospitals*; Hall, "Confederate Medicine," 489; Kantor and Kantor, *Sanitary Fairs*, 254; H. H. Cunningham, *Doctors in Gray*, 51; and Nash, "Some Reminiscences."

68. Massey, *Bonnet Brigades*, 47–48; Andrews, *Women of the South*, 127–30; Whites, *Crisis in Gender*, 91.

69. Medical Department Morning Reports of Patients in General Hospitals 1–4, 7–8, 10–20, CSGO, NARA.

70. Medical Department List of Employees, Chimborazo Hospital No. 2, CSGO, NARA.

71. For example, Charles R. Greenleaf (*Manual for the Medical Officers of the United States Army*, 19) said of Union matrons that "they perform the duty of laundresses."

72. Simkins and Patton, "Work of Southern Women," 481.

73. News and Courier, *Our Women in the War*, 151; Mason, "Memories," 316; Marshall, "Nurse Heroines," 327; Hall, "Confederate Medicine," 488.

74. Parsons, *Memoir*, 72.

75. Powers, *Hospital Pencillings*, 42, 154.

76. Quoted in Bacon and Howland, *Letters of a Family*, 2:594.

77. See, e.g., Powers, *Hospital Pencillings*, 120, and Parsons, *Memoir*, 62. White nurse Fannie Oslin Jackson (*On Both Sides*, 78) had to do the wash when the black laundresses for whom she was responsible were absent. Kate Cumming (*Kate*, 92) resorted to hiring civilian men. For the rigors of washing clothes in the field, see Wendel, "Washer Women," 36.

78. Elizabeth D. Leonard, "Civil War Nurse," 194; Rebecca Usher to Martha Usher Osgood, December 5, 1862, Usher Family Papers, Maine Historical Society, Portland (quotation).

79. The initial request was made on behalf of the laundresses by Surgeon John E. Crane to Dorothea Dix, July 5, 1864, Dix Nursing Papers, NARA. In his letter to Dix, Crane noted that the women were "intelligent & industrious, and truly deserving of favor." Yeatman responded to Dix, in July 1864, that "women who are or have been employed as Laundresses, are not the kind of women contemplated under Circular Order No. 8. It would be a fraud on government to employ Laundresses as Nurses." Ibid.

80. Cumming, *Kate*, 74, 192, 265. See also Simkins and Patton, "Work of Southern Women," 477, and News and Courier, *Our Women in the War*, 339.

81. Fannie Oslin Jackson, *On Both Sides*, 119.

82. For a description, see Wittenmyer's "Special Diet Kitchens," Box 13, Entry 740, Communications Received, 1862–65, Central Office, USCC, NARA, and Moss, *Annals of the United States Christian Commission*, 663–84. According to Elizabeth Leonard (*Yankee Women*, 92), Wittenmyer was aware of the low status attached to the label of "cook" and insisted that her workers be considered "managers."

83. See Pomroy, *Echoes*, 183–84.

84. See Roca, "Presence and Precedents."

85. Bradley Diary, June 11, 1862, DU.

86. Parsons, *Memoir*, 27, 58.

87. For evidence of nuns' custodial labor, see Sister Angela to Surgeon Ninian Pinkney, August 11, 1863, Pinkney Papers, LC, and Maher, *To Bind Up the Wounds*, 80–81. Although one of the Woolsey sisters noted that "whitewash and women on a hospital ship are both excellent disinfectants," it is not clear whether she meant that she herself performed heavy cleaning. Quoted in Bacon and Howland, *Letters of a Family*, 2:402. For more on the filthy condition of hospital ships, see Samuel McKinney Stafford to Abby Stafford, October 2, 1862, Stafford Papers, DU.

88. For evidence of contraband women carrying slops at Washington's Columbia College Hospital, see Pomroy, *Echoes*, 164.

89. Stearns, *Lady Nurse of Ward E*, 16, 24, 71. Jane Grey Swisshelm (*Crusader and Feminist*, 232) also described 18-hour days at Washington's Campbell Hospital in May 1863. The most serious cases in the Army of the Potomac were thought to land at Armory Square, where the mortality rate was a high 12.7 percent of admissions. *Medical and Surgical History*, 6:960.

90. Powers, *Hospital Pencillings*, 128.

91. Slave women helped tend the eight-acre garden at Clayton Hospital in Forsyth, Ga. See Davis, "Confederate Hospital." Kate Cumming (*Kate*, 70) reported that servants "do all the domestic work." Another elite white, Sarah Agnes Pryor (*Reminiscences*, 185), noted during the Seven Days battles that "efficient, kindly colored women assisted us."

92. See Marshall, "Nurse Heroines," 328. Janie Clarke, a nursing partner of Ada Bacot in Charlottesville, reported making candles at Midway Hospital. Clarke Diary, October 21, 22, 1862, DU.

93. Pember fired at least one ward matron for her alcoholism. It was customary for Confederate matrons to be in charge of the distribution of alcohol, which frequently put them at odds with stewards and surgeons. For the war over the whiskey barrel, see Pember, *Southern Woman's Story*, 6–7, 52, and News and Courier, *Our Women in the War*, 225.

94. For nurses who dispensed medicines, see, e.g., Stearns, *Lady Nurse of Ward E*, 16, 24, and Parsons, *Memoir*, 38. For those who dressed wounds, see, e.g., Eaton Diary, December 14, 1862, SHC-UNC; Bradley Diary, June 11, 1862, DU; and Morgan, *How It Was*, 107. For those who accompanied surgeons on rounds, see, e.g., Parsons, *Memoir*, 18, 20, and Von Olnhausen, *Adventures*, 123.

95. Amanda Rhoda Shelton Diary, May 23, 1864, SC-UI. See also Mason, "Memories," 315.

96. Powers, *Hospital Pencillings*, 123–24. For nurses who assisted in surgical operations, see, e.g., Newcomb, *Four Years*, 116; Beers, *Memories*, 90, 135–36; and Maher, *To Bind Up the Wounds*, 111.

97. The Dix Nursing Papers, NARA, contain many examples of women assigned to field hospitals, such as the depot hospital at City Point, Va., and the Sheridan field hospital in Winchester, Va. During General A. E. Burnside's expedition to North Carolina in 1862, the Union's Carrie Eliza Cutter worked in the field with the 21st Massachusetts, where her father, Calvin Cutter, was chief surgeon. See "Carrie Eliza Cutter, the Florence Nightingale of the 21st," n.d., Cutter Papers, Manuscript Division, LC. The Confederacy's Sallie Swope was in camp near Bristol, Va., as early as September 1861. See anonymous letter to Juliet Opie Hopkins, September 3, 1861, Hopkins Papers, ADAH.

98. See, e.g., Hobbs, "Excerpts from the Autobiography," and *Campaign of Mrs. Julia Silk*, 21–23. Confederate nurse Fannie Beers also foraged for food from a general hospital in Georgia late in the war. See Marshall, "Nurse Heroines," 322, 330.

99. See, e.g., G. T. Harrower to Hellen Harrower, June 23, 1863, Harrower Letters, LLMVC-LSU, and "Sister Anthony O'Connell," *NAW* 2:647–48.

100. At the request of Colonel Andrews, Hyatt carried wounded soldiers from Centerville to Fairfax Court House, a distance of eight miles, in August 1862. Holland, *Our Army Nurses*, 449–50. For other examples of nurses in the field encountering newly wounded men, see Eliza Chappell Porter's account of the battle of Sugar Creek, Ga., in May 1864, in Porter, *Memoir*, 190.

101. Barton, "Work and Incidents of Army Life," 1866, Barton Papers, LC.

102. Barton Diary, May 14, 1864, and miscellanies and speech fragments, ibid.

103. See Barton Papers, LC, and Elizabeth Brown Pryor, *Clara Barton*, 127.

104. Amy Morris Bradley to Sister, October 20, 1861, and Bradley Diary, October 7, 1861, Bradley Papers, DU.

105. Circular of April 3, 1863, Circulars and Circular Letters, USGO, NARA.

106. Circular of June 15, 1864, ibid.; Circular of August 27, 1864, Letters Received by Surgeon Lincoln R. Stone, USGO, NARA. White male nurses and cooks were to receive $24 per month, but at least some left the service because of the pay cut. See Kristie R. Ross, "'Women Are Needed Here,'" 111–12.

107. By April 1864 USCC agent Amanda Shelton was earning $20 per month, $2 more than government-paid women would have received after June 1864. See Amanda Rhoda Shelton Diary, April 16, 1864, SC-UI.

108. Ralph C. Gordon, "Nashville," 101.

109. Sarah A. Stevens et al. to Surgeon in Charge, Knight General Hospital, February 1, 1865, Dix Nursing Papers, NARA.

110. Emmeline D. Tenney to Dorothea Dix, January 28, 1865, ibid.

111. Ibid.; Hawks, *Woman Doctor's Civil War*, 211.

112. Hospital expenditures for November 1861–January 1862, Hopkins Papers, ADAH.

113. For the pay of Confederate women, see Simkins and Patton, *Women of the Confederacy*, 87, and Negroes Employed in Chimborazo No. 2, Medical Department List of Employees, Chimborazo Hospital No. 2, CSGO, NARA. For Confederate inflation, see, e.g., Cumming, *Journal of Hospital Life*, 200; Simkins and Patton, *Women of the Confederacy*, 129–31; and McPherson, *Battle Cry of Freedom*, 438–42.

114. Negroes Employed in Chimborazo No. 2, Medical Department List of Employees, Chimborazo Hospital No. 2, CSGO, NARA.

115. Alcott, *Louisa May Alcott*, 121. Alcott's tour of duty was cut short when she contracted typhoid.

116. Palmer, *Aunt Becky's Army Life*, 201. See also Dorothea Dix to Assistant Surgeon C. A. McCay, March 27, 1863, and Peter D. Bates to Surgeon General William Hammond, July 8, 1863, Letters Received, 1818–70, USGO, NARA.

117. Surgeon J. M. Bill to Surgeon General, February 6, 1863, Letters Received, 1818–70, USGO, NARA. See also George E. H. Lacy to Surgeon General, April 6, 1864, and Surgeon W. P. Daast to Surgeon General, June 22, August 25, 1864, ibid.

118. Surgeon E. B. Dalton to Brevet Lieutenant Colonel T. A. McPailin, December 4, 1864, and Superintendent J. W. Brinckerhoff to Brigadier General L. Thomas, July 25, 1865, Letters Received, 1818–70, USGO, NARA. See also Mary Phinney von Olnhausen's account of "destitute" black workers who had not been paid in Von Olnhausen, *Adventures*, 161.

119. Assistant Surgeon C. D. Dally to Surgeon General, November 5, 1863; Surgeon Z. E. Bliss to Surgeon General Joseph K. Barnes, March 23, 1865; and Surgeon E. W. Baily to Surgeon General, November 2, 1863, Letters Received, 1818–70, USGO, NARA. On pay irregularities for laundresses in the field, see Wendel, "Washer Women," 35.

120. See, e.g., Surgeon B. B. Breed to Surgeon General William Hammond, June 11, 1863, Letters Received, 1818–70, USGO, NARA, and Assistant Medical Director Sanford B. Hunt to Surgeon Lincoln R. Stone, June 4, 1864, Letters Received by Stone, USGO, NARA.

121. Mary Phinney von Olnhausen and Phoebe Yates Pember were two of many widows obliged to support themselves. See Agnes Brooks Young, *Women and the Crisis*, 193, and Pember, *Southern Woman's Story*.

122. See, e.g., Sarah Walker to Dorothea Dix, September 29, 1862, Dix Nursing Papers, NARA, and Mrs. N. Tinkham to "Secretary of the Christian Commission," November 28, 1864, Communications Received, 1862–65, Central Office, USCC, NARA (quotation).

123. For evidence of surgeons' preference for volunteer nurses, see, e.g., Surgeon D. W. Bliss to Surgeon General Hammond, February 11, 28, 1863, Letters Received, 1818–70, USGO, NARA; "Sarah Low," 4; and Parsons, *Memoir*, 44. For the pay of religious orders, see Barton, *Angels of the Battlefield*, 182–83.

124. Newcomb, *Four Years*, 34; McKay, *Stories*, 104.

125. Bradley Diary, July 7, 1862, DU.

126. Clara Barton to Commissioner D. P. Holloway, December 11, 1863, Barton Papers, LC.

127. News and Courier, *Our Women in the War*, 222; Beers, *Memories*, 126; Marshall, "Nurse Heroines" (on Tompkins), 325; Newcomb, *Four Years*, 95; Bacon and Howland, *Letters of a Family*, 2:550. For examples of nurses returning their wages to soldiers, see accounts of the Sisters of St. Joseph of Wheeling, W.Va., and the Holy Cross Sisters who earned fifty cents a day for service aboard the *Red Rover*, in Maher, *To Bind Up the Wounds*, 78, 91, 93.

## Chapter Two

1. Mary Elizabeth Massey (*Bonnet Brigades*, 44) was the first to note that nursing work provided women the opportunity to be useful outside of the home. See also more recent commentary in Faust, *Mothers of Invention*, 98–102, and Rable, *Civil Wars*, 121.

2. See, e.g., Conner et al., *South Carolina Women*, and Anderson, *North Car-*

*olina Women*. Both authors enumerate the contributions of every aid society in their respective state. See also Culpepper, *Trials and Triumphs*, chap. 7.

3. Attie, *Patriotic Toil*, 4. Attie limits her discussion to the Northern home front, though it could well apply to Confederate constructions of patriotism. See also *Charleston Courier*, July 16, 1863; *Charleston Mercury*, July 30, 1863; and Kate Whitebread to Juliet Opie Hopkins, June 10, 1861, Hopkins Papers, ADAH. Whitebread mentions seeing in Suffolk, Va., Hopkins's call for female nurses. Northern relief efforts also depended on the press to get the word out. In 1861 Clara Barton advertised for supplies for Union soldiers in the *Worcester Spy*. See Elizabeth Brown Pryor, *Clara Barton*, 81, and Endres, "Women's Press," 31–32, 37. See also "To the Patriotic Women of New Haven and Vicinity," Schlesinger Library, Cambridge. After Union seizure of the Sea Islands in 1862, the newly formed Freedman's Relief Association (FRA) circulated an announcement requesting women to start sewing circles and to send clothes for 15,000 contrabands among whom the "destitution" was "great." See FRA circular of February 22, 1862, Hawks Papers, LC.

4. Scales, "Civil War Letters," 170. See also Faust, *Mothers of Invention*, 20.

5. Cordelia Lewis Scales to Loulie, August 17, 1861, Scales Letters, MDAH.

6. Quoted in Holland, *Our Army Nurses*, 467.

7. Ibid., 315. Adelaide W. Smith (*Reminiscences*, 260) expressed a similar sentiment: "If I had been a man, I would have enlisted as a soldier." See also Culpepper, *Trials and Triumphs*, 23–24.

8. Quoted in Conner et al., *South Carolina Women*, 173.

9. James McPherson has argued that duty, honor, and patriotism motivated men who enlisted in the first two years of the war. See McPherson, *For Cause and Comrades*, esp. chaps. 1, 2.

10. Bucklin, *In Hospital and Camp*, 33–34, 47.

11. Holstein, *Three Years*, 10; Mildred Duckworth to Juliet Opie Hopkins, November 11, 1861, Hopkins Papers, ADAH; Alcott, *Louisa May Alcott*, 115; Ropes, *Civil War Nurse*, 29. See also Miss M. A. Ball to George Stuart, August 11, 1864, Communications Received, 1862–65, Central Office, USCC, NARA.

12. Susan E. D. Smith, *Soldier's Friend*, 49; *Campaign of Mrs. Julia Silk*, 5.

13. Faust, "Altars of Sacrifice," 1228.

14. Bacot Diary, December 12, 1860, SCL-USC.

15. Newsom, *Florence Nightingale of the Southern Army*, 58.

16. See W. M. Green to Juliet Opie Hopkins, October 8, 1862, Hopkins Papers, ADAH. In fact, women in both sections were frank about needing the money. Julia Silk of Ann Arbor, Mich., explained that because her "circumstances in life were very moderate," she "was willing to lend [her] assistance as far as lay in [her] power for whatever remuneration might be judged sufficient recompense for [her] services." *Campaign of Mrs. Julia Silk*, 5.

17. Phoebe Yates Pember to Eugenia Levy Phillips, September 13, 1863, Phillips Papers, LC. In spite of Pember's sensitivity on the subject, some historians

have argued that it became more acceptable in the South during the war for middle-class women to seek paid work. See, e.g., Faust, *Mothers of Invention*, 80, and Culpepper, *Trials and Triumphs*, 237.

18. A friend of Esther Hill Hawks admired her for the danger she imagined Hawks was in. See Amanda Harris to Esther Hill Hawks, March 28, 1864, Hawks Papers, LC.

19. Bucklin, *In Hospital and Camp*, 23. Women like Sarah Emma Edmonds or Belle Boyd, who wrote sensational narratives, were among those chastised for their "daring exploits" during the war.

20. Smith (*Soldier's Friend*, 295) lambasted a nurse who was in service "only for the doctors to play with."

21. Many social and medical histories of nineteenth-century health care institutions draw this conclusion. See, e.g., Rothman, *Discovery of the Asylum*; Starr, *Social Transformation*; and Pernick, *Calculus of Suffering*.

22. Cumming, *Kate*, 16, 18, 66.

23. Victoria Bynum (*Unruly Women*, 8) has argued that more potent patriarchal authority in the South was embedded in the home because it was, unlike the North, "the locus of economic production." See also Anne Firor Scott, *Southern Lady*; Rable, *Civil Wars*; Campbell and Rice, *Woman's War*, 77–78; and Fox-Genovese, *Within the Plantation Household*.

24. Cumming, *Kate*, 136.

25. Ibid., 178. For more on the hesitation of elite Southern women to serve as nurses, see Clinton, *Tara Revisited*, 82–85, and Faust, *Mothers of Invention*, 109.

26. Faust, *Mothers of Invention*, 107, 109.

27. Mason, "Memories," 480. Ada Bacot, Fannie Beers, Juliet Opie Hopkins, Ella Newsom, Sally Tompkins, Louisa McCord, and even Cumming and Pember themselves present plenty of evidence that they served alongside social peers.

28. Phoebe Yates Pember to Eugenia Levy Phillips, September 13, 1863, Phillips Papers, LC.

29. Pember, *Southern Woman's Story*, 146.

30. For a succinct discussion of how Southern society received nursing hopefuls, see Faust, "Altars of Sacrifice," 1214–16. Faust argues that women who chose to nurse were labeled masculine and thus sexually deviant.

31. Beers, *Memories*, 34–35, 39, 61. For evidence of opposition to young women's service, see, e.g., Simkins and Patton, *Women of the Confederacy*.

32. Lizzie D. Lewis to Juliet Opie Hopkins, June 11, 24, 1861, Hopkins Papers, ADAH. Hopkins advertised for female volunteers in the June 10, 1861, issue of the *Richmond Dispatch*.

33. Newsom, *Florence Nightingale of the Southern Army*, 93.

34. Sizer (*Political Work*, 96) argues that, in *Hospital Sketches*, Nurse Periwinkle's "playful" tone was calculated to ease home front anxiety.

35. John Lynch to Bessie Mustin, August 9, 1862, Lynch Letters, Historical Society of Pennsylvania, Philadelphia; Mary Shelton Diary, July 2, 1864, SC-UI;

Elizabeth Tuttle Letter, March 11, 1863, LL-IU. See also material on Indiana's Bettie Bates, a well-to-do woman who left home only at her father's consent, in Merrill, *Soldier of Indiana*, 254.

36. Clara Barton to Elvira Stone, [November or December] 1863, Barton Papers, LC.

37. Elizabeth Brown Pryor, *Clara Barton*, 83, 96; Oates, *Woman of Valor*, 41, 50.

38. Daly (*Diary of a Union Lady*, 131, 173) reported, "I had almost determined to go, but finding that others of more experience had volunteered, and having little or no experience myself in taking care of the sick, I did not offer myself."

39. Harriet Terry to Harriet Foote Hawley, January 5, 1863, and Kate Foote to Hawley, June 14, 1864, Hawley Papers, LC. Katharine Prescott Wormeley (*Other Side of the War*, 36) noted that a friend's mother looked at her disapprovingly for working.

40. Parsons, *Memoir*, 67–68. Emily Bliss Souder (*Leaves*, 19) wrote in the same vein to her husband Edward from Gettysburg: "We all feel sure that if you could see the terrible need here of women's hands, you would all feel quite satisfied that we are here."

41. *Harper's Weekly*, September 6, 1862, 568–69. Alice Fahs (*Imagined Civil War*, 140) draws a similar conclusion about public approval of female nursing by 1862.

42. Hoge, *Boys in Blue*, 111. Charles Peterson, editor of a popular women's magazine, concurred: "Nothing in the history of this war, is nobler than the devotion of women to the hospitals." Quoted in Endres, "Women's Press," 42.

43. George F. Allen to Adjutant General Allen C. Fuller, September 21, 1863, Bickerdyke Papers, LC. See also the 1866 report of the Indiana Sanitary Commission in Peggy Brase Seigel, "She Went to War," 24, which indicates that "the earlier prejudice against women nurses had greatly disappeared" by midwar.

44. Women like Cornelia Hancock and Emily Bliss Souder traveled without sanction to Gettysburg but later found official positions when they had proved their worth as workers.

45. Mary Ann Bickerdyke was sent by a church-run ladies' aid in Galesburg, Ill., and later became an agent of the Northwest Sanitary Commission.

46. See, e.g., pension files of Nancy Dodson Carter (#1416752), Maria Bear Toliver (#1161879), and Minerva Dillard Washington (#1330575), all of whom were contraband workers, in OIPF.

47. Agnes Brooks Young (*Women and the Crisis*, 96) notes that Union regiments could take two women as matrons and up to four more as cooks and laundresses. On Sarah Sampson, see MacCaskill and Novak, *Ladies on the Field*, 51–53.

48. See Millbrook, "Michigan Women Who Went to War," 13.

49. John W. Bell to Nancy Bell, June 15, 1862, Bell Papers, LLMVC-LSU. For evidence of other Confederate women joining regiments, see the account of Mrs. Johnson Hagood of Barnwell, S.C., in Conner et al., *South Carolina Women*, 2:51. For a detailed description of laundry equipment, see Wendel, "Washer Women," 35.

50. Constant Hanks to Mary Rose, September 26, 1862, Hanks Papers, DU.

51. See Lucy Campbell Kaiser's account of a stowaway she met on the way to Pittsburg Landing (Tenn.) who agreed to become laundress for her husband's regiment in exchange for food, in Holland, *Our Army Nurses*, 183.

52. Glymph, "'This Species of Property,'" 63.

53. Taylor, *Reminiscences*, 26, 21, 17. Julia Silk (*Campaign of Mrs. Julia Silk*, 6–7) of the 23rd Illinois and Clarissa Gear Hobbs ("Excerpts from the Autobiography," n.p.) of the 12th Iowa also emphasized their nursing activities.

54. Higginson, *Life in a Black Regiment*, 192. Thavolia Glymph ("'This Species of Property,'" 61) reports that six African American husbands and wives attempting to escape to Union gunboats were caught by Confederate forces and hanged.

55. Newcomb, *Four Years*, 37. Mary Logan (*Reminiscences*, 50–51) performed similar duty for her husband John's 31st Illinois, which came down with measles in camp at Cairo in 1861.

56. Forbes, *African American Women*, 45, from the *Christian Recorder*, July 22, 1865; Holland, *Our Army Nurses*, 277–79.

57. Godfrey also had four brothers in the regiment. See Eunice Norton Godfrey Mahaffey pension file (#478192), OIPF.

58. On Sullivan and Taylor, see Andrews, *Women of the South*, 112–16, 121–25. For Horne, see Conklin, *Women at Gettysburg*, 36–40. On Rose Rooney, an Irish immigrant to the United States in the 1840s who spent the war with the 15th Louisiana, see Beers, *Memories*, 217–20.

59. In particular, Annie Etheridge and Bridget Divers, also called "Irish Biddy," were known throughout the North for their courage and endurance. See Agnes Brooks Young, *Women and the Crisis*, 94–95, 113; and Moore, *Women of the War*, 513–18, 533–35.

60. Testimonial to Catherine Oliphant, September 8, 1865, Oliphant Papers, LC. Harriet Patience Dame was equally popular with the 2nd New Hampshire and shared its fortunes for fifty-six months, including capture by Confederate pickets in 1862. See Dame pension file (#279717), PSAC.

61. See Wheelock, *Boys in White*, 32. Alice Fahs (*Imagined Civil War*, 139–41) notes the representation of bereaved women turning to work in the popular literature of the time.

62. Stearns, *Lady Nurse*, 116. See also Hoge, *Boys in Blue*, 244, 268–69; Parsons, *Memoir*, 88; and Holland, *Our Army Nurses*, 111.

63. John D. St. John to Mr. and Mrs. St. John, March 26–27, 1862, St. John Papers, LC. For an account of other women caught in camp during the battle, see Agnes Brooks Young, *Women and the Crisis*, 167.

64. Susan E. D. Smith, *Soldier's Friend*, 57–60. Julia Morgan (*How It Was*) of Nashville went to her husband after he was wounded at Chickamauga in 1863 and transported him to Marietta, Ga., where family members were refugees. Morgan worked in Confederate hospitals in Georgia for the rest of the war.

65. Coker, *Story of the Civil War*.

66. Fanny Ricketts Diary, July 25–December 17, 1861, Manassas National Battlefield Park, Manassas, Va.

67. See, e.g., the response of Clara Barton to the offer of Nancy Willmartts. Clara Barton to Elvira Stone, n.d. [November or December], 1863, Barton Papers, LC.

68. See Sarah Low's ("Sarah Low," 4) recommendation to a friend to have "some responsible gentlemen to recommend you."

69. Mary J. Jordan to Hannah Carlisle, May 27, 1863, Carlisle Family Papers, MHC-UM.

70. Kate Whitebread to Juliet Opie Hopkins, June 10, 1861, and Lizzie D. Lewis to Hopkins, June 11, 1861, Hopkins Papers, ADAH.

71. Though men usually recommended experienced nurses, occasionally a woman in a prominent position would. See, e.g., Dorothea Dix to Surgeon General R. C. Wood, April 9, 1862, Letters Received, 1818–70, USGO, NARA.

72. Fannie Oslin Jackson, *On Both Sides*, 62.

73. N. McGowan to George A. Stuart, August 10, 1864, Communications Received, 1862–65, Central Office, USCC, NARA.

74. Edward L. Clark to Rev. Mr. Boardman, November 13, 1864, ibid.

75. Letter of introduction from John M. Cuyler to Dr. Palmer, n.d., Beck Papers, SHC-UNC. For other examples, see Horace L. Barnes to "Whom It May Concern," n.d., Dix Nursing Papers, NARA, and reference of Rev. Benjamin Excell quoted in Mrs. C. A. Briggs to J. K. Barnes, November 14, 1864, Letters Received, 1818–70, USGO, NARA.

76. Swisshelm, *Crusader and Feminist*, 250; see also 253. For evidence of applicants writing to established nurses, see Tisler, "War Time Diary of Mrs. Sarah Gregg," February 11, 1864, ISHL, and A. W. Knight to Mary Ann Bickerdyke, October 10, 1863, Bickerdyke Papers, LC. Having received a form letter rejection from James Yeatman, Knight wrote to Bickerdyke asking for more specific information about where nurses were needed.

77. See Miss M. Bruce to President Lincoln, December 25, 1863, Dix Nursing Papers, NARA. A Stockton, Ga., woman began with the chief executive of her state, asking him to assign her to the 12th Georgia Infantry. See Mrs. Emily Bostick to Gov. Joseph Brown, June 16, 1862, GDAH.

78. Mrs. Nathan Tinkham to "the Secretary of the Christian Commission," November 28, 1864, Communications Received, 1862–65, Central Office, USCC, NARA.

79. Acting Surgeon George E. Brickett to Amy Morris Bradley, August 3, 1861, and Surgeon G. S. Palmer to Bradley, August 11, 1861, Bradley Papers, DU. Even experienced nurses could not count on obtaining new work. An orphaned and widowed schoolteacher who referred to herself as a "Veteran Army Nurse" begged the Union surgeon general to reassign her to "some place of usefulness, *however humble*," after her assignment at Division No. 1 Hospital in Annapolis had ended. See Mrs. P. A. Bortell to Surgeon General, January 15, 1864, Dix Nursing Papers, NARA.

80. H. J. Alvord to Alpheus Felch, regarding Miss Alm[en]dinger, September 15, 1862, Felch Papers, MHC-UM. A form letter from the Western Sanitary Commission explained to another hopeful that "in the meantime, your name and address will be entered in a book . . . and your recommendations preserved, so that, should your services be needed hereafter, you can be notified." J. G. Forman to Mrs. A. M. Latham, January 25, 1864, Dix Nursing Papers, NARA. Even in the war's first months, Superintendent Dix had been compelled to rescind her order for volunteers due to the multitude of applicants. See Giesberg, *Civil War Sisterhood*, 35.

81. Mary Smith Reid to Robert Reid, July 14, 1862, Reid Letters, Swann Family Papers, SHC-UNC.

82. Bacot Diary, November 17, 1861, August 31, 1863, SCL-USC.

83. Newsom, *Florence Nightingale of the Southern Army*, 16.

84. See L. A. Hayward to Mary Ann Bickerdyke, April 5, 1865, Bickerdyke Papers, LC. For women who left babies with others, see the accounts of Estelle Johnson, who left a one-year-old daughter with relatives before joining the 4th Vermont, in Holland, *Our Army Nurses*, 208, and of Julia Silk, who left her one-year-old son with her mother before joining the 23rd Illinois, in Silk, *Campaign of Mrs. Julia Silk*, 6. Amanda Farnham and Matilda E. Morris also left children with relatives. See Holland, *Our Army Nurses*, 283, 391.

85. Livermore, *Story of My Life*, 471. Wendy Hamand Venet ("Emergence of a Suffragist," 144) has recently suggested that Livermore's obedience to convention would lessen during the course of the war.

86. Dorothea Dix to Surgeon General, April 14, 1865, Letters Received, 1818–70, USGO, NARA. Mrs. Spaulding left a fourth son stationed with the Army of the Potomac. Thirty-nine-year-old Hannah Carlisle, a mother of two, was called home from her post in Columbus, Ky., when her house in Buchanan, Mich., burned down. Just as urgent was the news of a sick child, which took Mary Banning and Julia Tompkins from the service. See Mary Banning to Dorothea Dix, October 19, 1864, Dix Nursing Papers, NARA, and Holland, *Our Army Nurses*, 107.

87. Pomroy, *Echoes*, 185–86; David Cumming to Kate Cumming, May 25, 1863, Cumming Papers, ADAH.

88. See Fannie Oslin Jackson, *On Both Sides*, 66. Annie Chamberlin, "the baby of the regiment," was the much petted daughter of the quartermaster in the 1st South Carolina Infantry. Higginson, *Life in a Black Regiment*, 139–47, and *Complete Civil War Journal*, 17. Nurse Periwinkle also expressed affection for the children of black laundresses at Hurly-Burly House (Union Hotel Hospital). See Alcott, *Hospital Sketches*, 59.

89. Parsons, *Memoir*, 62.

90. Fannie Oslin Jackson, *On Both Sides*, 63.

91. Kate M. Scott, *In Honor of . . . Army Nurses*; Pomroy, *Echoes*, 185–86; Ralph C. Gordon, "Nashville," 108. From her Union post in Paducah, Ky., Mrs. A. N. Stearns lamented that out of the eighteen months she had been in service, her young son Henry had "suffered during one whole year with Diarrhoea." Fan-

nie Beers left her post in Richmond to seek the aid of Confederate relatives when her son contracted typhoid. Mrs. A. N. Stearns to Mary Ann Bickerdyke, February [n.d.], 1864, Bickerdyke Papers, LC; Beers, *Memories*, 13; Marshall, "Nurse Heroines," 329. Alabama's Amelia Gayle Gorgas complained that constant attention to her seven children's ailments abbreviated the time she was able to spend with wounded soldiers after the battle of Chancellorsville. Josiah Gorgas to Amelia Gayle Gorgas, May 9, 1863, Gorgas Papers, WSHSC-UA.

92. According to James McPherson (*Battle Cry of Freedom*, 12), there were 9,000 railroad miles in the United States before 1850 and 21,000 after 1860. Although she does not address out-of-town travel per se, Mary Ryan (*Women in Public*, esp. chap. 2) argues that women occupied public space during the early nineteenth century, especially as urban planners created public spaces with women in mind. See also Schriber, "Julia Ward Howe."

93. Rable, *Civil Wars*, 51.

94. Pember, *Southern Woman's Story*, 112. Another Confederate observer reported that "after the war began, we thought nothing of scuffling along single-handed." News and Courier, *Our Women in the War*, 165.

95. See, e.g., Ella Reeve to Juliet Opie Hopkins, August 2, 1861, Hopkins Papers, ADAH. Reeve offered services, adding that her brother was willing to accompany her on the trip as chaperone.

96. Cumming, *Kate*, 51, 90.

97. Stearns, *Lady Nurse*, 67.

98. Alcott, *Hospital Sketches*, 12–13. Gail Hamilton (*Country Living*, 91) expressed a similarly bemused attitude about a man who purportedly escorted her during the war: "I was currently reported to be traveling *under the care* of Mr. Lakeman of Alabama; as if I couldn't take care of myself fifty thousand times better than that respectable stupidity could."

99. Powers, *Hospital Pencillings*, 2–3, 6–7.

100. G. S. Blodgett to M. C. Meigs, December 13, 1862, Lydia Pierce to Dorothea Dix, November 15, 1862, January 5, February 19, 1863, and "Report," n.d., Consolidated Correspondence File, 1794–1915, Quartermaster General's Office, NARA. Hannah Carlisle also had difficulty proving that she had served under legitimate authority and was denied transportation home after the war. See Hannah Carlisle to Daniel Carlisle, June 30, 1865, Carlisle Family Papers, MHC-UM.

101. See, e.g., Dorothea Dix communiqués to Quartermaster General, July 22, 24, 28, 1862, February 14, 1863, Consolidated Correspondence File, 1794–1915, Quartermaster General's Office, NARA; and Dix communiqués to Surgeon General, March 12, 1865, April 7, 10, 12, 14, 1865, Letters Received, 1818–70, USGO, NARA.

102. Haviland (*Woman's Life-Work*, 249–50, 268–69) noted that for relief workers operating alone, it was next to impossible to secure transportation. On laundress Caroline Steuber, of the 2nd Missouri, who fell ill at Camp Halleck in Rolla and needed transportation to St. Louis, see Report 867 1/2, Reports and Correspondence Regarding Contracts for Nurses, 1861–65, AGO, NARA.

103. Baker, *Cyclone in Calico*, 9–10; Fannie Oslin Jackson, *On Both Sides*, 127.

104. Mary Smith Reid to Robert R. Reid, July 14, 1862, Reid Letters, Swann Family Papers, SHC-UNC. Reid was funded by the Florida Soldiers' Relief Committee and the Lake City Aid Society, which gave her fifty dollars.

105. Marshall, "Nurse Heroines," 332; Cumming, *Kate*, 294; testimony of Susan E. D. Smith (*Soldier's Friend*, 185), who was stranded at war's end at Hill Hospital in Cuthbert, Ga.

106. See, e.g., Dorothea Dix to Surgeon General, August 10, 1865, Letters Received, 1818–70, USGO, NARA. In this letter, Dix requested transportation for Mrs. Phebe Miller from Washington to Keokuk, Iowa, a distance of 850 miles. Massachusetts native Emily Parsons traveled from hospitals in New York Harbor to her main post for the rest of the war in St. Louis, a distance of just under 1,000 miles.

107. See Dorothea Dix to Assistant Surgeon General Crane regarding Mrs. Ransom, March 16, 1865, Letters Received, 1818–70, USGO, NARA. For Ransom's account of the sinking of the *North America*—in which 194 of the 203 disabled soldiers on board perished—see Holland, *Our Army Nurses*, 511–14.

108. Phoebe Yates Pember frequently spoke of traveling by ambulance. Emily Bliss Souder daily rode four miles in an ambulance from her quarters to the Gettysburg hospitals. See Pember to Lou Gilmer, October 20, 1863, Pember Letters, SHC-UNC, and Souder, *Leaves*, 38–39.

109. See Newcomb, *Four Years*, 117, and Von Olnhausen, *Adventures*, 195. See also Charlotte McKay's (*Stories*, 50–51) description of a several days' journey from Washington to Gettysburg in a supply wagon.

110. See Glymph, "'This Species of Property,'" 64.

111. Barton Diary, January 1, 1863 (quotation), and Barton, "Work and Incidents," 1866, Barton Papers, LC; Elizabeth Brown Pryor, *Clara Barton*, 78–80. Matilda E. Morris of Randolph, Ohio, also encountered trouble when the train in which she was riding to Washington stopped unexpectedly in Wheeling, W.Va.—Rebel ambushes were reported farther down the line. See Holland, *Our Army Nurses*, 391–92.

112. Eaton Diary, October 19, 1862, SHC-UNC.

113. Eaton Diary, November 20, 1862, February 3, 1863, SHC-UNC.

114. Nurse Periwinkle is Alcott's fictionalized self in *Hospital Sketches* (1863).

## Chapter Three

1. Bradley Diary, June 29, 1862, DU.

2. Ella Wolcott to Harriet Foote Hawley, March 27, 1864, Hawley Papers, LC.

3. Powers, *Hospital Pencillings*, 137.

4. Barton Diary, April 22, 23, 1863, Barton Papers, LC. Six weeks later (Diary, June 8, 1863), her tune had not changed: "I fear I may be spending time to little purpose, no one really needs me here."

5. Holstein, *Three Years*, 11, 67. See also Mrs. L. Tilton to Mary Ann Bickerdyke, December 20, 1863, Bickerdyke Papers, LC. Tilton wrote: "Grateful to us! I could weep whenever a wounded soldier thanks me for any favor. Do we not owe every blessing we possess, next to God, to the brave men who are defending our homes, and securing by suffering and self-sacrifice all that renders those homes dear to us?"

6. Bradley Diary, June 11, 1862, DU.

7. Katharine M. Jones, *Heroines of Dixie*, 103 (McDonald); Sarah Agnes Pryor, *Reminiscences*, 181–82; Beers, *Memories*, 45.

8. Stearns, *Lady Nurse*, 255, 82. En route from New Orleans to Cairo, Laura Haviland (*Woman's Life-Work*, 343) was moved by the stoicism of soldiers having their wounds dressed: "It was hard to restrain tears in their presence, but we gave vent to them when in our state-room." See also Palmer, *Aunt Becky's Army Life*, 46.

9. Alcott, *Hospital Sketches*, 67.

10. Swisshelm, *Crusader and Feminist*, 263.

11. For evidence of church services in Armory Square Hospital, see Stearns, *Lady Nurse*, 38.

12. Pomroy, *Echoes*, 14, 25; Eaton Diary, November 27, 1862, SHC-UNC; Mary E. Shelton Diary, January 9, 1865, SC-UI.

13. News and Courier, *Our Women in the War*, 6. See also Mason, "Memories," 477.

14. Lawrence, *Autobiography*, 98–99. Judith Brockenbrough McGuire, Eudora Clark, and Jane Merrill Ketcham regularly read the Bible to patients. Another Confederate nurse recited the Lord's Prayer in French to a francophone soldier. Andrews, *Women of the South*, 157; Clark, "Hospital Memories," 329, 331; News and Courier, *Our Women in the War*, 250–51. For women administering last rites to soldiers, see Parsons, *Memoir*, 57; Beers, *Memories*, 85; News and Courier, *Our Women in the War*, 302; and Faust, *Mothers of Invention*, 185–86.

15. Haviland, *Woman's Life-Work*, 281 (first quotation); Barton, *Angels of the Battlefield*, 46; Bradley Diary, June 11, 1862, DU; Pomroy, *Echoes*, 129–30, 147–48, 237. For more on nurses' role in deathbed conversions, see *Notes of Hospital Life*, 41, 63–66, 88.

16. Eaton Diary, October 18, 1862, December 3, 4, 6, 1864, SHC-UNC. On another occasion, Eaton wrote after the baptism of three soldiers, "Oh! how thankful I am and shall be to all eternity that I came here." November 28, 1864., ibid.

17. Quoted from the O'Keefe narrative in Conklin, *Women at Gettysburg*, 217–18. See also Faust, "Christian Soldiers."

18. Cumming, *Kate*, 26; Porter, *Memoir*, 163; Harriet Foote Hawley to Cousin Belle, May 31, 1864, Hawley Papers, LC.

19. Bucklin, *In Hospital and Camp*, 146; Souder, *Leaves*, 31, 34; Tisler, "War Time Diary of Mrs. Sarah Gregg," June 5, 1863, ISHL. Union nurse Elizabeth Tuttle dissented from the pack at Gettysburg, praising Rebel soldiers for being "a great deal better behaved than our men both after they became prisoners and in

traveling through Pennsylvania and Maryland on the march with their own army." Tuttle letter, July 22, 1863, LL-IU.

20. Von Olnhausen, *Adventures*, 81. Harriet Whetten ("Volunteer Nurse," 141) admitted her fear of Rebel patients: "To tell the truth I was frightened. I could be alone with hundreds of our men and feel safe and happy, but these fellows looked different." Ohioan Matilda Morris was ordered to care for Rebels at Winchester, "but deep in my heart," she confessed, "I could not feel the same." Quoted in Holland, *Our Army Nurses*, 391.

21. Beers, *Memories*, 158–59.

22. Andrews, *Women of the South*, 105–11; Fannie Oslin Jackson, *On Both Sides*, 49; News and Courier, *Our Women in the War*, 227.

23. Wheelock, *Boys in White*, 205. During the Seven Days battles of 1862, Mrs. E. C. Kent, of Cincinnati, forbidden from aiding Union soldiers, was incensed when she observed Confederate military personnel selling bread and water to them. Ella Wolcott, a Union nurse, was barred from entering Rebel wards at Point Lookout, Md., in February 1865. See Kent, *Four Years in Secessia*, 15, and Wolcott to Dorothea Dix, February 16, 1865, Dix Nursing Papers, NARA.

24. Bradley Diary, June 11, 1862, DU.

25. For the account of Southern parents, see McKay, *Stories*, 120. Among Northerners who believed that Southern men were treated well in Union hospitals were Jane Hoge (*Boys in Blue*, 42), Eliza Chappell Porter (*Memoir*, 215), Eliza Woolsey Howland (Bacon and Howland, *Letters of a Family*, 2:407–8), and Abby Hopper Gibbons (*Life*, 1:316). Northern women also claimed that Rebel prisoners returning to Richmond on exchange spoke of being more kindly treated in Northern hospitals than in their own. See Kent, *Four Years in Secessia*, 14.

26. Cumming, *Kate*, 15, 283. Sophie Bibb of Montgomery and Kate Kern of Winchester, Tenn., insisted that enemy soldiers received equal treatment; Kern even established a correspondence with the mother of a Yankee soldier who had died in her presence. See Clinton, *Tara Revisited*, 83–84.

27. See Barton, *Angels of the Battlefield*, 98–99, 390–92. The Holy Cross sisters of St. Mary's, Ind., were not permitted to serve aboard the *Red Rover* until a time and place for daily devotions could be secured. See Sister Angela to Surgeon Ninian Pinkney, August 11, 1863, Pinkney Papers, LC. See also Georgeanna Woolsey's account of the Sisters of Charity, idle at White House Landing in June 1862, in Bacon and Howland, *Letters of a Family*, 2:426.

28. Emily Bliss Souder stayed in a private home near Gettysburg. Fannie Oslin Jackson rented a room in a house near the Union tent hospital outside Atlanta where she worked in the summer of 1864. Phoebe Yates Pember stayed in the attic of a private residence in Richmond without heat, light, or a carpet but paid monthly rent of sixty dollars. Surgeon John H. Brinton replaced his U.S. Army nurses with fifteen Sisters of Mercy whom he boasted would all sleep in one room. See Souder, *Leaves*, 14; Fannie Oslin Jackson, *On Both Sides*, 72; Phoebe Yates Pember to Lou Gilmer, October 20, 1863, Pember Letters, SHC-UNC; and Brinton, *Personal Memoirs*, 44–45.

29. Amanda Akin Stearns (*Lady Nurse*, 160) spoke with fondness of a house built next to Armory Square especially for female nurses.

30. Parsons, *Memoir*, 32.

31. See Ropes, *Civil War Nurse*, 39–40. New Hampshire's Sarah Low ("Sarah Low," 3) also commented on the poor ventilation and unsanitary conditions. Morning reports from the Clayton Hospital in Forsyth, Ga., noted that slops were thrown out of the kitchen windows, making the hospital grounds rank. See Davis, "Confederate Hospital."

32. Cumming, *Kate*, 146, 120. For Ella Newsom's account of sleeping in a private home after Shiloh, see Andrews, *Women of the South*, 135–36. For administrative correspondence regarding women's accommodations, see Acting Surgeon A. C. Bournonville to Medical Director W. S. King, August 12, 1862, and Surgeon William M. Breed to Surgeon General William Hammond, August 14, 1862, Letters Received, 1818–70, USGO, NARA.

33. Colonel B. O. Fry to Juliet Opie Hopkins, February 5, 1862, and Surgeon Q. M. Williams to Hopkins, March 19, 26, 1862, Hopkins Papers, ADAH.

34. Powers, *Hospital Pencillings*, 52, 157, 121; Parsons, *Memoir*, 28–29, 83. A pet cat at Benton Barracks was treated to a daily eggnog, but a Newfoundland retriever at Point of Rocks Hospital had to work for its food by ferrying baskets of meat to the cook. See Bucklin, *In Hospital and Camp*, 355–56. For other evidence of hospital pets, see Hoge, *Boys in Blue*, 217; *Notes of Hospital Life*, 187; and "Sarah Low," 9–10.

35. Alcott, *Hospital Sketches*, 50; Eaton Diary, October 21, 1862, SHC-UNC.

36. Clara Barton to Mary Norton, June 26, 1863, Norton Papers, DU. For the Union plunder of the Sea Islands, see Esther Hill Hawks to Soldiers Aid Society, November 26, 1862, Hawks Papers, LC.

37. Bradley Diary, September 15, 1861, DU.

38. E. W. Johns to Juliet Opie Hopkins, August 7, 1861, Hopkins Papers, ADAH; Phoebe Yates Pember to Lou Gilmer, December 30, 1863, February 19, 1864, Pember Letters, SHC-UNC. See also Cumming, *Kate*, 67–68, 73.

39. See Cumming, *Kate*, 248. Southern citizens fared no better, of course. For a complete account of Southern wartime shortages, see Massey, *Ersatz in the Confederacy*.

40. Clara Barton, "Work and Incidents," n.p., Barton Papers, LC; Eaton Diary, May 6, 1863, November 5, 1862, SHC-UNC. Barton would probably have taken a rain-soaked tent over no tent at all, however, as an incident from 1864 seems to bear out. A Massachusetts surgeon, "too indolent to provide comfortable quarters for himself," got a quartermaster to requisition Barton's tent, leaving her "at the mercy of the elements" for the night. Barton Diary, April 7, 1864, LC. Eaton became so accustomed to sleeping in a new place every night that she found it worth noting when she had the luxury of a bed. See also Hoge, *Boys in Blue*, 310; Cumming, *Kate*, 93; and Dannett, *Noble Women*, 170.

41. Mary Livermore quoted in Hoge, *Boys in Blue*, 270; Maria Mann to Eliza, February 10, 1863, Mann Papers, LC. The mud at Belle Plain, Va., was so deep in

December 1862 that two hundred ambulances carrying the wounded of Fredericksburg were sunk up to the wheel hulls, and "you saw nothing of any animal below his knees." Barton Diary, December n.d., 1862, and untitled draft of speech about the Christian Commission at Fredericksburg (quotation), Barton Papers, LC. See also Clarke Diary, April 14, 1862, DU.

42. Maria Mann to Mary Mann, April 7, 1863, Mann Papers, LC; Faust, *Mothers of Invention*, 104 (Crutcher); Von Olnhausen, *Adventures*, 201; Hawks, *Woman Doctor's Civil War*, 33; Culpepper, *Trials and Triumphs*, 343. Amanda Akin Stearns (*Lady Nurse*, 75) found mice in her trunk at Armory Square.

43. Clara Barton to Elvira Stone, October 20, 1864, Barton Papers, LC.

44. Hancock, *South after Gettysburg*, 91–97. Kate Cumming (*Kate*, 214, 220, 241) believed that it was bad luck whenever new hospital buildings were completed because the Army of Tennessee would inevitably be obliged to move on the next day. At Gettysburg, Charlotte McKay (*Stories*, 59–61) discovered looters in her tent who believed that the hospital had been abandoned. Similarly, Louisa May Alcott (*Hospital Sketches*, 29–30) noted that personal property was not safe at Union Hotel, Matron Hannah Ropes (*Civil War Nurse*, 69) adding that the poor inmates there "barely escape with life or clothes or money." For other examples of theft, see Adelaide W. Smith, *Reminiscences*, 94–95; Mason, "Memories," 310; and Holland, *Our Army Nurses*, 283.

45. Cumming, *Kate*, 231. A campfire was responsible for burning Fannie Oslin Jackson's (*On Both Sides*, 117) tent and her belongings in Chattanooga in the winter of 1865. Harriet Eaton's (Diary, December 17, 1862, SHC-UNC) dress began to burn at Fredericksburg as she prepared food in a snowstorm. See also Culpepper, *Trials and Triumphs*, 337.

46. Jennie Fyfe to Ellen Mott, June n.d., March 31, 1864; Fyfe Family Papers, MHC-UM. Ada Bacot (Diary, January 17, 1862, SCL-USC) wrote of a fire at Charlottesville's Monticello Hospital on January 17, 1862, in which doctors and orderlies carried patients to safety while nurses rescued clothes and medical supplies.

47. Eaton Diary, December 13, 1862, SHC-UNC; Glymph, "'This Species of Property,'" 68. During the siege of Vicksburg, Annie Turner Wittenmyer rode horseback under bombardment. See Gallagher, "Annie Turner Wittenmyer," 541, and Wittenmyer, *Under the Guns*, 15, 140. Mississippian Emma Balfour (Diary, May 23, 30, 1863, MDAH) and the Union's Charlotte McKay (*Stories*, 34, 37, 39) also wrote of nursing under bombardment—the former at Vicksburg, the latter delivering supplies in the midst of an artillery barrage at Chancellorsville.

48. Newcomb, *Four Years*, 42; Clara Barton, "Work and Incidents," Barton Papers, LC; Dannett and Jones, *Our Women of the Sixties*, 14; Brooks, *Civil War Medicine*, 56; Kate M. Scott, *In Honor of . . . Army Nurses*; Logan, *The Part Taken*, 373. Sarah Gregg reported that one of her party was grazed by a stray bullet at Vicksburg. Tisler, "War Time Diary of Mrs. Sarah Gregg," June 9, 1863, ISHL.

49. Brockett and Vaughan, *Woman's Work*, 509; Bradley Diary, April 16, 1862, DU; Eliza Chappell Porter to Mary Ann Bickerdyke, May 7, 1864, Bickerdyke Papers, LC. When making the ocean passage from Hilton Head island to Beau-

fort, Susie King Taylor (*Reminiscences*, 37–38) narrowly escaped drowning when her boat capsized; a two-year-old passenger did not. Mary Newcomb (*Four Years*, 46) reported on the tenuousness of water crossings when describing the drowning of Wisconsin governor Louis Harvey between hospital ships after Shiloh.

50. Bradley Diary, September 6, 1865, DU.

51. Tisler, "War Time Diary of Mrs. Sarah Gregg," January 27, 1863, ISHL.

52. Ropes, *Civil War Nurse*; Alcott, *Hospital Sketches*, 60; Sarah G. Beck to Harriet F. Hawley, August 26, 1865, Hawley Papers, LC; Beck Papers, SHC-UNC. USGO records indicate that Mrs. C. S. Rumsey requested permission to leave Union Hotel in October 1862—just three months before Ropes's death—"on account of ill health." Rumsey to Dorothea Dix, October 15, 1862, Dix Nursing Papers, NARA. Like Alcott and Beck, Mary Phinney von Olnhausen (*Adventures*, 127, 152) was sent home when she contracted yellow fever in a Morehead, N.C., hospital in October 1864. Emily Parsons (*Memoir*, 72), whose family lived a thousand miles away in Boston, had no choice but to recuperate in her St. Louis hospital when she came down with malaria in March 1863.

53. See, e.g., Surgeon Bernard Vanderkieft to Dorothea Dix, January 15, 1865, and G. S. Palmer to Dix, May 31, 1865; Dix Nursing Papers, NARA. Eudora Clark ("Hospital Memories," 336) noted that five of her nursing colleagues at Annapolis died of typhoid in the winter of 1864–65.

54. See Seigel, "She Went to War," 3; Mason, "Memories," 479; and Malinda McFarland Jackson pension file (#1151092), OIPF. From Helena, Ark., Maria Mann reported that "several of the many deaths have been traceable to the want of care from nurses & visits from surgeons at their smallpox quarters." Maria Mann to Mary Mann, n.d., Mann Papers, LC. For evidence of women choosing work in smallpox hospitals, see Powers, *Hospital Pencillings*, 42, and Mary F. Koch to Dorothea Dix, September 28, 1864, Dix Nursing Papers, NARA. Regimental workers like former slave Susie King Taylor (*Reminiscences*, 17) were obliged to care for men who came down with smallpox. Elizabeth Pickard Hunt survived the smallpox she contracted in a Keokuk hospital. See Kate M. Scott, *In Honor of . . . Army Nurses.*

55. See Mary Foushée to Juliet Opie Hopkins, August 6, 1861, Hopkins Papers, ADAH; Conner et al., *South Carolina Women*, 104–5; and Barton, *Angels of the Battlefield*, 108. See also Maher's account of Sister Coletta O'Connor's funeral in *To Bind Up the Wounds*, 119–20, and Walt Whitman's account of the military burial of Rose Billings in *Specimen Days and Collect*, 2:57.

56. Parsons, *Memoir*, 40; Palmer, *Aunt Becky's Army Life*, 158–59.

57. Hoge, *Boys in Blue*, 169. See also Cumming, *Kate*, 223; Palmer, *Aunt Becky's Army Life*, 34; and Barton, "Work and Incidents," Barton Papers, LC.

58. Jane Grey Swisshelm (*Crusader and Feminist*, 232–33) was the only woman among more than a thousand soldiers at Campbell Hospital in Washington after the battle of Chancellorsville. In the autumn of 1861 Carrie Cutter ("Carrie Eliza Cutter," Cutter Papers, LC) was the only woman to accompany the 21st Massa-

chusetts on an expedition to Roanoke Island and to nurse in the field hospital there.

59. Hawks, *Woman Doctor's Civil War*, 56, 65, 69.

60. Beers, *Memories*, 118, 184.

61. Pember, *Southern Woman's Story*, 74; Phoebe Yates Pember to Eugenia Levy Phillips, June 25, September 13, 1863, Phillips Papers, LC.

62. Maria Mann to Mary Mann, n.d., Mann Papers, LC.

63. Von Olnhausen, *Adventures*, 40–41; Morris, *Better Angel*, 110 (Hawley's dislike of Whitman).

64. Susan E. D. Smith, *Soldier's Friend*, 114; News and Courier, *Our Women in the War*, 225; Jennie Fyfe to Ellen Mott, May 24, 1864, Fyfe Family Papers, MHC-UM. From Armory Square, Sarah Low ("Sarah Low," 6) reported that on a June morning in 1864, 1,200 visitors had attempted to enter the hospital. See also Tisler, "War Time Diary of Mrs. Sarah Gregg," February 4, 5, 1864, March 30, 1865, ISHL, and Bucklin, *In Hospital and Camp*, 154–59.

65. Cumming, *Kate*, 93.

66. Henry Bryant to Surgeon General William Hammond, February 13, 1863, and Marcia J. Alexander to Surgeon General, February 11, 1863, Letters Received, 1818–70, USGO, NARA; Alcott, *Hospital Sketches*, 65; E. T. Perkins to Amy Morris Bradley, April 6, 1863, Bradley Letterbook, DU. Rebecca Pomroy was also known to give up her supper and bed to female visitors. See Pomroy, *Echoes*, 217, and Stearns, *Lady Nurse*, 95. The surgeon in charge of Park Barracks in Louisville reported that a woman who had come to nurse her husband's erysipelas slept on his cot and developed a "severe herpatic eruption." See Benjamin Woodward to M. Goldsmith, January 14, 1863, Bickerdyke Papers, LC.

67. Amanda Shelton Stewart Address, 14–15, SC-UI.

68. Higginson, *Life in a Black Regiment*, 192. For incidents involving the destitution of soldiers' families, see Forbes, *African American Women*, chaps. 5, 9.

69. Tisler, "War Time Diary of Mrs. Sarah Gregg," February 26, 1864, ISHL; Pember, *Southern Woman's Story*, 94. See also Stearns, *Lady Nurse*, 53. One of the more remarkable childbearing stories was recorded by Surgeon Thomas Azpell, who attended a woman aboard the hospital ship *Empress*. On April 11, 1862, several days after her husband had been killed at Shiloh and she herself wounded in the breast, she gave birth to a daughter and was given over to the ladies of Keokuk, Iowa—the destination of the *Empress*. Letterbook of Thomas F. Azpell, NARA.

70. Eaton Diary, October 30, 1862, SHC-UNC; Whites, *Crisis in Gender*, 93; Holstein, *Three Years*, 13; Andrews, *Women of the South*, 391–93. Eudora Clark ("Hospital Memories," 328) reported that surgeons left to her the job of telling fifteen-year-old William Miller of his impending death.

71. Stearns, *Lady Nurse*, 30; Clara Barton to Mary Norton, June 26, 1863, Norton Papers, DU. See also Barton Diary, Barton Papers, May 1, 1863, LC. Stephen Oates (*Woman of Valor*, Part 3) has speculated that Barton's solitary rides might have been a cover for her trysts with Colonel John Elwell.

72. Eaton Diary, November 7, 1862, October 31, November 12, 1864, SHC-UNC.

73. Hancock, *South after Gettysburg*, 17–18.

74. Beers, *Memories*, 121.

75. Hobbs, "Excerpts from the Autobiography," n.p. Amanda Akin Stearns (*Lady Nurse*, 18) drew the same conclusion at Armory Square: "We pass up and down among these rough men without fear of the slightest word of disrespect."

76. Holstein, *Three Years*, 55; Parsons, *Memoir*, 93. See also Palmer, *Aunt Becky's Army Life*, 93; McKay, *Stories*, 74–75; and Newcomb, *Four Years*, 117.

77. See introduction to Mitchell, *Vacant Chair*.

78. Gibbons, *Life*, 2:31; McKay, *Stories*, 53. See also Parsons, *Memoir*, 41, and Porter, *Memoir*, 170.

79. Amanda Rhoda Shelton Diary, May 17, 1864, SC-UI. For an insightful analysis of Shelton's unwitting entanglement, see Kristie R. Ross, "'Women Are Needed Here,'" 157–59.

80. Maria Mann to Mary Mann, n.d., Mann Papers, LC.

81. Glymph, "'This Species of Property,'" 58, 64–67.

82. Forbes, *African American Women*, 57, from an article in the *Liberator*, June 24, 1864.

83. Hawks, *Woman Doctor's Civil War*, 34.

84. Victoria Bynum (*Unruly Women*, 118) has suggested that "the context in which the dominant white society viewed rape made it impossible to identify rapists and determine the number and victims of rape during the Civil War." Assaults of white women ran the gamut from soldiers who brandished weapons to the rape of a Union woman searching for her wounded husband. See Eaton Diary, October 6, 1862, SHC-UNC; Cordelia Scales to Loulie, October 29, 1862, Scales Letters, MDAH; and Seigel, "She Went to War," 26. Reid Mitchell (*Vacant Chair*, 106–10) presents the symbolic "replacement" theory; he also notes the example of a Northern officer threatening the women of Selina and Sparta, Tenn., with rape unless they prepared food for his men (p. 103). See also Forbes, *African American Women*, 221–22, for the dismissal of six white officers from the 4th Louisiana Corps D'Afrique for the attempted rape of black laundresses at Fort Jackson in December 1863.

85. Bacot Diary, April 1, 30, July 18, 1862; Bradley Diary, June 29, 1862, January 17, 1863; Jennie Fyfe to Ellen Mott, n.d., Fyfe Family Papers, MHC-UM. Harriet Whetten ("Volunteer Nurse," 146) was flattered by the attentions of a male nurse who visited her and gave her his photograph.

86. Surgeon J. N. Huber to Dorothea Dix, April 4, 1864, Dix Nursing Papers, NARA.

87. Palmer, *Aunt Becky's Army Life*, 116–17; Phoebe Yates Pember to Lou Gilmer, April 16, 1864, Pember Letters, SHC-UNC. The soldier wrote to Bradley that he hoped "someday to meet you face to face when wife will not object to my giving you a kiss of welcome." E. D. Hulbert to Amy Morris Bradley, January 5, 1862, Bradley Papers, DU.

88. Rebecca Pomroy (*Echoes*, 141) noted this incident. Dix may have been refer-

ring to Amanda Farnham, of Vermont, who fell in love with Marshall Felch in the summer of 1862 and married him immediately after the war. See Marshall Felch pension file, quoted in Conklin, *Women at Gettysburg*, 87. See also Bucklin, *In Hospital and Camp*, 351–52; Minerva Trigg Dillard Washington pension file (#1330575), OIPF; and Christie, "'Performing My Plain Duty,'" 223–24. The matchmaker was New York's Adelaide Smith, who at City Point in 1864 did everything for the wedding of Annie Bain and Captain Robert C. Eden except marry the bride.

89. Stearns, *Lady Nurse*; Austin, *Woolsey Sisters*; Conklin, *Women at Gettysburg*, 303; Bacot, *Confederate Nurse*, 15, 182. Lois Dennett Dunbar and Lucy Campbell Kaiser also married soldiers they had nursed. See Holland, *Our Army Nurses*, 297; George A. Dunbar to Mary Ann Bickerdyke, April 9, 1863, Bickerdyke Papers, LC; *St. Charles Chronicle*, October 7, 1915; and Kaiser pension file (#1138563), OIPF.

90. On Margaret Hamilton, the Sister of Charity who married a soldier of the 19th Maine, see Kate M. Scott, *In Honor of . . . Army Nurses*. Sophronia Bucklin (*In Hospital and Camp*, 79–80) also mentioned the marriage of a Sister of Charity to a Union officer she met at Hammond General.

91. Alcott, *Hospital Sketches*, 38–46.

92. Beers, *Memories*, 123.

93. Paludan, "*People's Contest*," 330.

94. See, e.g., N. M. Daily letter, October 5, 1864, in Tisler, "War Time Diary of Mrs. Sarah Gregg," ISHL; Eaton Diary, March 14, 1863, SHC-UNC; Palmer, *Aunt Becky's Army Life*, 127; and Powers, *Hospital Pencillings*, 15.

95. Bradley Diary, November 28, 1861, DU; Newcomb, *Four Years*, 17.

96. See, e.g., Parsons, *Memoir*, 57; Hoge, *Boys in Blue*, 159; and Emily Mason's account of a soldier who died after selflessly insisting that she help another man in News and Courier, *Our Women in the War*, 151.

97. Alcott, *Hospital Sketches*, 44, 37; Parsons, *Memoir*, 56. See also Alice Fahs's discussion of John Suhre's heroism in *Imagined Civil War*, 115–16, 118.

98. Parsons, *Memoir*, 79; Livermore, *My Story of the War: A Woman's Narrative*, 103.

99. Mary Foushée to Juliet Opie Hopkins, August 6, 1861, Hopkins Papers, ADAH; Bacon and Howland, *Letters of a Family*, 2:371 (Woolsey); Livermore, *My Story of the War: A Woman's Narrative*, 325. See also Hoge, *Boys in Blue*, 268.

100. On the segregation of officers from the rank and file, see, e.g., Mary S. Foushée to Juliet Opie Hopkins, August 6, 1861, Hopkins Papers, ADAH.

101. See Schultz, "Inhospitable Hospital."

102. Pember, *Southern Woman's Story*, 39.

103. Livermore, *Story of My Life*, 473. See also *Notes of Hospital Life*, xii.

104. Barton Diary, December 5, 1863, LC; Mrs. L. Tilton to Mary Ann Bickerdyke, December 20, 1863, Bickerdyke Papers, LC; Pember to Lou Gilmer, June 22, 1864, Pember Letters, SHC-UNC. See also Daly, *Diary of a Union Lady*, 172, and "Sarah Low," 7.

105. Alcott, *Louisa May Alcott*, 116–17; Pember to Eugenia Levy Phillips, September 13, 1863, Phillips Papers, LC. Mary Newcomb (*Four Years*, 114) wrote, "[Having] seen soldiers in all possible circumstances, . . . all my associations with them made me like them better."

106. Jennie Fyfe to Ellen Mott, May 7, 24, 1864, Fyfe Family Papers, MHC-UM.

107. See Eudora Clark, "Hospital Memories," 324, 326. Clark served Native American soldiers from Michigan regiments in Annapolis.

108. Reed, *Hospital Life*, 80–82; Parsons, *Memoir*, 136, 88–89. For another account of a white nurse teaching black soldiers to read, see Pomroy, *Echoes*, 157.

109. Gibbons, *Life*, 1:365, 382–83, 2:34–35, 39–40.

110. Von Olnhausen, *Adventures*, 211. Amanda Shelton (Diary, May 5, 1864, SC-UI) also spoke of black regiments in glowing terms.

111. Hawks, *Woman Doctor's Civil War*, 51–52. Forbes (*African American Women*, 76) mentions the elite Mrs. Charles Reason in connection with fund-raising for the education of freedmen. If she was the wife or mother of the soldier Hawks cares for, then it is likely that Reason was light-skinned.

112. Hawks, *Woman Doctor's Civil War*, 54.

113. See, e.g., Alcott, *Hospital Sketches*, 53, and Stearns, *Lady Nurse*, 68.

114. Wormeley, *Other Side of the War*, 44; Hoge, *Boys in Blue*, 256–57; Beers, *Memories*, 82.

115. Bradley Diary, July 7, 1862, DU. Charles Stillé (*United States Sanitary Commission*, 475) confirmed that the hospital transport service made use of "loyal women of the highest social grade."

116. Pember to Lou Gilmer, December 30, 1863, Pember Letters, SHC-UNC; Pember, *Southern Woman's Story*, 35–36; Beers, *Memories*, 61, 63. For Southern nurses' class conflicts, see also George Rable, *Civil Wars*, 122–23.

117. Amanda Rhoda Shelton Diary, May 9, 1864, SC-UI; Hancock, *South after Gettysburg*, 55.

118. For more on Protestant nurses' conflict with Catholic sisters, see Kristie R. Ross, "'Women Are Needed Here,'" 175–80.

119. Cumming, *Kate*, 70.

120. Rebecca Pomroy (*Echoes*, 96) noted that a contraband woman was detailed as the nurses' cook at Columbia College Hospital in Washington.

121. Bradley to Sister, October 20, 1861, August 31, 1862, Bradley Letterbook, DU; Barton Diary, June 16, 1863, Barton Papers, LC; Von Olnhausen, *Adventures*, 138. See also Lee, *Wartime Washington*, 309, in which Elizabeth Blair Lee asks her husband if he "can pick up a good dining room servant."

122. Mann to Mary Tyler Peabody Mann, April 19, 1863, Mann Papers, LC; Von Olnhausen, *Adventures*, 191. For additional examples, see Hoge, *Boys in Blue*, 372, and Bucklin, *In Hospital and Camp*, 69.

123. For more on the racialization of nineteenth-century culture, see Riss, "Racial Essentialism and Family Values in *Uncle Tom's Cabin*."

124. Alcott, *Hospital Sketches*, 58–59.

125. Parsons, *Memoir*, 138–39. For examples of streetcar and rail discrimination against black female relief workers, see Forbes, *African American Women*, 149–53.

126. Alcott, *Hospital Sketches*, 58.

## Chapter Four

1. Hancock, *South after Gettysburg*, 87–88. From Campbell Hospital in Washington after Chancellorsville, Jane Grey Swisshelm (*Crusader and Feminist*, 232) expressed a similar sentiment: "I cannot leave the hospitals; am completely stuck fast and feel that here is my place."

2. Hawks, *Woman Doctor's Civil War*, 182.

3. Mason, "Memories," 310.

4. See Carded Service Records, NARA, and Hawks, *Woman Doctor's Civil War*, 182. Maria M. C. Hall, only twenty-three when the war began, served nearly four years—from September 1861 to May 1865—a tour of duty that included field work at Antietam. Although few spent all four years in service, pension depositions show that a significant number of women did. See Logan, *The Part Taken*, 371.

5. Cumming, *Kate*, 122; Bucklin, *In Hospital and Camp*, 296.

6. See Pernick, *Calculus of Suffering*, 21, 26, 29, 138, 242–47. For other accounts of nineteenth-century medicine's stormy history, see Starr, *Social Transformation*, 7–8, 27, 93–102, and Rosenberg, "Therapeutic Revolution."

7. See Adams, *Doctors in Blue*, 34–35.

8. On Hammond's trials as Union surgeon general, see Stillé, *United States Sanitary Commission*, 58, 130–36; Gillett, *Army Medical Department*, 177–78, 225–26; and Adams, *Doctors in Blue*, 27–41.

9. See Cunningham, *Doctors in Gray*, 33–34. Note also that nepotism was rife in the Union army medical service. Surgeon Daniel Holt (*Surgeon's Civil War*, 80) was passed over for promotion to head surgeon of his New York regiment several times, while men of lesser merit were promoted. "Kissing goes by favor," he noted derisively in March 1863.

10. Kate Cumming and the surgeons for whom she worked complained regularly about orders to move just as the staff was settling into new accommodations. Phoebe Yates Pember, accustomed to general hospital life in Richmond, was shocked by the disorganization of the Gulf area facilities she visited in 1864. See Cumming, *Kate*, 119, 137–38, and Cunningham, *Doctors in Gray*, 62, 66–67. By the same token, medical historians have noted that this "flying hospital" system paved the way for mobile army surgical hospital (MASH) units in the twentieth century. See Schroeder-Lein, *Confederate Hospitals on the Move*.

11. See J. B. Hern to Juliet Opie Hopkins, November 13, 1863, Hopkins Papers, ADAH, which alludes to problems that Hopkins was having with "those in authority." Virginia's Emily Mason ("Memories," 314, 476–77), who was given "carte blanche" early in the war to supply and manage her own hospital, found hos-

pital life at Camp Winder much more stressful. In addition to the decreasing value of women in the hospitals as a centralized medical system was forged, some Confederate surgeons complained that Moore removed too many able practitioners from the field for more sedentary administrative jobs, thereby robbing infantry regiments of adequate medical organization. See Cunningham, *Doctors in Gray*, 249.

12. Rable, *Civil Wars*, 123–26.

13. In April 1861, after her own petition to become a Union army nurse had been denied, Dr. Elizabeth Blackwell of the New York Infirmary gave a small group of women a four-week session on basic nursing techniques at the behest of the Woman's Central Relief Association. Georgeanna Woolsey, a daughter of the well-connected New York family most of whose members nursed during the war, was one of Blackwell's pupils. Ultimately, the USSC's skepticism about Blackwell's wish to professionalize female relief workers and its putative acknowledgment of Dorothea Dix's authority as nurse handler squashed Blackwell's initiative. See Giesberg, *Civil War Sisterhood*, 40–50; Kalisch and Kalisch, *Advance of American Nursing*, 94; and Mottus, *New York Nightingales*, 27–28. Emily Parsons (*Memoir*, 4) took a "crash course" in nursing at Massachusetts General Hospital in 1861 before leaving for her first post at Fort Schuyler, N.Y. The Confederacy's Ella Newsom reported having received nurses' training at Memphis City Hospital as early as 1861 before beginning service in Bowling Green, Ky., late in the year. See Simkins and Patton, "Work of Southern Women," 480.

14. Ruth Abram points out that physicians needed neither license nor medical degree to practice in nineteenth-century America. See Abram, "Soon the Baby Died," 17, and *Doctors in Blue*, 10–11. Many surgeons themselves complained about their own lack of experience or the incompetence of coworkers. See, e.g., Keen, "Surgical Reminiscences"; Surgeon William Watson to Ella Watson, January 4, 1863, in Watson, *Letters*, 46; and Holt, *Surgeon's Civil War*, 28, 30, 34.

15. See Holzman, "Sally Tompkins."

16. Pember, *Southern Woman's Story*, 22, 26.

17. Von Olnhausen, *Adventures*, 39, 71. Sophronia Bucklin (*In Hospital and Camp*, 125) expressed a similar sentiment about the dangers of complaining about hospital conditions at Point Lookout, Md.

18. Stearns, *Lady Nurse*, 250, 49, 36. Other nurses who took matters into their own hands were less lucky: a Mrs. Harris was dismissed for prescribing for a patient when she had only been on the job for three days. See Surgeon B. Randall to Dorothea Dix, April 4, 1862, Dix Nursing Papers, NARA.

19. Hoge, *Boys in Blue*, 110, 188; Amanda Rhoda Shelton Diary, April 22, 1864, and Amanda Shelton Stewart Address, 7–8, SC-UI; Bucklin, *In Hospital and Camp*, 124.

20. Woolsey quoted in Dannett, *Noble Women*, 88. Lyde Sizer (*Political Work*, 183) observes that Woolsey's later essay "How I Came to Be a Nurse," in USSC's *Spirit of the Fair* (a newspaper published for New York's Metropolitan Fair), April 8, 1964, is even more critical of surgeons. See her discussion of nurses' confidence about their "indispensability" to surgeons.

21. See, e.g., Dorothea Dix to Surgeon General R. C. Wood, April 9, June 9, 1862, and Surgeon Roberts Barthalow to Surgeon General Hammond, October 30, 1862, Letters Received, 1818–70, USGO, NARA.

22. Dorothea Dix to Mary Ann Bickerdyke, February 26, 1863, Bickerdyke Papers, LC. Dix wrote: "I have *long* wished to learn your address—and to day am surprised to hear you are in Washington but your residence I have not ascertained—I write on the chance of opening a communication with you. I wish very *much* to see you for many solid reasons."

23. Beers, *Memories*, 39, 61; Cumming, *Kate*, 12, 65; Simkins and Patton, "Work of Southern Women," 484–85.

24. M. C. Bass to Juliet Opie Hopkins, October 26, 1862, Hopkins Papers, ADAH.

25. Handwritten account of Mary Ann Bickerdyke, General Miscellany, Bickerdyke Papers, LC.

26. Parsons, *Memoir*, 54. Among those who managed other women's work were Eliza Chappell Porter (*Memoir*, 167) and Mary Livermore (*Story of My Life*, 2:472), both of whom, as USSC agents, had the power to appoint nurses and then travel with them to the sometimes distant sites of their employment. Kate Cumming was responsible for contracting laundresses as she moved through the Confederate interior with the Army of Tennessee. See David Cumming to Kate Cumming, May 7, 1863, Cumming Papers, ADAH. Coincidentally, surgeons on the *City of Alton*, who so valued Emily Parsons's help, made a similar gesture to Mary Newcomb during the evacuation of Union soldiers at Shiloh. See Newcomb, *Four Years*, 65.

27. Parsons, *Memoir*, 9; James Yeatman to Dorothea Dix, July 14, 1863, Dix Nursing Papers, NARA.

28. See Barton, *Angels of the Battlefield*, 144–59. Emily Mason ("Memories," 315) noted that she learned a good deal about nursing from the Sisters of Mercy of Charleston, S.C., whom she employed at her Virginia hospital. More typically, lay nurses criticized nuns for poor culinary and domestic skills. Some even maintained that soldiers did not like to be cared for by nuns. See, e.g., Gibbons, *Life*, 1:355, 357. See also Maher, *To Bind Up the Wounds*, 46, and Billings, "Medical Reminiscences," on surgeons' preference for Catholic sisters.

29. See Stillé, *United States Sanitary Commission*, 303. After her own service on hospital transports, New York nurse Harriet Whetten ("Volunteer Nurse," 221) became superintendent of nurses at Carver Hospital in Washington. For the connection between class privilege and selection of female attendants for hospital transport work, see Wormeley, *Other Side of the War*, 44, and Kristie R. Ross, "Arranging a Doll's House." For Bradley's promotions, see Bradley Diary, DU, and Cashman, *Headstrong*.

30. See Grimké, *Journal*, 138–40; Forbes, *African American Women*, 131; and Maria Bear Toliver pension file (#889647), Toliver and Louisa Frazer depositions, October 11, 1897, and Betsey Lawson deposition, February 12, 1895, OIPF.

31. Truth, *Narrative*, 1991 ed., 181–87; Painter, *Sojourner Truth*, 212–17; Mabee, *Sojourner Truth*, 117–22.

32. See Harriet Ross Tubman Davis (#415288), OIPF, NARA, and Quarles, "Tubman's Unlikely Leadership," 1136.

33. See John Milton Hawks to Esther Hill Hawks, May 17, 1862, Hawks Papers, LC, and Maria R. Mann to Mary Mann, February 10, 1863, Mann Papers, LC.

34. See Matilda Cleaver John pension file (#1139370), OIPF. White women, like Janie Clarke of Charleston, S.C., expressed unwillingness to care for ailing coworkers when soldiers demanded their time and "servants" might be available to do the work: "It is impossible," wrote Clarke (Diary, December 27, 1862, DU) "to attend to the House and Mrs. Rion also[.] I am up and down all night."

35. See, e.g., C. J. Clark to Juliet Opie Hopkins, December 10, 1862; A. B. Moor to Hopkins, September 10, 1861; Gov. John Gill Shorter to Hopkins, June 4, 1862; and George L. Hutchinson to Hopkins, August n.d., 1862—all in Hopkins Papers, ADAH. Hopkins also fielded correspondence from nursing hopefuls, like the wife of the mayor of Selma, and from physicians offering their services.

36. Parsons, *Memoir*, 95; Pember, *Southern Woman's Story*, 74.

37. Reasons given for dismissing nurses were "disobedience of orders," an "uncontrollable tongue," "incompetency," and "inefficiency." See card on Miss Terry, September 20, 1864; Surg. J. Mouz (?) to Dorothea Dix, January 16, 1863; card on Mary Olmstead, March 31, 1865; card on Caroline M. Christian, May 21, 1864; and card on Miss Brock, March 6, 1863—all in Dix Nursing Papers, NARA.

38. See, e.g., James E. Yeatman to Dr. Irwin, June 6, 1863, and John V. Farrell, B. F. Jacobs, and Robert Patterson to Nathan Bishop, December 24, 1864, Bickerdyke Papers, LC.

39. Barton Diary, December 5, 1863, Barton Papers, LC.

40. Ibid.

41. See, e.g., Barton Diary, August 6, 1864, Barton Papers, LC.

42. Taylor, *Reminiscences*, 31. See also Harriet Eaton's (Diary, December 25, 1862, SHC-UNC) description of walking by the cot of a dead man all day long.

43. The Army Medical Department created the position of medical cadet in 1861 so that young medical students could get on-site experience as wound dressers. See Gillett, *Army Medical Department*, 155. As female nurses learned to dress wounds, they could relieve the burden on cadets, who were also needed as ambulance attendants.

44. Powers, *Hospital Pencillings*, 123–24.

45. Stearns, *Lady Nurse*, 287.

46. Newcomb, *Four Years*, 116. Phoebe Pember believed that she was better able to endure her own infirmities because "the constant sight of amputations" made her more "courageous." Pember to Eugenia Levy Phillips, September 13, 1863, Phillips Papers, LC. See also Mason, "Memories," 315, and Elizabeth Brown Pryor, *Clara Barton*, 99.

47. Hancock, *South after Gettysburg*, 8, 15; Parsons, *Memoir*, 40. Amanda Akin Stearns (*Lady Nurse*, 39) saw not only distance from the past but also a new self emerging: "It seemed as if I were entirely separated from the world I had left behind. Certainly, 'I am not myself at all.'"

48. Fyfe to Ellen Mott, February 15, 1865, Fyfe Family Papers, MHC-UM.

49. A Miss Hadley quoted in Hurn, *Wisconsin Women*, 112; *Notes of Hospital Life*, 18. See also Beers, *Memories*, 150. Michael Fellman (*Inside War*, 147–51) observes a similar character-splitting phenomenon among Missouri guerrillas and Union soldiers. When taken into custody and isolated, guerrillas would claim that their brutal acts came from the "not-me," whereas their peace-loving selves were the "real-me." What Fellman refers to as "coarsening" among Union soldiers can be compared to the "hardening" process I describe nurses passing through.

50. Eaton Diary, January 24, 20, 1863, SHC-UNC. As Eaton contemplated her own son's fate later that spring, her morale remained low: "Oh why this dreadful war! he bears no malice to his Southern brother, can he deliberately take his life? I cannot bear the thought. Can a Christian nation conscienciously [*sic*] kill each other? Will our Maker approve? Why is this, let us ask why?" (April 15, 1863).

51. Bradley Diary, February 22, 23, 1863, DU. For other examples of winter doldrums, see Cumming, *Kate*, 90, and Pomroy, *Echoes*, 173.

52. Cumming, *Kate*, 263.

53. Barton Diary, March 29, April 19, 1864, Barton Papers, LC.

54. Stearns, *Lady Nurse*, 190, 127, 262. Kate Cumming and Jennie Fyfe also referred to their charges in private writing by number instead of name.

55. Harriet Eaton (Diary, February 14, 1863, SHC-UNC) spoke of being "homesick to get back to my work" with Maine regiments in Maryland. See also Alcott, *Hospital Sketches*, 69; *Notes of Hospital Life*, 162.

56. Brinton, *Personal Memoirs*, 44. Kristie Ross ("'Women Are Needed Here,'" 169) observes that Brinton's harsh criticism of female nurses may have been enabled by the passage of thirty years. He probably would not have risked such candor at the time of the war. Surgeon Simon Pollack of the Western Sanitary Commission in St. Louis was equally disappointed in the members of the Union Ladies' Aid Society, "who, impelled by a patriotic feeling, are loud in professions of doing good work, [but] it is all a sham. To work is neither to their taste or their habit." Quoted in Parrish, "Western Sanitary Commission," 26–27.

57. A. Bolus to Surgeon General Hammond, May 24, 1863, Letters Received, 1818–70, USGO, NARA; James E. Yeatman to Dorothea Dix, April 11, 1865, Dix Nursing Papers, NARA.

58. Circular letter of Surgeon J. R. Smith, October 28, 1862, Circulars and Circular Letters, USGO, NARA.

59. Surgeon Thomas F. Azpell to Surgeon General, November 6, 1862, Letterbook of Azpell, NARA. Thomas McParlin, medical director of the Army of the Potomac, expressed similar sentiments, seeing women as better suited to diet-kitchen work than ward duty. See Gillett, *Army Medical Department*, 240. Correspondence to Dorothea Dix indicates that female nurses were unhappy to be restricted to work in the hospital linen room or kitchen. For instance, Mrs. E. J. Bushnell resigned her position as matron of Hospital No. 2 in Quincy, Ill., "owing to orders which deprived her of service upon the sick and confined her to the linen room." Bushnell to Dix, n.d., Dix Nursing Papers, NARA.

60. Surgeon J. H. Baxter to Surgeon General William A. Hammond, March 16, 1863, Letters Received, 1818–70, USGO, NARA. See also Surgeon E. B. Dunning to Dorothea Dix, October 28, 1863, Dix Nursing Papers, NARA. There were, of course, exceptions. Union surgeons at City Point requested more female nurses in June 1864 but were told by the medical director that "an increase in the number would be detrimental to the service." See Medical Director E. B. Dalton to Surgeon G. A. Wheeler, July 8, 1864; Wheeler to Dalton, June 30, 1864; and Surgeon F. F. Burmeister to Surgeon General, June 30, 1864—all in Letters Received, 1818–70, USGO, NARA.

61. James E. Yeatman to Colonel T. P. Robb, December 29, 1864, January 31, 1865, Dix Nursing Papers, NARA.

62. Surgeon J. Bond Peale to Dorothea Dix, December 2, 1864, ibid., citing the bravery of Sarah Palmer.

63. Surgeon George Rex to Dorothea Dix, February 2, 1864, ibid.

64. Surgeon E. Smith to Dorothea Dix, June 5, 1864, ibid., praising "Miss Gorton."

65. Assistant Surgeon Walter Ure to Dorothea Dix, February 9, 1865, ibid.

66. Schuyler Colfax to Dorothea Dix, December 19, 1861, ibid.

67. Surgeon J. M. Palmer to Dorothea Dix, April 21, 1865, ibid.

68. Bradley Diary, January 17, 1863, and Surgeon Sanford Hunt to Fred Knapp, June 1, 1863, Bradley Letterbook, DU.

69. Stearns, *Lady Nurse*, 52, 235.

70. Barton Diary, July n.d., 1864, Barton Papers, LC. For other praise of surgeons by nurses, see Mary Ann Bickerdyke's (General Miscellany, Bickerdyke Papers, LC) account of the siege at Fort Donelson, Eudora Clark's ("Hospital Memories," 331) praise of Bernard Vanderkieft's bedside manner at Annapolis, and Abby Hopper Gibbons's (*Life*, 1:375) praise of Dr. Douglas at Point Lookout.

71. Maria Mann to Mary Mann, May 18, 1863, Mann Papers, LC.

72. Parsons, *Memoir*, 20, 29.

73. Ella Wolcott to Dorothea Dix, February 1, 1865, Dix Nursing Papers, NARA.

74. See cards of March 6, 1863, ibid.

75. Susan E. D. Smith, *Soldier's Friend*, 69, 75.

76. Hoge, *Boys in Blue*, 179; Powers, *Hospital Pencillings*, 208.

77. Beers, *Memories*, 95–96. Beers lambasted Yankee surgeons at Newnan, Ga., for their rough treatment of Confederate patients (pp. 157–58).

78. Pember, *Southern Woman's Story*, 80.

79. Ibid., 35–36.

80. Isabella Stuart and L. S. Johns to Juliet Opie Hopkins, August 13, 1861, Hopkins Papers, ADAH. See also Simkins and Patton, "Work of Southern Women," 488.

81. Hawks, *Woman Doctor's Civil War*, 55.

82. Eaton Diary, January 21, 1863, SHC-UNC.

83. Bacon and Howland, *Letters of a Family*, 2:406.

84. For examples of conflict over food and supplies, see Swisshelm, *Crusader*

*and Feminist*, 239–40; Tisler, "War Time Diary of Mrs. Sarah Gregg," June 10, 1865, ISHL; Wheelock, *Boys in White*, 131–34; McKay, *Stories*, 54–56; Powers, *Hospital Pencillings*, 127, 130; and Lawrence, *Autobiography*, 102.

85. Annie Turner Wittenmyer, "Instructions to Managers of Special Diet Kitchens," Communications Received, 1862–65, Central Office, USCC, NARA.

86. Special Order No. 21, January 23, 1864, from Headquarters, General Field Hospital, Chattanooga, Bickerdyke Papers, LC. For evidence of the court-martial of an unruly laundress, see Wendel, "Washer Women," 33.

87. See, respectively, Pomroy, *Echoes*, 49, 176; Newcomb, *Four Years*, 62, 112; and Wittenmyer, *Under the Guns*, 193–201.

88. Newcomb, *Four Years*, 98–99.

89. Surgeon Harvey E. Brown to Medical Director W. J. Sloan, August 30, 1862, Letters Received, 1818–70, USGO, NARA.

90. See, e.g., a surgeon's response to Elvira Powers's poultice, in Powers, *Hospital Pencillings*, 64. In Surgeon John Patterson's Clayton Hospital in Forsyth, Ga., Rebel soldiers forged prescriptions to obtain liquor without staff consent. See Davis, "Confederate Hospital."

91. See, e.g., Pember, *Southern Woman's Story*, 6–7; Gibbons, *Life*, 1:305, 324, 2:36; Haviland, *Woman's Life-Work*, 261; and Von Olnhausen, *Adventures*, 33.

92. See Elizabeth D. Leonard, *Yankee Women*, 38–39, 123–24; Snyder, *Dr. Mary Walker*, 32; Jolly, *Nuns of the Battlefield*, 48; and Newcomb, *Four Years*, 35. Although nurses believed that surgeons were too quick to amputate, Surgeon John Shaw Billings ("Medical Reminiscences," 120) maintained that "the great majority were timid" in this regard.

93. Barton Diary, May 29, 30, 1864, Barton Papers, LC.

94. See, e.g., Fannie Beers's (*Memories*, 97) and Eudora Clark's ("Hospital Memories," 324–25) accounts of administering blisters to men given up by surgeons and ultimately saving them, Emily Mason's ("Memories," 317) account of a man already pronounced dead whom she still believed to be alive, and Rebecca Pomroy's (*Echoes*, 38–39, 220) account of at least two soldiers whom she saved despite surgical opposition.

95. On sentimentality and death, see Ann Douglas, *Feminization of American Culture*, esp. chap. 6.

96. Watson, *Letters*, 60, 63, 65, 72. See also Keen, "Surgical Reminiscences."

97. Thrall, "Iowa Doctor in Blue," esp. letter of November 15, 1862.

98. Cyrus Bacon, "Daily Register," 383. See also John Gill's ("Union Surgeon Views the War," 274–75) description of typhoid patients in Kentucky.

99. Alcott, *Hospital Sketches*, 29.

100. Holt, *Surgeon's Civil War*.

101. Mrs. S. A. M. Blackford to O. H. Browning, January 25, 1865, and to Abraham Lincoln, February 16, 1865; and Medical Inspector R. H. Coolidge to Assistant Surgeon General R. C. Wood, n.d.—all in Letters Received, 1818–70, USGO, NARA. Lincoln never acted on Blackford's letter.

102. In January 1863 Louisa May Alcott (*Louisa May Alcott*, 117) noted that

Union Hotel had "no competent head . . . to right matters" and that "a jumble" of other attendants "complicate[d] the chaos still more." When it first opened as a military hospital, Union Hotel was headed by Indiana surgeon John Shaw Billings, who went on to distinguish himself in the profession. He was transferred in the spring of 1862, before the Seven Days battles near Richmond, to establish Cliffburne Hospital. See Billings, "Medical Reminiscences."

103. Ropes, *Civil War Nurse*, x. Abby Hopper Gibbons (*Life*, 1:344–45) also maligned the Union surgeon general for his "coarseness" and "roughness" when she solicited his help in a transfer.

104. Ropes, *Civil War Nurse*, 77.

105. Ibid., 82.

106. Ibid., 86.

107. Ibid., 93.

108. John A. Brown to Surgeon General Joseph K. Barnes, May 6, 1865, Letters Received, 1818–70, USGO, NARA.

109. Gibbons, *Life*, 1:350, 354.

110. Maria Mann to Mary Mann, n.d., 1863, Mann Papers, LC. Mann reported that the patients had "no outhouse" nor "proper assistants" to help them.

111. Letter of Mary Ann Bickerdyke to "the proper authorities!," December 24, 1863, Bickerdyke Papers, LC.

112. Bucklin, *In Hospital and Camp*, 125.

113. See Dorothea Dix to William Hammond, March 2, 1863, Letters Received, 1818–70, USGO, NARA, and C. Wagner to Hammond, March 6, 1863, Dix Nursing Papers, NARA.

114. Sizer, *Political Work*, 208.

115. Bucklin, *In Hospital and Camp*, 240.

116. Ibid., 241.

117. Ibid., 289.

118. Ibid., 292.

119. Ibid., 296.

120. Barton Diary, December 5, 1863, Barton Papers, LC.

121. Cumming, *Kate*, 123–24.

## Chapter Five

1. Mary Gillett (*Army Medical Department*, 251) notes that by June 1865, 170 of the 204 general hospitals the Union established were closed. Despite the rapid closing of hospitals after Appomattox, thousands of soldiers in the remaining hospitals were not well enough to be sent home. And where soldiers were sick, female workers remained to care for them. Modenia McCall, for example, was still on duty in August 1865 at the Memphis Smallpox Hospital where she had served for twenty months. Annie Webb Peck deposition, September 3, 1890, and Modenia McCall Weston pension file (#1129677), OIPF.

2. Cumming, *Gleanings*, 257.

3. In her recent book, *The Political Work of Northern Women Writers*, Lyde Sizer argues that despite the war's having "produced a revolution in 'woman's sense of herself,'" it had produced no immediate corresponding revolution in society" (p. 4).

4. Wrote one celebrant, "When the war closed [nurses] went quietly to their homes, and took up again the daily routines of woman's work." Kate M. Scott, *In Honor of . . . Army Nurses*, 1. See also Hanaford, *Daughters of America*, 165–93.

5. Brockett and Vaughan, *Woman's Work*, 93.

6. Mary Ryan argues that women were visible in the public domain throughout the nineteenth century, despite the somewhat circumscribed notions of "women's sphere" historians, whose public/private schematic all too often consigned women to private space. Although women were visible in public forums before the war, it was not really until after the war that a sizable number of middle-class women began to seek work outside of the home. Ryan, *Women in Public*, esp. introduction.

7. See Mary Tyler Mann to Dorothea Dix, n.d., 1865[?], Mann Papers, LC.

8. See Wormeley, *Other Side of the War*, and "Katharine Prescott Wormeley," *NAW* 3:674–75.

9. Hancock, *South after Gettysburg*, 171.

10. Cornelia Hancock to Frank Moore, April 12, 1866, Moore Papers, DU. For a full discussion of the development of freedmen's schools, see Jacqueline Jones, *Soldiers of Light*.

11. Ginzberg, *Work of Benevolence*, 134–36, 172–73. Ginzberg notes that the transition to national politics was a move away from the religious authority that had previously governed their work.

12. Jeanie Attie (*Patriotic Toil*, chap. 4) has gone the furthest to reveal the complex grid of interests that impelled USSC president Henry Bellows and Woman's Central Relief Association liaison Louisa Lee Schuyler to misinterpret public disenchantment with the Sanitary Commission's big business approach. Fed up with rumors about the USSC's mishandling of supplies and the huge salaries paid to its wealthy leaders, female producers on the home front sought more reliable conduits for their "patriotic toil." For the questionable humanitarian loyalties of the USSC, see Frederickson, *Inner Civil War*, chap. 7.

13. See Rena Littlefield Miner pension file (#1130970), OIPF; Mary Gardner Holland to Elizabeth Avery Kime, March 18, 1895, Bickerdyke Papers, LC; and Holland, *Our Army Nurses*, 138–41.

14. Maria Bear Toliver pension file (#1161879), OIPF; see also Forman, *Guide to Civil War Washington*, 45–46, 50. Whether Freedman's was the contraband hospital attached to Camp Barker or Campbell Hospital, which became Freedman's Hospital in 1865, is not clear.

15. For evidence of job opportunities for ex-slaves, see, e.g., Taylor, *Reminiscences*; Jacobs, *Incidents in the Life of a Slave Girl*; Deborah Gray White, *Ar'n't I a Woman?*, 160–67; and Jacqueline Jones, *Labor of Love*, esp. chaps. 2–4. A small number of former slaves, including Harriet Jacobs, were able to get postwar work

as freedmen's teachers in the South. See Jacqueline Jones, *Soldiers of Light*, 34, 63–64.

16. Thomas Dublin (*Transforming Women's Work*, 159–60, 236–38) makes this argument about black women in New England. See also Gilmore, *Gender and Jim Crow*, 21–27.

17. H. E. Sterkx (*Partners in Rebellion*, 137) notes, for example, that Alabama women employed in wartime factories lost their livelihood with the destruction of factories and mills.

18. See "Sally Louisa Tompkins," *NAW* 3:471–72.

19. See Cumming Diary, October 1865–April 1867, Cumming Papers, ADAH.

20. "An Appeal to the Patriotic People of the South," Cumming Papers, ADAH. For other impoverished Confederate hospital workers, see Andrews, *Women of the South*, 127–28; Paquette, "A Bandage in One Hand"; and Holzman, "Sally Tompkins." Cumming's *Gleanings* resisted the nationalist impulse toward reunion of North and South. For more on the sentimentalization of reunion, see Schultz, "From Avenging Angel to 'Clara Barton of the Confederacy,'" and Silber, *Romance of Reunion*.

21. See "Ella King Newsom Trader," *NAW* 3:475–76. In her diary entry of May 24, 1862, Chesnut (*Chesnut's Civil War*, 350) wrote: "Coûte que coûte—and come what will, survive or perish—we will not go into one of the departments. We will not stand up all day at a table and cut notes apart, ordered round by a department clerk. We will live at home with our families and starve as a body."

22. Cumming, *Journal of Hospital Life*, 184.

23. Bridges, "Alabama Hospitals in Richmond."

24. Rable addresses these issues in *Civil Wars*, esp. chaps. 1, 11–12.

25. Massey (*Bonnet Brigades*, 109–10) and Rable (*Civil Wars*, 28–29) confirm the social acceptability of teaching for Southern women.

26. See Anne Firor Scott, *Southern Lady*, 110, and Massey, *Bonnet Brigades*, 142–43. For examples of Confederate women in wartime clerical work, see Conner et al., *South Carolina Women*, 31, 180. In Washington, D.C., women moved into government clerical jobs as early as the 1850s. After a stint as a schoolteacher in the 1850s, Clara Barton left her Massachusetts home to take a lucrative job in the U.S. Patent Office—evidence that even before the war, a small percentage of women was already performing such work. See Elizabeth Brown Pryor, *Clara Barton*, 77, and Oates, *Woman of Valor*, 10–13.

27. Massey, *Bonnet Brigades*, 121, 132–35; Rable, *Civil Wars*, 131.

28. After serving with the Army of the Potomac, Ann Eliza Gridley found a postwar position in the Patent Office, which she kept for thirty years. See Kate M. Scott, *In Honor of . . . Army Nurses*, n.p. See also Massey, *Bonnet Brigades*, 135–36, and Rable, *Civil Wars*, 132. Rable addresses Confederate women in Richmond government offices during the war years but notes similar salary and "spoils" dynamics.

29. Harriet Patience Dame pension file (#524192), PSAC.

30. See Mary Morris Husband pension file (#520821) and S. Rept. 710, June

18, 1884, PSAC. After working in the 1870s to establish an orphanage in Bath, Maine, Sarah Sampson in 1883 left home for the Pension Office (two years after the death of her husband), where she worked for twenty-three years—until her death in 1907. See MacCaskill and Novak, *Ladies on the Field*, 77–78.

31. For studies on gender and labor in the northern United States, see, e.g., Dublin, *Women at Work* and *Transforming Women's Work*; Kessler-Harris, *Out to Work*, esp. chaps. 3–5; and Foner, *Factory Girls*.

32. Husband to Frank Moore, January 30, 1866, Moore Papers, DU. Husband noted that Etheridge was from "a poor but respectable family." See also Conklin, *Women at Gettysburg*, 102–4. There is not much agreement about the year in which Etheridge was born, but from census evidence, it would appear to be 1839.

33. Taylor, *Reminiscences*, 61–76. For Taylor's dependence on female family members, see Elizabeth Young, *Disarming the Nation*, 201–2.

34. See Miss E. M. Granahan to the Pension Commissioner, Nancy Dodson Carter pension file (#1416752), Margaret A. Haynes deposition, August 17, 1896, and Rachael Anderson pension file (#1162327), OIPF.

35. Porter, *Memoir*; "Eliza Emily Chappell Porter," *NAW* 3:86–88. Pennsylvania's Salome Myers was happy to return to the classroom after the war, as was Mother Angela Gillespie. Myers nursed wounded men in her Gettysburg home and went on to marry Henry Stewart, the brother of a soldier who had died there. Widowed after only a year, Myers resumed her teaching work in 1868, anxious to support herself and her infant son. Gillespie directed the academic program at St. Mary's College near South Bend, Ind., and in the 1870s founded convent schools in Baltimore, Salt Lake, Washington, and Austin, Tex. Kate M. Scott lists many women who made teaching their careers, like Ada Johnson, who had nursed in St. Louis and on hospital transports, and taught for thirty years after the war. For more on Johnson and Myers (Stewart), see Kate M. Scott, *In Honor of . . . Army Nurses*, n.p., and Conklin, *Women at Gettysburg*, 117–20. See also "Mother Angela Gillespie," *NAW* 2:34–35.

36. See Cashman, *Headstrong*; "Amy Morris Bradley," *NAW* 1:220–22; and Correspondence from J. B. Abbott (September 1, 1864), Surgeon G. L. Sutton (August 26, 1864), and George E. Scott (August 17, 1864), Bradley record book, Bradley Letterbook, DU. Another war nurse, Sarah Chamberlin (Eccleston), who had served one year in Nashville, traveled to Argentina to establish kindergartens in the postwar years. See Kate M. Scott, *In Honor of . . . Army Nurses*.

37. Taylor, *Reminiscences*, 5–6; Haviland, *Woman's Life-Work*, 425–29, 515–16. For other war workers who went on to teach in freedmen's schools, see Hanaford, *Daughters of America*, 188.

38. Penn School Papers, SHC-UNC; Towne, *Letters and Diary*; "Laura Matilda Towne," *NAW* 3:472–74.

39. Grimké, *Journal*; "Charlotte Forten Grimké," *NAW* 2:95–97.

40. My reference is to Emily Dickinson's poem no. 709, which conveys the sense that to put one's intellect intentionally before a promiscuous assembly is to pollute oneself. For examples of unsigned Southern narratives, see Conner et al.,

*South Carolina Women*, 2:218, and News and Courier, *Our Women in the War*, 165, 173, 302.

41. After publishing *Hospital Sketches* in 1863, Alcott pursued a course that made her name a household word in less than a decade. The war figured prominently in *Little Women* (1868), *Work* (1872), and other stories, but her output was limited neither to juvenilia nor the war; the "Children's Friend" wrote seductive thrillers under various pseudonyms and used the profits to support her parents and sisters.

42. For publication statistics, see Drew Faust's introduction to Wilson's *Macaria*, xv–xvii, xxvii–xxviii. Wilson used royalties from *Macaria* and *St. Elmo* to sponsor orphanages in Alabama and Washington after the war.

43. Evans's financial situation—already promising by 1866—improved when she married wealthy Lorenzo Wilson in 1868. See Fidler, *Augusta Evans Wilson*; Faust, Introduction to *Macaria*; and "Augusta Jane Evans Wilson," *NAW* 3:625–26. Faust (*Mothers of Invention*, 178) argues that Evans surrendered her more radical position on female independence in the novels after *Macaria*.

44. Sutherland, *Confederate Carpetbaggers*, 36–40, 226–28; Harrison, *Recollections Grave and Gay*; "Constance Cary Harrison," *NAW* 2:146–47.

45. See Sutherland, *Confederate Carpetbaggers*, 259. Alice Fahs ("Feminized Civil War") argues that the work of Southern women writers became popular in the late 1870s after initial postwar acclaim for Northern women writers.

46. Cary scrapbook, correspondence from William Dean Howells to Cary in the 1880s, and Elizabeth Stoddard to Cary, January 1, 1891, Harrison Papers, LC. Virginian Sarah Pryor's trajectory was similar to Harrison's. Though she served in Richmond hospitals in 1862, Pryor's main commitment was to raising her seven children. At the end of the war she remained in Petersburg while her husband Roger tried to build a law practice in New York City. No easy task for an ex-Confederate who had edited a pro-secession newspaper, Roger Pryor slowly gained the goodwill of his former enemies, and his family was able to join him by 1868. Establishing herself initially as a music teacher, Sarah Pryor worked her way into New York society through participation in charities and historic preservation groups. When she ultimately sat down to write in her seventies, she produced works about Old Virginia—most notably her 1903 biography of Mary Washington, the first president's mother, and her 1907 history of the Jamestown settlement. See Pryor, *Reminiscences*; "Sara Agnes Rice Pryor," *NAW* 3:103–4; and Karen Manners Smith, "Recapturing Southern Identity."

47. The woman was Rachel Holton of Charlotte. See Anderson, *North Carolina Women*, 86.

48. Swisshelm, *Crusader and Feminist*; "Jane Grey Cannon Swisshelm," *NAW* 3:415–17. Like Swisshelm, Charlestonian Louisa McCord was at the end of a meteoric career as journalist, essayist, and translator when the war began. An economic correspondent for *DeBow's* and the *Southern Quarterly Review*, she wrote columns in defense of slavery and against woman suffrage in the 1850s. After managing a hospital in Columbia and losing her only son at Second Manassas in

1862, she retired from public life. "Louisa Susannah Cheves McCord," *NAW* 2:450–52.

49. See Lebsock, *Free Women of Petersburg*, 215, and Friedman, *Enclosed Garden*, xi–xiii, chap. 1.

50. See Venet, "Emergence of a Suffragist," 159.

51. Linus P. Brockett to Clara Barton, August 4, 1877, Barton Papers, LC.

52. "Harriet Tubman," *NAW* 3:481–83.

53. Gibbons, *Life*.

54. "Abby Hopper Gibbons," *NAW* 2:28–29.

55. See Ginzberg, *Work of Benevolence*, 155–56, 159–60, 175–76, and "Jane Currie Blaikie Hoge," *NAW* 2:199–201.

56. Livermore, *My Story of the War: The Civil War Memoirs*; Brockett and Vaughan, *Woman's Work*, 577–89; "Mary Ashton Rice Livermore," *NAW* 2:410–13.

57. See Paludan, *"People's Contest,"* 387–88, and "Mary Ashton Rice Livermore," *NAW* 2:410–13.

58. For Bickerdyke's involvement in the woman suffrage campaign, see Anna L. Clapp to Mary Ann Bickerdyke, September 16, 1869, and Bickerdyke speech, May 30, 1893, Bickerdyke Papers, LC.

59. Bickerdyke Papers, LC; Baker, *Cyclone in Calico*; "Mary Ann Ball Bickerdyke," *NAW* 1:144–46.

60. See USCC documents on special diet kitchens, Communications Received, 1862–65, Central Office, USCC, NARA, and Elizabeth D. Leonard, *Yankee Women*, chap. 2.

61. Wittenmyer, *Under the Guns*; Gallagher, "Annie Turner Wittenmyer"; "Annie Turner Wittenmyer," *NAW* 3:636–38. Though they were ultimately under government purview, women designed the day-to-day workings of such homes, leaving the imprint of female benevolence on them. See Patrick J. Kelley, *Creating a National Home*, 10–11.

62. Pomroy, *Echoes*, 249. Anna L. Boyden—a friend of Pomroy's—was the editor of Pomroy's published letters. But Pomroy, who was still working in 1884 when the collection was published, would have had to hand over the letters to Boyden and give her permission for publication to have taken place. Neither Pomroy's nor Boyden's motives are made clear in the collection, although it was not uncommon for those wary of self-promotion to seek ambassadors to the public.

63. See Conklin, *Women at Gettysburg*, 114–15, and Beers, "Camp Nichols," *Memories*, 319–23. Camp Nichols opened in 1884.

64. See Mottus, *New York Nightingales*, 40–41.

65. See Kalisch and Kalisch, *Advance of American Nursing*, 96.

66. See Mottus, *New York Nightingales*, 42–43, and Woolsey, *A Century of Nursing*, 94, 137–62. Significantly, no former Southern worker associated herself with nursing education or the professionalization of the field in the postwar years. Faust (*Mothers of Invention*, 111) notes that "the Cummings, Pembers, and Newsoms of the South wrote their memoirs and faded away."

67. Since the 1850s classes in nursing had been offered at several women's medical colleges, including Emily and Elizabeth Blackwell's New York Infirmary for Women and Children. See Kalisch and Kalisch, *Advance of American Nursing*, 94.

68. For a history of discriminatory practices in nurse training and hiring, see Hine, *Black Women in White*; Melosh, *Physician's Hand*, 76; and Reverby, *Ordered to Care*, esp. chap. 9.

69. For nursing educators' wish to professionalize nursing, see Melosh, *Physician's Hand*, 29–30.

70. See Kalisch and Kalisch, *Advance of American Nursing*, 110. The Carded Service Records list ten women named "Billings." Von Olnhausen's partner was most likely Sarah Billings of Massachusetts, born in 1818 like Von Olnhausen. Linus Brockett reported in 1877 that Mary Morris Husband headed up a nurse training school in St. Louis, and in 1881 that the training school was in New York City, but I have found no other reference to that activity. See Brockett to Clara Barton, August 4, 1877, November 18, 1881, Barton Papers, LC.

71. Linus Brockett wrote to Clara Barton in 1877 that Parsons was ensconced in her Cambridge hospital. Brockett to Barton, August 4, 1877, Barton Papers, LC. See also Parsons, *Memoir*, and "Emily Elizabeth Parsons," *NAW* 3:21–23.

72. See Barton, *Angels of the Battlefield*; Jolly, *Nuns of the Battlefield*; and "Sister Anthony O'Connell," *NAW* 2:647–48.

73. See Maher, *To Bind Up the Wounds*, 36, 70–72.

74. "Abby Howland Woolsey," "Jane Stuart Woolsey," and "Georgeanna Muirson Woolsey," *NAW* 3:665–68; Mottus, *New York Nightingales*, 33, 49, 51.

75. "Abby, Jane, and Georgeanna Woolsey," *NAW* 3:665–68.

76. See Morantz-Sanchez, *Sympathy and Science*; Walsh, *"Doctors Wanted"*; Abram, *"Send Us a Lady Physician"*; and Blake, "Women and Medicine." Mary Elizabeth Massey (*Bonnet Brigades*, 63) notes that the barriers against women in medicine eroded more quickly during the war years.

77. The three Southerners were Ella Cooper, Elizabeth Carraway Holland, and Orrie R. Moon. The thirteen Northerners were Mary Blackmar, Chloe Annette Buckel, Caroline Burghardt, Sarah Chadwick Clapp, Susan Edson, Harriet Dada Emens, Esther Hill Hawks, Nancy Maria Hill, Frances M. Nye, Mary Jane Safford, Vesta Ward Swarts, Mary Edwards Walker, and Caroline Brown Winslow.

78. For Zakrzewska's alliance with the Blackwells, her travails with Gregory, and her establishment of the New England Hospital for Women and Children, see Morantz-Sanchez, *Sympathy and Science*, 82–84, and Abram, *"Send Us a Lady Physician,"* 90–92.

79. The historian in question is Edward Warren, quoted in Hall, "Confederate Medicine," 498. See also Marshall, "Nurse Heroines," 320.

80. According to Mary Elizabeth Massey (*Bonnet Brigades*, 63), the Chicago Hospital for Women and Children opened in 1863 under the direction of Dr. Mary H. Thompson, but it would appear that Buckel was actually its founder in 1859.

81. See C. Annette Buckel pension bill, S. Rept. 2325, April 18, 1904, PSAC;

Seigel, "She Went to War," 19; Powers, *Hospital Pencillings*, 95; "Cloe [*sic*] Annette Buckel," *NAW* 1:265–67; and Massey Papers, Winthrop College Archives, Rock Hill, S.C.

82. Esther Hill Hawks, *Woman Doctor's Civil War*, 11; John Milton Hawks Diary, September n.d., 1864, Hawks Papers, LC.

83. For more on the WNLL, see Venet, *Neither Ballots nor Bullets*, 101–22.

84. Hawks, *Woman Doctor's Civil War*, 270–82.

85. See Rable, *Civil Wars*, 127–28. The third Confederate doctor was Elizabeth Carraway Holland, of New Bern, N.C., about whom little is known. See Anderson, *North Carolina Women*, 18.

86. See Moldow, *Women Doctors*, 12, 17, 107; Brockett and Vaughan, *Woman's Work*, 444–47; and Logan, *The Part Taken*, 358.

87. See Adelaide W. Smith, *Reminiscences*, 140; *Michigan Women in the Civil War*, 106–7; and Conklin, *Women at Gettysburg*, 270–72.

88. See Nancy Maria Hill pension file (#1138537), OIPF; Holland, *Our Army Nurses*, 82–85; Stimson and Thompson, "Women Nurses with the Union Forces," 219; and Logan, *The Part Taken*, 374.

89. See Caroline Assenath Grant Burghardt pension file (#550210) and S. Rept. 2217, February 12, 1891, PSAC; Holland, *Our Army Nurses*, 558–60; and Moldow, *Women Doctors*, 23.

90. See Brockett and Vaughan, *Woman's Work*, 431–39, and Conklin, *Women of Gettysburg*, 272–74.

91. See Adelaide W. Smith, *Reminiscences*, 95.

92. See Livermore, *My Story of the War: The Civil War Memoirs*, 206–16; Fischer, "Cairo's Civil War Angel"; "Mary Jane Safford," *NAW* 3:220–22; and Mary J. Safford to Clara Barton, March 6, 1870, Barton Papers, LC.

93. See Vesta Ward Swarts pension files (#965256 and #1006153), OIPF, and Holland, *Our Army Nurses*, 144–46.

94. See Elizabeth D. Leonard, *Yankee Women*, 120, and "Mary Edwards Walker," *NAW* 3:532–33.

95. See Assistant Surgeon J. N. Green to Surgeon General (December 11, 1861), Surgeon George E. Cooper to Surgeon General (September 10, 1863), and Surgeons F. H. Gross, J. Perkins, and Roberts Barthalow to Surgeon General (March 8, 1864), Papers Relating to Dr. Mary E. Walker, OAGVSB, NARA. See also the excellent account of Walker's trials with the medical bureaucracy in Elizabeth D. Leonard, *Yankee Women*, 131–34.

96. For a detailed account of this incident, see Schultz, "Women at the Front," 3. See also Elizabeth D. Leonard, *Yankee Women*, 138–40.

97. See, e.g., B. J. Semmes to Jorantha Semmes, April 12, 1864, Massey Papers, Winthrop College Archives, Rock Hill, S.C., and Rowland Journal, April 14, 1864, Special Collections, Emory University, Atlanta. For Walker's incarceration, see "Memoirs of Brigadier-General William Montgomery Gardner," Elizabeth McKinne, ed., #mf 036, n.d., GDAH.

98. Elizabeth Leonard (*Yankee Women*, 140) has argued that Walker was in ill health at the time she was released from Castle Thunder and that this and other incidents of exposure hastened the end of her medical practice.

99. For Barton's lecture tour, see Barton Miscellany, Barton Papers, LC, and Oates, *Woman of Valor*, 373–81.

100. For a full description of these proceedings, see Snyder, *Dr. Mary Walker*, 114–19.

101. For notice of Walker's Medal of Honor, see *New York Herald*, November 23, 1865. See also W. H. DeMotte to President Andrew Johnson, June 12, 1865, and Mary E. Walker to President Johnson, January 24, 1866, Papers Relating to Dr. Mary E. Walker, OAGVSB, NARA. A 1977 act of Congress reinstated Walker's medal posthumously.

102. I make this argument in greater detail in Schultz, "Inhospitable Hospital."

103. See Cashin, *Family Venture*; Faust, "Trying to Do a Man's Business"; and Anne Firor Scott, *Southern Lady*, 109. Suzanne Lebsock has noted that the black and white women of Petersburg, Va., had worked in cotton and tobacco production in the antebellum years, but that industrial expansion tended to exclude them. Moreover, industrial jobs were scarce throughout the South immediately after the war. See Lebsock, *Free Women of Petersburg*, 10–11, and chap. 6, and Ayers, *Promise of the New South*, chap. 5.

104. See Conklin, *Women at Gettysburg*, 36–40.

## Chapter Six

1. See Isabella Fogg pension file (#129830), PSAC; Moore, *Women of the War*, 125–26; and MacCaskill and Novak, *Women on the Field*, 47–50. From a hospital in Cincinnati, Fogg arranged for her soldier-son Hugh, recovering from a leg amputation, to be transferred from his own hospital bed in Baltimore to one in Philadelphia, where she thought he would receive better care.

2. Martha Spicer pension file (#457620), OIPF. For an example of coordinating a special act of Congress, see J. H. Campbell to Mary Ann Bickerdyke, December 31, 1885, Bickerdyke Papers, LC.

3. Elizabeth Martin Handy pension file (#1128485), OIPF. For how illiteracy affected pension applicants, see Shaffer, "'I Do Not Suppose That Uncle Sam Looks at the Skin,'" 135, 137.

4. See Sanders, "Paying for the 'Bloody Shirt,'" 138.

5. See WRC pamphlet, Barton Miscellany, Barton Papers, LC.

6. Silber, *Romance of Reunion*. Gaines Foster (*Ghosts*) and LeeAnn Whites (*Crisis in Gender*) also observe this phenomenon.

7. See Glasson, *Military Pension Legislation*, 16–17, and McClintock, "Civil War Pensions," 463.

8. See Sanders, "Paying for the 'Bloody Shirt,'" 139.

9. Ibid., 142–44; McClintock, "Civil War Pensions," 464.

10. See Gordon, "New Feminist Scholarship"; Sapiro, "Gender Basis of

American Social Policy"; Mink, "The Lady and the Tramp"; and Nelson, "Origins of the Two-Channel Welfare State."

11. Theda Skocpol (*Protecting Soldiers*, 102, 110, 132) argues that what had been military pensions awarded on the basis of war-related injury became a de facto old-age pension program, with some similarities to our present Social Security system.

12. See ibid., 143–45, and McClintock, "Civil War Pensions," 471–79.

13. Sanders ("Paying for the 'Bloody Shirt,'" 151–52) notes a similar trend in the pensioning of soldiers and their families: By 1890, the greatest number of pensions went to Americans of Anglo-Saxon heritage.

14. The Surgeon General's Order No. 23 of 1864 stated that only persons of African descent could be hired as cooks. See Surgeon Warren Webster to Dorothea Dix, February 26, 1864, Dix Nursing Papers, NARA.

15. Surgeon General John Moore to Secretary of War, April 8, 1890, Classified Schedule of Female Hospital Employes [*sic*] Record and Pension Division, War Department, NARA.

16. My count of the raw data in the Union Carded Service Records, NARA, revealed 21,208 workers. By dividing the number who requested pensions into the total number of women who appear in the Carded Service Records, I concluded that approximately one in nine female workers requested pensions. The Carded Service Records include only women who appeared on hospital payrolls; many who donated their services do not appear. Therefore the total number of female workers is likely to have been greater than 21,208, which would render even smaller the percentage of those requesting pensions. Moreover, not all of the 2,448 pension applicants served in the Civil War. A few appear to have been active in the Spanish American War, and some of the names are those of men who presumably were applying for pensions because they, too, were army nurses. Therefore the estimate of one in nine, based on dividing 2,448 claims by 21,208 workers, may be slightly inflated. See OIPF. No scholar has tabulated how many of the 2,448 workers actually received pensions. Several turn-of-the-century works celebrate the Army Nurses Pension Act but do not provide any statistical summary. See, e.g., Kate M. Scott, *In Honor of . . . Army Nurses* (1910), and *Woman's Relief Corps Red Book* (1897).

17. In a study of Civil War widows' pensions, Amy E. Holmes ("'Such Is the Price We Pay'") contends that by 1886 widows were receiving twelve dollars per month. But Skocpol (*Protecting Soldiers*, 106–7) dismisses the notion of any standard pension amount for widows.

18. The WRC saw to it, for example, that a bill be introduced in Congress in 1885 on behalf of celebrated nurse Mary Ann Bickerdyke. See Abbie M. Gannett to Mary Ann Bickerdyke, September 8, 1885, Bickerdyke Papers, LC, and S. Rept. 351, March 31, 1886, 49th Cong., 1st sess., Bickerdyke pension file (#574178), PSAC. In the same congressional session, Adeliza Perry also was pensioned by special act, appealing to legislators on the basis of ill health. Because she had contracted malaria in the service, she had been "greatly hindered and impeded in the performance of anything like remunerative labor" in the intervening two decades.

See H. Rept. 3071, June 25, 1886, 49th Cong., 1st sess., Adeliza Perry pension file (#599919), PSAC.

19. See H.R. 1610, May 20, 1884, 48th Cong., 1st sess., Harriet Patience Dame pension file (#524192), and S. Rept. 2217, February 12, 1891, 51st Cong., 2d sess., Caroline Burghardt pension file (#992181), PSAC.

20. See, e.g., the special acts of Congress for Mary Morris Husband, who spent $2,000 of her own money, and Annie Turner Wittenmyer and Harriet Stinson Pond, who spent $3,000, in PSAC.

21. See special act of July 13, 1868, Harriet Stinson Pond pension file (#116340), PSAC. For comparison, see the 1867 pension claim of Sarah Wilcox Roberts (#130221), OIPF. Roberts filed as a soldier's dependent, even though she rendered service as a regimental worker.

22. Caroline Burghardt pension file (#550210), PSAC. Anna Morris Holstein, who applied only two months before the act, was also pensioned at this amount. The special acts pensioning Adeliza Perry in 1866 and Harriet Dada Emens and Mary C. Upton in 1890 were also funded at $12 per month. See Holstein (#1126339), Perry (#599919), Emens (#778849), and Upton (#776090) pension files, PSAC.

23. Fanny Titus-Hazen pension file (#1130928), OIPF.

24. Dr. Vesta M. Swarts to James F. Davenport, February 7, 1913, Swarts pension file (#1140543), OIPF.

25. Swarts to Davenport, February 28, 1913, Swarts deposition, February 27, 1914, and Swarts pension file, OIPF.

26. Swarts to Davenport, March 3, 1913, Swarts pension file, OIPF.

27. See Elizabeth Leonard's ("Civil War Nurse," 204–5) discussion of Mary Newcomb's widow's pension, which enabled her to volunteer her nursing services.

28. See WRC pamphlet, Barton Miscellany, Barton Papers, LC.

29. For the National Asylum movement (later the National Home for Disabled Volunteer Soldiers), see Patrick J. Kelley, *Creating a National Home*.

30. Kate B. Sherwood to Clara Barton, February 21, 1890, Barton Papers, LC. On the petition itself, see George Fuller to Barton, February 12, 1890, Barton Papers, LC.

31. See Skocpol, *Protecting Soldiers*, 121.

32. Sarah E. Fuller to Clara Barton, February 10, 1890, Barton Papers, LC.

33. Kate M. Scott, *In Honor of . . . Army Nurses*, 1. Echoing the sentiment that nurses deserved a pension as much as soldiers was Mrs. E. L. Norton, who had served with Mary Ann Bickerdyke at Pittsburg Landing (Shiloh) and was shocked to discover public disapprobation on the subject of a pension for nurses. See Norton to Bickerdyke, February 16, 1886, Bickerdyke Papers, LC.

34. This was the case with Pennsylvania relief worker Anna Morris Holstein, whose husband was a USSC agent. See Holstein, *Three Years*, and Holstein pension file (#1126339), PSAC.

35. Cornelia Hancock to Commissioner of Pensions William Lochren, February 20, 1895, Hancock pension file (#1162959), OIPF.

36. See Sanders, "Paying for the 'Bloody Shirt,'" 143. In addition to carrying the pensions of Civil War veterans and their kin, the Pension Bureau in 1886 was still carrying 13,397 widows of soldiers who had fought in the War of 1812. Each widow received $12 per month. See Glasson, *Military Pension Legislation*, 24, 37–38, 64–65, 91.

37. S. Rept. 2317, February 24, 1892, 52d Cong., 1st sess., Classified Schedule of Female Hospital Employes [*sic*], Record and Pension Division, War Department, NARA. The graduated scale was proposed as follows: nurses with three months to one year of service would receive $12 per month; from one year to three years, $20 per month; and more than three years, $25 per month.

38. H.R. 7294, March 16, 1892, 52d Cong., 1st sess., ibid.

39. See, e.g., Circular No. 3, June 24, 1893, AGO Document File, Box 69, Department of the Interior, NARA; Pension Commissioner William Lochren to Colonel L. C. Ainsworth, Record and Pension Division, July 5, 1893, AGO Document File, ibid.; and H.R. 9603, December 14, 1896, 54th Cong., 2d sess., Classified Schedule of Female Hospital Employes [*sic*], Record and Pension Division, War Department, NARA.

40. See Conklin, *Women at Gettysburg*, 314–15. Neither Esther Hill Hawks, who worked with African American troops in the Sea Islands, nor Jane Hoge, who traveled throughout the western theater as a USSC agent, appears in the records, for example.

41. See WRC brochure of 1906, Miscellany, Barton Papers, LC.

42. Elizabeth Nichols to Pension Bureau, September 23, 1862, and Green B. Raum to Nichols, January 23, 1893, Nichols pension file (#1131954), OIPF.

43. "History of Claimant's Disability," August 18, 1898, Nichols pension file (#1131954), OIPF. I cannot account for the more standardized spelling and grammar of the later testimony. Perhaps Nichols sought editorial help in drafting her 1898 affidavit.

44. See H.R. 1418, February 11, 1892, 52d Cong., 1st sess., and H.R. 950, January 17, 1895, 53d Cong., 3d sess., AGO Document File, Box 69, Department of the Interior, NARA.

45. Sarah A. Clapp to Pension Commissioner Warner, September 9, 1907, and Pension Bureau to Clapp, October 18, 1907, Clapp pension file (#610330), OIPF.

46. Surgeon General William Hammond statement, June 16, 1862, Surgeon General to Commissioner of Pensions, March 15, 1894, and Lavinia Payne statement, March 23, 1897, H.R. 1921, 55th Cong., 3d sess., Payne pension file (#1152578), PSAC.

47. Circular No. 3, Department of the Interior, June 24, 1893, Army Nurse Corps Historical Data File, USGO, NARA.

48. Mary Ann Bickerdyke corresponded with soldiers she had nursed during the war well into the 1890s. See, e.g., H. W. Rood to Bickerdyke, September 26, 1891, and N. B. Hood to Bickerdyke, December 9, 1895, Bickerdyke Papers, LC.

49. Michigan's Jennie Fyfe, a USSC nurse stationed in Paducah, Ky., had a similar problem. Papers of the northwestern branch of the commission had been

donated to the Chicago Historical Society shortly after the war, but the collection perished in the Great Fire of 1871, along with proof of Fyfe's service. See Fyfe pension file (#1150420), OIPF.

50. See Annie Turner Wittenmyer to Commissioner William Lochren, November 29, 1893, Christian Newcomer to "Whom It May Concern," December 26, 1893, and Ruth Danforth to William Lochren, July 21, 1893, Danforth pension file (#1140928), AGO Document File, Box 69, Department of the Interior, NARA. See also Annie Turner Wittenmyer to Mary Ann Bickerdyke, November 22, 1897, Bickerdyke Papers, LC.

51. War Department to Ruth Danforth, n.d., Danforth pension file (#1140928), AGO Document File, Box 69, Department of the Interior, NARA. The Pension Bureau responded similarly to Dr. Vesta Swarts's use of testimony from Wittenmyer and USCC president George H. Stuart, neither of whom it believed had authority to hire nurses. See Swarts pension file (#1140543), OIPF.

52. Annie Turner Wittenmyer to Mary Ann Bickerdyke, June 24, November 22, 1897, Bickerdyke Papers, LC.

53. See H.R. 210, January 20, 1898, 55th Cong., 2d sess., Wittenmyer pension file (#1207237), PSAC.

54. Usher even cited references to her nursing activities in the commemorative volume by Linus P. Brockett and Mary Vaughan, *Woman's Work*, but the Pension Bureau did not find these examples persuasive. See Rebecca Usher pension file (#1132097), OIPF.

55. In my earlier account of this case, I misidentified Jane C. Hoge Patton as the Jane C. B. Hoge described in Chapter 5. See Schultz, "Race, Gender, and Bureaucracy," 51–52.

56. Patton could only remember having served "on the battle fields & in tents. . . . in one Hospital where I was they bomb shelled it[.] I dont remember where it was as my mind & memory has failed me so." See Commissioner J. L. Davenport to Jane Hoge Patton, April 16, 1913, and Patton to Commissioner of Pensions, April 20, 1913, Patton pension file (#1408621), OIPF.

57. See Miss E. M. Granahan to "Dear Sir," February 1, 1915, Nancy Dodson Carter pension file (#1416752), OIPF.

58. WRC proceedings indicate that unpensioned nurses were occasionally aided by this means. The WRC in Kansas paid the mortgage of former regimental worker Eunice Norton Godfrey Mahaffey in the 1890s when her husband died and Mahaffey was left to support her ninety-five-year old mother. Records indicate that Mahaffey never applied for a nurse's pension, even though her service with the 11th Kansas Volunteers would have entitled her to one. Anna Lawrence Platt was able to supplement her $12 pension with WRC monies when she was ill in the late 1890s. The WRC also established a home in Madison, Ohio, which had thirteen of the "dear old women" living there in 1891. Mahaffey pension file (#W.O. 478192), OIPF; unknown correspondent from Delevan, Ill., to Mary Ann Bickerdyke, December 7, 1891, and Anna Lawrence Platt to Bickerdyke, January

21, 1900[?], Bickerdyke Papers, LC. See also *Journal of the 28th National Convention of the Woman's Relief Corps*, 359, and Logan, *The Part Taken*, 343.

59. Margaret O'Donnell affidavit, January 4, 1893, O'Donnell pension file (#1130043), AGO Document File, Box 69, Department of the Interior, NARA.

60. George Avery affidavit, January 4, 1893, and Brevet Lieutenant Colonel S. B. Lamoreaux to Mrs. O'Donnell, October 12, 1865, O'Donnell pension file, ibid. The testimonial was "a token of our respect for your attention and kindness during the time we have been, as it were, a member of your family."

61. John M. Reynolds, Assistant Secretary, to "The Commissioner of Pensions," n.d. [May 1894?], O'Donnell pension file, ibid.

62. Commissioner William Lochren to A. D. Wilkinson, May 19, 1894, O'Donnell pension file, ibid.

63. Letter of September 8, 1865 from officers of the 3rd Maryland Cavalry, and Catherine Oliphant service record dated September 7, 1865, Oliphant Papers, LC.

64. Letter of Junius Turner, August 2, 1916, ibid.; Catherine Oliphant pension file (#574007), OIPF.

65. One can cross-reference pension rosters with the Carded Service Records in NARA, but racial data were not always recorded on the cards. An unscientific search in the pension index for 204 black women named in the Carded Service Records yielded only 12 who filed applications with the Pension Bureau. Of those 12, only 4 actually received pensions, suggesting that less than 6 percent of black workers applied, and only one-third of that 6 percent (or fewer than 2 percent of black workers overall) were awarded pensions. Because racial categories were probably assigned by the hospital administrators hiring female workers or the clerks registering them on staff, the records are not definitive and should be approached with caution.

66. Henry Glasson (*Military Pension Legislation*, 119) estimated that the names of 650 army nurses were on the rolls by 1900, but pension claims continued to be filed well into the 1920s. As late as 1913, the pension commissioner explained to widow's pension applicant Vesta Swarts that "a separate record showing the number of army nurse pensioners is not kept by the Bureau." Commissioner of Pensions James F. Davenport to Dr. Vesta Swarts, February 25, 1913, Swarts pension file (#1140543), OIPF.

67. See Shaffer, "'I Do Not Suppose That Uncle Sam Looks at the Skin,'" for an intriguing discussion of the particular disadvantages facing African American soldiers in the pensioning process, many of which also applied to African American relief workers.

68. Maria Mann, a white teacher in a freedmen's camp in Helena, Ark., noted in 1863 that simply establishing a daily routine was her charges' greatest challenge. See correspondence of Maria R. Mann to Mary Mann, Mann Papers, LC.

69. For the problems of race and textual mediation, see Musher, "'The Way the Almighty Wants It,'" esp. 2–5, 10–14.

70. Even among nurses who were thought to have liberal views on race, black

workers were seldom described individually. Louisa May Alcott referred to the laundresses at Georgetown's Union Hotel Hospital as "a knot of colored sisters." And Emily Elizabeth Parsons, matron at Benton Barracks near St. Louis, spoke of wards "where we have colored women and children; it is very funny, the queerest little pickaninnies!" Although Parsons would institute a program to train black nurses, none of her correspondence mentioned individual black women. Alcott, *Hospital Sketches*, 22; Parsons, *Memoir*, 132–33, 135, 144.

71. William H. Mullins to Commissioner William Lochren, March 15, 1895, Malinda McFarland Jackson pension file (#1161092), OIPF. Mullins went on to say that all of his Civil War records had been destroyed in a fire, making it impossible for him to corroborate the applicant's testimony even if he had remembered her.

72. The USCC, for whom Wittenmyer worked, employed only white women in its diet kitchens. For the number 618, see Wittenmyer to Mary Ann Bickerdyke, November 22, 1897, Bickerdyke Papers, LC.

73. Parsons, *Memoir*, 133–35, 144, and Bradley Diary, entries for December 1862 and January 1863, DU.

74. See S. Rept. 2239, April 18, 1904, 58th Cong., 2d sess., Buckel pension file (#1314124), PSAC.

75. For more on the working relations between black and white hospital workers, see Schultz, "Seldom Thanked, Never Praised, and Scarcely Recognized."

76. Margaret A. Haynes deposition taken by Special Examiner James H. Clements, October 9, 1896, Rachel Anderson pension file (#1162327), OIPF. In the case of black soldiers, Shaffer ("'I Do Not Suppose That Uncle Sam Looks at the Skin,'" 141) argues that "a few ex-slaveholders perjured themselves in the hopes of derailing a claim," a motive similar to that of Haynes's employer.

77. Though neither Alcott nor Ropes mentions Cleaver in their accounts of the war, during the period that Cleaver served at Union Hotel Hospital, both women contracted typhoid. Ropes died in the hospital; fearful surgeons requested that Alcott be sent home lest the death of another female employee give the hospital a bad name. Alcott, whose service was cut to only six weeks by the illness, was carried back to Massachusetts to complete her recovery. See Alcott, *Hospital Sketches*, and Ropes, *Civil War Nurse*.

78. Matilda Cleaver John to Andrew Davidson, February 17, 1893, John pension file (#1139370), OIPF.

79. J. W. Patterson to Commissioner of Pensions, February 27, 1893, ibid.

80. See deposition of Sarah Thompson Gammon, November 5, 1897, Gammon pension file (#1159071), OIPF.

81. Webster Davis to Commissioner of Pensions, n.d., ibid.

82. Maria Bear Toliver deposition taken by Special Examiner W. H. Hamsberger, October 11,1897, Toliver pension file (#1161879), OIPF.

83. Louisa Frazer deposition taken by Special Examiner W. H. Hamsberger, October 11, 1897, ibid.

84. Betsey Lawson deposition taken by Special Examiner A. H. Thompson, May 11, 1895, ibid.

85. See McClintock, "Civil War Pensions," 471–72.

86. Amanda Jones deposition taken by Special Examiner R. S. McCall, October 7, 1903, Jones pension file (#W.O. 756912), OIPF.

87. Minerva Dillard Washington deposition taken by Special Examiner N. H. Nicholson, October 9, 1905, Washington pension file (#1330575), OIPF.

88. Cynthia Franklin Shields and Annie Ragan Carmickles depositions, January 17, 1905, ibid.

89. N. H. Nicholson to Commissioner of Pensions, November 20, 1905, ibid.

90. Ibid.

91. Surgeon Henry W. Brown affidavit, June 6, 1894, and Brown to Commissioner of Pensions, July 16, 1894, Jones pension file (#W.O. 756912), OIPF.

92. For African American army marriages in the South and the social restrictions made possible through marriage, see Frankel, "Southern Side of 'Glory,'" 31.

93. Special Examiner E. D. Narrington to Commissioner of Pensions, January 31, 1903, Jones pension file (#W.O. 756912), OIPF.

94. Chaplain Reed's testimony reported by Special Examiner R. S. McCall to Commissioner of Pensions, October 8, 1903, ibid. For problems that arose regarding ex-slave surnames, see Shaffer, "'I Do Not Suppose That Uncle Sam Looks at the Skin,'" 136–38.

95. Special Examiner P. J. McCall to Commissioner of Pensions, October 8, 1903, Jones pension file (#W.O. 756912), OIPF.

96. Amanda Jones deposition taken by Special Examiner E. D. Narrington, October 7, 1903, ibid.

97. Special Examiner E. D. Narrington to Commissioner of Pensions, January 31, 1903, ibid.

98. Amanda Jones deposition, October 7, 1903, ibid.

99. Special Examiner R. S. McCall to Commissioner of Pensions, October 8, 1903, ibid.

100. Special Examiner E. D. Narrington to Commissioner of Pensions, January 31, 1903, ibid.


## Chapter Seven

1. Mary E. Walker to Frank Moore, May 4, 1866, Moore Papers, DU.

2. Judge Advocate General Joseph Holt to Secretary of War Edwin Stanton, October 30, 1865, Papers Relating to Dr. Mary E. Walker, OAGVSB, NARA.

3. Elizabeth Leonard (*Yankee Women*, 155–56) has suggested that Congress awarded the medal to rid the capital of Walker once and for all.

4. In fact, the Southern Historical Association was formed in 1869 to counteract the cultural impact of Northern-inflected narratives. See Cullen, *The Civil War in Popular Culture*, 109, 111.

5. Beers, "The Confederate Reunion at Dallas," *Memories*, 314.

6. See Beers, *Memories*, frontispiece.

7. The phrase comes from Nina Silber's essay "Intemperate Men, Spiteful Women."

8. Blight, "Quarrel Forgotten," 154–56.

9. Brockett and Vaughan, *Woman's Work*, 781.

10. Powers, *Hospital Pencillings*, 30; Hoge, *Boys in Blue*, 14.

11. Henry W. R. Jackson's *Southern Women of the Second American Revolution*, published in 1863 in the hope of stimulating more widespread participation in war relief, included no first-person narratives of hospital life.

12. News and Courier, *Our Women in the War*, 426. See also accounts of workers' responses to having to nurse Union soldiers (pp. 227, 249).

13. Blight ("Quarrel Forgotten," 157, 164–69) has observed a similar phenomenon in his account of the fiftieth anniversary of the battle of Gettysburg.

14. See Blight, *Race and Reunion*; Reardon, *Pickett's Charge*; and Savage, *Standing Soldiers, Kneeling Slaves*.

15. Blight, *Race and Reunion*; Reardon, *Pickett's Charge*; and Savage, *Standing Soldiers, Kneeling Slaves*; Eicher, *Mystic Chords of Memory*.

16. If one compares the soldier's national monument at Gettysburg, erected in 1869, with the Confederate soldiers' pyramid at Hollywood Cemetery in Richmond, constructed in the 1880s, the difference in conceptualization becomes apparent. James Mayo (*War Memorials*, 174–75) notes that early monuments to the Civil War are much more graphic and realistic in their depiction of soldiers than the more distant and abstract portrayals of later monuments. See also Eicher, *Mystic Chords of Memory*, 92, 138.

17. For nineteenth-century domesticity, see, e.g., Bleser, *In Joy and in Sorrow*; Cashin, *Family Venture*; Cott, *Bonds of Womanhood*; Fox-Genovese, *Within the Plantation Household*; Friedman, *Enclosed Garden*; Mary Kelley, *Private Woman, Public Stage*; and Sklar, *Catherine Beecher*.

18. A photograph of the Bickerdyke monument can be found in the *Galesburg (Ill.) Daily Republican Register* for May 23, 1907. The monument at Macon is pictured in Conklin, *Women at Gettysburg*, 34.

19. James Mayo (*War Memorials*, 171) states that most Southern monument building was not done until the twentieth century, as one of the legacies of Southern defeat. The Columbia monument is dedicated to all of the women of South Carolina and does not single out its hospital workers. See photograph and inscription in Campbell and Rice, *Woman's War*, 172–73. For the monuments at Rome, Columbia, and Baltimore, see photographs in Conklin, *Women at Gettysburg*, 34, 39, 370.

20. The bas-relief is located at the junction of M Street and Rhode Island Avenue in the northwest quadrant of the city.

21. See Coski and Feely, "Monument to Southern Womanhood," 137.

22. Gaines Foster makes this point in *Ghosts*, 38. Patrick Kelley (*Creating a National Home*, chap. 3) has observed a corresponding gender dynamic in the USSC's sponsorship of soldiers' homes in 1865 and the increasingly male administration of such facilities in the 1870s.

23. Gaines Foster (*Ghosts*, 39, 42–43) notes a similarly named cemetery established by the LMA of Raleigh. LMAs from Fredericksburg to Columbus, Ga., celebrated Confederate Memorial Day in May, when citizens would file to cemeteries, decorate graves, and listen to speeches by local dignitaries. See also Napier, "Montgomery during the Civil War," 116, and Coski and Feely, "Monument to Southern Womanhood," 134–37.

24. Quoted in Lebsock, *Free Women of Petersburg*, 249.

25. Whites, *Crisis in Gender*, 13–14, 160–65, 186.

26. On Maine relief workers, see Sudlow, *A Vast Army of Women*.

27. See Foster, *Ghosts*, 135, and Ayers, *Promise of the New South*, 334–35. See also Clinton, *Tara Revisited*, 185–86. One group was known as the Children of the Confederacy.

28. Foster, *Ghosts*, 128–29.

29. See Charles Reagan Wilson, *Baptized in Blood*, 51, 140–41, and Foster, *Ghosts*, 116, 120, 172–75.

30. Charles Reagan Wilson, *Baptized in Blood*, 105–6; Foster, *Ghosts*, 172 (UDC membership statistics). Clinton (*Tara Revisited*, 182–83) reports that from 1900 to 1920 UDC membership rose from 17,000 to 70,000. In 1937 the UDC's sponsorship of a Harpers Ferry monument to a slave raised considerable internal opposition. Similarly, Augustus Saint-Gaudens's 1897 bronze relief of the 54th Massachusetts Infantry has inspired poetic and cinematic analyses of white racial anxiety. See Timothy Sweet's discussion of Robert Lowell's 1962 "For the Union Dead" in *Traces of War*, 201–5, and Jim Cullen's of the 1989 film *Glory* in *The Civil War in Popular Culture*, 143–71.

31. Army nurses were also expected to pay $1 annual dues to the organization. See WRC proceedings from the headquarters of the NAAN, Phoenixville, Pa., 1899, Bickerdyke Papers, LC. For the GAR encampment of 1892, see Lawrence, *Autobiography*, 169.

32. See souvenir program of the NAAN, printed matter file, Bickerdyke Papers, LC, and 1907 brochure of the WRC, Barton Miscellany, Barton Papers, LC.

33. Clinton, *Tara Revisited*, 186–87.

34. Cullen, *The Civil War in Popular Culture*, 12; Coski and Feely, "Monument to Southern Womanhood," 138, 149–51.

35. Books like Tony Horwitz's *Confederates in the Attic* (1998) show the extent to which Americans North and South buy into the reactionary values of the Confederate past.

36. *St. Louis Post-Dispatch*, June 2, 1996. One hundred and fifty women were expected to attend a DUV convention held in Indianapolis. *Indianapolis Star*, August 11, 1991.

37. Holland's (*Our Army Nurses*, 89) account of Emma L. Simonds of Dekalb, Ill., is one page long, whereas Moore's (*Women of the War*, 415–53) account of Amy Morris Bradley is thirty-seven pages.

38. Gerald Schwartz, for example, published the diary and letters of New Hampshire physician Esther Hill Hawks in 1984, long after her death. See Hawks,

*Woman Doctor's Civil War.* No one to my knowledge has ever attempted to publish Barton's Civil War diaries, I suspect, because of the editorial conundrum they present: they consist of multiple two-inch by three-inch volumes written in a minuscule hand with numerous ambiguities of date. On the other hand, scores of biographies have been written about Barton, owing as much to her work in the American Red Cross as to her wartime labors. More than any other Civil War relief worker, she remains a subject of historical curiosity. Three major accounts of Barton's life have appeared since 1987 alone: Elizabeth Pryor's *Clara Barton: Professional Angel* (1987), Stephen Oates's *Woman of Valor: Clara Barton and the Civil War* (1994), and David Burton's *Clara Barton: In the Service of Humanity* (1995).

39. The Confederates who published were Fannie Beers, Kate Cumming, Constance Cary Harrison, Judith Loughborough, Emily Mason, Cornelia Peake McDonald, Julia Morgan, Phoebe Yates Pember, Sarah Pryor, Susan E. D. Smith, and Cornelia Phillips Spencer. The Union women were Louisa May Alcott, Sophronia Bucklin, Eudora Clark, Maria Lydig Daly, Abby Hopper Gibbons, Laura Haviland, Jane Hoge, Anna Morris Holstein, Mrs. E. C. Kent, Catherine Lawrence, Mary Livermore, Mary Simmerson Logan, Charlotte McKay, Mary Newcomb, Sarah Palmer, Rebecca Pomroy, Eliza Chappell Porter, Elvira Powers, Sarah Edmonds Seelye, Julia Silk, Adelaide Smith, Emily Bliss Souder, Amanda Akin Stearns, Jane Grey Swisshelm, Susie King Taylor, Sojourner Truth, Julia Wheelock, Annie Turner Wittenmyer, Georgeanna Woolsey, Jane Woolsey, Katharine Prescott Wormeley, and the anonymous author of *Notes of Hospital Life.*

40. Of course, many more monograph-length accounts were published by friends, relatives, and historians, but I consider here only those accounts published by the workers themselves. Altogether I am aware of sixty-seven monograph-length accounts, excluding collections of letters and accounts in serials and commemorative volumes, but there is undoubtedly a larger number extant.

41. Loughborough, *Cave Life*, vii. According to Drew Faust (*Mothers of Invention*, 158), Southern women put their faith in Northern publishers whom they believed would more fully market their books. Alice Fahs (*Imagined Civil War*, chap. 1) has suggested that Northern publishing dominance artificially limited the availability of texts that represented a Southern viewpoint.

42. Mrs. J. L. Colt to Frank Moore, February 17, 1866, Moore Papers, DU.

43. Almira Fales to Frank Moore, May 17, 1866, and J. M. Sweat to Moore, March 15, 1866, ibid. Harriet Eaton minimized her achievements as a state relief agent whose work "differed materially from that of a nurse." Eaton to Moore, April 11, 1866, ibid.

44. Maria M. C. Hall to Frank Moore, April 6, 1866, ibid.

45. *Campaign of Mrs. Julia Silk*, 22–23.

46. Lawrence, *Autobiography*, 68–74, 95–99.

47. Eaton Diary, December 26, 1862, January 15, 1863, November 15, 1864, SHC-UNC.

48. Maria Mann to Mary Tyler Mann, May 18, [July or August n.d.], 1863, Mann Papers, LC.

49. See Simkins and Patton, "Work of Southern Women," 496.

50. E. C. Bissell to Frank Moore, September 1, 1866, Moore Papers, DU.

51. Cumming, *Journal of Hospital Life*, 3.

52. Hoge, *Boys in Blue*, 37.

53. *Notes of Hospital Life*, dedication, xiii.

54. Livermore, *My Story of the War: The Civil War Memoirs*, iii, 8.

55. *Notes of Hospital Life*, vii. Jane Hoge also sought the ambassadorial services of a clergyman, Rev. T. M. Eddy of Chicago, for her account. Catherine Lawrence (*Autobiography*, 3) and Mary Newcomb (Newcomb, *Four Years*, v) published books in 1893 in which they also capitulated to the wishes of friends.

56. Cumming, *Journal of Hospital Life*, 5; Beers, *Memories*, 5. Beers also dedicated her memoir to the soldiers (p. 3).

57. Taylor, *Reminiscences*, v–vi.

58. Morgan, *How It Was*, 105–6; Newcomb, *Four Years*, v.

59. Livermore, *My Story of the War: The Civil War Memoirs*, 11; Adelaide W. Smith, *Reminiscences*, 11.

60. Stearns, *Lady Nurse*, 45. Charlotte McKay's *Stories of Hospital and Camp* (1876) also depended on a journal; see p. 92.

61. Pomroy, *Echoes*, 155–56.

62. Livermore, *My Story of the War: The Civil War Memoirs*, 11; Venet, "Emergence of a Suffragist," 151–52; Swisshelm, *Crusader and Feminist*, 30. Swisshelm privately published an autobiography, *Half a Century*, in 1880; a second edition was brought out in the same year by the Chicago House of Jansen, McClurg. The relatives who published *Crusader and Feminist* in 1934 used material from *Half a Century*.

63. *Notes of Hospital Life*, xiii; Hoge, *Boys in Blue*, 13; Mary Walker to Frank Moore, May 4, 1866, Moore Papers, DU; Powers, *Hospital Pencillings*, vi.

64. Edmonds, *Nurse and Spy*, 6. Edmonds grew up in Canada.

65. Sarah Emma Edmonds Seelye pension file (#526889), OIPF.

66. See Fornell, "A Woman in the Union Army." Publication figures also are quoted in Sizer, "Acting Her Part," 126.

67. Souder, *Leaves*, 8.

68. Stearns, *Lady Nurse*, 92. Whitman had published "The Great Army of the Sick" in the *New York Times* in February and was anxious to ride the wave of *Hospital Sketches* later in the year. See Morris, *Better Angel*, 146–47, and Fahs, *Imagined Civil War*, 114.

69. Alcott, *Louisa May Alcott*, 125–26.

70. Bacon and Howland, *Letters of a Family*, 2:534.

71. Cumming to John Morton, May 21, 1866, Cumming Papers, ADAH.

72. Cumming to "My Dear Brother," July 2, 1866, and to J. B. Lippincott, August 24, 1866, ibid. On July 29, 1867, Lippincott declined to take Cumming's book, reporting that the market for such works was "flooded."

73. F. P. Wellford to Cumming, February 11, 1867, Cumming Papers, ADAH.

74. Cumming Diary, February 13, 1867, ibid.

75. Cumming to William H. Fariss, May 20, 1867, ibid.

76. Notice from Harper and Brothers to Cumming, August 26, 1867, ibid.; Cumming, *Kate*, 81, 23. Susan Smith (*Soldier's Friend*, 152) had chosen a Memphis publisher in 1866, but it is likely that she sold even fewer volumes than Cumming in light of references to "ten thousand . . . depredations, committed on our soil by those merciless invaders."

77. Cumming, *Kate*, 183, and *Gleanings*, 160.

78. Quoted in Newsom, *Florence Nightingale of the Southern Army*, 38.

79. Powers, *Hospital Pencillings*, preface; Bucklin pension file (#1138431), OIPF; Elizabeth D. Leonard, *Yankee Women*, 160–62, 265–66. Spinster Julia Wheelock published *The Boys in White* in 1870, echoing Jane Hoge's 1867 account, *The Boys in Blue*.

80. Alice Fahs (*Imagined Civil War*, 313) argues that the 1870s saw the nadir of war publications but that the market improved in the 1880s, which my evidence also corroborates.

81. Burton's book was called *The Woman Who Battled for the Boys in Blue: Mother Bickerdyke* (1886). There are fourteen full-length biographies of Bickerdyke, including one for children.

82. Livermore, *My Story of the War: The Civil War Memoirs*, 7.

83. Annie Turner Wittenmyer to Mary Ann Bickerdyke, June 24, 1897, Bickerdyke Papers, LC.

84. Anna Lawrence Platt to Mary Ann Bickerdyke, January 21, [1898?], Bickerdyke Papers, LC. According to the National Union Catalogue, Platt never published a monograph.

85. Lawrence, *Autobiography*, 4.

86. A sampling of these works included Moore's own *Rebellion Record: A Diary of American Events, with Documents, Narratives, Illustrative Incidents, Poetry, etc.* (1861–63), Brockett's *The Camp, the Battle Field, and the Hospital* (1866), and Richard Miller Devens's *Pictorial Book of Anecdotes and Incidents of the War of the Rebellion* (1866).

87. Nine of the eighty-seven individuals commemorated in *Woman's Work* went on to publish their own monographs: Abby Hopper Gibbons, Jane Hoge, Anna Morris Holstein, Mary Livermore, Charlotte McKay, Eliza Chappell Porter, Annie Turner Wittenmyer, Jane Woolsey, and Katharine Prescott Wormeley.

88. See Mary Gardner Holland to Elizabeth Avery Kinne, March 18, 1895, Bickerdyke Papers, LC. For an excellent discussion of gender relations in nineteenth-century publishing circles, see Coultrap-McQuin, *Doing Literary Business*, esp. chap. 2.

89. Edward P. Smith to Mary Ann Bickerdyke, February 8, May 22, 1866, Bickerdyke Papers, LC; Smith to Frank Moore, January 29, May 31, 1866; A. M. Brown to Moore, March 18, 1866—all in Moore Papers, DU. Ultimately, Bickerdyke did provide a draft to Smith in late May 1866. Brockett and Vaughan (*Woman's Work*, 111) included a segment on Barton but were no more successful

than Moore in winning her as a correspondent: "In the preparation of this sketch," they wrote, "we have availed ourselves . . . of a paper prepared for us by a clerical friend of the lady, who had known her from childhood."

90. See, e.g., Charlie Kendall to Frank Moore, March 10, 1866, M. B. Goodwin to Moore, February 15, 1866, Moore Papers, DU. The soldier who wrote about his mother was John H. Burnham in a letter to Moore dated March 23, 1866.

91. The four soldiers who wrote to Moore in 1866 about Husband were George Brown (January 31), John S. Lockwood (March 17), George Spencer (March 26), and Horace S. Shepard (April 2). See also Mary Morris Husband to Moore, January 30, February 17, 1866, Moore Papers, DU. It later came to light that Husband was preparing her own monograph, which might have accounted for her standoffishness.

92. Anonymous letter to Frank Moore, November 9, 1866, Moore Papers, DU; Moore, *Women of the War*, 536.

93. George Brown to Frank Moore, January 31, 1866, Moore Papers, DU.

94. Husband to Moore, January 30, February 17, 1866, ibid.

95. Georgiana Willetts to Frank Moore, March 26, 1866, ibid.

96. Quentin Danielle to Frank Moore, July 31, 1866, and E. F. Morris to Moore, June 16, 1866, ibid.

97. Jane Hoge to Frank Moore, January 24, February 9, April 17, October 25, 1866, ibid.

98. Cornelia Hancock to Frank Moore, April 12, 1866, ibid.

99. Hannah Stevenson to Gov. John A. Andrew, January 20, 1866, ibid.

100. Katharine P. Wormeley to Frank Moore, March 3, 1866, ibid.

101. Isabella Fogg to Frank Moore, March 17, April 11, 1866, ibid. For evidence of Fogg's impoverished state, see Edward P. Smith to Moore, May 31, 1866, ibid. See Chapter 6 for a discussion of Fogg's pension case.

102. Elvira J. Powers to Frank Moore, April 29, 1866, Moore Papers, DU.

103. Lyde Sizer (*Political Work*, 208) has speculated that Powers and Sophronia Bucklin were excluded from *Women of the War* because they had gained the reputation of troublemakers; it is just as likely that negotiations over money soured Moore, whose middle-class values made him mistrust women seeking pay.

104. Amy Morris Bradley to Frank Moore, January 15, 1866, Moore Papers, DU.

105. C. S. Shepherd to Frank Moore, February 22, 1866, ibid. Mary Morris Husband noted that even while in the service, soldiers would take up subscriptions for Etheridge, since she was not on a payroll. Husband to Frank Moore, January 30, 1866, ibid.

106. In addition to Mary Walker and Annie Etheridge, Mary Morris Husband planned to publish her diary, but never did so. Ibid.

107. Katharine P. Wormeley to Frank Moore, March 3, 1866, ibid.

108. See Barton Diary, October 27, 1865, Barton Papers, LC. Clara Barton and Linus Brockett, a physician, were friends and correspondents.

109. Edward P. Smith to Frank Moore, May 31, 1866, Moore Papers, DU.

110. Moore, *Women of the War*, 22, 177.

111. See Fahs, *Imagined Civil War*, 118. Alcott's "The Brothers" was published in *Atlantic Monthly*, November 1863; Cooke's "A Woman," which recounted Josephine Addison's nursing service, appeared in *Atlantic Monthly*, December 1862.

112. Bucklin, *In Hospital and Camp*, 82–83, 91–93.

113. Ibid., 125.

114. Ibid., 241. The surgeon claimed that Bucklin had disobeyed orders in accompanying a widow to the depot whom the surgeon had just propositioned (p. 240).

115. C. Wagner to Surgeon General William Hammond, March 6, 1863, Dix Nursing Papers, NARA; Bucklin, *In Hospital and Camp*, 321.

116. Bucklin, *In Hospital and Camp*, 292–93.

117. On anger in the nursing memoir, see Sizer, *Political Work*, 196.

118. Newcomb, *Four Years*, v, 14.

119. Brinton, *Personal Memoirs*, 44; Newcomb, *Four Years*, 34.

120. Newcomb, *Four Years*, 35, 99, 14.

121. Beers, *Memories*, 61, 39.

122. Cumming, *Kate*, 39, 70, 270; *Gleanings*, 219.

123. Cumming, *Kate*, 124, 143; *Gleanings*, 115, 117–18.

124. Cumming, *Gleanings*, 118.

125. See Sizer's (*Political Work*, 211–14) discussion of the class inflections in Palmer's narrative.

126. For analyses of female subjectivity in nineteenth-century American literature, see Baym, *Woman's Fiction*; Mary Kelley, *Private Woman, Public Stage*; and Smith-Rosenberg, *Disorderly Conduct*.

## Appendix

1. Douglas, "The War within a War," 206–7. See also Nina Bennett Smith, "Women Who Went to the War."

2. Faust, "Ours as Well as That of the Men," 240.

3. See Bynum, *Unruly Women*; Whites, *Crisis in Gender*; Schwalm, *Hard Fight for We*; Clinton, *Tara Revisited*; and Edwards, *Scarlet Doesn't Live Here Anymore*. Susan Lebsock, whose 1984 book, *The Free Women of Petersburg*, broke new ground in a more diverse reading of Southern women in the antebellum era, must also be included here.

4. Southern historians have demonstrated that gender, race, and class relations in elite and yeoman households must be understood as regionally discrete configurations. See, e.g., Faust, "'Trying to Do a Man's Business'"; McCurry, "Politics of Yeoman Households"; Fox-Genovese, *Within the Plantation Household*; and Clinton, *Plantation Mistress*.

5. Elizabeth D. Leonard, *Yankee Women*, 198–99.

6. Attie, *Patriotic Toil*, 52, 89.

7. Giesberg, *Civil War Sisterhood*, 11–13; Ginzberg, *Work of Benevolence*, 8–10.

8. Sizer, *Political Work*, 7, 12, 4–5.

9. See, e.g., Michael Fellman's "Women and Guerrilla Warfare" and Peter Bardaglio's "Children of Jubilee."

10. Mitchell, *Vacant Chair*, xiii, chap. 1.

11. See Forbes, *African American Women*.

12. See Silber, *Romance of Reunion*.

13. Diffley, *Where My Heart Is Turning Ever*, xvii–xviii; *To Live and Die*, 16.

14. Fahs, *Imagined Civil War*, 4–11, 311, 315.

15. Elizabeth Young, *Disarming the Nation*, 6, 10, 17, 15.

16. Elizabeth D. Leonard, *All the Daring of the Soldier*, 18–19, 274–75.

17. Blanton and Cook, *They Fought Like Demons*, 1–7.

# Bibliography

## Primary Sources

*Manuscripts and Manuscript Collections*

Ann Arbor, Mich.
  Bentley Historical Library, Michigan Historical Collections, University
      of Michigan
    Carlisle Family Papers
    Alpheus Felch Papers
    Fyfe Family Papers
Atlanta, Ga.
  Georgia Department of Archives and History
    Emily Bostick Letter to Governor Joseph Brown, June 16, 1862, Incoming
        Correspondence
    Elizabeth McKinne, ed., "Memoirs of Brigadier-General William Mont-
        gomery Gardner," n.d.
  Special Collections, Emory University
    Kate Whitehead Rowland Journal
Baton Rouge, La.
  Louisiana and Lower Mississippi Valley Collections, Louisiana State
      University
    John W. Bell Papers
    G. T. Harrower Letters
Bloomington, Ind.
  Lilly Library, Indiana University
    Elizabeth Tuttle Letters
Cambridge, Mass.
  Schlesinger Library, Radcliffe College
    "To the Patriotic Women of New Haven and Vicinity: An Appeal for the
        Sick and Wounded in the Army"
Chapel Hill, N.C.
  Southern Historical Collection, Wilson Library, University of North
      Carolina
    Sarah G. Beck Papers
    Mary White Beckwith Diary

Harriet H. A. Eaton Diary
Phoebe Yates Pember Letters
Penn School Papers
Mary Smith Reid Letters, Swann Family Papers
Columbia, S.C.
Manuscripts, South Caroliniana Library, University of South Carolina
Ada Bacot Diary
Durham, N.C.
Manuscripts, Perkins Library, Duke University
Amy Morris Bradley Diary and Letterbook, 1861–65
Janie Clarke Diary
Constant Hanks Papers
Walter M. Howland and George S. Tilton Papers
Gertrude Jenkins Papers, Margaret Elizabeth Clewell, "A Volunteer Nurse"
McCutchen Family Papers
Frank Moore Papers
Mary Norton Papers
Abby Stafford Papers
Indianapolis, Ind.
Indiana State Library, Manuscripts
Jane Chambers McKinney Graydon Letters
Jane Merrill Ketcham Papers
Lewis King Papers
Iowa City, Iowa
Special Collections, University of Iowa
Shelton Family Papers
Amanda Rhoda Shelton Diary
Mary E. Shelton Diary
Amanda Shelton Stewart Address
Jackson, Miss.
Mississippi Department of Archives and History
Emma Balfour Diary
Cordelia Lewis Scales Letters
Manassas, Va.
Manassas National Battlefield Park, U.S. Department of the Interior
Fanny Ricketts Diary
Montgomery, Ala.
Alabama Department of Archives and History
Kate Cumming Papers
Juliet Opie Hopkins Papers
Philadelphia, Pa.
Historical Society of Pennsylvania
John W. Lynch Letters

Portland, Maine
  Maine Historical Society
    Maine Camp Hospital Association Papers
    Usher Family Papers
Raleigh, N.C.
  North Carolina Department of Archives and History
    James B. Brickell Papers, Harriet R. Greentree Letter, November 20, 1865
    John Heritage Bryan Papers, Letter to E. G. Speight, November 1, 1861
Richmond, Va.
  Archives Division, Virginia State Library
    William F. Broaddus Diary
    Sally Tompkins Letters
Rock Hill, S.C.
  Winthrop College Archives
    Mary Elizabeth Massey Papers
Springfield, Ill.
  Illinois State Historical Library
    Lovicy Ann Eberhart, "Reminiscence of the Civil War, 1861 to 1865"
    ——— [first name unknown] Tisler, ed., "The War Time Diary of
      Mrs. Sarah Gregg"
Tuscaloosa, Ala.
  W. S. Hoole Special Collections, Gorgas Library, University of Alabama
    Amelia Gayle Gorgas Papers
    B. W. Simmons Family Papers
    Sturdevant-Hall Papers
    Augusta Evans Wilson Papers
Washington, D.C.
  Manuscript Division, Library of Congress
    Clara Barton Papers
    Mary Ann Ball Bickerdyke Papers
    Breckinridge Papers
    Carrie E. Cutter Papers
    Burton Harrison Papers
    John Milton and Esther Hill Hawks Papers
    Joseph Roswell Hawley Papers
    Mary Tyler Peabody Mann Papers
    Benjamin F. and Catherine Oliphant Papers
    Philip Phillips Papers
    Ninian Pinkney Papers
    Bela T. St. John Letters
    U.S. Sanitary Commission Papers
    Annie Turner Wittenmyer Papers

Adjutant General's Office Document File. Box 69. Records Pertaining to Army Nurses Pension Act of August 2, 1892. Department of the Interior. Record Group 94.

Adjutant General's Office Document File, #1643286. Provost Marshal General's Office, Circular 25, June 26, 1864. War Department. Record Group 94.

Army Nurse Corps Historical Data File, 1898–1947. Entry 103. Union Surgeon General's Office. Record Group 112.

Card Index for Female Contract Nurses, 1861–65. Adjutant General's Office. Record Group 94.

Carded Service Records of Union Hospital Attendants, Matrons, and Nurses, 1861–65. Entry 535. Adjutant General's Office. Record Group 94.

Circulars and Circular Letters, 1861–65. Entry 63. Union Surgeon General's Office. Record Group 112.

Classified Schedule of Female Hospital Employes [*sic*]. Adjutant General's Office Document File, Box 69. Record and Pension Division, War Department. Record Group 94.

Colored Contract Nurses, July 16, 1863–June 14, 1864. Medical Department Register. Record Group 94.

Communications Received, 1862–65. Central Office, U.S. Christian Commission. Record Group 94.

Consolidated Correspondence File, 1794–1915. Box 258. Quartermaster General's Office. Record Group 92.

Dorothea Dix Nursing Papers, 1–430, Record Group 94.

General Order No. 351, October 29, 1863. Adjutant General's Office, War Department, Record Group 112.

Letterbook of Thomas F. Azpell, Surgeon, U.S. Volunteers, 1862–76. Entry 227. Union Surgeon General's Office. Record Group 112.

Letters Received, 1818–70. Entry 12. Boxes 10–14, 26–28. Union Surgeon General's Office. Record Group 112.

Letters Received, 1861–65. Entry 20. Quartermaster General's Office. Record Group 92.

Letters Received, 1861–65. Confederate Secretary of War. Record Group 109.

Letters Received by Surgeon Lincoln R. Stone. Entry 228. Union Surgeon General's Office. Record Group 112.

Letters Sent, 9-18-369. Confederate Secretary of War. Record Group 109.

Letters Sent, Vol. 258/591, Department of the Missouri. Records of the U.S. Army Continental Commands, 1821–1920. Record Group 393.

Medical Department List of Employees and Register of Patients, Chimborazo Hospital, Richmond, Va., 1861–64, Chap. VI, Vol. 33. Confederate Surgeon General's Office. Record Group 109.

Medical Department List of Employees, Chimborazo Hospital No. 1, Richmond, Va., 1862–63, Chap. VI, Vol. 79. Confederate Surgeon General's Office. Record Group 109.

Medical Department List of Employees, Chimborazo Hospital No. 2, Richmond, Va., 1862–65, Chap. VI, Vol. 85. Confederate Surgeon General's Office. Record Group 109.

Medical Department Morning Reports of Patients in General Hospitals 1–4, 7–8, 10–20, 22–23, 25–27, Chap. VI, Vol. 711. Confederate Surgeon General's Office. Record Group 109.

Medical Department Morning Reports of Patients and Attendants, Robertson Hospital, Richmond, Va., Chap. VI, Vol. 717. Confederate Surgeon General's Office. Record Group 109.

Monthly Returns of Contract Nurses, 1861–65. Entry 578. Adjutant General's Office. Record Group 94.

Office of Female Nurses, Hospital Papers 1-430. Adjutant General's Office. Record Group 94.

Orders and Circulars, Trans-Mississippi Department, 1861–65. Adjutant General's Office. Record Group 94.

Organization Index to Pension Files, Film Series T289. Pension Files Relating to 2,448 Army Nurses. Veterans Administration. Record Group 15.

Papers Relating to Dr. Mary E. Walker. File W2068, Box 94. Office of the Adjutant General Volunteer Service Branch, 1863. Record Group 94.

Pensions by Special Acts of Congress. [Mary Ann Bickerdyke, Chloe A. Buckel, Caroline Burghardt, Emmeline J. Bushnell, Harriet Dada, Harriet P. Dame, Anna M. Holstein, Mary Morris Husband, Mary Shelton Huston, Lavinia M. Payne, Adeliza Perry, Harriet Stinson Pond, Rebecca Wiswell, Annie Turner Wittenmyer.] U.S. Bureau of Pensions, Department of the Interior. Record Group 15.

Ramsey, Samuel. "Remarks on Legislation for the Benefit of Army Nurses," May 23, 1890. Adjutant General's Office Document File. Box 69. Records Pertaining to Army Nurses Pension Act of August 2, 1892. Department of the Interior. Record Group 94.

Records Concerning the Conduct and Loyalty of Army Officers, Civilian Employees of the War Department, and Citizens during the Civil War. Record Group 107.

Registers of Applications for Appointments, July 1863–March 1865. Records of the Confederate Secretary of War. Record Group 109.

Reports and Correspondence Regarding Contracts for Nurses, 1861–65. #1-1198. Adjutant General's Office. Record Group 94.

Union Provost Marshals' File of Papers Relating to Individual Citizens [Dr. Mary E. Walker]. Record Group 109.

Alcott, Louisa May. *Hospital Sketches*. Boston: James Redpath, 1863.

———. "My Contraband." In *Hospital Sketches and Camp and Fireside Stories*. Boston: Roberts Brothers, 1869.

———. *Louisa May Alcott: Her Life, Letters, and Journals*. Edited by Ednah D. Cheney. Boston: Little, Brown, 1928.

Anderson, Lucy Worth. *North Carolina Women of the Confederacy*. Fayetteville, N.C.: Cumberland, 1926.

Andrews, Matthew Page. *The Women of the South in War Times*. Baltimore: Norman, Remington, 1920.

Bacon, Cyrus. "The Daily Register of Dr. Cyrus Bacon, Jr.: Care of the Wounded at the Battle of Gettysburg." Edited by Walter M. Whitehouse and Frank Whitehouse Jr. *Michigan Academician* 8, no. 4 (Spring 1976): 373–86.

Bacon, Georgeanna Woolsey. *Three Weeks at Gettysburg*. New York: Anson Randolph, 1863.

Bacon, Georgeanna Woolsey, and Eliza Woolsey Howland. *Letters of a Family during the War for the Union, 1861–1865*. 2 vols. New Haven: Tuttle, Morehouse, and Taylor, 1899.

Bacot, Ada. *A Confederate Nurse: The Diary of Ada W. Bacot*. Edited by Jean V. Berlin. Columbia: University of South Carolina Press, 1994.

Beers, Fannie A. *Memories: A Record of Personal Experience and Adventure during Four Years of War*. Philadelphia: J. B. Lippincott, 1888.

Billings, John Shaw. "Medical Reminiscences of the Civil War." *Transactions of the College of Physicians of Philadelphia*, 3d ser., 27 (1905): 115–21.

Boyd, Belle. *Belle Boyd in Camp and Prison*. 1865. Reprint, with a new foreword by Drew Gilpin Faust and a new introduction by Sharon Kennedy-Nolle, Baton Rouge: Louisiana State University Press, 1998.

Brinton, John H. *Personal Memoirs of John H. Brinton, Major and Surgeon, U.S.V., 1861–1865*. New York: Neale, 1914.

Brockett, Linus P. *The Camp, the Battlefield, and the Hospital; or, Lights and Shadows of the Great Rebellion*. Philadelphia: National Publishing Co., 1866.

Brockett, Linus P., and Mary C. Vaughan. *Woman's Work in the Civil War*. Philadelphia: Zeigler, McCurdy, 1867.

Browne, Junius H. *Four Years in Secessia: Adventures Within and Beyond the Union Lines*. Chicago: G. and C. W. Sherwood, 1865.

Bucklin, Sophronia E. *In Hospital and Camp*. Philadelphia: John E. Potter, 1869.

*The Campaign of Mrs. Julia Silk, Formerly of Ann Arbor, Michigan*. Ann Arbor: Ann Arbor Courier Print, 1892.

Chesnut, Mary. *Mary Chesnut's Civil War*. Edited by C. Vann Woodward. New Haven: Yale University Press, 1981.

Clark, Eudora. "Hospital Memories." *Atlantic Monthly* 20 (September 1867): 324–36.

Coker, Hannah Lide. *A Story of the Civil War*. Edited by Nathaniel Clenroy Browder. Raleigh, N.C.: N.p., 1984.

Conner, Mrs. James, et al. *South Carolina Women in the Confederacy*. Columbia, S.C.: State, 1907.

Crotty, Daniel G. *Four Years Campaigning in the Army of the Potomac*. Grand Rapids, Mich.: Dygert Brothers, 1874.

Cumming, Kate. *A Journal of Hospital Life in the Confederate Army of Tennessee*. Louisville, Ky.: J. P. Morton, 1866.

———. *Gleanings from Southland*. Birmingham, Ala.: Roberts and Son, 1895.

———. *Kate: The Journal of a Confederate Nurse*. Edited by Richard Barksdale Harwell. Baton Rouge: Louisiana State University Press, 1959.

Daly, Maria Lydig. *Diary of a Union Lady, 1861–1865*. Edited by Harold Earl Hammond. New York: Funk and Wagnalls, 1962.

Devens, Richard Miller. *The Pictorial Book of Anecdotes and Incidents of the War of the Rebellion: Civil, Military, Naval, and Domestic*. Hartford, Conn.: Hartford Publishing Co., 1866.

Edmonds, Sarah E. *Nurse and Spy in the Union Army: Comprising the Adventures and Experiences of a Woman in Hospitals, Camps, and Battle-Fields*. Hartford, Conn.: W. S. Williams, 1865.

———. *Memoirs of a Soldier, Nurse, and Spy*. Edited by Elizabeth Leonard. Northern Illinois University Press, 1999.

Gibbons, Abby Hopper. *Life of Abby Hopper Gibbons: Told Chiefly through Her Correspondence*. 2 vols. Edited by Sarah Hopper Emerson. New York: Putnam's, 1896–97.

Gill, John C. "A Union Surgeon Views the War from Kentucky, 1862." Edited by Harry F. Lupold. *Register of the Kentucky Historical Society* 72, no. 3 (July 1974): 272–75.

Greenleaf, Charles R. *A Manual for the Medical Officers of the United States Army*. Philadelphia, 1864. Reprint, San Francisco: Norman Publishing, 1992.

Grimké, Charlotte Forten. *The Journal of Charlotte Forten: A Free Negro in the Slave Era*. Edited by Ray Allen Billington. London: Dryden, 1953.

———. *The Journals of Charlotte Forten Grimké*. Edited by Brenda Stevenson. New York: Oxford University Press, 1988.

Hamilton, Gail. *Country Living and Country Thinking*. Boston: Ticknor and Fields, 1862.

———. "A Call to My Country-Women." *Atlantic Monthly* 11 (1863): 345–49.

Hanaford, Phebe A. *Daughters of America; or, Women of the Century*. Cincinnati: Forshee and McMakin, 1883.

Hancock, Cornelia. *South after Gettysburg: Letters of Cornelia Hancock, 1863–1868*. Edited by Henrietta Stratton Jaquette. New York: Thomas Y. Crowell, 1937.

Harrison, Constance Cary. *Recollections Grave and Gay*. New York: Scribner's, 1912.

Harvey, Cordelia. *My Story of War: A Woman's Narrative of Life and Work in Union Hospitals*. New York: Longmans, Green, 1885.

Haviland, Laura S. *A Woman's Life-Work: Labors and Experiences of Laura S. Haviland*. 1881. Reprint, Salem, N.H.: Ayer, 1984.

Hawks, Esther Hill. *A Woman Doctor's Civil War: Esther Hill Hawks' Diary*. Edited by Gerald Schwartz. Columbia: University of South Carolina Press, 1984.

Higginson, Thomas Wentworth. *Army Life in a Black Regiment*. 1870. Reprint, East Lansing: Michigan State University Press, 1960; also edited by R. D. Madison. New York: Penguin, 1997. References are to 1960 ed.

———. *The Complete Civil War Journal and Selected Letters of Thomas Wentworth Higginson*. Edited by Christopher Looby. Chicago: University of Chicago Press, 2000.

Hobbs, Clarissa Emily Gear. "Excerpts from the Autobiography of Clarissa Emily Gear Hobbs." *Journal of the Illinois State Historical Society* 17, no. 4 (1928): 611–714.

Hoge, Jane. *The Boys in Blue; or, Heroes of the "Rank and File."* New York: E. B. Treat, 1867.

Holland, Mary Gardner. *Our Army Nurses*. Boston: B. Wilkins, 1895.

Holstein, Anna Morris. *Three Years in Field Hospitals of the Army of the Potomac*. Philadelphia: J. B. Lippincott, 1867.

Holt, Daniel M. *A Surgeon's Civil War: The Letters and Diary of Daniel M. Holt, M.D.* Edited by James M. Greiner, Janet L. Coryell, and James R. Smither. Kent, Ohio: Kent State University Press, 1994.

Hoole, William Stanley, and Addie S. Hoole. *Confederate Norfolk: The Letters of a Virginia Lady to the Mobile Register, 1861–1862*. University, Ala.: Confederate Publishing, 1984.

Jackson, Fannie Oslin. *On Both Sides of the Line*. Edited by Joan F. Curran and Redena K. Mallory. Baltimore: Gateway Press, 1989.

Jackson, Henry W. R. *The Southern Women of the Second American Revolution*. Atlanta: Intelligencer Steam Power Presses, 1863.

Jacobs, Harriet. *Incidents in the Life of a Slave Girl*. Edited by Jean Fagan Yellin. Cambridge: Harvard University Press, 1987.

Keen, W. W. "Surgical Reminiscences of the Civil War." *Transactions of the College of Physicians of Philadelphia*, 3d ser., 27 (1905): 95–114.

Kent, Mrs. E. C. *Four Years in Secessia: A Narrative of a Residence at the South previous to and during the Southern Rebellion*. N.p., 1864.

Lauderdale, John Vance. *The Wounded River: The Civil War Letters of John Vance Lauderdale, M.D.* Edited by Peter Josyph. East Lansing: Michigan State University Press, 1993.

Lawrence, Catherine S. *Autobiography*. Albany, N.Y.: Amasa J. Parker, 1893.

Lee, Elizabeth Blair. *Wartime Washington: The Civil War Letters of Elizabeth Blair Lee*. Edited by Virginia J. Laas. Urbana: University of Illinois Press, 1991.

Livermore, Mary A. *My Story of the War: of Four Years Personal Experience*. Hartford, Conn.: Worthington, 1889.

———. *The Story of My Life*. 2 vols. Hartford, Conn.: Worthington, 1899.

———. *My Story of the War: The Civil War Memoirs of the Famous Nurse, Relief Organizer, and Suffragette*. Edited by Nina Silber. New York: Da Capo Press, 1995.

Locke, E. W. *Three Years in Camp and Hospital*. Boston: George D. Russell, 1870.

Logan, Mary Simmerson. *The Part Taken by Women in American History*. Wilmington, Del.: Perry-Nalle Publishing Co., 1912.

———. *Reminiscences of a Soldier's Wife*. New York: Scribner's, 1913.

Loughborough, Mary W. *My Cave Life in Vicksburg*. New York: D. Appleton, 1864.

Mason, Emily V. "Memories of a Hospital Matron." *Atlantic Monthly* 90 (September–October 1902): 305–18, 475–85.

McDonald, Cornelia. *A Diary with Reminiscences of the War and Refugee Life in the Shenandoah Valley, 1860–1865*. Nashville: Cullom and Ghertner, 1934.

McKay, Charlotte E. *Stories of Hospital and Camp*. Philadelphia: Claxton, Remsen and Haffelfinger, 1876.

Moore, Frank. *The Rebellion Record: A Diary of American Events, with Documents, Narratives, Illustrative Incidents, Poetry, etc.* New York: G. P. Putnam, 1861–63.

———. *Women of the War: Their Heroism and Self-Sacrifice*. Hartford, Conn.: S. S. Scranton, 1866.

Morgan, Julia. *How It Was: Four Years among the Rebels*. Nashville: Publishing House of the Methodist Episcopal Church, South, 1892.

Nash, Herbert M. "Some Reminiscences of a Confederate Surgeon." *Transactions of the College of Physicians of Philadelphia*, 3d ser., 28 (1906): 122–44.

Newcomb, Mary A. *Four Years of Personal Reminiscences of the War*. Chicago: H. S. Mills, 1893.

News and Courier. *Our Women in the War: The Lives They Lived, the Deaths They Died*. Charleston, S.C.: News and Courier Book Press, 1885.

Newsom, Ella King. *The Florence Nightingale of the Southern Army: Experiences of Mrs. Ella K. Newsom, Confederate Nurse*. Compiled by J. Fraise Richard. New York, Baltimore: Broadway Publishing, 1914.

*Notes of Hospital Life from November, 1861, to August, 1863*. Philadelphia: J. B. Lippincott, 1864.

Palmer, Sarah A. *The Story of Aunt Becky's Army Life*. New York: John F. Trow, 1867.

Parsons, Emily. *Civil War Nursing: Memoir of Emily Elizabeth Parsons*. New York: Garland, 1984.

Pember, Phoebe Yates. *A Southern Woman's Story: Life in Confederate Richmond*. 1879. Edited by Bell I. Wiley. Reprint, Jackson, Tenn.: McCowat-Mercer, 1959.

Pomroy, Rebecca R. *Echoes from Hospital and White House: A Record of Mrs. Rebecca R. Pomroy's Experience in War-Times.* Edited by Anna L. Boyden. Boston: D. Lothrop, 1884.

Porter, Eliza Chappell. *Eliza Chappell Porter: A Memoir.* Chicago, New York: Fleming H. Revell, 1892.

Potter, William W. *One Surgeon's Private War: Doctor William W. Potter of the 57th New York.* 1888. Edited by John Michael Priest. Reprint, Shippensburg, Pa.: White Mane, 1996.

Powers, Elvira J. *Hospital Pencillings.* Boston: Edward L. Mitchell, 1866.

Pryor, Sarah Agnes. *Reminiscences of Peace and War.* New York: Macmillan, 1905.

Reed, William Howell. *Hospital Life in the Army of the Potomac.* Boston: William V. Spencer, 1866.

Ridgway, Frank. "From the Wilderness to Petersburg: The Diary of Surgeon Frank Ridgway." Edited by James J. Heslin. *New-York Historical Society Quarterly* 45, no. 2 (April 1961): 113–40.

Ropes, Hannah L. *Civil War Nurse: The Diary and Letters of Hannah L. Ropes.* Edited by John R. Brumgardt. Knoxville: University of Tennessee Press, 1980.

Scales, Cordelia. "The Civil War Letters of Cordelia Scales." Edited by Percy L. Rainwater. *Journal of Mississippi History* 1, no. 1 (1939): 169–81.

Scott, Kate M. *In Honor of the National Association of Army Nurses.* Atlantic City: N.p., 1910.

Simkins, Francis Butler, and James Welch Patton. *The Women of the Confederacy.* Richmond: Garrett and Massie, 1936.

Smith, Adelaide W. *Reminiscences of an Army Nurse during the Civil War.* New York: Greaves Publishing, 1911.

Smith, Susan E. D. *The Soldier's Friend: Being a Thrilling Narrative of Grandma Smith's Four Years' Experience and Observation, as Matron, in the Hospitals of the South, during the Late Disastrous Conflict in America.* Memphis: Bulletin Publishing, 1867.

Souder, Emily Bliss. *Leaves from the Battle-field of Gettysburg.* Philadelphia: C. Sherman, 1864.

Spencer, Cornelia Phillips. *The Last Ninety Days of the War in North Carolina.* New York: Watchman Publishing, 1866.

Stanton, Elizabeth Cady, Susan B. Anthony, and Matilda Joslyn Gage, eds. *The History of Woman Suffrage.* 2 vols. New York: Fowler and Wells, 1882.

Stearns, Amanda Akin. *The Lady Nurse of Ward E.* New York: Baker and Taylor, 1909.

Stoney, John Safford. "Recollections of John Safford Stoney, Confederate Surgeon." Edited by Samuel G. Stoney. *South Carolina Historical Magazine* 60, no. 4 (October 1959): 208–20.

Swisshelm, Jane Grey. *Crusader and Feminist: Letters of Jane Grey Swisshelm, 1858–1865.* St. Paul: Minnesota Historical Society, 1934.

Taylor, Susie King. *Reminiscences of My Life in Camp.* Boston: N.p., 1902. Edited by Anthony G. Barthelemy. Reprint, New York: Oxford University Press, 1988.

Thrall, Seneca. "An Iowa Doctor in Blue: The Letters of Seneca Thrall, 1862–1864." Edited by Mildred Throne. *Iowa Journal of History* 58, no. 2 (April 1960): 97–188.

Towne, Laura. *Letters and Diary of Laura M. Towne.* Edited by Rupert S. Holland. Cambridge, Mass.: Riverside, 1912.

Truth, Sojourner. *The Narrative of Sojourner Truth.* New York: Arno Press and New York Times, 1968.

———. *The Narrative of Sojourner Truth: A Bondswoman of Olden Time: With a History of Her Labors and Correspondence Drawn from Her "Book of Life."* Edited by Olive Gilbert. New York: Oxford University Press, 1991.

Underwood, John L. *The Women of the Confederacy.* New York: Neale, 1906.

Velasquez, Loreta Janeta. *The Woman in Battle: The Civil War Narrative of Loreta Janeta Velasquez: Cuban Woman and Confederate Soldier.* 1876. Reprint, with a new introduction by Jesse Alemán, Madison: University of Wisconsin Press, 2003.

Von Olnhausen, Mary Phinney. *Adventures of an Army Nurse in Two Wars: Edited from the Diary and Correspondence of Mary Phinney, Baroness von Olnhausen.* Edited by James Phinney Munroe. Boston: Little, Brown, 1904.

Watson, William. *Letters of a Civil War Surgeon.* Edited by Paul Fatout. West Lafayette, Ind.: Purdue University Studies Humanities Series, 1961.

Welch, Spencer Glasgow. *A Confederate Surgeon's Letters to His Wife.* New York and Washington: Neale, 1911.

Wheelock, Julia S. *The Boys in White: The Experience of a Hospital Agent in and around Washington.* New York: Lange and Hillman, 1870.

Whetten, Harriet D. "A Volunteer Nurse in the Civil War: The Letters of Harriet Douglas Whetten." Edited by Paul H. Hass, *Wisconsin Magazine of History* 48, no. 2 (Winter 1964–65): 131–51, and 48, no. 3 (Spring 1965): 205–21.

Whitman, Walt. *Specimen Days and Collect: Complete Poetry and Prose of Walt Whitman.* 2 vols. Edited by Malcolm Cowley. Garden City, N.Y.: Garden City Books, 1954.

———. *Memoranda during the War.* Cambridge, Mass.: Applewood Books, 1993.

Wittenmyer, Annie Turner. *Under the Guns: A Woman's Reminiscences of the Civil War.* Boston: E. B. Stillings, 1895.

Woolsey, Jane Stuart. *Hospital Days.* Privated published, 1868. Reprint, New York: Van Nostrand, 1870.

Wormeley, Katharine Prescott. *The Other Side of the War with the Army of the Potomac.* Boston: Ticknor, 1889.

*Charleston Courier* (Charleston, S.C.), July 16, 1863

*Charleston Mercury* (Charleston, S.C.), July 30, 1863

*Chicago Record Herald*, February 1902

*Daily Republican Register* (Galesburg, Ill.), May 23, 1907

*Detroit Free Press*, October 30, 1881

*Farmers Advocate* (Charles Town, W.Va.), July 30, 1898

*Frank Leslie's Illustrated Newspaper*, August 17, 31, December 7, 1861; July 19, November 22, 1862; March 7, April 4, October 31, 1863; July 16, November 5, 1864; July 7, 1866

*Harper's Weekly*, September 6, 1862; April 4, 1863

*Indianapolis Star*, August 11, 1991

*New York Herald*, November 5, 1861; April 21, October 31, November 5, 17, 1862; June 17, September 16, 21, 23, 24, November 3, 1863; January 7, March 19, April 25, August 12, 14, September 2, November 26, 1864; February 20, July 1, 1865

*Richmond Dispatch*, June 10, 1861

*Richmond Enquirer*, March 7, 1862

*Richmond Examiner*, September 3, 1864

*St. Charles Chronicle* (St. Charles, Ill.), October 7, 1915

*St. Louis Post-Dispatch*, June 2, 1996

*Sandusky Register* (Sandusky, Ohio), December 12, 1864

*Washington Chronicle* (Washington, D.C.), March 30, 1865

*Woman's Journal* (Boston), August 31, 1907

## Secondary Sources

*Books and Monographs*

Abel-Smith, Brian. *A History of the Nursing Profession*. London: Heinemann, 1960.

Adams, George Worthington. *Doctors in Blue: The Medical History of the Union Army in the Civil War*. New York: Henry Schuman, Inc., 1952.

Ashley, Jo Ann. *Hospitals, Paternalism, and the Role of the Nurse*. New York: Columbia University Press, 1976.

Attie, Jeanie. *Patriotic Toil: Northern Women and the American Civil War*. Ithaca: Cornell University Press, 1998.

Austin, Anne L. *The Woolsey Sisters of New York: A Family's Involvement in the Civil War and a New Profession*. Philadelphia: American Philosophical Society, 1971.

Ayers, Edward L. *The Promise of the New South: Life After Reconstruction*. New York: Oxford University Press, 1992.

Baker, Nina Brown. *Cyclone in Calico: The Story of Mary Ann Bickerdyke.* Boston: Little, Brown, 1952.

Barton, George. *Angels of the Battlefield: A History of the Labors of the Catholic Sisterhood in the Late Civil War.* Philadelphia: Catholic Art Publishing, 1898.

Baym, Nina. *Woman's Fiction: A Guide to Novels by and about Women in America, 1820–1870.* Ithaca: Cornell University Press, 1978.

Berlin, Ira, Barbara J. Fields, Steven F. Miller, Joseph P. Reidy, and Leslie S. Rowland. *Free at Last: A Documentary History of Slavery, Freedom, and the Civil War.* New York: New Press, 1992.

Blanton, DeAnne, and Lauren M. Cook. *They Fought Like Demons: Women Soldiers in the American Civil War.* Baton Rouge: Louisiana State University Press, 2002.

Blanton, Wyndham B. *Medicine in Virginia in the Nineteenth Century.* Richmond: Garrett and Massie, 1933.

Bleser, Carol. *In Joy and in Sorrow: Women, Family, and Marriage in the Victorian South, 1830–1900.* New York: Oxford University Press, 1991.

Blight, David W. *Race and Reunion: The Civil War in American Memory.* Cambridge: Belknap Press of Harvard University, 2001.

Brooks, Stewart. *Civil War Medicine.* Springfield, Ill.: Charles C. Thomas, 1966.

Burton, David. *Clara Barton: In the Service of Humanity.* Westport, Conn.: Greenwood Press, 1995.

Burton, Margaret Davis. *The Woman Who Battled for the Boys in Blue: Mother Bickerdyke.* San Francisco: A. T. Dewey, 1886.

Bynum, Victoria E. *Unruly Women: The Politics of Social and Sexual Control in the Old South.* Chapel Hill: University of North Carolina Press, 1992.

Campbell, Edward D. C., Jr., and Kym S. Rice, eds. *A Woman's War: Southern Women, Civil War, and the Confederate Legacy.* Richmond: Museum of the Confederacy, and Charlottesville: University Press of Virginia, 1996.

Cashin, Joan E. *A Family Venture: Men and Women on the Southern Frontier.* New York: Oxford University Press, 1991.

Cashman, Diane Cobb. *Headstrong: The Biography of Amy Morris Bradley.* Wilmington, N.C.: Broadfoot Publishing, 1990.

Clinton, Catherine. *The Plantation Mistress: Woman's World in the Old South.* New York: Pantheon, 1982.

———. *Tara Revisited: Women, War, and the Plantation Legend.* New York: Abbeville, 1995.

Clinton, Catherine, and Nina Silber, eds. *Divided Houses: Gender and the Civil War.* New York: Oxford University Press, 1993.

Conklin, Eileen F. *Women at Gettysburg, 1863.* Gettysburg, Pa.: Thomas Publications, 1993.

Cott, Nancy F. *The Bonds of Womanhood: Woman's Sphere in New England, 1780–1835.* New Haven: Yale University Press, 1977.

Coultrap-McQuin, Susan. *Doing Literary Business: American Women Writers in the Nineteenth Century*. Chapel Hill: University of North Carolina Press, 1990.

Cullen, Jim. *The Civil War in Popular Culture: A Reusable Past*. Washington, D.C.: Smithsonian Institution Press, 1995.

Culpepper, Marilyn Mayer. *Trials and Triumphs: The Women of the American Civil War*. East Lansing: Michigan State University Press, 1991.

Cunningham, H. H. *Doctors in Gray: The Confederate Medical Service*. Baton Rouge: Louisiana State University Press, 1958.

Dannett, Sylvia G. L. *Noble Women of the North*. New York: Thomas Yoseloff, 1959.

Dannett, Sylvia G. L., and Katharine M. Jones. *Our Women of the Sixties*. Washington: U.S. Civil War Centennial Commission, 1963.

Denney, Robert E. *Civil War Medicine: Care and Comfort of the Wounded*. New York: Sterling, 1994.

De Pauw, Linda Grant. *Battle Cries and Lullabies: Women in War from Prehistory to the Present*. Norman: University of Oklahoma Press, 1998.

Diffley, Kathleen. *Where My Heart Is Turning Ever: Civil War Stories and Constitutional Reform, 1861–1876*. Athens: University of Georgia Press, 1992.

———, ed. *To Live and Die: Collected Stories of the Civil War, 1861–1876*. Durham: Duke University Press, 2002.

Dolan, Josephine A. *History of Nursing*, 12th ed. Philadelphia: W. R. Saunders Co., 1968.

Douglas, Ann. *The Feminization of American Culture*. New York: Knopf, 1977.

Drachman, Virginia G. *Hospital with a Heart: Women Doctors and the Paradox of Separatism at the New England Hospital, 1862–1969*. Ithaca: Cornell University Press, 1984.

Dublin, Thomas. *Women at Work: The Transformation of Work and Community in Lowell, Massachusetts, 1826–1860*. New York: Columbia University Press, 1979.

———. *Transforming Women's Work: New England Lives in the Industrial Revolution*. Ithaca: Cornell University Press, 1994.

Edwards, Laura F. *Scarlett Doesn't Live Here Anymore: Southern Women in the Civil War Era*. Urbana: University of Illinois Press, 2000.

Eicher, David J. *Mystic Chords of Memory: Civil War Battlefields and Historic Sites Recaptured*. Baton Rouge: Louisiana State University Press, 1998.

Elbert, Sarah. *A Hunger for Home: Louisa May Alcott and Little Women*. Philadelphia: Temple University Press, 1984.

Enloe, Cynthia. *Does Khaki Become You? The Militarisation of Women's Lives*. London: South End Press, 1983.

Fahs, Alice. *The Imagined Civil War: Popular Literature of the North and South, 1861–1865*. Chapel Hill: University of North Carolina Press, 2001.

Faust, Drew Gilpin. *Mothers of Invention: Women of the Slaveholding South in the American Civil War*. Chapel Hill: University of North Carolina Press, 1996.

Fellman, Michael. *Inside War: The Guerrilla Conflict in Missouri during the American Civil War*. New York: Oxford University Press, 1989.

Fidler, William P. *Augusta Evans Wilson, 1835–1909: A Biography*. Tuscaloosa: University of Alabama Press, 1951.

Foner, Philip. *The Factory Girls: A Collection of Writings on Life and Struggles in the New England Factories of the 1840s*. Urbana: University of Illinois Press, 1977.

Forbes, Ella. *African American Women during the Civil War*. New York: Garland, 1998.

Forman, Stephen M. *A Guide to Civil War Washington*. Washington, D.C.: Elliott and Clark, 1995.

Foster, Gaines Milligan. *Ghosts of the Confederacy: Defeat, the Lost Cause, and the Emergence of the New South, 1865–1913*. New York: Oxford University Press, 1987.

Fox-Genovese, Elizabeth. *Within the Plantation Household: Black and White Women of the Old South*. Chapel Hill: University of North Carolina Press, 1988.

Frankfort, Roberta. *Collegiate Women: Domesticity and Career in Turn-of-the-Century America*. New York: New York University Press, 1977.

Frederickson, George M. *The Inner Civil War: Northern Intellectuals and the Crisis of the Union*. New York: Harper Torchbooks, 1965.

Friedman, Jean. *The Enclosed Garden: Women and Community in the Evangelical South, 1830–1900*. Chapel Hill: University of North Carolina Press, 1985.

Gallman, J. Matthew. *Mastering Wartime: A Social History of Philadelphia during the Civil War*. Philadelphia: University of Pennsylvania Press, 2000.

Giesberg, Judith. *Civil War Sisterhood: The U.S. Sanitary Commission and Women's Politics in Transition*. Boston: Northeastern University Press, 2000.

Gillett, Mary C. *The Army Medical Department, 1818–1865*. Washington, D.C.: Center of Military History, 1987.

Gilmore, Glenda. *Gender and Jim Crow: Women and the Politics of White Supremacy in North Carolina, 1896–1920*. Chapel Hill: University of North Carolina Press, 1996.

Ginzberg, Lori D. *Women and the Work of Benevolence: Morality, Politics, and Class in the Nineteenth-Century United States*. New Haven: Yale University Press, 1990.

Glasson, William Henry. *History of Military Pension Legislation in the United States*. New York: Columbia University Press, 1900.

Gooding, James Henry. *On the Altar of Freedom: A Black Soldier's Civil War Letters from the Front*. Amherst: University of Massachusetts Press, 1991.

Greenbie, Marjorie Barstow. *Lincoln's Daughters of Mercy*. New York: G. P. Putnam's, 1944.

Hanley, Lynne. *Writing War: Fiction, Gender, Memory*. Amherst: University of Massachusetts Press, 1991.

Hewitt, Nancy A. *Women's Activism and Social Change: Rochester, New York, 1822–1872*. Ithaca: Cornell University Press, 1984.

Higgonet, Margaret Randolph, Jane Jenson, Sonya Michel, and Margaret Collins Weitz, eds. *Between the Lines: Gender and the Two World Wars.* New Haven: Yale University Press, 1987.

Hine, Darlene Clark. *Black Women in White: Racial Conflict and Cooperation in the Nursing Profession, 1890–1950.* Bloomington: Indiana University Press, 1989.

Horan, James David. *Desperate Women.* New York: Putnam, 1952.

Horwitz, Tony. *Confederates in the Attic.* New York: Vintage, 1998.

Hurn, Ethel Alice. *Wisconsin Women in the War between the States.* Wisconsin History Commission, Original Papers, no. 6, May 1911.

James, Edward T., ed. *Notable American Women.* 3 vols. Cambridge: Harvard University Press, 1971.

Jolly, Ellen Ryan. *Nuns of the Battlefield.* Providence, R.I.: Providence Visitor Press, 1927.

Jones, Jacqueline. *Soldiers of Light and Love: Northern Teachers and Georgia Blacks, 1865–1873.* Chapel Hill: University of North Carolina Press, 1980.

———. *Labor of Love, Labor of Sorrow: Black Women, Work, and the Family from Slavery to the Present.* New York: Basic Books, 1985.

Jones, Katharine M. *Heroines of Dixie.* Indianapolis: Bobbs-Merrill, 1955.

Jones, Wilbur D. *Giants in the Cornfield: The 27th Indiana Infantry.* Shippensburg, Pa.: White Mane, 1997.

*The Journal of the 28th National Convention of the Woman's Relief Corps, Auxiliary to the Grand Army of the Republic.* Boston: E. B. Stillings, 1910.

Kalisch, Philip A., and Beatrice J. Kalisch. *The Advance of American Nursing,* 2d ed. Boston: Little, Brown, 1986.

———. *The Changing Image of the Nurse.* Menlo Park, Calif.: Addison Wesley, 1987.

Kantor, Alvin R., and Marjorie S. Kantor. *Sanitary Fairs: A Philatelic and Historical Study of Civil War Benevolences.* Glencoe, Ill.: S F Publications, 1992.

Kelley, Mary. *Private Woman, Public Stage: Literary Domesticity in Nineteenth-Century America.* New York: Oxford University Press, 1984.

Kelley, Patrick J. *Creating a National Home: Building the Veterans' Welfare State.* Cambridge: Harvard University Press, 1997.

Kessler-Harris, Alice. *Out to Work: A History of Wage-Earning Women in the United States.* New York: Oxford University Press, 1982.

Lebsock, Suzanne. *The Free Women of Petersburg: Status and Culture in a Southern Town, 1784–1860.* New York: Norton, 1984.

Leonard, Elizabeth D. *Yankee Women: Gender Battles in the Civil War.* New York: Norton, 1994.

———. *All the Daring of the Soldier: Women of the Civil War Armies.* New York: Norton, 1999.

Leonard, Thomas C. *Above the Battle: War-Making in America from Appomattox to Versailles.* New York: Oxford University Press, 1978.

Long, Lisa. "The American Civil War and Cultural Disease." Ph.D. diss., University of Wisconsin, 1997.

Mabee, Carleton. *Sojourner Truth: Slave, Prophet, Legend*. New York: New York University Press, 1993.

MacCaskill, Libby, and David Novak. *Ladies on the Field: Two Civil War Nurses from Maine on the Battlefields of Virginia*. Livermore, Maine: Signal Tree Publications, 1996.

Maher, Sister Mary Denis. *To Bind Up the Wounds: Catholic Sister Nurses in the U.S. Civil War*. Westport, Conn.: Greenwood Press, 1989.

Massey, Mary Elizabeth. *Bonnet Brigades*. New York: Knopf, 1966.

———. *Ersatz in the Confederacy: Shortages and Substitutes on the Southern Homefront*. 1952. Reprint, Columbia: University of South Carolina Press, 1993.

Mayo, James M. *War Memorials as Political Landscape: The American Experience and Beyond*. New York: Praeger, 1988.

McMillen, Sally G. *Motherhood in the Old South: Pregnancy, Childbirth, and Infant Rearing*. Baton Rouge: Louisiana State University Press, 1990.

McPherson, James. *The Negro's Civil War: How American Negroes Felt and Acted during the War for the Union*. New York: Pantheon Books, 1965.

———. *Battle Cry of Freedom: The Civil War Era*. New York: Ballantine, 1988.

———. *For Cause and Comrades: Why Men Fought in the Civil War*. New York: Oxford, 1997.

*The Medical and Surgical History of the War of the Rebellion*. 1875–88. 12 vols. Reprinted as *The Medical and Surgical History of the Civil War*, Philadelphia: Broadfoot, 1990–92. All page references are to the reprint.

Melosh, Barbara. *The Physician's Hand: Work, Culture, and Conflict in American Nursing*. Philadelphia: Temple University Press, 1982.

Merrill, Catharine. *The Soldier of Indiana in the War for the Union*. Indianapolis: Merrill, 1866.

*Michigan Women in the Civil War*. Lansing: Michigan Civil War Observance Commission, 1963.

Mitchell, Reid. *The Vacant Chair: The Northern Soldier Leaves Home*. New York: Oxford University Press, 1993.

Moldow, Gloria. *Women Doctors in Gilded Age Washington: Race, Gender, and Professionalization*. Urbana: University of Illinois Press, 1987.

Morantz-Sanchez, Regina. *Sympathy and Science: Women Physicians in American Medicine*. New York: Oxford University Press, 1985.

Morris, Roy, Jr. *The Better Angel: Walt Whitman in the Civil War*. New York: Oxford University Press, 2000.

Moss, Lemuel. *Annals of the United States Christian Commission*. Philadelphia: J. B. Lippincott, 1868.

Mottus, Jane E. *New York Nightingales: The Emergence of the Nursing Profession at Bellevue and New York Hospital, 1850–1920*. Ann Arbor, Mich.: UMI Research Press, 1981.

Oates, Stephen B. *A Woman of Valor: Clara Barton and the Civil War*. New York: Free Press, 1994.

O'Brien, Frank. *Forgotten Heroines.* Lansing: Michigan Historical Commission, 1916.

Painter, Nell Irvin. *Sojourner Truth: A Life, a Symbol.* New York: Norton, 1996.

Paludan, Phillip Shaw. *"A People's Contest": The Union and Civil War, 1861–1865.* New York: Harper and Row, 1988.

Pernick, Martin. *A Calculus of Suffering: Pain, Professionalism, and Anesthesia in Nineteenth-Century America.* New York: Columbia University Press, 1985.

Pryor, Elizabeth Brown. *Clara Barton: Professional Angel.* Philadelphia: University of Pennsylvania Press, 1987.

Rable, George. *Civil Wars: Women and the Crisis of Southern Nationalism.* Urbana: University of Illinois Press, 1989.

Randall, James G., and David Donald. *Civil War and Reconstruction.* Boston: Heath, 1961.

Reardon, Carol. *Pickett's Charge in History and Memory.* Chapel Hill: University of North Carolina Press, 1997.

Reverby, Susan M. *Ordered to Care: The Dilemma of American Nursing, 1850–1945.* London: Cambridge University Press, 1987.

Richmond Civil War Centennial Commission. *Confederate Military Hospitals.* Official Publication No. 22. Richmond: Richmond Civil War Centennial Commission, 1964.

Ross, Ishbel. *Rebel Rose: Life of Rose O'Neal Greenhow: Confederate Spy.* New York: Harper, 1954.

———. *Angel of the Battlefield: The Life of Clara Barton.* New York: Harper, 1956.

Ross, Kristie R. "'Women Are Needed Here': Northern Protestant Women as Nurses during the Civil War, 1861–1865." Ph.D. diss., Columbia University, 1993.

Rothman, David. *The Discovery of the Asylum: Social Order and Disorder in the New Republic.* Boston: Little, Brown, 1990.

Ryan, Mary P. *Cradle of the Middle Class: The Family in Oneida County, New York, 1790–1865.* New York: Cambridge University Press, 1981.

———. *Women in Public: Between Banners and Ballots, 1825–1880.* Baltimore: Johns Hopkins University Press, 1990.

Savage, Kirk. *Standing Soldiers, Kneeling Slaves: Race, War, and Monument in Nineteenth-Century America.* Princeton: Princeton University Press, 1997.

Scarborough, Ruth. *Belle Boyd: Siren of the South.* Macon, Ga.: Mercer University Press, 1983.

Schroeder-Lein, Glenna R. *Confederate Hospitals on the Move: Samuel H. Stout and the Army of Tennessee.* Columbia: University of South Carolina Press, 1994.

Schultz, Jane E. "Women at the Front: Gender and Genre in Literature of the American Civil War." Ph.D. diss., University of Michigan, 1988.

Schwalm, Leslie. *A Hard Fight for We: Women's Transition from Slavery to Freedom in South Carolina.* Urbana: University of Illinois Press, 1997.

Scott, Anne Firor. *The Southern Lady: From Pedestal to Politics, 1830–1930*. Chicago: University of Chicago Press, 1970.

Silber, Nina. *The Romance of Reunion: Northerners and the South, 1865–1900*. Chapel Hill: University of North Carolina Press, 1993.

Sizer, Lyde Cullen. *The Political Work of Northern Women Writers and the Civil War, 1850–1872*. Chapel Hill: University of North Carolina Press, 2001.

Sklar, Kathryn Kish. *Catherine Beecher: A Study in American Domesticity*. New York: Norton, 1973.

Skocpol, Theda. *Protecting Soldiers and Mothers: The Political Origins of Social Policy in the United States*. Cambridge: Belknap Press of Harvard University, 1992.

Smith, Nina Bennett. "The Women Who Went to the War: The Union Army Nurse in the Civil War." Ph.D. diss., Northwestern University, 1981.

Smith-Rosenberg, Carroll. *Disorderly Conduct: Visions of Gender in Victorian America*. New York: Knopf, 1985.

Snyder, Charles McCool. *Dr. Mary Walker: The Little Lady in Pants*. New York: Vantage Press, 1962.

Solomon, Barbara Miller. *In the Company of Educated Women: A History of Women and Higher Education in America*. New Haven: Yale University Press, 1985.

Stansell, Christine. *City of Women: Sex and Class in New York, 1789–1860*. Urbana: University of Illinois Press, 1987.

Starr, Paul. *The Social Transformation of American Medicine*. New York: Basic Books, 1982.

Sterkx, H. E. *Partners in Rebellion: Alabama Women in the Civil War*. Rutherford, Ala.: Fairleigh Dickinson University Press, 1970.

Stillé, Charles J. *History of the United States Sanitary Commission*. New York: Hurd and Houghton, 1866, 1868.

Straubing, Harold Elk. *In Hospital and Camp: The Civil War through the Eyes of Its Doctors and Nurses*. Harrisburg, Pa.: Stackpole Books, 1993.

Sudlow, Lynda L. *A Vast Army of Women: Maine's Uncounted Forces in the American Civil War*. Gettysburg, Pa.: Thomas Publications, 2000.

Sutherland, Daniel. *The Confederate Carpetbaggers*. Baton Rouge: Louisiana State University Press, 1988.

Sweet, Timothy. *Traces of War: Poetry, Photography, and the Crisis of the Union*. Baltimore: Johns Hopkins University Press, 1990.

Trustram, Myna. *Women of the Regiment: Marriage and the Victorian Army*. Cambridge: Cambridge University Press, 1984.

Venet, Wendy Hammand. *Neither Ballots nor Bullets: Women Abolitionists and the Civil War*. Charlottesville: University Press of Virginia, 1991.

Walsh, Mary Roth. *"Doctors Wanted: No Women Need Apply"; Sexual Barriers in the Medical Profession, 1835–1975*. New Haven: Yale University Press, 1977.

Warren, Robert Penn. *The Legacy of the Civil War*. New York: Random House, 1961.

Wheeler, Marjorie Spruill. *New Women of the New South: The Leaders of the Woman Suffrage Movement in the Southern States.* New York: Oxford University Press, 1993.

White, Deborah Gray. *Ar'n't I a Woman? Female Slaves in the Plantation South.* New York: Norton, 1985.

White, Hayden. *Tropics of Discourse: Essays in Cultural Criticism.* Baltimore: Johns Hopkins University Press, 1978.

———. *The Content of the Form: Narrative Discourse and Historical Representation.* Baltimore: Johns Hopkins University Press, 1987.

Whites, LeeAnn. *The Civil War as a Crisis in Gender: Augusta, Georgia, 1860–1890.* Athens: University of Georgia Press, 1995.

Wiley, Bell. *Confederate Women.* Westport, Conn.: Greenwood Press, 1975.

Wilson, Charles Reagan. *Baptized in Blood: The Religion of the Lost Cause, 1865–1920.* Athens: University of Georgia Press, 1980.

Wilson, Dorothy Clarke. *Stranger and Traveler: The Story of Dorothea Dix: American Reformer.* Boston: Little, Brown, 1975.

Woloch, Nancy. *Women and the American Experience.* New York: Knopf, 1984.

*The Woman's Relief Corps Red Book.* Boston: E. B. Stillings, 1897.

Woolsey, Abby Howland. *A Century of Nursing.* New York: Putnam's, 1876.

Young, Agnes Brooks [Agatha Young, pseud.]. *The Women and the Crisis: Women of the North in the Civil War.* New York: McDowell, Obolensky, 1959.

Young, Elizabeth. *Disarming the Nation: Women's Writing and the American Civil War.* Chicago: University of Chicago Press, 1999.

*Articles*

Abram, Ruth J. "Soon the Baby Died: Medical Training in Nineteenth-Century America." In *"Send Us a Lady Physician": Women Doctors in America, 1835–1920,* edited by Ruth J. Abram, 17–20. New York: Norton, 1985.

Attie, Jeanie. "Warwork and the Crisis of Domesticity in the North." In *Divided Houses: Gender and the Civil War,* edited by Catherine Clinton and Nina Silber, 247–59. New York: Oxford University Press, 1993.

Austin, Anne L. "Wartime Volunteers—1861–1865." *American Journal of Nursing* 75 (May 1975): 816–18.

Bardaglio, Peter. "The Children of Jubilee." In *Divided Houses: Gender and the Civil War,* edited by Catherine Clinton and Nina Silber, 213–29. New York: Oxford University Press, 1993.

Berkeley, Kathleen C. "'Colored Ladies Also Contributed': Black Women's Activities from Benevolence to Social Welfare, 1866–96." In *Black Women in American History,* edited by Darlene Clark Hine, 61–83. Brooklyn: Carlson Publishing, 1990.

Berlin, Ira, Leslie S. Rowland, and Steven F. Miller. "Afro-American Families in the Transition from Slavery to Freedom." In *Black Women in American*

*History*, edited by Darlene Clark Hine, 84–117. Brooklyn: Carlson Publishing, 1990.

Blake, John B. "Women and Medicine in Ante-bellum America." *Bulletin of the History of Medicine* 39, no. 2 (March–April 1965): 99–123.

Blight, David W. "Quarrel Forgotten or a Revolution Remembered? Reunion and Race in the Memory of the Civil War, 1875–1913." In *Race and Reunion: The Civil War in American Memory*, edited by David W. Blight, 151–79. Cambridge: Belknap Press of Harvard University, 2001.

Blustein, Bonnie Ellen. "'To Increase the Efficiency of the Medical Department': A New Approach to U.S. Civil War Medicine." *Civil War History* 33, no. 1 (March 1987): 22–41.

Brav, Stanley R. "The Jewish Woman, 1861–1865." *American Jewish Archives* 17, no. 1 (April 1965): 34–75.

Bridges, Edwin C. "The Alabama Hospitals in Richmond." A paper generously provided by the author.

Bullough, Vern, and Bonnie Bullough. "The Origins of Modern American Nursing: The Civil War Era." *Nursing Forum* 2, no. 2 (1963): 12–27.

Christie, Jeanne Marie. "'Performing My Plain Duty': Women of the North at City Point, 1864–1865." *Virginia Cavalcade* 47, no. 2 (Summer 1997): 214–24.

Conrad, Earl. "I Bring You General Tubman." In *Black Women in American History*, edited by Darlene Clark Hine, 268–73. Brooklyn: Carlson Publishing, 1990.

Coski, John M., and Amy R. Feely. "A Monument to Southern Womanhood: The Founding Generation of the Confederate Museum." In *A Woman's War: Southern Women, Civil War, and the Confederate Legacy*, edited by Edward D. C. Campbell Jr. and Kym S. Rice, 131–63. Richmond: Museum of the Confederacy, and Charlottesville: University Press of Virginia, 1996.

Culpepper, Marilyn Mayer, and Pauline Gordon Adams. "Nursing in the Civil War." *American Journal of Nursing* 88, no. 7 (July 1988): 981–84.

Cunningham, Constance. "The Sin of Omission: Black Women in Nineteenth-Century American History." In *Black Women in American History*, edited by Darlene Clark Hine, 275–86. Brooklyn: Carlson Publishing, 1990.

Davis, Stephen. "A Confederate Hospital: Surgeon John Patterson and the Clayton during the Atlanta Campaign, 1864." *Journal of the Medical Association of Georgia* 75, no. 1 (1986): 14–24.

Deutrich, Bernice M. "Propriety and Pay." *Prologue* 3, no. 2 (Fall 1971): 66–72.

Douglas, Ann. "The War within a War: Women Nurses in the Union Army." *Civil War History* 18, no. 3 (September 1972): 197–212.

———. "'The Fashionable Disease': Women's Complaints and Their Treatment in Nineteenth-Century America." *Journal of Interdisciplinary History* 4, no. 1 (Summer 1973): 25–52.

Endres, Kathleen L. "The Women's Press in the Civil War: A Portrait of Patriotism, Propaganda, and Prodding." *Civil War History* 30, no. 1 (March 1984): 31–53.

Fahs, Alice. "The Feminized Civil War: Gender, Northern Popular Literature, and the Memory of the War, 1861–1900." *Journal of American History* 85, no. 4 (March 1999): 1461–94.

Faust, Drew Gilpin. "Christian Soldiers: The Meaning of Revivalism in the Confederate Army." *Journal of Southern History* 53, no. 1 (February 1987): 63–90.

———. "Altars of Sacrifice: Confederate Women and the Narratives of War." *Journal of American History* 76, no. 4 (March 1990): 1200–1228.

———. Introduction to Augusta Evans Wilson's *Macaria*. Baton Rouge: Louisiana State University Press, 1992.

———. "Trying to Do a Man's Business: Gender, Violence, and Slave Management in Civil War Texas," *Gender and History* 4, no. 2 (Summer 1992): 197–214.

———. "'Ours as Well as That of the Men': Women and Gender in the Civil War." In *Writing the Civil War: The Quest to Understand*, edited by James McPherson and William J. Cooper, 228–40. Columbia: University of South Carolina Press, 1998.

Fellman, Michael. "Women and Guerrilla Warfare." In *Divided Houses: Gender and the Civil War*, edited by Catherine Clinton and Nina Silber, 147–65. New York: Oxford University Press, 1993.

Fischer, Leroy H. "Cairo's Civil War Angel: Mary Jane Safford." *Illinois State Historical Society Journal* 54 (Autumn 1961): 229–45.

Fladeland, Betty. "Alias Franklin Thompson." *Michigan History* 42, no. 4 (December 1958): 435–62.

———. "New Light on Sarah Emma Edmonds, Alias Franklin Thompson." *Michigan History* 47, no. 4 (December 1963): 357–62.

Fornell, Earl W. "A Woman in the Union Army." *American-German Review* 26–27 (February–March 1961): 13–15.

Frankel, Noralee. "The Southern Side of 'Glory': Mississippi African-American Women during the Civil War." *Minerva: Quarterly Report on Women and the Military* 8, no. 3 (Fall 1990): 28–36.

Gabrielson, Rosamond L. "Two Centuries of Advancement: From Untrained Servant to Skilled Practitioner." *Journal of Advanced Nursing* 1, no. 4 (1976): 265–72.

Gallagher, Ruth A. "Annie Turner Wittenmyer." *Iowa Journal of History and Politics* 29, no. 4 (October 1931): 518–69.

Gallman, J. Matthew. "Volunteerism in Wartime: Philadelphia's Great Central Fair." In *Toward a Social History of the American Civil War*, edited by Maris Vinovskis, 93–116. Cambridge: Cambridge University Press, 1990.

Gilbert, Sandra. "Soldier's Heart: Literary Men, Literary Women, and the Great War." *Signs* 8, no. 3 (Spring 1983): 422–50.

Glymph, Thavolia. "'This Species of Property': Female Slave Contrabands in the Civil War." In *A Woman's War: Southern Women, Civil War, and the Confederate Legacy*, edited by Edward D. C. Campbell Jr. and Kym S. Rice, 55–71. Richmond: Museum of the Confederacy, and Charlottesville: University Press of Virginia, 1996.

Gordon, Linda. "The New Feminist Scholarship on the Welfare State." In *Women, the State, and Welfare*, edited by Linda Gordon, 9–35. Madison: University of Wisconsin Press, 1990.

Gordon, Ralph C. "Nashville and the U.S. Christian Commission in the Civil War." *Tennessee Historical Quarterly* 60, no. 2 (Summer 1996): 98–112.

Guyot, Sister Henrietta. "The Nurse in Civil War Literature." *Nursing Outlook* 10, no. 5 (May 1962): 311–14.

Hacker, Barton C. "Women and Military Institutions in Early Modern Europe: A Reconnaissance." *Signs* 6, no. 4 (Summer 1981): 643–71.

Hall, Courtney Robert. "Confederate Medicine: Caring for the Confederate Soldier." *Medical Life* 42, no. 9 (September 1935): 445–508.

Henle, Ellen Langenheim. "Clara Barton: Soldier or Pacifist?" *Civil War History* 24, no. 2 (June 1978): 152–60.

Holmes, Amy E. "'Such Is the Price We Pay': American Widows and the Civil War Pension System." In *Toward a Social History of the American Civil War*, edited by Maris Vinovskis, 171–95. Cambridge: Cambridge University Press, 1990.

Holzman, Robert S. "Sally Tompkins: Captain, Confederate Army." *American Mercury* 88 (March 1959): 127–30.

James, Janet Wilson. "Isabel Hampton and the Professionalization of Nursing in the 1890s." In *The Therapeutic Revolution: Essays in the Social History of American Medicine*, edited by Charles E. Rosenberg and Morris J. Vogel, 201–44. Philadelphia: University of Pennsylvania Press, 1979.

Kalisch, Philip A., and Beatrice J. Kalisch. "Untrained but Undaunted: The Women Nurses of the Blue and the Gray." *Nursing Forum* 15, no. 1 (1976): 4–33.

Kalisch, Philip A., and Margaret Scobey. "Female Nurses in American Wars: Helplessness Suspended for the Duration." *Armed Forces and Society* 9, no. 2 (Winter 1983): 215–44.

Leonard, Elizabeth D. "Civil War Nurse, Civil War Nursing: Rebecca Usher of Maine." *Civil War History* 41, no. 3 (September 1995): 190–207.

Marshall, Mary Louise. "Nurse Heroines of the Confederacy." *Bulletin of the Medical Librarians' Association* 45 (July 1957): 319–36.

McClintock, Megan J. "Civil War Pensions and the Reconstruction of Union Families." *Journal of American History* 83, no. 2 (September 1996): 456–80.

McCurry, Stephanie. "The Politics of Yeoman Households in South Carolina." In *Divided Houses: Gender and the Civil War*, edited by Catherine Clinton and Nina Silber, 22–38. New York: Oxford University Press, 1993.

Melosh, Barbara. "Every Woman Is a Nurse: Work and Gender in the Emergence of Nursing." In *"Send Us a Lady Physician": Women Doctors in America, 1835–1920*, edited by Ruth J. Abram, 121–28. New York: Norton, 1985.

Millbrook, Minnie Dubbs. "Michigan Women Who Went to War." In *Michigan Women in the Civil War*, 12–30. Lansing: Michigan Centennial Civil War Observance Commission, 1963.

Mink, Gwendolyn. "The Lady and the Tramp: Gender, Race, and the Origins of the American Welfare State." In *Women, the State, and Welfare*, edited by Linda Gordon, 92–122. Madison: University of Wisconsin Press, 1990.

Morantz, Regina Markell. "The 'Connecting Link': The Case for the Woman Doctor in Nineteenth-Century America." In *Sickness and Health in America*, edited by Judith Walzer Leavitt and Ronald Numbers, 117–28. Madison: University of Wisconsin Press, 1978.

Morantz, Regina Markell, and Sue Zschoche. "Professionalism, Feminism, and Gender Roles: A Comparative Study of Nineteenth-Century Medical Therapeutics." *Journal of American History* 67, no. 3 (December 1980): 568–88.

Musher, Sharon Ann. "Contesting 'The Way the Almighty Wants It': Crafting Memories of Ex-Slaves in the Slave Narrative Collection." *American Quarterly* 53, no. 1 (March 2001): 1–31.

Napier, John. "Montgomery during the Civil War." *Alabama Review* 41, no. 2 (April 1988): 103–31.

Nelson, Barbara J. "The Origins of the Two-Channel Welfare State: Workmen's Compensation and Mothers' Aid." In *Women, the State, and Welfare*, edited by Linda Gordon, 123–51. Madison: University of Wisconsin Press, 1990.

Newman, Kathy. "Wounds and Wounding in the American Civil War: A (Visual) History." *Yale Journal of Criticism* 6, no. 2 (1993): 63–86.

Paquette, Patricia. "A Bandage in One Hand and a Bible in the Other: The Story of Captain Sally L. Tompkins." *Minerva: Quarterly Report on Women and the Military* 8, no. 2 (Summer 1990): 47–54.

Parrish, William E. "The Western Sanitary Commission." *Civil War History* 36, no. 1 (March 1990): 17–35.

Perkins, Linda M. "The Education of Black Women in the Nineteenth Century." In *Women and Higher Education in American History*, edited by John Mack Faragher and Florence Howe, 64–86. New York: Norton, 1988.

Quarles, Benjamin. "Harriet Tubman's Unlikely Leadership." In *Black Women in American History*, edited by Darlene Clark Hine, 1132–47. Brooklyn: Carlson Publishing, 1990.

Rable, George. "'Missing in Action': Women of the Confederacy." In *Divided Houses: Gender and the Civil War*, edited by Catherine Clinton and Nina Silber, 134–46. New York: Oxford University Press, 1993.

Riss, Arthur. "Racial Essentialism and Family Values in *Uncle Tom's Cabin*." *American Quarterly* 46, no. 4 (December 1994): 513–44.

Robertson, Mary D., ed. "The Dusky Wings of War: The Journal of Lucy G. Breckinridge, 1862–1864." *Civil War History* 23, no. 1 (March 1977): 26–51.

Roca, Steven. "Presence and Precedents: The USS *Red Rover* during the American Civil War, 1861–1865." *Civil War History* 44, no. 2 (June 1998): 91–110.

Rosenberg, Charles E. "Florence Nightingale on Contagion: The Hospital as Moral Universe." In *Healing and History*, edited by Charles E. Rosenberg, 116–36. New York: Science History Publications, 1979.

———. "The Therapeutic Revolution: Medicine, Meaning, and Social Change in Nineteenth-Century America." In *The Therapeutic Revolution: Essays in the Social History of American Medicine*, edited by Charles E. Rosenberg and Morris J. Vogel, 3–25. Philadelphia: University of Pennsylvania Press, 1979.

Ross, Kristie R. "Arranging a Doll's House: Refined Women as Union Nurses." In *Divided Houses: Gender and the Civil War*, edited by Catherine Clinton and Nina Silber, 97–113. New York: Oxford University Press, 1993.

Ruoff, John C. "Frivolity to Consumption; or, Southern Womanhood in Antebellum Literature." *Civil War History* 18, no. 3 (September 1972): 213–29.

Sanders, Heywood T. "Paying for the 'Bloody Shirt': The Politics of Civil War Pensions." In *Political Benefits: Empirical Studies of American Public Programs*, edited by Barry S. Rundquist, 137–59. Lexington, Mass.: Lexington Books, 1980.

Sapiro, Virginia. "The Gender Basis of American Social Policy." In *Women, the State, and Welfare*, edited by Linda Gordon, 36–54. Madison: University of Wisconsin Press, 1990.

"Sarah Low: Dover's Civil War Nurse." Northam Colonist Historical Society, Dover, N.H., 1962.

Sauls, Diana. "The Sunset Gun: The Story of Mary Ann Bickerdyke: Civil War Nurse." *North South Medical Times* 9, no. 3 (May–June 1996): 12–20.

Schriber, Mary Suzanne. "Julia Ward Howe and the Travel Book." *New England Quarterly* 62, no. 2 (June 1989): 264–79.

Schultz, Jane E. "Mute Fury: Southern Women's Diaries of Sherman's March to the Sea, 1864–1865." In *Arms and the Woman: War, Gender, and Literary Representation*, edited by Helen M. Cooper, Adrienne Auslander Munich, and Susan Merrill Squier, 59–79. Chapel Hill: University of North Carolina Press, 1989.

———. "The Inhospitable Hospital: Gender and Professionalism in Civil War Medicine." *Signs* 17, no. 2 (Winter 1992): 363–92.

———. "From Avenging Angel to 'Clara Barton of the Confederacy': Kate Cumming's Southern Reconstruction." Paper presented at the Southern Association of Women Historians Conference, Rice University, Houston, June 1994.

———. "Race, Gender, and Bureaucracy: Civil War Army Nurses and the Pension Bureau." *Journal of Women's History* 6, no. 2 (Summer 1994): 45–69.

———. "'Are We Not All Soldiers?': Women in the Civil War Hospital Service, 1861–1865." *Prospects: A Journal of American Cultural Studies* 18 (1995): 39–56.

———. "Seldom Thanked, Never Praised, and Scarcely Recognized: Gender and Racism in Civil War Hospitals." *Civil War History* 48, no. 3 (September 2002): 220–36.

Seigel, Peggy Brase. "She Went to War: Indiana Women Nurses in the Civil War." *Indiana Magazine of History* 86 (March 1990): 1–27.

Shaffer, Donald R. "'I Do Not Suppose That Uncle Sam Looks at the Skin': African Americans and the Civil War Pension System, 1865–1934." *Civil War History* 46, no. 2 (2000): 132–47.

Shryock, Richard H. "Nursing Emerges as a Profession: The American Experience." *Clio Medica* 3 (1968): 131–47.

Silber, Nina. "Intemperate Men, Spiteful Women, and Jefferson Davis." In *Divided Houses: Gender and the Civil War*, edited by Catherine Clinton and Nina Silber, 283–305. New York: Oxford University Press, 1993.

Simkins, Francis B., and James W. Patton. "The Work of Southern Women among the Sick and Wounded of the Confederate Armies." *Journal of Southern History* 1, no. 4 (November 1935): 475–96.

Sizer, Lyde Cullen. "Acting Her Part: Narratives of Union Women Spies." In *Divided Houses: Gender and the Civil War*, edited by Catherine Clinton and Nina Silber, 114–33. New York: Oxford University Press, 1993.

Sloan, Patricia E. "Early Black Nursing Schools and Responses of Black Nurses to Their Educational Programs." In *Black Women in American History*, edited by Darlene Clark Hine, 1285–1304. Brooklyn: Carlson Publishing, 1990.

Smith, Karen Manners. "Recapturing Southern Identity: Mary Virginia Terhune and the Construction of the Mary Washington Monument." Paper presented at the Great Lakes American Studies Association Conference, Indiana University, Bloomington, March 1997.

Smith-Rosenberg, Carroll, and Charles Rosenberg. "The Female Animal: Medical and Biological Views of Woman and Her Role in Nineteenth-Century America." *Journal of American History* 60, no. 2 (September 1973): 332–56.

Stimson, Julia C., and Ethel C. S. Thompson. "Women Nurses with the Union Forces during the Civil War." *Military Surgeon* 62, no. 1 (1928): 208–30.

Strauss, Anselm. "The Structure and Ideology of American Nursing: An Interpretation." In *The Nursing Profession: Five Sociological Essays*, edited by Fred Davis, 60–108. New York: John Wiley, 1966.

Tierney, Roberta. "The Beneficent Revolution: Hospital Nursing during the Civil War." In *Florence Nightingale and Her Era: A Collection of New Scholarship*, edited by Vern Bullough, Bonnie Bullough, and Marietta Stanton, 138–51. New York: Garland, 1990.

Tomes, Nancy. "'Little World of Our Own': The Pennsylvania Hospital Training School for Nurses, 1895–1907." *Journal of the History of Medicine and Allied Sciences* 33, no. 4 (October 1978): 507–30.

Venet, Wendy Hammand. "The Emergence of a Suffragist: Mary Livermore, Civil War Activism, and the Moral Power of Women." *Civil War History* 48, no. 2 (June 2002): 143–64.

Verbrugge, Martha H. "Women and Medicine in Nineteenth-Century America." *Signs* 1, no. 4 (Summer 1976): 957–72.

Wedin, Carolyn. "The Civil War and Black Women on the Sea Islands." In *Southern Women*, edited by Caroline Matheny Dillman, 71–80. New York: Hemisphere Publishing, 1988.

Wendel, Vickie. "Washer Women." *Civil War Times Illustrated* 38, no. 4 (August 1999): 31–36.

Werlich, Robert. "Mary Walker: From Union Army Surgeon to Side Show Freak." *Civil War Times Illustrated* 6, no. 3 (1967): 46–49.

Whites, LeeAnn. "The Civil War as a Crisis in Gender." In *Divided Houses: Gender and the Civil War*, edited by Catherine Clinton and Nina Silber, 3–21. New York: Oxford University Press, 1993.

Wiley, Bell. "Women of the Lost Cause." *American History Illustrated* 8, no. 8 (1973): 10–23.

Williams, Katherine. "From Sarah Gamp to Florence Nightingale: A Critical Study of Hospital Nursing Systems from 1840 to 1897." In *Rewriting Nursing History*, edited by Celia Davies, 41–75. London: Croon Helm, 1980.

Young, Elizabeth. "Warring Fictions: *Iola Leroy* and the Color of Gender." In *Subjects and Citizens: Nation, Race, and Gender from Oroonoko to Anita Hill*, edited by Michael Moon and Cathy N. Davidson, 293–318. Durham: Duke University Press, 1995.

———. "Confederate Counterfeit: The Case of the Cross-Dressed Civil War Soldier." In *Passing and the Fictions of Identity*, edited by Elaine K. Ginsberg, 181–217. Durham: Duke University Press, 1996.

———. "A Wound of One's Own: Louisa May Alcott's Civil War Fiction," *American Quarterly* 48, no. 3 (September 1996): 439–74.

# Index

dations, 81–82, 83, 85, 276 (n. 40); and solace, 90, 279 (n. 71); and relationships among workers, 103; and hospital administrators, 119–20, 132–33, 140; and surgeons, 126–27; as teacher, 159; and Brockett, 165; U.S. lecture tour of, 177, 179; and pension, 188; and Army Nurse Pension Act, 191; memoirs of, 211; diaries of, 220, 308 (n. 38); and Moore, 232

Bass, Mrs. M. C., 115

Battlefields, 3, 15, 16, 33, 55, 69–71, 257 (n. 26). *See also* Field hospitals; Regimental women

Baxter, J. H., 125

Beck, Sarah, 86

Beers, Anna L., 183

Beers, Fannie: and pay, 44; and nursing applications, 52–53; and hospital-life adjustments, 75–76; and enemy soldiers, 78; and isolation, 88; and sexual vulnerability, 90; and maternal feelings, 95; and relationships among workers, 100; and surgeons, 115, 128–29; as writer, 162; war memoirs of, 213, 226, 242; and Confederate reunions, 219

Bellinger, Sarah Hails, 18

Bibb, Sophie, 218

Bickerdyke, Mary Ann "Mother": children of, 64; and travel, 68; and Dix, 115, 285 (n. 22); and surgeons, 115–16; and lack of class status, 117–18; and military authority, 119, 137; and reform movements, 155, 167–68; and hospital work, 164, 167–68; and Safford, 176; and pension, 189, 299 (n. 18); and monuments, 217; biography of, 230; and Platt, 231; and Moore, 232

Billings, John Shaw, 289 (n. 92), 290 (n. 102)

Billings, Sarah, 170, 296 (n. 70)

Blackman, George C., 39

Blackmar, Mary, 175

Blackwell, Elizabeth, 1, 175, 177, 254 (n. 2), 284 (n. 13), 296 (n. 67)

Blanton, DeAnne, 251

Blight, David, 214, 216

Bliss, D. W., 43, 126, 175

Boate, Henrietta Wellington, 45

Boyden, Anna L., 211

Bradley, Amy Morris: as matron, 2, 116–17; and convalescent camp, 2, 117, 126, 159; and managerial experience, 2, 159–60; and relief work, 2, 218; and relationships among workers, 36, 103; and hospital-life adjustments, 39, 73, 74, 75, 77, 78–79, 85, 89, 94, 95; and pay, 43, 100; and nursing applications, 62–63; and relationship with hospital administrators, 107; as teacher, 159; and African American women, 202; and war memoirs, 236–37

Brasier, George, 208

Brinton, John, 18, 25, 123, 241, 287 (n. 56)

Brockett, Linus P., 19, 148, 165, 214, 215, 223, 231

Brown, A. M., 232

Brown, Harvey E., 131–32

Brown, Henry W., 207

Buckel, Chloe Annette, 166, 173–74, 175, 202, 236

Bucklin, Sophronia, 47, 94, 109, 114, 137–41, 230, 240–41, 243, 311 (n. 103), 312 (n. 114)

Burghardt, Caroline, 175, 189

Burton, Margaret Davis, 230

Butler, Benjamin F., 26, 39

Bynum, Victoria, 248

Carded Service Records, 20, 21–31, 184, 188, 260 (nn. 58, 59), 299 (n. 16), 303 (n. 65)

Carlisle, Hannah, 160

Carter, Martha Milledge Flournoy, 38
Carter, Nancy Dodson, 157, 198
Cary, Constance, 17, 162–63
Chamberlain, Joshua, 184
Charity work, 6, 15, 148–49, 150, 153
Chase, Nelly M., 233
Chesnut, Mary Boykin, 153
Children, 5, 46, 63–65, 66, 271 (n. 84)
Children's aid societies, 149
Churches, 14, 18, 21, 68, 164
Civil service jobs, 155, 157, 185
Clapp, Sarah Chadwick, 194, 195
Clark, A. M., 134, 136
Class issues: and job assignments, 3, 4, 5, 34, 35–37, 118, 187–88, 203; and relationships among workers, 5, 35–37, 99–102, 240, 248; and veterans' organizations, 7; and women volunteers, 17, 42–43, 100, 241–42; and pay, 40, 42–43, 47, 48–49, 100, 266–67 (n. 17); and shunning of hospitals, 49; and domestic arrangements, 65; and hospital-life adjustments, 74, 76, 87–88; and sexual vulnerability, 90; and soldiers' conduct, 92; and nurse patient bond, 97–98, 102, 105; and hospital administrator/worker relationship, 141; and women's postwar work, 150, 162; and nursing training, 170; and job classification, 185, 187, 188; and pensions, 187, 209; and war memoirs, 216
Clerical work, 6, 153, 154, 155, 159, 160, 168, 179, 292 (nn. 26, 28)
Clinton, Catherine, 220, 248, 249
Confederate hospitals: and class issues, 4; and state hospitals, 14, 17, 111; and Newsom, 14, 111, 153; number of women serving in, 20–21, 31–32; and matrons, 31, 32, 33, 40, 51; and home-based relief work, 31, 33, 108; centralization of, 111, 113, 283–84 (n. 11); restationing

of, 111, 283 (n. 10); and war memoirs, 213
Confederate surgeon general, 20–21, 31, 111, 283–84 (n. 11)
Conlan, Consolata, 87
Contrabands: as hospital workers, 36, 55; and domestic arrangements, 63; clothing for, 68; and travel, 70; Union commanders' attitudes toward, 92–93; and nurse-patient bond, 98; and class issues, 102, 103; and relationships among workers, 103–4; and Washington, D.C., 151; and Porter, 159; and O'Connell, 171; and Union army, 184
Convalescent camp, 2, 117, 126, 159
Convalescent soldiers: and gender roles, 3, 217; as hospital nurses and orderlies, 18–19; preference for women nurses, 19, 116; as cooks, 34–35; and job assignments, 37; and relationships with nurses, 94; and sympathy for other soldiers, 95; place in military hierarchy, 97; and return to regiments, 123; brutal handling of, 136. See also Patient care
Cook, Lauren, 251
Cooke, Rose Terry, 143, 239
Cooks: and pensions, 7, 187, 192, 195, 203, 209; and surgeons, 17, 110; and job assignments, 20, 34; number of, 21; African American women as, 22, 187, 188; and Confederate hospitals, 33, 35; convalescent soldiers as, 34–35; pay of, 40, 41; for regiments, 56, 57; and domestic arrangements, 64; and isolation, 88
Cooper, Ella, 174
Crane, Stephen, 250
Crutcher, Emma, 83
Cultural memorialization. See Monuments; War memoirs
Cumming, David, 64, 152

Cumming, Kate: and soldiers' preference for female nurses, 19; and hospital staff supervision, 35, 285 (n. 26); and job assignments, 38; and stigma of working, 40, 49–50; and nurses' children, 64; and travel, 66, 68, 152; and religious faith, 77; and nursing enemy soldiers, 79; and hospital accommodations, 80, 83; and family visitors, 89; and African Americans' class issues, 102; and military authority, 109, 116; and surgeons, 115, 140; and isolation, 122; and nurse-patient bond, 140; and postwar era, 146, 152; and teaching, 152, 154; and Hopkins, 153; war memoir of, 223, 225–26, 228–30, 242–43; and transience of hospitals, 283 (n. 10)

Custodial workers, 7, 21, 35–36, 102, 155, 187–88. *See also* Cooks; Laundresses

Daffin, Sallie, 118
Daly, Maria Lydig, 54
Dame, Harriet Patience, 20, 155, 183, 189
Danforth, Ruth, 196, 206
Daughters of Confederate Veterans, 219
Daughters of Union Veterans (DUV), 218, 219, 220
Davenport, James F., 190
Davis, Jefferson, 219, 220
Davis, Mollie, 125
Davis, Webster, 203–4
De Bruler, J. P., 18–19
Deforest, J. W., 250
De Pauw, Linda Grant, 251
Dependent Pension Act of 1890, 186, 191, 199
Dependents' pensions, 185, 186, 187, 188
Diffley, Kathleen, 250

Dillard, Henry, 94, 205, 206
Dix, Dorothea: and surgeons, 15, 115, 123, 126; and dress, 15, 255 (n. 3); selection standards of, 15–16, 187, 257 (n. 23); and number of women serving, 21, 260 (nn. 58, 59); and pay, 40, 41; and women volunteers, 43; and Boate, 45; and nursing applicants, 62, 271 (n. 80); and furloughs, 64; and travel expenses, 67–68, 273 (n. 106); and nurses' health, 86; and nurses' relationships with soldiers, 94, 280–81 (n. 88); and Bickerdyke, 115, 285 (n. 22); and Yeatman, 116; and Barton, 120; and Wolcott, 128; and Bucklin, 137, 138–39, 240; and Pomroy, 169; and job classification, 188; and Ex-Nurse's Association, 191; as competent authority, 195; and John, 203; and Lawrence, 223; and Newcomb, 242; and Blackwell, 284 (n. 13); and job assignments, 287 (n. 59)

Domesticity: nursing equated with, 3, 20, 44, 91, 109, 255 (n. 6); and military hospitals, 5, 96, 104–5, 123; and women's postwar work, 6; and war memoirs, 7, 217; and postwar era, 12; military domesticity as woman's province, 54; and domestic arrangements of relief workers, 63–65; and Northern soldiers, 249

Domestic work, 6, 17, 31, 102, 151, 157, 179
Douglas, Ann, 247–48
Duckworth, Mildred, 47
Dulaney, Evalina, 78

Eaton, Harriet: and travel, 70–71; and hospital-life adjustments, 76, 77, 81, 83, 85, 89, 90; and hospital accommodations, 82, 276 (n. 40); and low morale, 122, 287 (n. 50); and

supplies, 130, 257 (n. 16); and reform movements, 165; and relief
work, 218; and private correspondence, 224; war journal of, 236
Edmonds, Sarah, 227
Edson, Susan, 174–75
Edwards, Laura, 248
Elite women: and relief work, 1–2;
and war memoirs, 6, 21, 221, 237;
and postwar era, 6, 146, 147, 153,
248; as hospital workers, 12, 18,
50–51; and social connections, 16,
36; and job assignments, 17, 36, 51,
187; and publicity, 19; as cooks, 35;
and relationships among workers,
35–37, 99–100, 105; and pay, 40,
48–49; motivation of, 47–48; and
domestic arrangements, 65; and
hospital-life adjustments, 74, 87–
88, 90; isolation of, 87–88; and
nurses' status, 97; and nurse-
patient bond, 102; and hospital
administrator/worker relationship,
137; and charity work, 148–49,
150; and free African Americans,
160; and reform movements, 165
Ellis, Mary A., 57
Emens, Harriet Dada, 175–76
Emens, Peter, 175–76
Etheridge, Annie, 155, 157, 233, 237,
311 (n. 105)

Fahs, Alice, 239, 250
Faust, Drew Gilpin, 47, 50, 162, 248
Female intelligence workers, 3, 118,
166, 227
Female physicians, 16, 98–99, 147,
173–77, 179, 194, 212
Femininity: and women's war work, 3;
and self-sacrifice, 47–48, 217; and
military nursing, 54, 115, 119, 148;
and religious faith, 150; and war
memoirs, 217, 224, 239; and writers, 225

Fern, Fanny, 224
Field hospitals, 18, 27, 31, 33, 34,
38–39, 108–9, 111, 258 (n. 33), 284
(n. 11). *See also* Regimental women
Fifield, Almira, 126
Fifteenth Amendment, 180
Fogg, Isabella, 85, 165, 184, 189, 218,
236, 239, 298 (n. 1)
Forbes, Ella, 249–50
Former slaves: as laundresses, 2; and
postwar work, 6; and class issues,
102, 157, 203; and postwar era, 146,
151; and pensions, 196, 200, 205,
206, 207; and Southern war mem-
oirs, 214
Forrest, Nathan Bedford, 83
Forten, Charlotte, 16–17, 118, 160
Fourteenth Amendment, 180
Foushée, Mary, 96
Fox-Genovese, Elizabeth, 250
Frazer, Louisa, 205
Free African Americans: as hospital
workers, 12; resistance to service of,
16–17; pay of, 41; as regimental
women, 57; and soldiers' conduct,
93–94; and class issues, 101–2;
schools for, 108, 149, 160, 166; and
pensions, 203
Freedmen's Relief Association (FRA),
40, 103, 266 (n. 3)
Front, 7–8
Frush, Mary Smith, 193
Fry, B. O., 80
Fry, Rose W., 214–15
Fuller, Sarah E., 191
Fyfe, Jennie, 83, 88, 94, 97–98,
121–22, 160, 301–2 (n. 49)

Gage, Matilda Joslyn, 1, 247
Gammon, Sarah Thompson, 203–4,
206
Gender identities: and relief work,
3; and class issues, 102; and white
women, 105; and Southern women,

tance to women hospital workers, 4, 18, 114–16; and job classifications, 7, 102, 187–88; and middle-class women, 43, 129, 131; and nursing applications, 60, 62; and hospital accommodations, 80, 82; and hospital workers' assertiveness, 115–16; and managerial positions, 118–19; and job assignments, 125; and morality, 130–40 passim

Hospital-life adjustments: and relationships among workers, 3, 5, 7, 99–101, 244; and nurses' relationships with soldiers, 16, 94–95, 105; and gendered infighting, 74–75; and religious faith, 75, 76–78; and tears, 75–76; and nursing enemy soldiers, 78–79, 274–75 (nn. 19, 20, 21); and accommodations, 79–87, 108, 275 (n. 28), 276 (n. 31); and theft, 83, 277 (n. 44); and disease, 85–87, 192, 278 (nn. 52, 54); and isolation, 87–88, 108, 122, 278–79 (n. 58); and family visitors, 88–90, 279 (nn. 64, 66); and solace, 90; and soldiers' conduct, 90–94; and maternal feelings for soldiers, 95–96, 102, 137; and soldiers as comrades, 96, 105; and hardening process, 120–23, 146, 287 (n. 49); and low morale, 122–23

Hospitals: general hospitals, 3, 5, 15, 33; hospital ships, 16, 36–37; field hospitals, 18, 27, 31, 33, 34, 38–39, 108–9, 111, 258 (n. 33), 284 (n. 11); as charitable institutions, 49. *See also* Military hospitals

Hospital workers: significance of, 1, 3; and pensions, 2, 6–7, 20, 157, 169, 187; characteristics of, 2, 12; number of, 5, 19–27, 31, 260 (n. 58), 299 (n. 16); and pay, 5, 44, 47; women seeking positions as, 12, 14, 15–16; and military service, 47; and

domesticity, 54; public perception of, 62; confidence of, 74, 105, 108; friction among, 74–75; and power, 105, 109, 113, 130, 137, 141, 244, 247; training of, 113, 170, 284 (n. 13); dismissal of, 119, 125, 127, 131, 134, 137, 138, 286 (n. 37); and professionalization of nursing, 173; and postwar medical careers, 175; war memoirs of, 216–17, 220. *See also* Cooks; Hospital administrator/worker relationship; Hospital-life adjustments; Laundresses; Matrons; Nurses and nursing

Howard, Oliver Otis, 184
Howe, Julia Ward, 78
Howells, William Dean, 163
Hunt, Sanford, 126
Husband, Mary Morris, 155, 157, 232, 233, 237, 296 (n. 70), 311 (n. 91)
Hyatt, Elizabeth, 39

Immigrant women, 17, 57, 100–101, 223
Independent workers, 70, 188, 195
Industrial work, 6, 151, 155, 179

Jackson, Fannie Oslin, 35, 61, 65, 68, 78
Jackson, Malinda McFarland, 87, 202
Job assignments: and relief work, 2; and class issues, 3, 4, 5, 34, 35–37, 118, 187–88, 203; and Confederate hospitals, 33, 38; and working-class women, 34, 37, 187–88; and laundresses, 34, 202, 204, 262 (n. 79); and nurses, 34, 262 (n. 79), 287 (n. 59); and Union hospitals, 37–38; and slaves, 38, 263 (n. 91); and hospital-life adjustments, 74; and hospital administrator/worker relationship, 125
John, Matilda Cleaver, 80, 94, 118, 203

129, 199 (n. 16), 255 (n. 6); as administrators of relief work, 14, 256 (n. 10); and memorial work, 218; and war memoirs of nurses, 232–33. *See also* African American soldiers; Convalescent soldiers; Surgeons

Messeroll, Maggie, 125

Middle-class women: and travel, 5, 71; motivation of, 5, 192; and pensions, 7, 180, 187, 210; and relief work, 12; and job assignments, 34; as cooks, 35; and socially stigmatized work, 35–36; and pay, 40, 42–43, 49, 150, 266–67 (n. 17); and hospital administrators, 43, 129, 131; and propriety of military nursing, 53; and regimental women, 57; as nursing applicants, 60–61; and domestic arrangements, 63; and isolation, 88; and sexual vulnerability, 90; and nurse-patient bond, 97–98; and relationships among workers, 99, 240; and postwar era, 146–47, 157, 181; and reform movements, 148; and nursing training, 170; and propriety of war memoirs, 232; and Moore, 237

Military authority: and hospital administrator/worker relationship, 3, 105, 108, 109, 116, 128, 130, 134, 140, 141, 248; and relationships among workers, 102, 105; and surgeons, 110, 114, 127; and Union surgeon general, 111; and Bickerdyke, 119, 137; and Barton, 119–20

Military hospitals: and relief work, 2; and domesticity, 5, 96, 104–5, 123; bureaucracies of, 6, 7; number of Union women serving in, 20, 21–31, 261 (n. 61); and job classification, 21–22, 31, 97, 100, 102, 109–10, 185; number of, 24, 261 (nn. 62, 63); number of patients in, 33–34;

and homeopathy, 195; postwar closing of, 290 (n. 1). *See also* Confederate hospitals; Hospital-life adjustments; Hospital workers; Northern hospitals

Military nursing: and sexual vulnerability, 5, 16, 49, 50, 51–52, 54, 61, 62, 90, 92, 95, 124, 125; and femininity, 54, 115, 119, 148. *See also* Nurses and nursing

Military service: definition of, 7; women's desire for, 46–47

Millen Wayside Home, 18, 31

Miller, Albert, 176

Miller, Ophelia, 61

Miner, Rena Littlefield, 151, 175

Mitchell, Edward L., 230

Mitchell, Reid, 249

Monuments, 217, 218, 219, 220, 306 (n. 16)

Moon, Orrie R., 173

Moore, Frank: and number of hospital workers, 19; seeks war narratives from women, 149–50, 211, 212, 223, 227; and propriety of women's writing, 221; and women's financial needs, 223–24, 230, 236–37, 239, 311 (n. 103); and women's modesty, 225, 233–36, 237, 238; editions of work, 231; and men's accounts of caregivers, 232–33

Moore, John, 188

Moore, Samuel Preston, 111, 113, 284 (n. 11)

Morality: and women's war work, 1; and hospital workers, 6, 187; and nursing applicants, 15, 61, 62; and women volunteers, 43; and hospitals, 49; and propriety of military nursing, 52, 125; of African American women, 93; and hospital administrator/worker relationship, 130–31, 134, 136, 137, 138–39, 140; and Swisshelm, 164; and widowed pensioners, 186–87; and war memoirs, 216, 223, 234, 240, 243, 244

Morantz-Sanchez, Regina, 173

Morgan, Julia, 226

Morton, John, 229

Morton, Oliver, 19

Mullins, William H., 202

Mustin, Bessie, 53

Narrington, E. D., 207, 208, 209

National American Woman Suffrage Association, 167

National Association of Army Nurses (NAAN), 189, 191–92, 218, 219–20

Native Americans, 98

Nativism, 101, 223

Newcomb, Mary: as volunteer, 43, 44; and regiment, 57; and travel, 69; and safety, 85; and maternal feelings, 95; and hardening process, 121; and surgeons, 131, 136, 241–42, 243, 285 (n. 26); and war memoir, 226, 241–42, 243, 309 (n. 55)

Newsom, Ella: and Confederate hospitals, 14, 111, 153; and slaves, 17, 63; and self-sacrifice, 48; as matron, 53; and class issues, 118–19; and postwar era, 152–53; and nursing training, 284 (n. 13)

New York State Charities Aid Association, 165, 171

Nichols, Elizabeth, 193–94

Nicholson, N. H., 206

Nightingale, Florence, 47, 50, 54, 169–70

Northern hospitals, 4, 111

Northern women: as hospital workers, 2, 4, 12, 19, 20, 21–31, 33, 37–38, 108, 261 (n. 61); and race issues, 4–5, 118; and travel, 5, 66–68, 155; as nursing applicants, 15–17, 62, 63; and opposition to service, 53;

and hospital-life adjustments, 65, 75, 80–81, 88, 92; and nursing enemy soldiers, 78–79, 274–75 (nn. 19, 20, 21); and nurse-patient bond, 98, 105; and relationships among workers, 100, 103–4; and postwar era, 146–47, 155, 181; and charity work, 148–49, 150, 164; as writers, 162; and war memoirs, 212, 215, 220–21, 243, 244, 308 (n. 39); Southern characterizations of, 215–16; memorial societies of, 218–19; and propriety of publishing, 224

Nuns: as hospital workers, 12, 21, 25–26; and pay, 21, 43; as nurses, 22, 24, 25–26, 116, 171, 285 (n. 28); and number of patients, 33; and job assignments, 37; and propriety of nursing, 50; and religious conversions, 77; and disease, 86–87; and family visitors, 89; and relationships with soldiers, 94, 281 (n. 90); and relationships among workers, 100–101; training of, 113; managerial responsibilities of, 116; and hospital development, 171; memorial to, 217

Nurse-patient bond, 5, 95–98, 102, 104–5, 140, 217

Nurses and nursing: and training, 1, 113, 124, 147, 169–71, 173, 284 (n. 13), 296 (n. 67); men as nurses, 3, 18–19, 113, 116, 129, 199 (n. 16), 255 (n. 6); and domesticity, 3, 20, 44, 91, 109, 255 (n. 6); and region and ethnicity, 4; military nursing, 5, 16, 49, 50, 51–52, 54, 61, 62, 90, 92, 95, 115, 119, 124, 125, 148; and pensions, 6, 7, 186–200, 219–20; and New York sanitary fair workers, 8; and applicants, 12, 14, 15–17, 60–63, 271 (n. 80); and uniforms, 12, 255 (n. 3); comparison of men and women as nurses, 18, 19, 259 (n. 40); and number of nurses, 21; African American women as nurses, 22; definition of, 33, 200, 204, 206–7, 209, 210, 247; and job assignments, 34, 262 (n. 79), 287 (n. 59); and pay, 39–44, 49, 62, 100, 108, 170, 190, 236, 266–67 (n. 17); women's right to nurse, 49–50; and hardening process, 120–21; and professionalization of nursing, 173, 179; memorials to, 219, 220; and war memoirs, 223–24. *See also* Hospital workers; Patient care

Nurses Pension Act of 1892, 6–7
Nurturing, 1, 3, 54, 102
Nye, Frances M., 176
Nye, Francis M., 176

Oates, Stephen, 54
O'Brien, Frank, 21
O'Connell, Sister Anthony, 39, 171
O'Donnell, Margaret, 198–99, 207
O'Keefe, Sister Camilla, 77
Oliphant, Catherine, 59, 198–99
Orderlies, 18–19, 111
Otis, Rebecca, 65

Pacifism, 244
Palmer, J. M., 126
Palmer, Sarah, 41, 94, 230, 243
Paludan, Phillip Shaw, 95
Parsons, Emily: and soldiers' preference for female nurses, 19; and African American women, 25, 202, 304 (n. 70); and number of patients, 33–34; and job assignments, 36; and social stigma of nursing, 54; and isolation, 73, 87; and hospital accommodations, 80; and food, 81; and sexual vulnerability, 90; and maternal feelings, 95–96; and nurse-patient bond, 98; and relationships among workers, 104; managerial re-

sponsibilities of, 116, 119, 285 (n. 26); and surgeons, 127–28; and postwar era, 145; and reform movements, 165; and nursing training, 170, 284 (n. 13); and charity hospital, 170–71

Patient care: and nurses as advocates, 3, 6, 7, 105–6, 109, 123, 129, 136, 243, 247–48; and hospital administrator/worker relationship, 3, 6, 105–6, 109–10, 113, 116, 129, 130–41, 248, 289 (nn. 92, 94); and nurse-patient bond, 5, 95–98, 102, 104–5, 140, 217; and patient's body as battleground, 6, 136, 243; and diet, 35, 38, 109, 114, 129–30, 131, 134, 137–40; improvements in, 109, 116; and low morale, 122

Patriotism: and relief work, 3, 46; and hospital workers, 12, 47; and women volunteers, 43; and domestic arrangements, 63, 64; and war memoirs, 215, 216, 221, 227, 235

Patton, James, 33, 215
Patton, Jane Hoge, 198, 302 (n. 56)
Pay. *See* Women's paid work
Payne, Lavinia, 194–95
Pember, Phoebe Yates: as matron, 32, 38, 119, 263 (n. 93); and number of patients, 33; and stigma of working, 40, 48–49, 50, 51–52; and travel, 66, 221, 273 (n. 108); and hospital food, 82; and isolation, 88, 119; and soldiers' conduct, 94, 280 (n. 87); and nurses' status, 97; and class issues, 100, 118–19; and hospital administrators, 113, 129, 221; and surgeons, 132; war memoir of, 229, 230, 240; and amputations, 286 (n. 46)

Pension and Relief Committee (PRC), 191, 193
Pension Bureau, 7, 184, 192, 200, 303 (n. 66)

Pension eligibility: and job classification, 7, 185–86, 199, 203, 204, 207, 209; and payroll records, 20, 193; and witness testimonials, 184, 194, 195–96, 198, 200, 203, 206–7; and length of service, 185, 194, 210; and competent authority, 195, 196, 199, 200, 201–2, 209; and definition of nurse, 200, 204, 206–7, 209, 210

Pensions: and hospital workers, 2, 6–7, 20, 157, 169, 187; and African American women, 7, 180, 184, 187, 188, 198, 200–209, 210, 303 (n. 65); and women volunteers, 20, 188, 191–94, 196, 198, 210; and regimental women, 59, 188, 193, 194, 195, 200; and government work, 155, 157; and special acts of Congress, 184, 185, 188–89, 191; dependents' pensions, 185, 186, 187, 188; veterans' pensions, 185, 189–90, 191, 218; widowed pensioners, 186–88, 190–92, 205, 207, 208, 299 (n. 17); and race issues, 187, 198, 200–209, 210; ban on second pensions, 188, 192–93; applications for, 188, 299 (n. 16); increases in, 189–90, 219–20; varying amounts of, 189–90, 300 (n. 22); graduated scale for, 192, 301 (n. 27)

Perry, Adeliza, 299–300 (n. 18)
Phelps, Elizabeth Stuart, 249
Philips, Bettie Taylor, 57, 145
Pierce, Lydia, 67
Platt, Anna Lawrence, 231
Point, Mary G., 41
Political life: and reform movements, 2; and elite women, 6; and middle-class women, 146–47; and Southern women, 185; and war memoirs, 216; and pensions, 219–20; and women's political rights, 249, 251; and women's writing, 250. *See also* Reform movements

Pollack, Simon, 287 (n. 56)
Pomroy, Rebecca, 76, 77, 101, 169, 226, 295 (n. 62)
Pond, Harriet Stinson, 189
Porter, Eliza Chappell, 77–78, 85, 159, 285 (n. 26)
Porter, Felicia Grundy, 15, 115
Porter, Jeremiah, 159
Postwar era: and hospital workers, 1, 2; and return to private life, 3, 6, 12, 146–48, 181, 245; and teachers, 6, 148, 150, 159, 293 (n. 35); and economy, 146, 152, 153, 155, 181, 212, 215; and Southern women, 146, 152–53, 180, 248, 295 (n. 66), 298 (n. 103); and women's paid work, 146–47, 153–54, 181; and Northern women, 146–47, 155, 181; and reform movements, 148, 150, 164–67, 291 (n. 12). *See also* War memoirs

Potter, Alonzo, 225
Powell, Hannah, 87
Powers, Elvira: and number of patients, 34; and job assignments, 37–38; and travel, 67, 68; and confidence in work, 74; and food, 81; and hardening process, 121; and surgeons, 128; war memoirs of, 214, 227, 230, 236, 311 (n. 103)
Pritchard, James, 207
Prostitution, 57, 93
Pryor, Elizabeth, 54
Pryor, Sarah, 75, 294 (n. 46)

Rable, George, 66, 111, 113, 153, 248
Race issues: and relief work, 3; and job assignments, 4, 34, 37, 118, 187–88; and Northern women, 4–5, 118; and job classifications, 21–22, 102, 185, 187, 200, 203; and management of custodial labor, 35–36; and hospital-life adjustments, 74; and nurse-patient bond, 98–99,

105; and relationships among workers, 99–100, 102–4, 248; and hospital administrator/worker relationship, 141; and reform movements, 164; and nursing training, 170; and pensions, 187, 198, 200–209, 210; and war memoirs, 215, 216, 223

Ransom, "Mother" Elnora, 69

Reardon, Carol, 216

Reason, Charley, 98–99

Reconstruction, 151, 152, 155, 180, 206

Redpath, James, 228

Reed, Martha Smith, 183

Reform movements: and relief work, 2, 12, 255–56 (n. 5); and Ropes, 134; and postwar era, 148, 150, 164–67, 291 (n. 12); and middle-class women, 157; and dress, 176–77; and gender identities, 249

Regimental women: and Carded Service Records, 20; and job assignments, 33, 34, 38–39; and travel, 39, 69–70; and pay, 40; characteristics of, 56–57, 59–60; white women as, 57, 80; and pensions, 59, 188, 193, 194, 195, 200; and hospital accommodations, 83. *See also* Field hospitals

Reid, Mary Smith, 14, 63, 68

Relief work: feminists' analysis of, 1–2; and reform movements, 2, 12, 255–56 (n. 5); significance of, 3, 8; obstacles to, 4, 44, 46, 49–50, 53–54, 153; home-based relief work, 5, 8, 14, 18, 21, 31, 33, 63, 108; motivations for, 5, 14, 46–47, 49; and travel, 5, 17, 65–70; men as administrators of, 14, 256 (n. 10); and mass production of household goods, 46, 266 (n. 3); and pay, 47, 48, 61; and domestic arrangements, 63; celebrants of, 147; and war memoirs, 215–16; monuments to, 217.

*See also* United States Christian Commission; United States Sanitary Commission; Women's Central Relief Association

Religion: and nurse-patient bond, 5; and duty, 12, 20, 43, 46, 47, 52, 54, 76, 105; and churches, 14, 18, 21, 68, 164; and hospital-life adjustments, 75, 76–78; and relationships among workers, 100–101; and hospital workers' longevity, 108; and women's war work, 150

Ricketts, Fanny, 60, 239

Ricketts, James, 60

Rooney, Rose, 169

Ropes, Hannah, 47, 80, 86, 107, 118, 134–36, 137, 203, 304 (n. 77)

Russell, Ira, 116

Ryan, Mary, 291 (n. 6)

Safford, Mary Jane, 176

Salina, Sally, 41

Sampson, Sarah, 56, 293 (n. 30)

Savage, Kirk, 216

Scales, Cordelia, 46–47

Schools: and local aid societies, 14; as field hospitals, 18, 258 (n. 33); for African Americans, 108, 145, 149, 157, 160, 166. *See also* Teachers and teaching

Schuyler, Louisa Lee, 165, 170, 291 (n. 12)

Schwalm, Leslie, 248

Scott, Anne Firor, 247

Scott, Kate, 191–92

Sea Islands: and Hawks, 16, 83, 93, 108, 174; and travel, 68; and Barton, 74, 81–82; and nurses' relationships with officers, 94; and patient care, 97, 140; and Forten, 118; and soldiers' conduct, 130; and teachers, 160; and Tubman, 166

Sectional reunion, 20, 185, 212, 250

Sedgwick, Catharine Maria, 224

Segregation, 4, 26, 152
Self-sacrifice: as motivation, 12, 49,
    51; and femininity, 47–48, 217; and
    class issues, 119; and Wilson, 162;
    and pensions by special acts of Con-
    gress, 188–89; and Army Nurses
    Pension Act negotiations, 192; and
    war memoirs, 217, 227, 239
Settlement work, 149
Sexual vulnerability: and propriety of
    military nursing, 5, 16, 49, 50, 51–
    52, 54, 61, 62, 90, 92, 95, 124, 125;
    and surgeons, 90, 92, 124, 138, 139;
    and soldiers' conduct, 90, 92, 280
    (n. 84); and family rhetoric, 96
Shelton, Amanda, 38, 92, 100, 114
Shelton, Mary, 53, 54, 76
Sherman, William T., 8, 78, 119
Shields, Cynthia Franklin, 206
Silber, Nina, 185, 249, 250
Silk, Julia, 47, 223, 266 (n. 16), 271
    (n. 84)
Simkins, Francis, 33, 215
Simmons, Barbara Moore, 18, 221
Sisters of Charity, 21, 43, 54, 79, 87,
    94, 171, 188, 281 (n. 89)
Sisters of Mercy, 87
Sizer, Lyde Cullen, 138, 249
Skocpol, Theda, 186
Slave narratives, 201
Slaves: as hospital workers, 12, 17, 31,
    87, 118; and job assignments, 38,
    263 (n. 91); runaway slaves, 56, 64–
    65, 89, 164; and domestic arrange-
    ments of relief workers, 63; and sol-
    diers' conduct, 93; and class issues,
    101–2; and pensions, 203; memori-
    als to, 219, 307 (n. 30)
Smith, Adelaide, 176, 226
Smith, Edward P., 65, 232
Smith, Hannah Cleaver, 40, 65
Smith, Nathan R., 133
Smith, Susan E. D. "Grandma," 47,
    49, 60, 88, 128, 229, 310 (n. 76)

Social service, 148, 150, 151, 155, 157,
    165
Social welfare policy, 209, 218
Soldiers. See African American sol-
    diers; Convalescent soldiers; Pa-
    tient care
Sons of Confederate Veterans, 219
Souder, Emily, 228
Southern women: as hospital workers,
    2, 4, 17, 19–21, 31–32, 33, 35, 38,
    108; and class issues, 4–5, 17, 21,
    50–51, 102, 118; and home-based
    relief work, 5, 8, 18, 21, 63; North-
    ern characterizations of, 8, 214,
    215, 223; as nursing applicants, 14,
    61, 62; and field hospitals, 18, 31,
    33, 38, 111, 258 (n. 33), 284 (n. 11);
    and war memoirs, 21, 213–14,
    220–21, 224, 225–26, 228–29,
    243, 244, 308 (n. 39); and pay, 40,
    44; and obstacles to relief work, 50;
    and propriety of military nursing,
    51–53; as regimental women, 57;
    and domestic arrangements, 63,
    65; and travel, 66, 67, 68, 71, 272
    (n. 94); and hospital-life adjust-
    ments, 75–76, 78, 79, 86–88, 92;
    and relationships among workers,
    100, 102; and nurse-patient bond,
    105; and hospital administrators,
    129–30; and postwar era, 146,
    152–53, 180, 248, 295 (n. 66), 298
    (n. 103); and clerical work, 153, 154,
    155, 292 (n. 26); as writers, 162;
    and pensions, 185; monuments to,
    217, 306 (n. 19); organizations of,
    218; propriety of publishing, 224
Southworth, E. D. E. N., 224
Spencer, Cornelia Phillips, 229
Spicer, Martha, 184
Stanton, Edwin, 136, 194
Stanton, Elizabeth Cady, 1, 247
State relief organizations, 14–15, 257
    (n. 16)

Stearns, Amanda Akin: and Whitman, 25; and job assignments, 37; and travel, 66; and hospital-life adjustments, 76; and solace, 90; and patients' diets, 114; and hardening process, 121, 123, 286 (n. 47); and surgeons, 126; war memoir of, 226, 228; and soldier conduct, 280 (n. 75)

Stevenson, Hannah, 235

Stillé, Charles, 1

Stoddard, Elizabeth, 163

Stowe, Harriet Beecher, 103, 224, 231

Strong, George Templeton: wife of, 16, 100; and Cary, 163

Stuart, Isabella, 130

Suhre, John, 95, 99

Sullivan, Betsy "Mother," 57

Surgeon general. *See* Confederate surgeon general; Union surgeon general

Surgeons: and conflict with nurses, 6, 7, 109, 110, 113, 114–16, 123–25, 133, 136–41, 284 (n. 20); and ethics, 6, 110, 111, 129, 131, 134, 136, 283 (n. 9); and nursing applicants, 12, 14, 15, 62; and Dix, 15, 115, 123, 126; and nurses' job assignments, 17, 38; comparison of men and women as nurses, 18, 259 (n. 40); and nurses' pay, 41–42, 62; and women volunteers, 43; and nurses' domestic arrangements, 64, 65; and hospital food, 81; and family visitors, 88, 89; and nurses' sexual vulnerability, 90, 92, 124, 138, 139; nurses' relationships with, 92, 94; and patient care, 97, 110, 131–33, 289 (n. 94); and relationships among workers, 102; military rank of, 110–11, 127; deficiencies in abilities of, 113, 284 (n. 14); and nurses' bravery, 126; and Newcomb, 131, 136, 241–42, 243, 285 (n. 26);

and Walker, 177, 212; nurses hired by, 188; as competent authority, 195, 198, 207; and African American women, 202; and war memoirs, 216, 240, 241, 242–43, 244, 312 (n. 114)

Swarts, David, 176, 190

Swarts, Vesta Ward, 176, 190

Swisshelm, Jane Grey, 62, 163–64, 224, 226, 309 (n. 62)

Taylor, Mrs. Thomas, 211

Taylor, Susie King: as regimental woman, 56–57; and white officials' abuse of former slaves, 93; and hardening process, 120; and school for African Americans, 145, 157, 160; and postwar work prospects, 180; excluded from commemorative volumes, 215; war memoir of, 226

Teachers and teaching: and postwar era, 6, 148, 150, 159, 293 (n. 35); as hospital workers, 12, 157, 159; and Cumming, 152, 154; and pay, 154–55; training for, 160. *See also* Schools

Tenney, Emmeline, 40

Terry, Harriet, 54

Thomas, Gertrude, 89

Thrall, Seneca, 133, 134

Tinkham, Mrs. Nathan A., 45, 62

Titus-Hazen, Charles, 189–90

Titus-Hazen, Fanny, 16, 47, 189–90

Toliver, Henry, 151

Toliver, Maria Bear, 118, 151, 204–5, 206

Tompkins, Sally, 31, 44, 94, 113, 152

Towne, Laura, 149, 160

Trader, Ella Newsom. *See* Newsom, Ella

Travel: and relief work, 5, 17, 65–70; and Southern women, 17, 66, 67, 68, 71, 272 (n. 94); nurses' travel expenses, 67–68, 273 (n. 106); and battlefield, 69–71

Trigg, Minerva, 94, 205
Truth, Sojourner, 103, 118
Tubman, Harriet, 118, 165–66
Turner, Eliza Preacher, 57
Turner, Junius, 199–200
Tuttle, Elizabeth, 53, 54, 274–75 (n. 19)
Twain, Mark, 11

Underwood, John L., 19, 215
Union surgeon general: and United States Sanitary Commission, 14; and nursing applicants, 15; and nurses' furloughs, 64; and nurses' travel, 69; and nurses' pay, 93; and therapeutic practices, 111; and surgeons' evaluation of nurses, 124–25; and Ropes, 135–36; and job classification, 185, 187, 200; and payroll records, 193
United Confederate Veterans, 217
United Daughters of the Confederacy (UDC), 152, 153, 218, 219, 220
United States Christian Commission (USCC), 14, 39–40, 131, 188, 227
U.S. Congress: special acts of, 184, 185, 188–89, 191
United States Sanitary Commission (USSC): and Blackwell, 1, 254 (n. 2); New York fair, 8, 12; male administrators of, 14, 256 (n. 10); and nurses' pay, 39; and Bickerdyke, 68, 119; and class issues, 100, 149; and Hancock, 108; and Hammond, 111; and reform movements, 150, 291 (n. 12); and Porter, 159; and Livermore, 166; nurses' deputized by, 188; and nurses' pensions, 196; and war memoirs, 227, 228; and Wormeley, 235; and women's charitable work, 249; and women as managers, 285 (n. 26)
Usher, Rebecca, 34, 198, 219

Vanderkieft, Bernard, 221
Vaughan, Mary, 19, 148, 214, 215, 223, 231
Velasquez, Loreta, 228
Veterans, 186, 191
Veterans' organizations, 6, 7, 217–18, 219
Veterans' pensions, 185, 189–90, 191, 218
Von Olnhausen, Mary Phinney: and hospital accommodations, 69–70, 83; and enemy soldiers, 78; and class issues, 88; and African American soldiers, 98, 99; and laundresses, 103–4; and supplies, 113–14; reputation of, 126; and nursing profession, 170

Wagner, C., 138
Walker, Mary Edwards: as patient advocate, 132; as physician, 174, 176–77, 212, 298 (n. 98); and clerical work, 179; and Congressional Medal of Honor, 212; war memoirs of, 212, 227
Walsh, Mary Roth, 173
War Department, 111, 188, 194
Ward masters, 109, 113–14, 240, 242
War memoirs: and commemorative volumes, 7, 19, 162, 220, 221, 231; representations of conflict in, 7, 216; and domesticity, 7, 217; and propriety of writing, 19, 162, 221, 224–28, 232, 233, 243; and Southern women, 21, 213–14, 220–21, 224, 225–26, 228–29, 243, 244, 308 (n. 39); and Wormeley, 149, 237; and financial need, 162, 223–24, 225, 228, 229–31, 236–37, 239, 243, 244, 311 (n. 103); and Northern women, 212, 215, 220–21, 243, 244, 308 (n. 39); and publishing industry, 212, 221, 228, 229–32, 237, 308 (n. 41); of Beers, 213, 226, 242;

and martial values, 217, 235, 244;
and triumphal narrative, 223–24,
228, 237, 239–40, 244
Warner, Charles Dudley, 11
Warren, Robert Penn, 215–16
Washington, Minerva Trigg Dillard,
205–7
Watson, William, 133, 134
Welch, Lizzie Breed, 174
Wheeler, Elizabeth, 47
Wheelock, Julia, 59, 78
Whetten, Harriet, 54
Whites, LeeAnn, 248
White women: and relief work, 1–2,
12; and cross-racial alliances, 5; and
pensions, 7, 180, 187; slaves' nursing of, 17; as Union hospital workers, 19, 23, 25, 27, 28, 30, 31, 32;
and job assignments, 22, 34, 187; as
Confederate hospital workers, 32,
118; as cooks, 35; pay of, 39, 41, 42;
and regimental women, 57, 80; and
domestic arrangements, 63, 65; and
travel, 70; and hospital-life adjustments, 74; and isolation, 88; and
sexual vulnerability, 90, 92, 280
(n. 84); and nurse-patient bond, 98,
105; and relationships among workers, 99, 102, 202; and hospital administrators, 129, 141; and postwar
era, 146–47, 181; and nursing training, 170; and war memoirs, 215
Whitman, Walt, 25, 88, 228
Willets, Georgiana, 233
Williams, W. S., 227
Wilson, Augusta Evans, 53, 162, 294
(n. 43)
Winslow, Caroline Brown, 174, 175
Wittenmyer, Annie Turner: and special diet kitchens, 35, 168, 206; and
reform movements, 164, 167, 168–
69; and pensions, 196, 198, 202,
206; war memoir of, 231
Wolcott, Ella, 74, 128, 138

Woman's Central Relief Association,
1, 14, 113, 165, 177, 284 (n. 13)
Woman's Christian Temperance
Union (WCTU), 167, 168
Woman's National Loyal League
(WNLL), 174
Woman's Relief Corps (WRC), 168,
169, 185, 191–93, 198, 218, 219,
231, 302–3 (n. 58)
Woman suffrage, 166, 167, 168, 174,
177
Women's paid work: wider acceptance
of, 6, 7; and pensions, 20, 209; and
nurses, 39–44, 49, 62, 100, 108,
170, 190, 236, 266–67 (n. 17); and
class issues, 40, 42–43, 47, 48–49,
100, 150, 266–67 (n. 17); and postwar era, 146–47, 153–54, 181; and
Miner, 151; and teachers, 154–55;
and industrial work, 155
Women's Relief Society of the Confederate States, 15
Women volunteers: as hospital workers, 15, 42–43; and class issues, 17,
42–43, 100, 241–42; and pensions,
20, 188, 191–94, 196, 198, 210
Wood, R. C., 15
Woolsey, Abby Howland, 170, 171
Woolsey, Caroline, 171
Woolsey, Eliza, 16, 44, 171
Woolsey, Georgeanna: and hospital
ships, 16; and job assignments, 34;
as volunteer, 44, 149; and surgeons,
115; and reform movements, 165;
and nursing training, 171, 173, 284
(n. 13); war memoir of, 228
Woolsey, Jane Stuart, 16, 44, 96, 130–
31, 149, 165, 171, 230
Working class, 6, 7, 243
Working-class men, 90, 97–98
Working-class women: as Confederate
hospital workers, 17, 87; and job assignments, 34, 37, 187–88; motivation of, 47; and domestic arrange-

ments, 64; and relationships among workers, 105, 240; and Wormeley, 149; and domestic work, 157, 179; and postwar era, 180–81; and pensions, 188, 198–99

Wormeley, Katharine Prescott, 99–100, 149, 150, 235–37

Writers and writing: and letterwriting, 2, 34, 37, 38, 54; and middle-class women, 157; and literature, 162–63, 224, 250; and journalism, 163–64; and femininity, 225. *See also* War memoirs

Yeatman, James, 34, 116, 125

Young, Elizabeth, 250

Zakrzewska, Marie, 173, 175

DATE DUE

| APR 2 7 2016 | |
| 2/23/2017 | |
| 4/25/17 | |
| 11/27/17 | |
| 2/22/2020 | |
| 3/19/2020 | |
| | |
| | |
| | |
| | |
| | |
| | |
| | |
| | |
| | |
| | |

PRINTED IN U.S.A.

KIRTLAND COMMUNITY COLLEGE
LIBRARY
4800 W. FOUR MILE RD.
GRAYLING, MI 49738
989.275.5000 x 246